SPIRITUAL CRISIS

SPIRITUAL CRISIS

VARIETIES AND PERSPECTIVES OF
A TRANSPERSONAL PHENOMENON

Fransje de Waard

Translated by Jo Nesbitt

imprint-academic.com

Published in the UK by Imprint Academic
PO Box 200, Exeter EX5 5YX, UK

Published in the USA by Imprint Academic
Philosophy Documentation Center
PO Box 7147, Charlottesville, VA 22906-7147, USA

ISBN 9 781845 402013

A CIP catalogue record for this book is available from the
British Library and US Library of Congress

'As one tone does not produce a harmony,
neither is a truth which stands alone complete.'

Emanuel Swedenborg, *Arcana Coelestia*, 4197

This book is dedicated to:

those who find themselves in a spiritual crisis
and must go to great lengths to emerge whole again;

those who find themselves in a spiritual crisis, but do not
find the help that they need;

those who support them in word and deed, with
understanding and compassion.

Contents

Acknowledgements

For their contribution to the first phase of my research, when it still concerned a master's thesis — Ingrid Sell, David Lukoff, William Braud, Guy Albert, Jennifer Elam, Marius Romme and Sandra Escher, Paul Jerry, Isabel and Chris Clarke: thank you.

For their contribution to the genesis of this book — Maaike Meijer, for your co-reading and your literary advice; Stephan Sanders, for your reflective input; Marieke van Geldermalsen and Monika Jaeckel, for your accomodation; Joost Ritman for your books and your study-room; David Lukoff, for your ongoing pioneering work then, and your foreword now; Jo Nesbitt, for the sensitivity you brought to the job of translating my brand of Dutch; Anthony Freeman, for your ready proposition to publish; an entire crowd of family, friends, teachers, acquaintances and others, for the moral support, perhaps without your knowing, and for the opportunity to bounce about all this stuff every now and then; all those who have told me their stories, for your openness and trust; and of course Mieke van Kasbergen, without whom I would have never made it to the finish line anyhow. For everything: thank you, thank you, thank you.

Foreword

The theme of this book is close to my heart as I underwent a spiritual crisis which impaired my ability to function in consensual reality and everyday social life. Joseph Campbell once said if there was a sign in a hallway that said 'Lecture on God turn right. Meet God turn left', most people would go to the lecture. I not only turned left to meet God but became God — or at least Buddha and Christ. This happened in 1971 when, at the age of twenty-three, after ingesting LSD for the first time, I spent two months firmly convinced that I was a reincarnation of both Buddha and Christ. Over five sleepless nights I held conversations with the 'spirits' of eminent thinkers in the social sciences and humanities. I had discussions with contemporary persons including R. D. Laing, Margaret Mead, and Bob Dylan, as well as individuals no longer living, such as Plato, Rousseau, Freud, and Jung. Based on the wisdom they imparted to me, I compiled a collection of their teachings into a 'Holy Book' that would unite all the peoples of the world. I then made photocopies of the book and gave them to my family and friends.

For those two months, my episode met the diagnostic criteria for Acute Schizophrenic Reaction in the *Diagnostic and Statistical Manual-II*, which was the current edition at that time. In the current *DSM-IV*, that experience could be diagnosed as a Hallucinogen Induced Delusional Disorder or a Brief Psychotic Disorder.[1]

I was fortunate to be supported by friends who took me in for weeks at a time. They provided a sanctuary for me and helped me to get grounded in the everyday social world and consensual reality again. Without their help, I might have been confined in a psychiatric hospital, diagnosed with a lifelong psychotic disorder, and 'treated' with medication. Being supported by caring friends is one of the many experiences in my life for which I am deeply grateful.

However, for a long time, I kept silent about this experience. No one had responded to me about my gift of the 'Holy Book'. I was intensely embarrassed about having believed myself to be such grandiose figures and distributed that book. For years I talked with absolutely no one about my experience — not my wife, not my parents, not even the first therapist I saw. But I now consider that episode to be my spiritual awakening. It is a touchstone experience in my life, and set me on a spiritual journey to understand what happened. How could I, raised in a very non-devout Jewish family, have believed myself to be Buddha and Christ, about whom I really knew very little?

I started to read books by Carl Jung, and by Joseph Campbell, many of whose workshops I attended in order to understand my experience. I also worked with shamans and Native American medicine chiefs who taught me how to control entry and exit from such ecstatic states, as well as their value. Six years after this episode I entered Jungian analysis, and one night I had a dream in which a large red book appeared. My analyst asked for my associations to the book. Memories of my 'Holy Book' leaped into my consciousness. I had not ever discussed my episode with anyone, and my heart raced at the prospect of sharing my story with someone in my own profession. Recognizing therapy as a sacred place where one can safely tell secrets, I blurted out the details — about believing myself to be a reincarnation of Buddha and Christ whose mission was to save the world by writing the new 'Bible'. To show that I was now a sane member of the psychology profession, I described these as 'grandiose delusions' and 'hallucinations'. At the end of my description she said, 'Well, I don't think that's craziness. Sounds like something important was happening to you on a deep level'. She invited me to bring the book to the next session, where I got to tell my story for the first time. In overcoming my own shame and reluctance to discuss it, I discovered that the valid spiritual dimensions of my experience could be salvaged through psychotherapy. Jungian analyst John Perry, MD, noted that following a psychotic episode, 'What remains ... is an ideal model and a sense of direction which one can use to complete the transformation through his own purposeful methods.'[2]

'Recovery means recovering the divine from within the disorder, seeing that its contents are authentically religious', James Hillman declared.[3] I began my own process of 'recovering the divine' by exploring Buddhism, Christianity, and other forms of spirituality (see Lukoff, 1990, for a fuller account).[4] I believe that my ability to effectively conduct therapy with other individuals who are having, or have had similar experiences, was aided by being given a rare opportunity to journey through the complete cycle and phenomenology of a naturally-resolving psychotic episode. Thus, beyond serving as a spiritual awakening, my journey held within it the archetypal gift of the Wounded Healer, providing me with the ability to connect more deeply with persons recovering from episodes of mental problems. As I have illustrated in several case studies, by eliciting the client's perspective and offering an individualized treatment strategy, as therapists we can help clients integrate their episode as a part of their spiritual journey and achieve a full recovery.

Some people who have spiritual crises become visionaries and social leaders, as the anthropologist Wallace has documented in several cultures. Many of the founders of psychology and psychiatry have been 'wounded healers' whose 'creative illness' involved a spiritual crisis that ultimately was transformative.[5] Since writing about this experience in *Shaman's Drum*, I have been contacted by many mental health professionals, and others in training, who have told me about their similar experiences.[6] As in my own case, these spiritual crises served as 'callings' into their vocations as psychologists, social workers, etcetera.

My critical episode launched my concern about others who have similar experiences, but end up in hospitals and are forcibly medicated. During the past thirty years of clinical work as a psychologist at UCLA-Neuropsychiatric Institute, Camarillo State Mental Hospital, and the San Francisco Veterans Medical Center as well as in private practice, I have often found myself face-to-face with individuals in the same state of consciousness that I had been in: convinced that they were reincarnations of Buddha, Christ, or other spiritual figures, reporting communication with such beings, believing they had a messianic mission to save the world, and preparing a 'Holy Book' that would form the basis for a new religion.

In 1980, this concern led me to start working with the Spiritual Emergency Network (SEN), a referral network organized by Stanislav and Christina Grof at Esalen Institute in California, which provided a telephone crisis hotline and provided referrals for people experiencing spiritual crises.[7] Dick Price, co-founder of Esalen, who seeded the development of the SEN by providing staff support and office space for its founding, personally had such experiences. He was not as lucky as I had been, however, and twice landed in a psychiatric hospital. The harsh treatment he received at these facilities led to his support for creating SEN.

Stanislav and Christina Grof coined the term *'spiritual emergency'* in 1978 to identify a variety of psychological difficulties, particularly those associated with the Asian spiritual practices and psychedelic drugs that had became popular in the West starting in the 1960s. They define spiritual emergencies as:

> crises when the process of growth and change becomes chaotic and overwhelming. Individuals experiencing such episodes may feel that their sense of identity is breaking down, that their old values no longer hold true, and that the very ground beneath their personal realities is radically shifting. In many cases, new realms of mystical and spiritual experience enter their lives suddenly and dramatically, resulting in fear and confusion. They may feel tremendous anxiety,

have difficulty coping with their daily lives, jobs, and relationships, and may even fear for their own sanity.[8]

Grof and Grof also note that 'Episodes of this kind have been described in sacred literature of all ages as a result of meditative practices and as signposts of the mystical path.'[9] It was obvious, however, that any familiarity with these phenomena was very hard to come by in the mental health sector. And so my work with SEN provided the initial impetus for proposing a new category for the fourth edition of the *Diagnostic and Statistical Manual*, which was due in 1994. Along with two psychiatrists, Francis Lu, MD and Robert Turner, MD, both on the faculty at University of California, San Francisco Department of Psychiatry, I viewed such an addition as the most effective way to increase the sensitivity of healthcare professionals to spiritual crises.

When the manual was published, articles on this new category appeared in *The New York Times, San Francisco Chronicle, Psychiatric News*, and the *APA Monitor*; it was described as indicating an important shift in the mental health profession's stance toward religion and spirituality. What did not receive attention in the media is that this new diagnostic category has its roots in the transpersonal psychology movement's attention to spiritual emergencies.

While I am not surprised, it is to Fransje de Waard's credit that her quest to understand the nature of spiritual crises brought her squarely into the field of transpersonal psychology, first as a student at the Institute of Transpersonal Psychology and then in this book. The core assumption of transpersonal psychology is that individuals are essentially spiritual beings, rather than simply a self or a psychological ego.[10] The psychological and spiritual dimensions of human experience are seen as different, although at times overlapping, with the spiritual as foundational.[11] The Association for Transpersonal Psychology (ATP), for which I have served as the Co-President for the past eight years, was formed in 1971 by many of the original founders of the Association for Humanistic Psychology; they saw the need for a psychology that was willing to study and explore transpersonal experiences in which the sense of identity extends beyond the individual, or personal, to encompass wider aspects of humankind, the natural world, and the cosmos. Such states are notoriously difficult to study, as William James pointed out in *Exceptional Mental States*.[12] James's philosophy of radical empiricism argued that a true science must be based on the study of all human experiences, not just those that can be manipulated in a laboratory. The discipline of transpersonal psychology attempts to scientifically study the reports of transpersonal experiences and behaviors.[13] In its journals and related books it has built a foundation of theory and research on transpersonal experiences including spiritual crises (as people in the UK prefer) or spiritual emergencies (as the literature from the USA uses).

Surveys show that mental health professionals routinely see clients with spiritual issues. In one survey, psychologists reported that 4.5% of their clients brought a mystical experience into therapy within the past year.[14] But surveys of mental health professionals also show that most do not have appropriate training. Scott Peck, a psychiatrist who has written several books on the spiritual dimensions of life, including the best selling *The Road Less Traveled*, gave an invited address which drew a standing-room only crowd at the 1992 Annual Meeting of the American Psychiatric Association. He pronounced that psychiatrists are 'ill-equipped' to deal with either spiritual pathology or health. Continuing to neglect spiritual issues, he claimed, would perpetuate the predicaments that are related to psychiatry's traditional neglect of these issues: 'occasional, devastating misdiagnosis; not infrequent mistreatment; an increasingly poor reputation; inadequate research and theory; and a limitation of psychiatrists' own personal development'.[15]

Yet polls conducted over the past thirty-five years have shown a dramatic increase in the percentages of people who report intense spiritual experiences including mystical, near-death, psychic, and 'alien abduction' experiences, all of which can assume a crisis level of intensity. Research on near-death experience (NDE), which is the most well-researched spiritual crisis, shows that most individuals experience anger, depression, and interpersonal difficulties after the NDE, even though research finds mostly positive outcomes after five years. Like many others experiencing a spiritual crisis, they could benefit from both a greater cultural acknowledgment of what such spiritual crises entail, and therapy with a sensitive and knowledgeable clinician.

De Waard's book is based on careful interviews conducted for her masters thesis with people who had a spiritual crisis, as well as several years of additional research and probing the extant literature. It serves as an invitation to a dialogue, first within oneself about the nature of spiritual crises, which are present in everyone at some level and part of the human existential condition, and then with anyone else who views themselves as on a spiritual journey. For the therapist, it is an ice breaker for mutual exploration about a client's experience of a spiritual crisis.

David Lukoff

Professor of Psychology, Institute of Transpersonal Psychology, Palo Alto, CA
Co-President of the Association for Transpersonal Psychology
Founder and instructor of the accredited
Spiritual Competency Resource Center

Notes

1 American Psychiatric Association (1994). *Diagnostic and Statistical Manual*, 4th edn (Washington, D.C.: American Psychiatric Association).
2 Perry, J. (1974). *The Far Side of Madness* (Englewood Cliffs, NJ: Prentice Hall). In the 1970s Perry founded an innovative residential treatment home called Diabasis for first-episode psychotic patients. It treated such people as visionaries in the making by facilitating the movement and expression of their psychotic experiences to a personally meaningful resolution.
3 Hillman, J. (1983). *Healing Fiction* (New York: Station Hill Press).
4 Lukoff, D. (1990). 'Divine Madness: Shamanistic Initiatory Crisis and Psychosis', *Shaman's Drum*, 22, 24–9.
5 Goldwert, M. (1992). *The Wounded Healers: Creative Illness in the Pioneers of Depth Psychology* (Lanham, MD: University Press of America).
6 Lukoff, D. (1990).
7 Prevatt, J., & Park, R. (1989). 'The Spiritual Emergence Network (SEN)', in S. Grof & C. Grof (eds), *Spiritual Emergency: When Personal Transformation Becomes a Crisis* (Los Angeles: J. P. Tarcher), 225–32.
8 Grof, S., & Grof, C. (eds) (1989). *Spiritual Emergency: When Personal Transformation Becomes a Crisis* (Los Angeles: Tarcher).
9 Grof & Grof (1989), back cover.
10 Sperry, L. (2001). *Spirituality in Clinical Practice* (Philiadelphia, PA: Brunner-Routledge).
11 Cortright, B. (1997). *Psychotherapy and Spirit: Theory and Practice in Transpersonal Psychotherapy* (Albany, NY: SUNY Press).
12 Taylor, E. (1983). *William James on Exceptional Mental States: The 1896 Lowell Lectures* (New York: Scribner).
13 Krippner, S. (1990). 'Beyond the Blind and Dumb', *Transpersonal Psychology Interest Group Newsletter* 3: 3.
14 Allman, L. S., De La Roche, O., Elkins, D. N., & Weathers, R. S. (1992). 'Psychotherapists's Attitudes Towards Clients Reporting Mystical Experiences, *Psychotherapy* 29: 564–9.
15 Peck, S. (1993). *Further Along the Road Less Traveled* (New York: Simon and Schuster).

Introduction

In 1994 the American Psychiatric Association published the fourth edition of the *Diagnostic and Statistical Manual of Mental Disorders*, the DSM-IV. This handbook forms the standard work *par excellence* on psychopathology, in the United States as well as beyond. Like a field guide to disorders and abnormalities, it systematically leads to the relevant diagnosis by means of a list of characteristics, thus providing a frame of reference for psychiatrists and clinical psychologists alike. Regular revisions reflect the gradually changing insights and views of the profession. Sometimes the impact of the latter is not restricted to the medical sphere alone — proof positive of the authority of the handbook. One of the most talked-about examples of such a spring-cleaning session was the DSM-II's scrapping of homosexuality as mental illness in 1973. The above-mentioned fourth edition aimed specifically at greater cultural sensitivity. The spirit of the age showed that a strictly medical-biological perspective does not necessarily do justice to the cultural nuances of mental suffering and discomfort. For example, the handbook would classify certain behaviour of non-western individuals as pathological, whereas the patients' own cultural context might endow it with a totally different significance and specific value. Discussion on this theme was initiated by anthropologists, and by social psychiatrists who found themselves increasingly approached by non-western immigrants with their mental troubles. Culture appeared to be an important factor, therefore, and clinicians with an eye for cultural nuances would be better able to assess the abnormality of their patients' behaviour, convictions or experiences.

This cultural refinement of the handbook was brought one step closer by the introduction of the category 'religious or spiritual problem'. Since the DSM-IV this category has been classified as V62.89. Known as a 'V-code', it concerns 'associated problems', not pathological in themselves but all the more alarming for that very reason. The published text is as follows:

V62.89 Religious or spiritual problem

> This category can be used when the focus of clinical attention is a religious or spiritual problem. Examples include distressing experiences that involve loss or questioning of faith, problems associated with conversion to a new faith, or questioning of other spiritual values which may not necessarily be related to an organized church or institution.

The ICD, the classification which forms the official standard in the Netherlands, has incorporated the article under the code Z71.8. The degree to which this category fits into the revised handbook however is less clearly visible in the official Dutch translation. After all, the translation of a 'spiritual' problem as a 'mental' problem — in such a work as the DSM, of all places — does not really help matters. It is as if an otherwise detailed field guide devoted an article to 'a plant'. But since its publication we in the Netherlands are casting aside our diffidence about 'spirituality' at high speed, and with its focus on 'spiritual crises' the use of language in this book blithely zeroes in on this. And then it becomes clear that V62.89 does carry some weight. After all, religious and spiritual customs, convictions, considerations, relations, portrayals of mankind, world views, values, morals, rituals and symbols form recognisable threads in the fabric of a particular culture. Conversely, many cultural phenomena in their turn can be traced back to religious and spiritual foundations. Even in the secular west one can detect the earlier religious background without much trouble. Not everyone would happily endorse this, but that does not alter the fact. It was surprising, however, to find religion and spirituality classified in the DSM as non-pathological. Religion and psychiatry? A simple free-association exercise would probably bring up the theme of religious mania in no time, and indeed, religiously charged passions and obsessions are all in a day's work for mental health professionals. The above-mentioned V-code refers nonetheless to other contexts. This is rather a strange attitude; after all, we would not expect the handbook to state that although there is a whole spectrum of eating disorders which people really do suffer from, eating as such is not necessarily a pathological symptom. With the introduction of V62.89, however, that is different; this can not be disentangled from the historical relationship between the two referees of the human mind: religion and spirituality on the one side, versus psychology and psychiatry on the other. To this very day these two parties are not always on the best of terms.

As empirical sciences, of course, psychology and psychiatry historically emerged from Enlightenment thought, which held that by reason man could at last free himself permanently from the prison of his own superstition. In the course of time science took over the monopoly of truth from religion, and the two became mutually exclusive. In spite of the little-known fact, incidentally, that most pioneers of this scientific field were exceptionally devout characters, who regarded their quest for knowledge of the true nature of things as a direct consequence of their faith. At a certain stage however it was accepted that all religion and spirituality was by definition an obstacle to progress, and organised religion certainly played its part in creating this idea. Over the centuries ecclesiastical organisations condemned various scientific breakthroughs and succeeded in making the lives of the diligent researchers behind them considerably difficult. Galileo, for example, who had the audacity to revise the authorised definition of the celestial motions, spent the last ten years of his life under house arrest, and the Roman Catholic inquisition kept a close eye on many a man who experimented too much with metals, minerals and herbal concoctions. Nowadays this mutual suspicion has resurfaced as strong as ever in the tug-of-war between creationists and evolutionary theorists, and the influence on education which each feels entitled to exert.

The mind sciences themselves meanwhile have little truck with the supernatural. That has been essentially so from the beginning; Freud himself had little time for God, nor was he much impressed by heavenly experiences. In his view, for example, the 'oceanic experience' of mystics was nothing more than regression to infantile helplessness and primary narcissism.[2] In the course of time Freud's colleagues supplemented his orderly interpretation with similar theories, varying from borderline psychosis to dysfunction of the temporal lobe.[3, 4] During those years the religious impulse was generally interpreted psychologically as the fulfilment of subconscious desires by projecting these onto parental figures of a 'higher' power: churches figured hereby as the socially sanctioned embodiment of this collective neurosis. And to summarize with the invective of Albert Ellis, the founder of cognitive behavioural therapy: 'Spirit and soul is horseshit of the worst sort. Obviously there are no fairies, no Santa Clauses, no spirits. What there is, is human goals and purposes ... But a lot of transcendentalists are utter screwballs.'[5]

We can hardly expect a balanced answer from Ellis on the identity of these screwballs. Even so, the group lumped together by him would also include the initiators of the above-mentioned DSM article. This group represented the psychological tendency which, nota bene, owes its rationale to something as idiotic as transcendentalism. For when Abraham Maslow — the man behind the human needs pyramid and peak experiences — could develop no further under the flag of humanism, he planted a new flag in 1969: that of transpersonal psychology. Over twenty years later, clinical psychologist David Lukoff (1948), together with two like-minded colleagues, lodged a proposal with the DSM-IV committee.[6]

They came armed with a pile of documentation on diverse forms of religious crisis and spiritual distress. Their aim: consensus on the social services' ingrained ignorance about religion and spirituality, in order to improve service to clients suffering, for example, from long-term breakdowns after transcendental experiences. Their original proposal was worded as follows:

Psychoreligious or psychospiritual problem

Psychoreligious problems are experiences that a person finds troubling or distressing and that involve the beliefs and practices of an organized church or religious institution. Examples include loss or questioning of a firmly held faith, change in denominational membership, conversion to a new faith, and intensification of adherence to religious practices and orthodoxy. Psychospiritual problems are experiences that a person finds troubling or distressing and that involve that person's relationship with a transcendent being or force. These problems are not necessarily related to the beliefs and practices of an organized church or religious institution.Examples include near-death experience and mystical experience. This category can be used when the focus of treatment or diagnosis is a psychoreligious or psychospiritual problem that is not attributable to a mental disorder.

Compared to this proposal, thus, the published article (see above) is not only less than half as long, but above all remarkably vague; it is all about religious and moral doubts. There is not the slightest trace of transcendentalism to be found, and specific examples of experiences have been omitted, so that the original text loses much of its force. Furthermore, documentation on this sort of experience from a wide variety of cultures is available, which could have increased the diagnostic depth of field in this area. Rational arguments, these, which did not weigh heavily enough for the committee at that time. For naturally, there was opposition. Great opposition, probably. What would have become of the whole field of study if the near-death experience had slipped into this sacred text? To what outer darkness would the psychiatric profession have been banished if it had taken the mystical experience seriously? No, it would never commit such a profanity.

But what would go through a psychiatrist's mind if one of those interviewed in this book came into the consulting room with his or her story? Such as the student of business economics, who was working himself to death, had slept badly for weeks, and was taking a walk one night when suddenly the heavens opened and he was overwhelmed by love: he took months to recover from this resounding blow, but ever since then he has known with absolute certainty that each and every one of us in the universe is made of love. Or if a middle-aged woman, from a terraced house in a small provincial town, should read out an excerpt from her diary, a dry and painstaking account of a physically almost unbearable ordeal, lasting several weeks, during which she felt an intense sensation of fire creeping up her spine, she heard a voice instructing her to drink only apple juice and to earth her energy by holding on to the shower rail, and she gradually became convinced that she was a winged being, adept in the mysteries? What on earth would a university-educated DSM-user make of that?

Now many people who tell their stories in this book actually avoided clinicians and therapists as much as possible, even though for weeks or even months at a time they did not know where to turn. Some of them were incapable of anything throughout this period, while others barely managed to keep going. Some felt themselves vanishing into nothingness, others were deluged by thoughts and emotions that did not seem to be their own. And of those who were driven to the consulting room by sheer desperation, most kept their mouths firmly shut on certain topics. Otherwise, they thought, the doctor would take down that hefty volume from the shelf and nod understandingly, without understanding in the least, as they rambled on about energies or apparitions or voices. And because deep down they knew that they were not mad, although sometimes this was the only thing that they *did* know. The few who decided to put all their cards on the table and to confide their experiences in bewildering new dimensions to a professional, were met by a glassy stare and sometimes a new prescription. All in all, the chance that a doctor or psychologist would be at a loss is thus not so very big. Which is somewhat disturbing, since that of course is what this V-code was meant for.

On the other hand, however, is the fact that the people in this book all came safely through their experiences. Often — though not always — with the support of family or friends, through physical activity or complete rest, through expressing their feelings or remaining silent, by seeking distraction or by entering the inner darkness. But always steering by their own compass. And all without exception say that they emerged better for the experience, richer, more clear-sighted, more loving, more impassioned, more complete. That it was difficult, severe or even devastating, but that they are now *more* human — and they know what that means for them. And here almost imperceptibly we leave the territory of accepted psychology once more. For by now the prevailing models of the psyche have taught us a thing or two about what and how and why people do what they do. But the same models leave us quite simply at a loss for words whenever we consider who or what a human being *is*. Who or what *are* we? What makes us human? A brain-pan full of spaghetti, to be seasoned according to taste with the right amount of hormones and neurotransmitters? Or a sophisticated reflex-gadget with a chip to supply the personal standard repertoire of emotions, thoughts and behaviour? These questions are far from new, and we could quite justifiably answer them with a 'yes', but it takes some nerve to suggest that that is all there is to it. At all events, the men and women in this book tell a very different story. Some of them were actively searching, and discovered that the spiritual life might turn out to be totally different from what they had imagined. Others were taken by surprise, and, unasked and sometimes under protest, allowed themselves to be gradually disarmed and swept along with the flow. For them, whether there is 'anything' more than spaghetti and chips is not so much a question, more of a scream.

In all sorts of ways, their accounts remind those familiar with such things of experiences and insights which we usually find in spiritual sources. Experiences of light, energy, vitality, immense power, dazzling beauty, unprecedented wisdom, pure innocence, fathomless depth, unutterable silence, of love which dissolves all boundaries. And then again waves of confusion, fear, panic, pain, coldness, emptiness, desolation, devastation, loss, sorrow, rage, loathing, hatred. No different from the accounts and reflections of the inner life of countless historical figures from the multicoloured palette of mystical traditions in the world — traditions drawn from Christianity, Judaism, Islam, Taoism, Hinduism, Buddhism — and of other spiritual systems, such as shamanist cultures. The experiences of Christian mystics such as Hildegard of Bingen, Meister Eckhart, Teresa of Avila and St John of the Cross can be bought on the high street, and that brings them closer to us, the people who shop there. But surely these mystics were exceptional individuals, who withdrew from the world in order to devote their lives completely to what was paramount for them? And by so doing, did they not leave behind unique, precious works which still move us and fill us with wonder centuries later? Even those who have not been officially canonized as yet — Hildegard got as far as beatification, while Eckhart died a suspected heretic and is still waiting for rehabilitation — are nevertheless regarded as saints. This makes it difficult for us to believe that we ourselves, or the man or woman beside us in the checkout queue, are susceptible to the same sort of experiences as these almost mythical beings. Or as Tibetan lamas or Indian *saddhus*, who sit meditating for years on mountain tops or in caves. But according to the people interviewed here, such things do happen now and then. And when they do — as we shall see — we don't quite know how to handle it.

It might have turned out differently in every case, as most of those interviewed are perfectly aware. They have lived to tell the tale; others in the same situation may have been less fortunate. Due to less support, less resilience, less insight; through those around them, their health, their history, by chance, whatever the reason. Several people said that admission into hospital would have made them 'really crazy', because then they could not imagine how they would ever have recovered. We must assume that in practice it does sometimes happen like that. And in those cases do we have sufficient knowledge and skill to make the right diagnosis? Do we have any way of telling whether we are dealing with someone in a non-pathological crisis as meant in the original proposal for V62.89, or with someone who is contending with one of the many other categories in the DSM? Can we distinguish between them? It is a difficult question – and a patient may in fact be suffering from both – but the answer at this moment can only be: no, we cannot distinguish between them. Not only because the original article is even less well-known than the published one, but because the mental health service is focused scarcely, if at all, on the recognition of spiritual crises and confusion. The watershed which formed between Jung and his preceptor Freud, precisely because of Jung's explicit interest in metaphysics, lies between official and alternative therapeutic practice. However curious it may sometimes seem, the roots of the mind sciences happen to lie in physics. Jung's analytical psychology, strongly influenced by his own crisis and further development, was only grudgingly admitted into the regular canon. For that reason most clinicians have simply never become acquainted with what some of them rather absurdly call 'the supernatural' – an observation which got as far as the *Tijdschrift voor Psychiatrie* (Journal of Psychiatry) but which remained a completely isolated case.[7] In clinical education, this department of the mind is a subject of no importance, and many practitioners feel awkward on the subject, one reason being that not a few of them come from a secular background themselves.[8] Outside of the regular sector we can of course take our spiritual indisposition to the alternative circuit, where by contrast you can get anything you want in the supernatural line. But the ability to distinguish between mental disorder and religious problem is no less necessary here, though the focus may be different. After all, not everyone who advertises their skill in patching up faded auras or sagging chakras is equally knowledgeable about the 'basics': object relations, cognitive development, personality types, moods, emotional management, social functioning etc, including the two-way traffic of transference transactions. This territory – significantly enough – is essentially still marked by what is known as the GAP Report of 1976 on the one hand, and by the message of antipsychiatry on the other.

The said GAP Report takes its name from the publisher: the *Group for the Advancement of Psychiatry*, an American society of psychiatrists, which explores subjects in and around the field of study through independent committees. Since 1947 the institute has presented the world with more than 200 reports; on the joys and sorrows of parenthood, on sex at university, on the abuse of psychiatry in the law courts, and on just about everything in between. At the time of the publication of *Mysticism: Spiritual Quest or Psychic Disorder?* the society had around 300 members; six of them—all of the male sex—formed the *Committee on Psychiatry and Religion*, which wrote the report.[9] The aim of the publication was to contribute to understanding the phenomenon of mysticism, which by then—in the mid 1970s—had become such a 'conspicuous social force'. The committee members saw a difficult task ahead, and restricted themselves to a small number of sources from a select number of traditions—the mystical tendencies in Christianity, Judaism and Hinduism. Their literary survey on this basis seems benevolent and sound, which makes the conclusions all the more startling, pervaded as they are with a quaint sort of fear of contamination. Now the country at this time was teeming with groups which claimed to be able to provide would-be mystics (male and female) with the celestial experience of oneness, and the committee members evidently identified instantly with the generation which took a dim view of their growing offspring's attraction to such groups. At all events, from the GAP point of view, both the aspiring mystic and the schizophrenic categorically rejected society, because he or she could not cope with the stress of everyday life; GAP made the distinction that the former took this step voluntarily, while the latter did not. To combat loneliness, the 'mystics' then banded together in low-budget fraternities, a life-style which they justified by alluding to their direct contact with the divine, with which no other authority could of course compete. Meanwhile the authors had unmasked the crucial experience as nothing more than a trancelike regression in which the world was obliterated and the gratification of infantile needs was hallucinated into existence. Those who could not avoid or reverse such a trance by willpower thereby stamped their own situation as psychotic. And as it was, the committee tied itself in diplomatic knots in its efforts to label the eccentrics concerned as severely disturbed, hysterical, schizophrenic or manic depressive, without actually taking responsibility for this approach. The report's hesitant epilogue does not clarify matters. After disclosing the fact that they were psychoanalysts, the worthy authors demonstrated a specimen of Freudian interpretation in a reflection on the experience of awe, which pervades so many mystical accounts. The core of this experience, they said, must surely lie in early childhood, on first beholding, that's right, the phallus—an adult specimen, that is to say—and as one man they agreed to this explanation of mystics' ecstatic powers. The text rambled on in clumsy Jungian jargon from diagnostic mistiness to misunderstood profundity—in short, the difficult birth of a misfit. Now from the beginning the committee had of course entangled itself in the tentacles of a dichotomy. In their view it was a black-and-white question – disorder or experience of salvation – and not surprisingly they failed to come up with a Judgement of Solomon. That they were aware of the paradox was revealed in the final paragraph of the report; this expressed a sort of covert respect for the mystic, who had mastered the art of living with contradictions.

Diametrically opposed to the GAP camp we find statements that we instantly associate with the 1960s and 1970s. Although the term 'antipsychiatry' for the relevant movement was rather unfortunate, this made its criticism of the whole psychiatric business no less harsh.[10] Following the example of the American Thomas Szasz and the British Ronald D. Laing in particular, the Dutch figurehead Jan Foudraine fulminated amidst loud applause against the medical model, against treatment in institutions, and against the psychiatrist's position of power. The fierce dispute raged through the whole country for a considerable time. This radical stock of ideas was an explosive mixture of Marxist cultural criticism and psychological humanism, that succeeded in inspiring experiments in institutions everywhere. In these experiments, 'lunatics' were no longer reduced to zombies by electric shocks but, as people with developmental difficulties, they were allowed to sit on the couch next to their 'supervisors' and discuss how to sort out their problems. The mothers of schizophrenic residents were particularly singled out for the sackcloth-and-ashes treatment, as they had produced nothing but sick patterns of communication. The derangement of their offspring was the only appropriate, indeed creative, answer to these patterns. Foudraine expressed further the idea that madness can be a fruitful affair. In those optimistic years this amounted to the idea that every psychosis was a toast to the freedom of the human spirit, and the idea of 'madness' was a perverse product of bourgeois anxieties. When he drew the logical conclusions from his vision, and entrusted his spiritual transformation to the good-time guru Baghwan Sri Rajneesh, not everyone was prepared to follow him so far. Although he later tried to pick up the thread of his first bestseller, his days as authority in the sector were over. In the wording and tone of his rhetoric, though, we recognise that of Ellis in the above quotation; as regards content they are opposites, rarely guilty of a nuance. And the time is now ripe for a little more nuance and reconsideration.

In such a situation some time ago Gemma Blok sketched a picture of antipsychiatry and its legacy in her doctoral thesis *Baas in eigen brein* (Master of your own Mind).[11] Here she concluded that the turbulent years foundered through excessive naivety, but that they undeniably acted as a catalyst. Since then, for example, the hierarchy has become more human, and forms of psychotherapy are a standard inclusion on the clinical agenda. A few years previously Agneta Scheurs published her book *Psychotherapie en Spiritualiteit*, in which she gives a detailed account of how she conducts group therapy from the spiritual viewpoint of Christian 'moderate orthodoxy'.[12] And the doctoral thesis of Jan Dirk Blom, entitled *Deconstructing Schizophrenia*, offers a rich and lucid insight behind the scenes of the psychiatric kitchen.[13] Little is hid from view. The cooks on duty are busy concocting the ultimate dish. While they are all busy stirring the contents of their pans they fail to realise that their cookery book is a pile of outdated recipes stapled together, that stocks of many ingredients have run out, and that they have never agreed on a formula for the restaurant. Guests are given a plate of food, but nobody really knows what brings them there. In terms of psychiatry, Blom argues that after decades of research into the causes of and therapeutic prospects for schizophrenia, so few patterns have been found that the illness as described in the textbooks does not exist. He is of course not the first to suggest that the *concept* of schizophrenia is unsound, while acknowledging that 'schizophrenics' may well be suffering from a genuine disorder. Blom however digs deeper into the evolution of the current model, samples the philosophical mindset surrounding it and dissects the structure. On this basis he contends, for example, that psychiatry overestimates the importance of certain aspects of reality, and is not open to the light which may filter through from quite different angles. By this he refers mainly to the assumption that there is a 'hard', organic cause of the illness out there somewhere, waiting to be found.

Meanwhile some 'voice-hearers' turn out to function remarkably well, detailed studies of the self from the East offer a comparative view of psychotic and mystical ecstasies, substantial surveys into near-death experiences demolish every physiological explanation, and forms of meditation appear on the therapeutic menu card. Along with philosopher of science Thomas Kuhn, known for his principal work *De structuur van wetenschappelijke revoluties* (The Structure of Scientific Revolutions) we are forced to conclude that a shift in the paradigm of the psyche is at hand.[14] Within the prevailing paradigm we keep getting bogged down in certain problems, while beyond it original suggestions are available; within it we raise more and more doubts and start more and more debates on fundamental questions, while outside it people are seething with curiosity about the implications of a broader and more fundamental perspective—this is all writing on the wall, signs that something is about to happen. Sooner or later a paradigm is defeated by a competitor. The latter needs to be armed with good rational arguments, admittedly, but these are never enough in themselves. The deciding factor in the end is that the competitor has an essentially different, better, broader and even more elegant story to tell. In this way the earth was dethroned by the sun as centre of the universe. In this way the mechanics of the colliding billiard balls was overtaken by quantum physics with its principle of uncertainty. And in this context that bigger, better story could well begin with the recognition, nearly a century later, that the same quantum physics also applies to the molecules in our very brains. The speculative models for the wave-like nature of brain activity thus deserve our undivided scientific attention. The cocksure researchers behind it, somewhat mildly reviled, have been arguing for years that empirical psychology's biggest blind spot is subjective experience, and that there lie the keys to understanding ourselves as humans, in our heights and in our depths. It is these areas of experience for which transpersonal psychology offers a broader perspective, as one of the players in a new field of science, where teams ranging from philosophers to neurocyberneticists gather round the great question of human consciousness.

This book was written as a sequel to my research into spiritual crises, within the framework of a distance master's degree at the *Institute of Transpersonal Psychology* in Palo Alto, California. I have never gone through such a crisis myself, but I have seen inwardly how close 'madness' lies to wholeness, as a sort of landscape in which nothing remains connected to anything else. Partly for this reason I became fascinated by the common ground and possible overlapping of both sorts of experience, and alert to references to them in literature. I was increasingly struck by references in spiritual literature to the 'deranged' behaviour of ecstatic figures, and in psychological sources to all sorts of 'religious psychopathology'. Usually, however, these were no more than brief notes which were not further developed. In this way authors seem to skirt around the subject. And yet my intuition proved to be less odd than I had first thought; others had already explored the subject. But the most important thing was that I succeeded in finding people who had undergone such a crisis, and who were willing and able to talk about it. In addition, David Lukoff, whose name is linked with the V62.89 article in the DSM-IV, was prepared to supervise my research as regards content. After finishing my study it was clear to me that these experiences were worth reading, and deserved to be read in the Dutch language in which they were originally described. Since then I have made a new series of visits to people who were prepared to tell me their story. The question which I put to them was always: have you ever had an experience in which you thought you were going 'mad', which sooner or later had spiritual significance for you?

Although at the thesis stage I was able to analyse the data qualitatively, in this book I have written from another motive, and for a different reader. The subject as such is ripe for closer acquaintance. Who knows, for some readers this may end up in a confrontation, which would not be so unlikely with this theme. For others it may turn out to be a feast of recognition, while still others might be in for a revelation. If there is one thing that is laid bare before, during and after a spiritual crisis, it is the ordinary take on the world. Now our collective view of ourselves and the world is undergoing a considerable shift at the moment, and it does not take much imagination to detect the contours of a spiritual crisis in that whole process too. Meanwhile there is no accepted Dutch term as yet for the sort of episode on which this book throws some light, such as the english phrase *spiritual emergency*. Understanding the phenomenon 'from back to front' is no doubt a step too far as well. And yet at first sight the way further leads through more or less familiar territory. To begin with, in Chapter 1 a fascinating historical case illustrates the limits of our usual field of vision. The three sub-chapters zoom in on 'the eyes of the beholder', the lenses through which we look at the complex, delicate and confusing episodes that spiritual crises generally are. In chapters 2 and 3 the focus is on science and religion respectively, as the primary frames of reference which have come down to us. Chapter 4 provides an outline of transpersonal psychology, as a school which in both theory and practice appears to offer a fruitful approach to this phenomenon. Scattered between these is the raw material itself: the first-hand accounts of 'out-of-the-ordinary' experiences and major spiritual crises which happened to 'ordinary' people. Within the limits of the printed text their experiences are recorded as directly and completely as possible, in order to let the reader sample something of them for himself — both of the extraordinary episodes themselves as well as of their impact on the ordinary lives in which they took place. If so wished, these stories can be read separately from the main text, but are intended to be read in combination with it, above all as food for the minds of those who do not wish to push this material aside as nonsense from the very start. In conclusion, a number of fundamental lines are developed a little further in a short discussion.

How pathological are spiritual experiences? How spiritual are pathological experiences? Although these questions served as framework for the whole project, it is far from my intention to provide definitive answers — if such things exist. I hope that the book as a whole will provoke more questions, and above all: discussion. And that it will do so for everyone who dares to read it: those who seek recognition for their own experiences, those who work at a particular level in the mental health service, psychologists and psychiatrists involved in research, members of religious orders, agnostics, philosophers of the mind, writers, creative individuals, but above all 'ordinary people', like most of those interviewed. Because for each of us, one and all, there is something to be learned from what they as ordinary people have experienced, even though we may not be able to place it or put it into words immediately. Let us, above all, keep our minds wide open.

Chapter One

Emanuel Swedenborg
and the Question of Diagnostics

Before focusing on the experiences of the people next to us in the supermarket queue, here is a historical case as introduction, which will be easier to examine separately from our own context. It so happens that there are psychiatrists to this day who view the case through a diagnostic magnifying glass and so illustrate a certain way of seeing. Nearly all of us, psychiatrists or not, have adopted this view. It is only one ingredient in the eclectic mixture of our highly personal outlook, which harbours all sorts of elements: from the Judaic-Christian body of thought, secular humanism, eastern spiritual traditions, classical mechanics and a smidgeon of quantum physics, from existential philosophies which exclude the time-honoured Supreme Being, post-modern modifications of all previous-isms, and from an even more modern 'somethingism', which make the space between heaven and earth just a little less empty. When someone claims to converse with God on a daily basis, however, sooner or later a thought along the lines of 'must be mad' pops into our heads. And if the individual in question really is 'mad', that means, to put it briefly: he or she is suffering from some or other diagnosable mental disorder or illness. Diabolical possession is passé, sin is old hat, deliberately asocial behaviour is tricky, illness is feasible. The American comedienne Lily Tomlin once observed with wonder that we call it 'praying' when we talk to God, and 'schizophrenia' when He replies. The 'case' of Emanuel Swedenborg speaks volumes in that respect—and in more than one sense. Firstly, the orthodox psychiatric evaluation of his case has produced various diagnoses over the years, none of which however are intellectually satisfying. The man lived a couple of hundred years ago, it is true, but his colourful history throws some light on controversies in ways of thinking about spiritual adventures and insanity. Secondly, his work is so rich, in both scope and colouring, that those who relish it can look forward to a feast.

1 The young scientist

Born in Stockholm in 1688 as the son of court preacher Jesper Swedberg, from his earliest years the young Emanuel was full of questions about life and death, God, suffering and salvation—themes which were never far from the surface in Lutheran circles. His father had little time for religion as an abstract doctrine. Jesper favoured a faith derived from man's inner experience, and was drawn to the pietist ideas of his time. Pietism is centred on inner devotion, motivated by love rather than fixed rules. His father's attitude must have encouraged his son Emanuel in his early search. The boy continually bombarded both his parents and the clergymen around him with questions and reflections, and at a certain stage he drew the conclusion that love is the essence of life. At the same time he was intensely interested in 'how things work'. When he left Uppsala university years later, he allowed his brother-in-law, a bishop, like Swedenborg's father by this time, to persuade him to study further in Europe. This brother-in-law was an enthusiastic amateur scientist, with contacts in various countries which he used to help Emanuel on his way. In 1710, accordingly, Emanuel travelled to London, which was then the biggest city in the world and the place to be for philosophical and scientific innovations. Here he continued his studies of mathematics and astronomy. He attended lectures by Isaac Newton, which greatly inspired him, listened to discourses on a variety of subjects, foraged in bookshops, and participated in London's rich intellectual life by entering wholeheartedly into discussion with other active minds. In addition he mastered various trades, including marble engraving, glass grinding, and the manufacture of measuring instruments. After London he spent some time in Leiden, then in France and Germany. He started work on the development of a navigational method, made a series of inventions, and designed the very first flying machine on paper. In addition to all this, he composed poetry in Latin. Then, determined to discover the truth of the universe through the empirical examination of physical reality, he returned to Sweden in 1715.

Once there he quickly made his way to King Karl XII with the proposal to build an observatory in the north of the country. The king, a dabbler in mathematics himself, did not see the immediate need for such a thing, but offered the bright young man a post in the ministry of mining. For the time being this appointment determined the focus of Emanuel's attention, and he put up a good show. In the following years he produced piles of articles, surveys, discoveries, innovations and inventions in the fields of geology, metalurgy, mineralogy and salt production, he laid the foundations of crystallography, constructed improved stoves, hearing aids and air guns, and designed the prototype of an 'underwater boat'. As engineer he was concerned with dykes and docks, and in his spare time he succeeded in organising the overland transport of a number of galleys for the king, in time to go to war with the Norwegians. When his family was raised to the nobility on account of his father's religious merits, and adopted the name of Swedenborg, Emanuel began his career as a worthy member of the House of Nobles. Among his achievements as politician, besides the introduction of duty on spirits — not all Swedes would thank him for that — are those of decimal currency and various innovations in the tax system and balance of trade. He gained widespread respect for his efforts and independent attitude. When the famous university of Uppsala offered him the prestigious chair of astronomy, however, he politely refused — in favour of Anders Celsius, the thermometer man — because he believed that he would be of greater use to Sweden as promoter of the mining industry.

2 Plumbing the depths on all fronts

Swedenborg's first important publications, on chemistry, mineralogy and the structure of matter, were based on the principle that physical reality originates from one invisible, infinite source. In passing he described the atomic structure of matter before John Dalton's name was linked to this theory, and the vibratory nature of light before Michael Faraday recorded his findings in various electromagnetic laws and units. Over the years Swedenborg's interest was channelled increasingly towards biology and then philosophy; he was searching for the soul within the temple of the body, for the link between the finite and the infinite, between man and God. In the foreword of one of his voluminous manuscripts he writes:

> I am determined not to allow myself a moment's rest before, through general study of the animal kingdom, I have penetrated to knowledge of the soul. Through an increasingly deeper contemplation within myself, I shall open all doors which lead to it, and in the end by divine grace I shall behold the soul itself.[1]

And later on, enlarging on his motivation:

> How would it serve my interests to wish to persuade someone to embrace my feelings? Let him be convinced by his own reason. I did not undertake this work for love of money or fame; I avoid both of these much more than I pursue them, since they disturb the soul and I am content with my lot; no, I undertook it for the sake of truth, which alone is indestructible.[2]

After his fundamental discoveries in inorganic matter, he was the first in the fields of anatomy and physiology, among others, to determine that brainwaves move synchronically with the lungs—not with the heart—that the brain regulates the internal secretion of hormones by the pituitary gland, and that organs and tissues obtain what they need not from the blood that is pumped into them, but by actively absorbing it themselves. He obtained such insights by combining other people's findings with his own research, and above all by his subtle and profoundly intuitive understanding of how things work. In many cases it was only much later that medical science could produce the hard evidence that he was right. For example, Swedenborg wrote hefty volumes on the human body, the senses, the organs, the circulation of the blood and the brain and, no less enthusiastically, on ethical principles, the *condition humaine*, the soul and metaphysics. His discoveries and reflections brought him a certain fame, but not the ultimate knowledge that he sought. Through analysis he had achieved his insights into the universe, at an increasingly higher level of integration—from separate particles via organic connections to flow fields. But, he began to realise, this method was inadequate when trying to penetrate to the essence of the correspondences between 'above' and 'below'. While he wrestled nevertheless with frustration at his fruitless search, he realised that he would need to draw on a more intuitive power of understanding.

3 Celestial visitation

Swedenborg's inner life had been becoming more intense for some time now. Increasingly often all sorts of remarkable dreams and spiritual experiences came bubbling to the surface, which he, always observing and dissecting, noted in his dream book. Then, one night in 1743, he had a vivid vision in his Delft hotel room. A man appeared to him in the guise of God the Father, and announced to him that he had been chosen to explain

Scripture anew to humanity. A year later a second vision followed, this time of Jesus, and Swedenborg could no longer evade his new vocation. He realised that love is the sought-for connection, which he could not find in reason. Perfectly content with his sense of being an ignorant child in this matter, he surrendered himself completely to what the Lord required of him. That proved to be quite a task, for it marked the beginning of his period as a visionary, which would continue to the end of his life.

From his first vision his inner eye was open to the spiritual world — even when wide awake, and talking to other people. He beheld what he called the spiritual world, a sort of parallel world in which, among other things, he was in direct contact with the dead. They told him how they had fared since their death, thus making it obvious to him that people on earth were in dire need of knowledge of the true state of affairs. Swedenborg performed his noble task to the full, and in the course of time published his next series of monumental works, in which for example he described heaven and hell in great detail, as became an exact scientist. When, in so doing, he fleshed out the ancient neo-platonic idea of correspondence between macro- and micro-cosmos, it was not at random; the consistency which he applied to the task, cutting right through all the various layers of reality, is quite simply mind-blowing. After teaching himself Hebrew he rewrote the biblical books of Genesis and Exodus in the process, so that mankind would be able to understand them at last. With the aid of an impressive notation system he commented on almost every word, replacing it with the real meaning. Through this fearsomely systematic exegesis, Genesis was transformed beneath his pen into the story of Jesus' life, and Exodus into the development of Christendom on earth. Swedenborg's use of language in this work consists of the dry account of the facts as he perceived them. One example of his many journeys through heaven:

> the paradisiacal gardens are situated in the first heaven, on the margin where the inner part of that heaven begins. They are representations which descend from the heaven above it, when the angels in the higher heaven are discussing the truth of the faith. In order to communicate with each other the angels make use of spiritual and celestial ideas which serve them as verbal expressions, a succession of representations, the beauty and charm of which are impossible to describe in any way. It is these wondrously beautiful and charming expressions of ideas which appear in the lower heaven as paradisiacal gardens.[3]

He encounters less pleasant places in the spiritual world, however, such as when he is offered a sightseeing tour through hell. Everywhere he finds illustrations of the principle that every person after his or her physical death end up in an environment — to continue the spatial metaphor for a moment — that reflects his or her earlier inner state; he or she feels quite at home there. The true inner kinship with others is thereby irrevocably revealed. Swedenborg repeatedly observes moreover that those who passed for devout individuals on earth — bishops for example — are not automatically accorded the places of honour. While the above fragment comes from a chapter on our visual sense, which manifests itself at a spiritual level as keen inward sight, in the following he deals with the perception of 'general atmospheres', which correspond with the physical sense of smell — as in the expression 'that reeks of … '

> but the odours which emanate from the perception of evil are extremely unpleasant. They are foul, they stink, like the smell of stagnant water, of excrement, corpses, or of people who give off the disgusting smell of mice or bodylice. In foul-smelling atmospheres like this live the inhabitants of hell. And strange to tell, those who live in it do not find it repellent. On the contrary, they find such tainted fumes delightful, and when they are present the residents of hell dwell in the atmosphere that affords them pleasure and enjoyment.[4]

4 Wildfire

The oeuvre that Swedenborg produced in this way is, to put it mildly, considerable. In thousands of pages he covered the nature of man, his divinity, the principle of regeneration, wisdom, love and sensuality and so on. As with his earlier scientific work he wrote in Latin, and published mainly in the Netherlands and Germany. In his new capacity, therefore, he was at first unknown in Sweden itself. Then at one stroke a dramatic incident created his later reputation as clairvoyant. Shortly after returning from abroad he was dining with friends in Gothenburg, but felt unable to swallow a morsel after six o'clock. He paced back and forth in the garden, and when the company anxiously questioned him, he told them that Stockholm was on fire. His mood gradually developed into panic, because the house of a friend had already been reduced to ashes, and his own was unlikely to escape the flames. Then around eight o'clock he cried out in relief that the fire — thank God — had stopped three houses away. Pressed by the alarmed governor, he told him exactly how the matter stood, how the fire started, how it spread and was then extinguished. Two days later a courier arrived and confirmed his story word for word.

   Sweden was astonished that the famous engineer, scientist and statesman now appeared to be amusing himself with the world of the mind as well. Over the years similar occurrences regularly took place. According to a well-documented story, the queen requested that if he happened to be talking to the dead, would he please send her regards to her dead brother? A few days later Swedenborg approached her and whispered in her ear. At this the queen blanched, crying out that only God and her brother could have known such a thing. The other famous incident, which also forms part of the canon of Swedenborg's powers, concerns a lost receipt. The Dutch ambassador's wife, Mevrouw de Marteville, who had been widowed a year by then, was driven to distraction when a goldsmith came knocking on her door for the sum of 25,000 florins, which her husband supposedly owed him. She was convinced that her husband, always a stickler for accuracy, had already paid the bill. But there was no trace of the receipt. At her wits' end, she diffidently called on Swedenborg and asked whether he had known her husband — he had not — and whether he could find out something from him in the hereafter. Swedenborg agreed to try, and a couple of days later he did manage to contact the deceased Meneer de Marteville and convey his wife's cry for help to him. De Marteville replied that he would look into it. One night the following week the lady dreamt about her husband, who pointed to a drawer in his desk and told her to pull it out completely. The receipt in question had been pushed to the back of it, and that's where she would find it. At this the lady woke up, went straight to his desk and found, of course, the missing document. With her mind at rest she went back to sleep. The following morning Swedenborg called on her. Before she could get a word in, he apologised for being no wiser about the case. Her husband, whom he had found with a group of people on that night, had told him that he had to rush off to his wife and tell her something important.

This case, and others less connected to high society, continued to witness to Swedenborg's unconventional knowledge. He himself took no notice of all the excitement, but talked in a friendly and courteous way to everyone who came to ask him anything. Many who arrived at his door as sceptics left as fervent admirers, greatly impressed by this devout and wise man. Swedenborg received regular visitors in his house on the Hoornstraat in Stockholm, showed them around his beautiful garden, and conversed with them over a cup of tea in a summer-house or arbour. To avoid gossip, he took care never to be alone in a room with a woman. He was extremely pleasant with children too. Now and then, for example, one of his neighbour's little daughters would come to the house, telling him more than once that she would love to see an angel. One day he confided to her that the time had come. They were in his summer-house and he told her to go and stand in front of a particular curtain. When he pulled it aside, she would see an angel. Astonished, she found herself gazing into a mirror.

5 Friction

Nevertheless his work led to a certain amount of controversy. Muttering was heard from the Lutheran doctrinal authority, focusing on a number of Swedenborg's intellectual friends who lacked his respectability and connections. The theologians were thoroughly convinced that Swedenborg's work would lead from bad to worse, but stubbornly refused to read anything by him. Their case was not a strong one, but with a bit of scheming it was brought before the judge years later, and two professors were sacked — no doubt creating much coveted vacancies. When Swedenborg marched to the king in high dudgeon, the latter took steps to rectify the injustice to some extent.

Swedenborg's revelations occurred at a period which was later seen as the lowest ebb of the whole Christian tradition, and people came up with various explanations for them. His admirer Heinrich Wilhelm Clemm, professor of mathematics and theology, distinguished three possibilities: 1) they were fantasies, 2) they were the delusions of an evil spirit, or 3) they were genuine.[5] Swedenborg's fiercest opponent, the Leipzig theologian Ernesti, contested irritably that there was a fourth possibility, namely that it was all a farrago of lies.[6] Swedenborg was not surprised that people cast doubt on his visions and refused to take him seriously, he had even prophesied this eventuality in his books, and regarded it as a matter between the doubters and God. But to be personally made out to be a fraud was another kettle of fish. He was hurt, he wrote to an Amsterdam acquaintance, but further regarded it as so beneath contempt that he took good care not to lose his dignity and behave 'like women of the lowest sort who, when quarreling, throw the mud of the street into each other's faces.'[7]

Perhaps the most famous affair concerning Swedenborg's credibility involved the German philosopher Immanuel Kant (1724–1804). The latter was struck by Swedenborg's scientific profundity, and particularly interested in the story of the queen and her late brother. As a pre-eminently critical thinker he saw it as the sort of proof which would give the described spiritual excursions the ring of truth. Kant sent various confidants to Sweden to check up on this and other stories; one by one they returned with a firm corroboration. Kant felt uneasy at this. As a philosopher he took the line that our highest cognitive power is pure reason, which does not give us access to metaphysical reality. We are therefore in no position to make pronouncements on the *Ding-as-sich*, but that was exactly what Swedenborg did, meticulously, page after page, with the conviction of a mathematician explaining the inscribed triangle. Kant could not afford to be linked in the eyes of friends and colleagues with the sort of superstitious speculations which the Enlightenment had just put behind it. A few years later, therefore, he expounded his position on the matter, exposing Swedenborg in the process. In Kant's 1766 pamphlet *Träume eines Geistersehers, erläutert durch die Träume der Metaphysik* (Dreams of a Spirit Seer, illustrated by thos of Metaphysics), he demolished this dreaming inveterate liar, who wrote books crammed with nonsense about the dead, ghosts and monsters and had done nothing useful in his life.[8] The tone of this remarkable publication caused amazement to put it mildly, and had the intended effect on contemporary German opinion on Swedenborg.

6 Lunacy

Besides the various interpretations of Swedenborg's work as heresy, fraud and balderdash, there is one more to consider, which is still current today. This one carries most weight in the context of this book, and is to the effect that the man wasn't right in the head, or to put it politely, suffered from a mental disorder. Kant also hinted at this, but the most prominent advocate of this evaluation was the Englishman John Wesley (1703–1791), the charismatic leader of the Methodists, who, in spite of the usual opposition from the Anglican bigwigs, established his church in America and made a success of it. In 1772 Wesley gave a detailed account in his journal *The Arminian Magazine* of Swedenborg's behaviour while staying with an acquaintance, one year after the Lord had appeared to him: he stood in the middle of the room, with hair standing on end and foaming at the mouth, crying that he was the Messiah and would offer himself to be crucified on behalf of the Jews. He then ran outside, tore off his clothes and rolled stark naked in the mud, ending by flinging all his money to the assembled onlookers. There is absolutely no concrete evidence to support this version of events, but Wesley certainly started a trend. This was in the eighteenth century, a period during which the time-honoured association of abnormal behaviour with diabolical possession had fallen into disuse. The religious diagnosis increasingly lost ground to scientific empiricism, and a century later, when psychopathology had developed a bit more, Swedenborg was post-humously presented with a real medical dossier. In 1869 the famous British pioneering psychiatrist Henry Maudsley (1835–1918) ascribed attacks of acute mania to him, in the case of his conversion experiences in 1743 and 1744, followed by chronic mania until his death.[9] In all, sufficient to evaluate his condition as a 'messianic psychosis'. This manifested itself primarily in Swedenborg's conviction that he was the second Messiah; his revelations of the spirit world were the typical hallucinations of a psychotic at the acute stage. A few years later James Howden, medical superintendent of Montrose Royal Lunatic Asylum in the Scottish city of Dundee, published a study of five cases of intense religious feeling among epileptics.[10] These included Swedenborg, Ann Lee — founder of the Shakers — and the prophet Mohammed. Around 1912 the Viennese physician Edward Hitschmann, an admirer and for a brief period the doctor of Freud, referring to Swedenborg's paranoia, hazarded a guess at his homosexual narcissism, a theme that was taken up for a while by a number of others;[11] ten years later no less a person than the German psychiatrist and philosopher Karl Jaspers (1883–1969) published a 'pathographical analysis' of 'creative schizophrenics' Strindberg, Hölderlin, Swedenborg and Van Gogh.[12] Later still, in 1970, Kenneth Dewhurst and A. W. Beard published five cases of conversion experiences among sufferers from temporal lobe epilepsy — the 'Dostoevski' variant; compared to these, though, Swedenborg's case did not seem watertight.[13] This did not prevent the German psychiatrist Karl Leonhard, however, from honouring the latter in his differentiated typology of endogenous psychoses with forty pages on his 'konfabulatorisch-phonemische Paraphrenie'.[14] In 1994 the British psychiatrist John Johnson re-examined Maudsley's pathography and concluded that it would remain a diagnostic riddle whether the ascertained manic messianism had been a question of acute schizophrenia or an epileptic psychosis after all.[15] In a 1996 edition of *Epilepsia*, Swedenborg's hallucinations caused undiminished amazement,[16] but it was only in the most recent article in this tradition, *Neuropsychology of Swedenborg's visions* of 1999, that the diagnostic specification was finally brought to a higher level. In this piece David T. Bradford, who once published a work on visual hallucinations, explained that when Swedenborg saw a light in the sky, he was actually experiencing a 'right-superior quadrantanopia, which corresponds with damage along the temporooccipital geniculocalcarine pathway and a probable lesion site within the temporal lobe of the left cerebral hemisphere'.[17] His long-lasting trances were probably ascribable to dissociative periods linked to the time lag of such attacks.

7 Test of criteria

Now most of these learned people do not fail to point out in the margin or epilogue that this diagnosing from a distance is a ticklish business to say the least. Perhaps we should see it therefore more as their own finger exercise in the nosology of their time. But some qualification is called for, if only because none of the authors ever set eyes on the 'patient'. Even John Wesley never actually met his contemporary Swedenborg, but apart from the status of his conclusions as a non-medical man, his switch from initially ambivalent admiration to rabid rejection can be ascribed without much difficulty to religious bickering. Considering Wesley's own mission as regenerator of the Word of God, and the symptoms that he displayed while fulfilling it—including dreams, visions, prophesies, miraculous cures, speaking in tongues and 'sacred fits of laughter'—he had his own interests in the matter. The reasoning behind the medical evaluations of Swedenborg's case however is of more significance.

Firstly, the 'patient' in question did not seem to suffer in the slightest from his condition. In strict psychiatric terms that could be interpreted as a lack of insight into and acceptance of his illness. This lands us however in an awkward circular argument, with one person declaring that the other is ill, thereby creating a framework in which all of the latter's behaviour is seen as symptomatic of his illness. David Rosenhan continues to wave an admonitory index finger since his experiment in 1972, in which one of his few voice-hearing simulators was caught in the act of 'writing behaviour' after admission.[18] Not very fruitful, thus, and without objective grounds. People can of course make things relatively easy for themselves by making things very difficult for others, but that doesn't get us very far either. There was no question of Swedenborg being a nuisance to others, unless it was the theological and moral headaches he caused for specific interest groups.

It is also striking that, according to historical tradition, from the beginning of his interaction with spirits and angels onwards Swedenborg never ended up in any kind of mental crisis. Throughout his life he continued to operate at a high practical, intellectual and moral level; respect and appreciation fell to his share. We are thus justified in ruling out the occurrence of psychotic symptoms within the framework of a chronic disorder.

The idea too that something was wrong with Swedenborg's contact with the physical consensus of reality—a stock criterion—cuts no ice at all in his case. This naturalist, who produced an atomic theory 200 years before Einstein did, the first nebular theory on the origin of the solar system, and theories on magnetism which would be empirically confirmed only decades later, unlocked one mystery after another on the material level.

Considering Swedenborg's good and flexible communication skills, the personality disorder theory can be dismissed too, along with the idea that he was a severely neurotic individual. His biography gives no indication of extreme mood swings, nor of a tendency to grandiosity. In his work for the mining ministry, his parliamentary work, and his work for the salvation of mankind there is no trace of any motive other than the desire to serve a good cause. Nowhere can he be caught out misusing his fame or edifying task for his own profit or glory. He never tired of explaining to those who came to interrogate him that the Lord had simply entrusted him with the task of communicating his knowledge of the hereafter, and that he was trying to fulfil this commission as well as possible. He himself regarded his extensive physical and philosophical research work which preceded his conversion as a preparation for this later visionary task, which he saw as his real destiny.

Just as deep-rooted was Swedenborg's lack of interest in founding or leading a new religious movement. Although as a prophetic author his writings frequently indicated the need for the transformation of languishing Christianity into a New Church, at no time did he cherish even the slightest ambition in that direction. Others set to work on that project, and then only after he had died. Not long after his death in 1772—which incidentally he foretold in detail—the contours of a new tendency began to take shape, in imitation of his revelations. This never amounted to more than a collection of splinters in the Christian universe, but nowadays, mainly in America, there are still ecclesiastical organisations which operate under the flag of the Swedenborgian body of thought.

8 An inconvenient truth?

Swedenborg's critics found new ammunition for the treatment which he initially received for his 'mental disturbance' in the posthumous publication of his dream diary. It was found in 1849 in the bequest of a professor, and was published ten years later by the Royal Library in Stockholm.[19] It was clearly a private piece of writing, and the use of it in the smear campaign aroused indignation in some quarters. Elise van Calcar for example wrote in the last century:

> And yet we find that some of Swedenborg's opponents have seized on this book with an animosity which hardly allows us to expect an impartial or calm judgement. But they forget that if they had written down their own temptations, trials and dreams, the criticism of their judges would have sounded unpleasantly in their ears! One can just as well hang a man without trial as a villain, as dismiss him as a lunatic, on the grounds of an outline of his dreams, especially when he is completely compos mentis when awake.[20]

Swedenborg made a statement himself, moreover, about the danger of going off the spiritual tracks inherent in the sort of communication in which he specialised. When Carl Robsahm, director of the Swedish Bank in Stockholm, once asked him whether others could possibly attain the same sort of state of consciousness, Swedenborg answered emphatically:

> Guard against any attempt to do so, for this is a way which would lead anyone who entered on it without authorisation straight to the madhouse, for he who attempted of his own accord to penetrate the spiritual mysteries would not be able in that situation to withstand the delusions of diabolical spirits, who in their turn however are able to attack the man who, naked as a natural human being, desires through his own speculations to get at the root of celestial things which are above his understanding.[21]

In short, while hard evidence is automatically ruled out, the circumstantial evidence is not in the least indicative of a chronic mental disorder. The basis for a credible diagnosis is by now so narrow that the whole concept of mental illness remains shaky. Posthumous attempts to declare Swedenborg ill are based therefore on nothing more than inconvenience. The inconvenience of symptoms which are 'odd', even impossible, within the favoured frame of reference. Swedenborg's inexplicable states of consciousness are put down to pathology, and no one has anything more to say about the newsworthiness of his celestial reports. Or only: he was such a creative man. None of this has led to a strong case so far; within psychological orthodoxy we are left with what remains a riddle.

Diana (1933)

From 1980 to 1986 I worked as a Wiccan, with other people in the area.[1] We performed lots of rituals. Then I read a book about Kundalini, where a man described how it caused him a lot of pain and misery, and drove him half mad; the whole business had lasted twelve years.[2] So I read that, and that was that. I'd borrowed it, but I could never find it again later. Another book I came across was called *Hypnosis for You and Me*, about self-hypnosis, and I started doing exercises from it, with another woman from the Wicca group. They were very intense relaxation exercises really, and after a while I could get into a deeply relaxed state with them very quickly. That affected me in all kinds of ways, I experimented with writing, movement, massage, playing the piano, all completely intuitive. And I started dancing. I'd just stand there and flick the switch, because there's a decisive moment, then my eyes would roll upwards a bit, and I'd wait till my arms and legs started moving of their own accord. That's not quite the same as 'just doing what comes into your head', it was being aware of an impulse here or an impulse there, and going with the flow. And whatever kind of music I played, my body reacted to it. All sorts of world music. I turned out to be fantastic at belly dancing to Egyptian music, for example. Fascinating, that was. With Finnish music I thought, no, that's not right, because my legs just kept walking round in circles. I had a Finnish pen-friend, as it happened, and she wrote to me quite by chance: Finnish folk dances are really boring, they just walk round in circles. Just like I'd done! And I once stood there fencing and conducting at the same time, to classical music. Someone who fenced and was studying conducting confirmed that.

So I was really intensely aware of what my body wanted to do. One winter night I was lying in bed and just for fun I gave my hands free rein. Suddenly they started doing something which made me think, hey, they're like snakes. My hands began to dance, it was a real snake dance. And I knew that the snake was the kundalini symbol. So I thought, hang on now, wait a minute. The next morning it happened again, and it became more and more agitated, and my eyes began to roll in all directions, in short, all kinds of things began to happen. I stayed in bed doing that, and at two o'clock in the afternoon I heard a voice saying: 'Now go to sleep'. After protesting a bit, I did. That afternoon I told the woman from the Wicca group that I was going to give up our hypnosis exercises, otherwise something else was going to happen to me. I was quite convinced that the kundalini fire was on the way and I thought: what am I going to do about it? Then I thought, this is a really calm period in my life, I'm in good health, I've only got one son still at home, I've got all the time in the world for myself, so if it's got to happen, now is the time. I was giving a sort of consent by doing this. I was perfectly aware that I was getting into something that could become pretty heavy, but that was a choice I made. I stayed in bed an awful lot so that I could be alert to what was going to happen. And I kept a detailed record of every-thing in my diary.

In the evening the snakes came again, and I also started having spontaneous orgasms, my whole body was on the go. At one point I had to look at a picture of the sun, and I heard the voice in my head again: 'This sun is not too strong for you to look at, just keep your eyes fixed on it. And don't read too much during the first few days.' Those snakes kept coming back, and it became more and more intense. My male Wicca partner came to see me regularly to keep me grounded, but he couldn't really guide me through it. He'd taught me an awful lot and he knew about this kind of thing, but he hadn't experienced it himself. So I had to figure it out for myself. He called round once, I was lying in bed and I began to prophesy, to talk in a strange dreamy way. About things that were going to happen to all sorts of friends and acquaintances — *none* of it came true, by the way. And then he said, 'I've heard people who were mentally ill talking like that.' That didn't really worry me, as I felt I was in good shape, but I did say, 'You've got to talk to my husband. Explain what's happening, because I think I can cope with it, but I don't want anyone around me to worry.'

I started responding more and more intuitively. If I was talking to some-one on the phone, the hand with the telephone would suddenly drop, so that was clear: stop the conversation. Now and then I felt a bit sick, and then suddenly I'd feel a real heat rising, from the base of my spine. I felt an energy starting to rise through me, and that was different from in the past few days. Then I really began to get scared. After all, I'd read in that book that if it went on it would be quite something. So I asked my Wicca partner to come, and he helped me to stay grounded, because I felt … wow, I'm get-ting dizzy. I started stammering, and had to really work at it to stay in the here and now. So he said, 'Stop, you're going too fast!' But I said, 'No, I won't stop.' Looking back I don't know if I had any control over it, but I'd declared myself ready to go through with it, even though I didn't know what to expect, how powerful it was going to get. I was tremendously alert, it was as if I was lying in bed and could literally see a snake in the corner of the room, that could attack any minute. So alert! I sat downstairs talking to him for a bit, and suddenly he said, 'Are you still there?' I was getting dizzy, not unconscious, but as if my soul was about to fly away, as if I was going mad or something. So that was actually a bit scary.

That night I lay there for hours, giving commands: back, back, back. It was so uncontrolled, like bolts of lightning through my body, from the base of my spine to my neck, sometimes for hours at a time, and then it would be quiet for a while. I felt safe lying next to my husband, but it was such a gigantic energy, as if 10,000 volts were shooting through my body. I thought, don't let it go to my head, not like this, not to my head. So in my mind I just lay there, willing it: back, back, back. Back to the base of my spine. And in my diary I wrote 'Slept about four hours, first round to me!'

Then eating became a very precise business. My hand would point at the things I ought to eat, mainly apples—russets—and rice wafers. Sometimes a russet apple, skin and all, washed or not, when it was really urgent. And I had to drink a lot, mainly apple juice. Suddenly the voice came into my head again, it said very emphatically: 'Lucia, Lucia, Lucia.' It was a real voice, quite different from a thought. Someone introduced herself as Lucia. I thought, I don't know who or what Lucia is, but if she can help me I'll do what she says. So far this voice had said sensible things. So I had a Lucia to rely on. I got very concrete instructions, like: 'Go and have a shower.' I had to do that a lot, I was having real fits, sometimes quite suddenly, zap! And just before that she'd say: 'Go and have a shower!' Once I had to do that at eight thirty in the morning, the boiler we had then held eighty litres of hot water and I showered until it was empty, then stood under the cold water so long that there was no steam left in the bathroom. 'Just a bit longer,' she said then. Well, I was completely frozen. But that was what I needed to do to earth the energy, apparently. Sometimes I had to hold on to the taps, and the water pipes—to earth myself, that's what it felt like. And after that I was allowed to rub myself with rose-scented hand-cream, and to oil my skin.

I had a small dental plate then, and that had to come out. She didn't tell me that, my hand did that. And I made my husband throw it in the rubbish bin, as if I would be getting new teeth. Well, he thought that was completely mad, but he did what I said. I fished the dental plate out again afterwards, to be on the safe side, though that felt like a lack of trust. But my husband stayed very calm the whole time, I'm still terribly grateful to him for that, that he stayed so cool and collected. All kinds of things happened as well when he or my son weren't there, self-healing movements and rolling my eyes and so on. As if they were being spared something, because it stopped if someone came into the room.

Now and then I used to go and hug a tree in the garden, to ground myself, but at one point I got a piece of piping out of the garage to use as an earth wire. I took it to bed as well. Because I hardly dared to go to sleep, I once woke up so suddenly with the idea, 'Quick, quick, quick, have a shower!' And I'd just finished showering and gone to sit on the sofa downstairs when Lucia said, 'Quick, have a shower!' So I said, 'Christ, Lucia, I've just finished having one!' 'Quick, have a shower!' So, I went and got in the shower again and whoosh! So it all made sense what she said.

The last violent attack was very bad, honestly, it was so heavy! Touch and go! That was five days after it started. I was lying stretched out on the floor, hands flat on the ground, feet flat on the ground, to ground myself completely, and then there came one wave after another, then another wave, and back again. Non-stop energy, it *flew* through my body, it was *so* intense! All I wanted to do was scream, to drain off all that immense tension. But I knew if I screamed, they'd come and get me. Then they might really take me away. Because I wouldn't be able to stop then, I'd have lost control. But it was so much tension, almost unbearable! So I lay flat on the ground and now and then I let my heels fall with a bang on the ground to get rid of it a bit. And my husband sat there reading the paper as if this was all in a day's work. Oh, he was so matter-of-fact … fantastic! And he helped me an awful lot by being like that, as if he was used to his wife going on like that! Of course, through the Wicca group I was used to managing energy in a very concentrated way. And to observe and wait and sense when something should stop. I lay there and sang and talked to him in the meantime, but I had to do my utmost to stay in control. I panted and sweated and it lasted at least an hour, then there was another severe attack, and then it was over. And then I wrote in my diary: 'Successful delivery!' So nonchalant! When I wrote that, so soon afterwards, I thought that it was a very accurate reflection of everything. But it didn't reflect the intensity of the whole business *at all*.

After that the snakes seemed to be tamed, and I felt like a priestess. I got my husband to pour me some orange juice and I offered a toast to the gods three times. Some time later I was lying on my back in bed, in my own room, and I felt a warm glow along my spine, that was a very pleasant feeling. It crept right up from the base of my spine to my neck. I said, 'Lucia, careful with my head … !' Then my head was pushed back a bit, and I felt the top of my head getting warm, as if the warmth had jumped from my neck to the top of my head. And I wrote down, 'It is done.' I lay there for a bit so I could greet and acknowledge everything with my eyes, as if I was seeing and accepting everything for the first time. That night I was wakened by a jolt inside my head, as if something had come to an end. And I had to say three times, 'I am a winged being.' That had to do with priests and priestesses in ancient Egypt, after their initiation they were called 'The winged ones'. After that I could just let the energy flow, the way was open. I could feel it as a power within myself, not as a snake outside of me any more. I had to be constantly on the alert that I didn't float off, it felt as though my consciousness could just disappear at any minute, I imagine you could go mad like that. And this energy still had to settle, to sink into every cell of my body, so I started doing all kinds of intuitive things again. Putting a glass of water on top of my head. Lucia soothed me, and told me to fetch a plastic shower cap and a plastic sanitary towel disposal bag, and a plastic sleeve from the cassette recorder, and something else from the table. I had to put that on my head, with the plastic shower cap over everything as if to stop it forcing its way out or something. As if my head needed protecting. I looked ridiculous, of course!

The apple juice had nearly run out, but I was allowed to dilute it with water, that made it homeopathic. And with all that plastic on my head I had to go to the toilet during the night and not sit on the seat but on the porcelain rim, and ground myself again. With my hands and feet on the stone floor. There I sat for one and a half hours, in the winter, frozen to the marrow. Then I'd go and warm up with my husband in bed, then go to my own room and greet everything again. In my room I had to write something down: 'Peace, and sleep well.' It was a sort of automatic writing. When I woke up again I felt a bit sick, and then another weird thing happened, I had to sit there with a chamber pot on my lap, to cough up a stomach tumour … ! I made all kinds of efforts to force something up, but nothing physical came out. The pot was supposedly full and I had to go and rinse it, along with everything else I'd touched, as if I was horribly infected. The toothbrush, soap, washing-up brush, breadboard, everything! I knew exactly how to do it. A clean cloth every time. Hand towels and tea towels on the kitchen mat, next to the clogs, the mat with all the cloths on the patio in the snow and then cover it all with more snow. That had to lie there for a day. I went shopping in the afternoon, I could manage that again, but I was still wearing the plastic hat, so I wore another hat on top of it.

I lost ten pounds in those ten days, by the way, so that energy really ate my energy.

Then the whole lot had to be cleaned up. Everything in a garbage bag, the chamber pot and garbage bags from the bed, towel, glass, and the plate with the face cloth, even a perfectly good tablecloth. And the bag had to be thrown out of the window, all without touching anything with my hands. And all the bedclothes as well, quick, outside, air the lot and then off to the dry cleaners. Downstairs I could hear the garbage men's lorry, I put my black coat on and I stood there in my bare feet in the snow with my plastic shower cap on just when the garbage men came round the corner. Without saying a word I handed over the bag, and they took it without a word. That was really odd, it was almost surreal. It was still dark and there I stood, but it wasn't even the day for garbage collection! Then the lorry turned round and drove off in the other direction. It wasn't supposed to be there at all! That was so odd. But I'd got rid of the bag. So I had a shower and washed my hair, then I got all dressed up. White jacket, white tights, black boots, silver belt, and I started dancing to disco music. Later I started singing something. *I can still feel the golden glow.* Then I suddenly realised everything that had happened, the pressure I'd been under. In my room I started playing that song on my cassette player and I cried my eyes out. Lucia sent me to my husband, I kept on crying with him. He patted me and said nothing, I sat on his knee and everything was all right.

I kept on feeling that energy, I'd wake up at night and I could feel that kundalini fire radiating out. I'd have to have a drink straight away, but otherwise I could handle it and just let it flow. And I could feel that this energy was working in my body, that it was doing something useful. Once I started doing a healing on my stomach, and Lucia said, 'Wonders never cease, the penny dropped!' I had whole discussions with her for days at a time about occult things and existential problems. God, what a lot I knew, I was getting *masses* of information! Cosmic information. Cosmic concepts, about mystical and occult things. I don't remember any of it now. And I thought, what on earth am I supposed to do with it? Should I pass it on to other people? Once I mentioned Seth, that was another one of these guides.[3] I said, 'Yes, but Seth says ... ' and then Lucia said, 'Yes, but Seth doesn't know everything.' And suddenly I thought, oh-oh. And I said, 'Lucia, do you know everything?' Dead silence. Oh dear ... then I started to worry, because I thought, if she's wrong about one thing, she might be wrong about everything! So then I started having my doubts about the wisdom she proclaimed. That didn't have much effect on what I did, but I had to start questioning the impulses I received. And it was the impetus to start thinking about things for myself.

For instance, I was having a shower once when I thought, God, I'm using an awful lot of water. And I'm always very careful with water. And then Lucia began to flatter me. She said, 'Oh, but a high priestess is entitled to use a lot of water.' And suddenly I thought, Oh really? I realised that she was flattering me, and that didn't fit in with her position as leader. So one step at a time I went back to my normal self. On one occasion I had a lot of tension in my left arm. So I went to ground myself in the snow by the sycamore tree, and I pressed myself right into the conifer. Suddenly I thought, I've been at this for six hours, I must be mad, I have to stop. I'd also started to write all sorts of weird words, it was supposed to be Atlantic.[4] After a while I suddenly thought, why on earth should I learn

Atlantic? What good is that? And how can I check if it really is Atlantic? What a waste of time. So I stopped doing that as well.

Once I had to see a doctor at the hospital, and everything had to be done just so! I was standing at the reception desk, I had to register. 'What's your name?' Oh, should I give my name as Diana or as Mrs Dijkstra? Doing the registration properly was very important, it had to be absolutely correct! Not giving the right name would have had a disruptive effect on something or other. But it was no longer clear where I could get it from, that absolute certainty, it had vanished. So I said,' I'll have to have a think.' I walked away from the reception desk, and all in all I took quite a time. Then I went back again but I still wasn't sure, so I went and sat down again, had a little think. If someone sees you like that they must think, 'Oh, she's not quite right in the head.' Then I had a difference of opinion with that doctor, and when I rang him up about it later he said, 'Well, you were behaving very oddly even at the reception desk.' Yet I began to find my feet again, as a person.

I was still very vulnerable, and I was terribly sensitive to energies. Music that didn't feel right would really upset me, for example. Those emotions were so extreme, so exaggerated, that I started to see things in proportion again. One night I started getting all sorts of ideas that undermined all my self-confidence. Everything that I'd done or thought until then, or not done and not thought, absolutely every mortal thing was completely demolished. And I mean *completely*, not a shred of me was left. For example: I'd done something and I'd meant well, hadn't I? — then I'd think, Yes, but you have to take this or that into account, so that means nothing. Everything was cancelled out, my ego was completely destroyed. I lay there and cried my eyes out. Everything that had been okay was now worthless. And then everything that I knew had been wrong became *so* incredibly heavy that it was almost unbearable. I think that's what hell is. For example our daughter had given her father some ear-warmers, but they were crazy things that he wouldn't be seen dead in, so I'd given them away. Well, at that moment it seemed like such an enormously huge fault, I'd hurt my daughter *so* much by doing it, it just grew out of all proportion. And then I thought, wait a minute, this is that old Christian guilt feeling that makes me feel completely worthless! I'm not having that, I won't accept it! Because it paralyses me, and that can't be the idea. Drop everything that seemed worth doing, okay, but it can't be right that those faults suddenly *do* count. And then I thought: now I could do three things. I could go mad — because if everything you've done and that you thought made sense is totally demolished, it can drive you completely round the bend. So that was one: I could go mad. Two: I could go straight off and join the church, then I'd have something to hold on to, or three: I can go ahead with nothing at all. Just nothing to hold on to any more. Okay then, I thought, I'll go ahead with nothing. I had enough inner strength left to do that. So from that standpoint I could distinguish between the destruction of the ego on the one hand, and that immense awareness of sin on the other. And when I realised that, it dissolved, it wasn't relevant any more. I knew, as Diana I no longer count for anything at all, but when all's said and done I'm a spark of the divine that can't be destroyed. What I realised then was that everything matters. Everything that's not in harmony has a disruptive effect on something, however small.

After that whole episode I didn't talk much about it. It was over and done with, more or less. There were very few people anyway who I could talk to about it. Not even about Wicca. I had to keep quiet about it to my brothers and sisters, it was so far removed from their experience. And even in my own family they had this attitude: oh, what bee has she got in her bonnet this time? I once told them about the rituals, but my son said to me, 'Mum, we think you're getting into something risky.' They were really worried as well, because of the whole business with magic and occultism. They didn't think much of my partner for a start, he lived nearby and often dropped in, and I often went round to his house. But he taught me such a lot, he opened up a whole new world for me. Still, because they were worried, I questioned things now and then in my mind. I'd not see him for a week, for example, so I could think things through. But then I'd start thinking: my intuition is my compass, and I have to go in this direction. When I stopped I'd feel so enormously unfaithful to myself, it felt like a sort of spiritual suicide. And it came to a point where they left me alone, because they knew that wild horses couldn't hold me back if I really went for something.

I didn't have anyone else to help me to come to terms with this afterwards, and to use it in one way or another. First of all I kept on seeing my Wicca partner, and new people came to take part in the rituals. But I noticed that I had become much more intuitive. But he had a huge amount of knowledge, intellectual knowledge, and technical knowledge of rituals and so on, but I'd outstripped him as regards experiential knowledge. We did healings together, for example, and he worked according to a plan, but I noticed that my hands wanted to do completely different things. And if I challenged him to use his powers more, he'd quit. That really shocked me. That's what happens if you see someone as your instructor, and the roles are reversed. He couldn't get used to it either. In '86 I stopped working with him and after that I went on alone, just with the skills that I had. If someone crossed my path whom I could help, I did so, by talking to them or whatever. Some people asked about this kind of experience, and I could say something useful about that. But it's not like I'm going to make a career out of it, it's more whatever comes my way at odd moments.

It did make me feel lonely, but I never had any doubts. About anything, even now. That whole process of awakening and being supervised by Lucia, it just made sense. And also that she made a thorough fool of me with her idiotic commands, to get the thinking part of me going again. At one stage I said, 'Well, thanks very much Lucia, I'm going to go it alone from now on.' At difficult moments I sometimes thought, I wish Lucia was here. I also had the feeling, if I need her she'll be there. But still, what could Lucia have been, my inner self? Did it manifest itself in a voice? What name could you put to that?

Of course this gave me a completely different idea of human potential. That is so immense. And I also realised: people who take up kundalini yoga need a really good teacher, because they have *no idea* what they're unleashing. I can also see the difference myself. A woman once said, 'When I sit down to meditate, I get really hot!' 'Oh', said the others, 'That's the shakti.'[5] I didn't say anything at the time, but I didn't believe a bit of it. Because if you just sit down and meditate, your mind calms down and all kinds of things start going on in your body for a while. That makes me feel hot as well. But it *really* isn't the kundalini experience. I once phoned up a woman who taught kundalini yoga, she came round here once. She never saw it happen so violently in her students. The whole thing happens much more gradually.

Deep, deep, deep down I think I have an enormous fear of death. I once had an operation when I was seventeen, I had half a lung removed. My worst fear was that I would wake up while they were still at it. And then I woke up, and I could feel very clearly that my body was only a box that I was inside of, and that I could shoot out of at any moment. I could feel the distinction. And I also realised, I mustn't go yet, they've got to hold me back. Somebody held my hand and the only thing I could do was move my hand, I thought, they've got to know that I'm conscious again, they've got to hold me back! So I know that death isn't the end of everything, but still I have a huge fear of death, somewhere very deep down. And yet in everyday life I do all kinds of things, in town once I tackled a man who was shouting and screaming and laying into someone. When that happens I feel this power, I'm not scared. I've also had a lot to do with death, in my family, with brothers, sisters, parents, sometimes I was there when they died, and that never scared me off. But I was once in hospital with a gigantic skin rash, and then I had a huge fear of death. I don't really know where it comes from. The moment when I said, 'Okay, I no longer exist as Diana, but I'm still the divine spark,' then I knew, 'If I let go of that, then I'll end up in this pitch black darkness.' And later I wondered, should I have found the courage? What would have happened if I had? That would have been absolutely total surrender. But perhaps I was just clutching at a safety belt.

I'd like to know what's happening with people who hear voices, whether this sort of process could be going on. People tend to put it in a particular pigeonhole, and that bothers me, because it can cause a lot of suffering. I knew what was going on more or less, but still I was so very near to screaming ... I don't even want to think about it. Because then they come and take you away and put you in an institution, and there's no doctor who can tell you anything about it. How do you ever get out? That must be horrible. Everybody has their life to live, of course, and I can't protect everybody from every mortal thing, and I don't want to either. And maybe other people just have to go through it, that's also possible. But I hope that people get more understanding of the connection between mind and body. That someone who goes mad isn't necessarily suffering from a disorder, but is maybe going through a developmental process, which can be an enormous growth process if it's well supervised. But you'd need spiritual doctors for that, who can understand that. They will come. People like Deepak Chopra.[6] I wrote to him about this, incidentally, and he wrote back too, he found it a fascinating story. Years later incidentally there was an appeal from the Correlatie Stichting to people who had had positive experiences with hearing voices.[7] I responded to it, because in my case all those instructions about taking showers and eating and drinking really helped to withstand the attacks. The person I spoke to found my story really fascinating, and I was quite prepared to talk about it at a symposium they were going to organise, but I didn't hear any more about it.

Hans (1974)

In my student days I went to the HEAO business institute in Amsterdam, and for part of the course I studied abroad as well. I was following in my father's footsteps really, he made a career in finance and is now a director of something or other. I thought, that's what you're supposed to do, so that's what I did. After the HES course, which I completed in four years, I still had a year of my grant left, so I enrolled at Nijenrode business college. I had a lot of stress in my life around the time I graduated. Never took a break, just kept slogging on and on. People around me said, 'It's amazing how you manage to keep going.' Once I got to Nijenrode it got really heavy, I had to study for about eighty hours a week, that was simply tremendous, and I was only twenty-three then.

As well as all this, my motivation was wavering, was this what I really wanted to do or not? With that intense pressure to study, and a busy social life into the bargain, plus a lot of beer-drinking and so on, I developed sleeping problems. At one stage I was only sleeping three or four hours a night, I was worrying all the time, I had thoughts racing through my head like mad. A sort of microprocessor in overdrive. My mind worked like lightning, I stumbled over my words, people could hardly follow me, I was simply heading for the brink. After a couple of months' study I had a rather emotional weekend, when I was made the new chairman of the rugby club, and on top of that I'd invited a girl to the gala in a month's time and she'd said yes. I was really happy about that, I really liked that girl. That made all the stress and intensity of the previous weeks melt away for a bit. But I still had problems sleeping. On Sunday evening that weekend I went to bed and woke up at four o'clock in the morning. That had been going on for a few weeks. But for some reason or another I felt I had to go outside that night, get a breath of fresh air, it was a strong inner urge. I'd never done that before, but I was wide awake anyway, so I got dressed and went out. I walked along a path for a while in those beautiful surroundings, with all those woods, and after maybe 150 yards I came to a crossroads. And right in the middle of the crossroads the heavens opened. I saw everything: total love. Everything was one, everything was connected. All wisdom was contained in it. I saw that I was born of my father and mother. And that love was the driving force behind the universe. It's hard to put such an experience into words, because it was all instinctive, or it took place in my mind. I didn't see a light or anything, but I felt total love. We were all created from love and I had a really strong feeling of a sort of *aha-erlebnis*, of aha … O how stupid! How stupid of me not to have seen it all the time, how stupid! Of course that's how it is, of course everything is created from love! It was also very creative, really immense creativity, everything is creation. And all wisdom was present, I had the answers to all questions. That all happened in the space of one and a half hours, in the middle of the night, in the middle of the Nijenrode campus. I stood there, and I suddenly became completely exalted, really inspired. I thought, I must go and convince those weird Nijenrodians. They're all so absorbed by their careers and business and making money. I must go and tell them that everything is love! And I thought, I'll make a sort of statement tomorrow to show them they're on the wrong track. But straight afterwards I thought, if I do that, they won't understand me, and then they might stick me in a lunatic asylum. And at that moment I got frightened. Very, very frightened. I saw that I might become a sort of Hitler or Stalin. I saw that I had that power, that potential inside me. That thought made me very, very frightened. I still had that microprocessor in my head, I could make connections quick as lightning, I saw the consequences of everything I could do as clear as crystal, and it all seemed very real. And I just became very, very frightened. Of being thought mad, of being mad.

Then I said to myself, 'Okay, Hans, get a grip on yourself, just stop all these ideas about tomorrow and the Nijenrodians.' I went back to my room and quickly wrote on a sheet of paper what I had to do. A sort of three-point plan, that I needed rest, love, and common sense. Feet on the ground. That was my father especially, he has both feet firmly on the ground. He's had quite a lot of experience with manic-depressive people, friends and family. There's also someone he knows well, he often has to help him and sometimes even drive him to the mental home. So I realised, I need my father, he can get me out of this. First thing the next morning I phoned him, he was on his way to work but he came and picked me up in Breukelen, and then we drove to the Hague, where I come from. And at the end of the same day I had a talk with a psychiatrist I knew, the mother of a good friend of mine. So that went really quickly, thank god. I told her a bit about what had happened to me, and she said, 'I believe in the things you've seen and in the ideas you have, I think it's all very fine, but you're staying here for the first couple of weeks to try and get the old Hans back again. And to do that you need sleep and rest, sleep and rest, lots and lots and lots of sleep.' Those were her instructions. The first night went well enough, but after that a whole lot of other things happened!

I had a heightened interpretative consciousness. For example, if shares went up I would think, that's my doing, because I feel this or that today. That kind of thing happened all the time. Ideas that passed through me and that I believed at the time — but there was always a sort of observer that watched everything happening and sometimes said, 'Hmm, that's a bit crazy, Hans.' But there were really beautiful things as well. I had a *very* pure contact with children. On one occasion I was at a social at my brother's basketball club somewhere, it was full moon and I felt … how can I put it … very light and a bit ethereal. And then a little girl came up to me, three or four years old, and she asked, 'Can I play with you?' And I thought, 'Eh, what?' I'd never seen that child before, but she reacted so purely to me! And more things like that. My psychiatrist had also told me, go and get some exercise, feel that body again. So I went jogging almost every day, and I experienced all kinds of things then. I also had a lot of emotions in that period, sometimes rather dark, heavy emotions and energies. I used to play with those a bit while I was jogging. If I stamped really hard, stomp stomp stomp, and breathed heavily, it got stronger, and if I was calm it died down. And on one occasion I had just got into one of those intense energies, when I ran out of a clump of trees and round the corner. Twenty yards or so further on stood a couple of small children. And the little girl screamed, 'Waaaaah!' and the other kid grabbed a stick and threw it at me. That gave me a real shock, so I raced off in the other direction. That kind of thing was really strong. That I'd be walking down the street and a child would come out of a door at the same moment, just look out of the door for a minute. I'd think, Oh, that'll be because of me. I also thought I could help people through using a sort of hypnosis. I remember standing in the supermarket a few yards away from an old man, and mentally trying to help him choose between two bars of chocolate. Or with telekinetic powers as well, I felt so connected to everything. I'd go and play football now and then, then the wind would get up and the ball would be blown around, and I'd think, keep still! And once I was sitting at the kitchen table, trying to make a fork stand on end without touching it. My father was watching and asked, 'What are you doing?' 'I'm trying to make the fork stand on end.' 'Well, that's a bit daft, Hans, maybe you need to have a rest.' And my reaction was, 'No, the reason it's not working is because you don't believe in it!'

I was very intuitive, and when I look back it sometimes seems as if we had a sort of *satsang* at home.[1] I used to sit on the sofa, with my father and mother beside me, and if we had people round I used to do a sort of interview and just blurt out what I saw about them. Then my father would step in, he felt that you shouldn't humour people when they're so overwrought, because otherwise you just reinforce the trip. But he wasn't too worried about me, because he could see from the beginning that I was doing everything I could to get through the process, to get well again, lucid. And he'd never seen me so disciplined. But I didn't know where I would end up either, just that I had to get through it, simple as that. And I was confident that it would work out all right. My mother was a bit less sure about it, she found that period pretty tough. I didn't suffer too much myself, it wasn't too bad. Sometimes I was in heaven, sometimes in hell, then it was really very dark and black. And it was as if I felt all forms of communication flowing through me, all e-mails and telephone calls and faxes. But the worst of all was the uncertainty. My psychiatrist once said to me, 'It's Monday today, where do you think you'll be at the weekend?' And I said, 'I'll either be dead or I'll be Jesus Christ.' That's really extreme, of course, but that's how it felt. There was also a lot of anxiety involved. But sometimes there was a deep belief that everything would turn out well. I drew a lot of strength from that particular moment, it was so full of love and so rich in wisdom, I knew: it can't have been anything but good. But it was very uncertain, that period.

After one and a half weeks I wanted to go back to Nijenrode after all to do an exam. But I was still much, much too susceptible for that, I couldn't even manage the whole trip on public transport. Something happened as soon as I got on the tram in the Hague, there was some vulgar type who was screaming her head off at her five- or six-year old child, 'Little bitch, loudmouth, get over here,' that sort of thing … ! And I thought, no wonder people are so wounded and so out of balance, what on earth will become of a child like that? All those city impressions, that was too much for me, so I got out halfway. I did succeed at the second attempt though, and I passed the exam as well!

Meanwhile I tried to rediscover the unconditional love that I'd felt during that experience. First of all with my parents, I wanted to surrender, for example, but then I'd see something in them freeze. Ah well, they live in their own world, they've got neuroses and defences of their own. After that I started projecting this unconditional love on the girl I invited to the gala, and it became obsessive. I was madly in love with her, but it was all a bit too much for her. Her mother had psychoses, that's odd as well, but she knew something about it, and maybe she thought: here we go again. Besides, she was about to go to America for a work placement. Our contact was normal and that was really good, but in fact she kept to a safe distance. We did go to the gala together, but nothing happened. Of course it went on until the small hours, and that upset my routine, I couldn't cope with it very well, so I became really sensitive again. Reality could come and go just like that, where normally you'd have any amount of defence mechanisms. And the following weekend I was so overwrought that I wanted to go and see Janneke, in the middle of the night. It was freezing, there was even snow on the ground, and my parents heard me slipping out of the house during the night. So there I stood in my boxer shorts—I'd put a woolly hat on though! But of course it gave them an awful shock. They said, 'Hans, where are you going?' And I said, 'I'm going to see Janneke.' Really innocent, really pure. For me my whole life centred on her. But they said something like, 'No no, come indoors, you can ring her tomorrow.'

The very next morning I had a dental appointment and my mother asked if I was okay now and let me go, but I really intended to go and see Janneke again. She wasn't at her own house, someone there said she was staying with her parents. I didn't know the address but I thought, I'll find it. I passed a house in a slightly wealthier area and thought, that's where she lives, so I went right up to it and started shouting, 'Janneke, come on out!' Just like that. Later it turned out that a girl I'd gone to secondary school with lived there, she had a psychosis two years after me, I talked to her about it afterwards. All very weird. Anyway, the people in that house thought it was peculiar and they phoned the police. They picked me up and took me to the police station. I thought, I'll just play along with them, I was also testing how far I could go. But for me the lunatic asylum was the limit, I didn't want to go that far. In the police car of course they had one of those police telephones, with all those numbers and codes, and I was convinced I could understand the codes. At the police station they questioned me, they rang my psychiatrist, and then my mother came to collect me. That was a really lovely meeting as well. I was sitting there in one of those cells, my mother opened the door and I just flew into her arms, and I said, 'Oh Mum, Grandma's dead, Grandma's dead!' And she said, 'Is she really? I haven't heard a thing, but as soon as we get home we'll ring up.' That was so pure as well, so … I don't know, so very innocent: Grandma's dead, isn't it awful! That wouldn't have been such a tragedy, actually, she was a woman of ninety-nine by then. And she turned out to be still alive, thank god!

Every night at that time I went through a birth-death, I was being reborn over and over, coming back alive from the dead. Dreaming and waking every time in a new world, and seeing that all your previous experiences don't matter, because they're different from reality as it is now. My star sign is Scorpio and at that period I was certainly very preoccupied with life and death. And, as my father put it, a few cans of worms got opened in my case. And also in my family's case, incidentally, because it spread like an oil slick, and of course I was the epicentre! For example, when I was eighteen I had a girlfriend and I got her pregnant and we arranged for an abortion. That sort of thing resurfaced with a vengeance. Sentences like: *am I my brother's keeper?* — when my brother came to visit. And to what extent can you make your own decisions about life and death? I told my psychiatrist about that as well, and I even had a session with her, together with my former girlfriend. I really used that time to clear up a lot of things.

After the police station incident my psychiatrist prescribed medication after all, an anti-psychotic drug, Cisordinol, but I had a super-violent reaction to it.[2] It was quite a low dosage but it gave me muscle cramps, and my lower jaw stuck out at an angle of nearly ninety degrees to the left. That was horribly painful. Two days later I rang her up, she sent me to the family doctor for a valium injection. And then pffff, the whole thing relaxed and I got a bit giggly. The anti-psychotic drug began with 20mg, but I was allowed to reduce it really quickly. For a while I was taking 4 or 2mg, and later on one or two pills if I was under stress. And that worked. But of course it flattened everything out, that was pretty boring, my enthusiasm for everything had really vanished then. After that really stormy period of a month or two, with all those emotions and energies flying in and out, I was very tired and listless for a long time. I wasn't depressed, but I used to lie around on the sofa and not take much interest in anything. My psychiatrist never actually said that it was a psychosis, incidentally. I asked her again at one stage but she called it a *temporary mental disorder*, something like that. I certainly had the symptoms of a psychosis, and I do wonder about it now and then, but I took a quite different view of it in the end.

I'd never had any interest in spirituality before, or in enlightenment, I knew absolutely nothing about it. But I had a friend who was an anthropologist, and that was another thing I saw during that one moment at Nijenrode—that I would go to India with him, and would sit in a cave with *saddhus*.[3] I still have that sometimes now, I'm busy doing something and suddenly I think, oh, I've seen that before, during that moment in Nijenrode. Anyway, I knew that he was going to write a thesis about these *saddhus*. I rang him a couple of weeks after that experience and told him I had no idea what was happening to me but that it might be a good idea to meet. So then I told him the whole story, and he said, 'Well, what happened to you, that's what a lot of monks sit meditating for all their lives; that's an enlightenment experience.' And he also said, 'I don't know how your psychiatrist deals with you, but you don't want to take too much notice of her, because if she says it's a psychosis or manic-depression, you might stick that label on yourself and then start developing it. That would stay with you your whole life, so be very careful about that.' That was really good for me; he was the first one who reflected back my ideas, and who showed me something about the spiritual side of life. His girlfriend is a medium, and from then on I used to go and see her too, and we would talk about it. I also meditated with her, that was really good, finally someone who gave me a bit of space, and didn't think what had happened to me was so bad. She'd been to India a lot, had also written a sort of ashram guide and had a lot to tell about it. That was a very important support for me. The two of them also lent me some books. There was one by Andrew Cohen, *Autobiography of an Awakening*. I saw it and I knew straight away, I have to have that, and when I read it, my whole life will change. And that's exactly what happened. Cohen hadn't been through such an overwrought, even psychotic, crazy period, but his experiences were very familiar, and I recognised them straight away.

In December I left Nijenrode, I really couldn't drum up the motivation any more. I was taking an exam and I thought, I've got to spend my time on other things, with what life is all about. Then I walked out of the exam and had my name taken off the register straight away. After that I went to live in Amsterdam again. The first few months I was pretty listless. I went walking in the countryside a lot, I always liked that. I was on benefit, which meant you weren't supposed to do jobs on the side but after a while I did it anyway, I got jobs in restaurants, I gradually built it up. After the summer I did a normal job, five days a week, in a very commercial job at a personnel bureau. A bit too much, as it turned out. You had to place people with a firm, and you got a bonus for every placement, the atmosphere was nice enough, all young people, but actually I found it horrible. I stuck it out for six months or so, then I packed it in and went to India. That's where my friend was, doing research for his thesis on the *saddhus* who lived in caves. He also did camerawork and was making a sort of documentary about it, I worked on that as well. I asked the questions while he recorded it. I asked about spiritual experiences, about oneness, I hadn't mastered the jargon yet but I learned a bit about it. The rest of the time we stayed in Rishikesh, at the foot of the Himalayas, a really spiritual city. It was really great just to be in India, because the spiritual is so much more a part of everyday life than it is here. After four weeks or so he went back to the Netherlands, and in the end I travelled around for another nine months. Mostly in the north, in Nepal as well, I stayed in monasteries, in Tibetan centres, all sorts of places. I travelled on my own, but in meditation centres you keep coming across the same people. It was great to do that on my own, as I was still very sensitive to crowds. This way I could do my own thing and be on my own sometimes, or else mix with people. I went to a workshop by Andrew Cohen when I was there, that was very inspiring. It lasted four days or so, and I asked questions now and then during *satsang*. That was great as well, I could finally talk to somebody about it at a high level.

But what I gained most from was a Buddhist monk, who I met in a monastery in Nepal where I was doing a four-week course. He was a westerner, from Switzerland, he'd been in Nepal for twenty years. He led the meditations, and I soon realised that he knew a lot about it. So I asked to see him in private, and he turned out to have had a similar 'opening' at the age of eighteen, when he went into a temple in Amritsar in India. And he was actually the first to say, 'Oh yes, that's what happened to you.' About the madness he said, 'I can well imagine that all kinds of strange things happen if your consciousness expands so gigantically in one go. It's actually quite logical for things to happen to you that you've never experienced before. But the opening that you had, you'll probably never have it again.' Later on Hans Laurentius said that in Zen you have big *kenshos* and small *kenshos*: openings, *satori* moments, enlightenment moments.[4] The small ones occur quite often, but a big one like that usually only happens once, and with me it was obviously a big one. After that I experienced all kinds of other things, but that moment never came back. It's better just to let it go, actually, you shouldn't keep searching for it.

That Indian trip was really the initiation of my spiritual search. At home in the Netherlands too I started actively searching and I shopped around at first for two years. I ended up before long at the *satsangs*, I've been to a whole lot of different teachers. I told a few of them my personal story, one to one. I still wanted to rid myself of the doubt about whether it was madness. Because then it might come back again. I was sometimes very afraid of that, if I was really stressed, and if I had a bit of a hangover or if my consciousness was either a bit cloudy or else particularly lucid, I sometimes had that fear. It's not as bad now, but when my girlfriend gets very emotional, for example, I can empathise and then sometimes I have a moment when I feel, oh help, I'm not going mad, am I? I have the tendency myself to rationalise everything, and it's good for me to be more in my body, to feel my emotions more, and that's what I'm doing at the moment, with yoga for example.

I once said to my psychiatrist, 'That whole India trip was actually a search into the question of what happened in my life during that one moment.' Because that moment itself, that was quite clear, that was quite simply an enlightenment experience. And the period afterwards, I was so wide open to life then that I thought I could make a fork stand on end, that I could read people's minds. I reckon that's actually possible, without being psychotic I mean. Some yogis and enlightened masters can do that. The things that my family and so on found so weird at the time, they really exist. Telekinesis, hypnosis, that sort of thing.

After that trip I worked for Greenpeace for two years, five days a week at first, then four, that suited me better. The best thing was working with groups and giving training courses and being with people. And now I'm going to train as a teacher, the shorter two-year course. I think working with children would be really good, that's such a pure contact. Apart from that, we'll see what happens, it's new to me after all. I won't be working full-time anymore. Working four days a week gives me so much more space, it's so much more relaxed, otherwise I get all stressed and then I sleep badly, I'm just susceptible to that. I'm now much more susceptible anyhow, I always was but that was never so obvious. I was a bit macho, I'm quite tall, long hair, I've done a lot of rugby, I was a bit of a tough guy. Since then my life has changed so enormously. I've got all kinds of other friends as well; I had a lot of college friends, but they're on a different trip. Besides working those four days a week, my life centres on spirituality, that was really a total shift after that trip. I did have a time when I made a strict distinction between the spiritual and the material life. I mean the really capitalist life, making a career, and working to earn more money in order to buy insurances to calm your fears. Because what is that all about, for heaven's sake? I used to have endless discussions with my ex-flatmate, when I was in India we used to mail each other about this sort of thing. He believed that you had to have proof of everything, in fact he was cynical about it, and now I just let him get on with it. It's his life.

I met my girlfriend at the *satsang*, so we really do this together. We go to regular retreats with Shantimayi, she's also become our teacher.[5] That's clear now. She belongs to the *sacha lineage*, that comes from Hinduism but it's a branch that stands a bit on its own. With her it's about realising your essential nature. But she hasn't much time for tendencies such as advaita, she thinks it's dangerous because you can really fool yourself with that. It's difficult to pin down her teaching, but it's about living with an open heart. My family can see of course that it isn't just a whim for six months or so, that it's here to stay, and that I'm going to go on with it. They've experienced the whole process of course, so they can fit it into some sort of framework now. But it's not the sort of experience you can pass on, sad to say. My mother once did a course in Buddhism, in order to understand me better, that's sweet. And she once came with me to *satsang*, so she goes into the subject in her own way. People tell me I'd be a good teacher. That frightened me off at first, I thought, oh no, don't say that, oh no, that's scary — that sort of thing. Also because I realised that my ego could get out of hand, and then it could go in the wrong direction. The images of Hitler and Stalin that I had that time, that was a sort of enlarged ego, of course. But that's all subsided a bit, I can put it into context better now.

The soul lives on after our physical death, that's clear to me. This body will die and be committed to the earth, but that doesn't matter in the least. I think it must be pleasant to be free of it, because now and again it's quite painful to be inside it. The idea of reincarnation really appeals to me. I can't verify it myself, but the Buddha saw it, for example, how the way in which you live determines what your next life will be like. That sounds very convincing to me. But anyway, every moment is life, death, life, death; every moment you die to the previous moment, everything is development.

It's good to talk about it, to sort it out a bit more for myself, a sort of healing. I had a really good talk about it this summer with Shantimayi, she said, 'Hans, you're not mad, you're not psychotic. I can feel it in your aura, in your psyche. There are a few people in my *sangha* who are psychotic, or manic-depressive, and I pick that up, I experience it as well. But you haven't got that at all, you don't have to worry about it at all. On the contrary, you're very strong and stable.' And for her it was beyond dispute that it was an enlightenment experience. It felt really good to hear that, she said it so firmly and clearly. That 'crazy period' was a logical consequence of my expansion of consciousness, and the experience itself was an enlightenment experience.

Josine (1954)

When I was eleven, my parents got divorced. My father and mother were pretty violent at that time and we really had to run for it, with my mother. There were years of custody hearings after that, and all the while my sister and brother and I were being sent from pillar to post. The world wasn't a good place. I thought, if I have to live in this world I'll do away with myself, because this is impossible, this isn't living, this can't be how it's meant to be. So I invented God for myself. I thought, there must be something greater than my parents, because I couldn't depend on them at all. Something greater than me. Because I could take my own life, but who made me in the first place? Even as a fourteen-year-old I used to wonder: what's the truth? What's the meaning of life? My upbringing hadn't given me any frame of reference at all. My father was anti-Christian, if he'd had his way he'd have turned the garden-hose on the 'bible-bangers' and washed them off the streets on Sundays. My mother was 'nothing', she wasn't geared to any faith at all, she was more of a humanist. But for me God was the force that gave us all life. And for me that was the answer that helped me go on living.

From then on I was always having confrontations with my father, because if I didn't see the point of something, I wanted to know why he wanted me to do it. I also wanted to run away, I thought, why do I have to live here? And I was different, I wasn't obedient. But he thought that a child like me had no business worrying about what the truth was anyway, and from then on he started calling me a psychopath. The rest of the family agreed with him, because I used to have violent reactions to what was going on. Later on I got involved with the Bhagwan, and of course they regarded him as no good, a cult figure. So I was getting involved in weird things, in their eyes I was really mad.

That urge to find the truth about life led me to study psychology. But after I graduated, seven years later, all the knowledge I'd acquired began to disintegrate. Everything was at odds with everything else. What I knew intuitively and what I'd acquired as knowledge, they didn't tally, and that caused a lot of stress. I found the course of study far too limited so I did various things besides. I went to summer camp with the Sufis, for example, I did all kinds of weekends with the Bhagwan, and rebirthing, you name it … I wanted to be a social worker, and if I was going to counsel people, I needed to know what it was all about, after all. You didn't learn anything about that on the course, you just sat there with your nose glued to your books. So I thought, right, I'll go and experience it for myself. And I didn't do that by halves! At the Sufi group I met a man who was also in the Rosicrucians, and I said to myself, I ought to take a definite direction.[1] So then I joined the Rosicrucians; I was also initiated there. And then I developed a sort of hypersensitivity. I was doing a lot of yoga at that time, and Tai Chi, and I read a lot of Sri Aurobindo, I explored my dreams, homeopathy, yin-yang philosophy, and so on, so I was very open to things, I think.[2] I could feel all sorts of cosmic vibrations, shall we say, but at a human level as well everything came at me in the form of energies. And that was quite something. I had the feeling I'd been boxed in on all sides. As if I was standing at a crossroads, with maybe ten streets all converging on that one centre, and really heavy traffic charging towards me from all sides. And that's what you have to contend with. I foresaw certain events before they happened. I saw images of other people, things that someone else had dreamed, or a horrific accident that someone had had. Or if I sat down on the sofa after someone else, I sensed how that person had been feeling — the sort of physical condition they were in. So I became clairvoyant and clairsentient, and of course I started thinking that I was mad myself, because who on earth ever senses things like that? In those days I lived in a commune, so I had ten or twelve people around me every day, and I started sensing all kinds of things, that was really incredible. That was so much! The commune was pretty idealistic, very easy-going. There was a rabbit hutch in the living room, along with a bike and the leeboard of a sailing boat, nobody minded that, but the fact that I experienced things that weren't usual, that was mad. That was rubbish. They were all academics who were either studying or already working, and that's how they all reacted. And I wasn't too sure myself, I thought maybe they're right. So that really made me start doubting.

Meanwhile I used to go around with the weirdest types, everyone else thought they were nuts, but I didn't; so I was able to counsel them a bit. But when I was at college I always gave a wide berth to anything and anyone to do with psychoses. Because I thought, once you get mixed up in that ... so when I started doubting because all those things were coming at me, I didn't know the first thing about it. I was frightened of it as well. I remember a joke from when I was seven or so. Sam thought he was a grain of corn and Moses said he should go to the lunatic asylum. So Sam did, and after a while he was cured and they let him out again. Then he ran into Moses again and Moses asked him if he realised now that he wasn't a grain of corn. And Sam said, 'Yes, I know I'm not a grain of corn, but does that hen know that?' Well, I thought that was a nasty joke even then. And later on when I could put myself in other people's shoes and feel what they felt, I no longer knew who I was, the hen or the grain of corn. I was both, actually, but at the time I couldn't see that as a spiritual *tour de force*; I thought I was mad. In the commune, if I sat down next to someone who was having trouble with his knee, I would ask about it, and he wouldn't understand how I knew about it, but then it would turn out that he'd had a fall the week before. Then I'd be stuck for the rest of the day with a pain in my knee. And someone would be sitting opposite me with something wrong with his eye, or his stomach, and I'd feel it all.

At first this sensitivity was just a nuisance. I also looked into a clairvoyant group which met now and then. Well, each of them was madder than the last, so I realised: this is not what I'm after either. But what I was after, I really didn't have a clue. So I got more and more isolated. I only used it to help other people, because I knew what was going on inside them. And often what was going to happen as well, or ought to happen. But it had some odd effects; there was one guy for example who thought I had power over him. So he started using his power against me, that was really nasty.

There were positive things as well. A friend of mine lived a few houses further down the street, and my contact with him was very telepathic. He was much younger than I was and came from a strict Evangelical family. There was something really Christ-like about him. He was tremendously open-minded, and he had such empathy with people, he knew exactly what was going on in their minds. And he was a carpenter — we were just like Joseph and Mary! My family said so too, when we had dinner with them once! He was quite a bit younger than me but intellectually we were equals. Each of us knew what the other was thinking, we felt completely at home with each other, we really were one person. I found that very affirming, with regard to the sort of impressions I was receiving. I was a sort of medium really, I wrote all kinds of things down, it was as if they had been transmitted to me. He read them and thought it was all fantastic; then he fell in love with me. And all of a sudden he wanted to marry me. And then I thought, now I'm going round the bend. Because okay, we were one person, but what did *that* have to do with it? It made no sense at all to me. But he was under enormous pressure from his family, so I had to let him go. But that meant that I had nothing left to hold onto, and then I really fell into a hole. I got into the same sort of state as when my parents got divorced. Everything fell apart, I had to run for my life — only this was inside me. I had really ghastly dreams, that a witch flew into my room. It seemed quite real, when I went into my room I could feel a freezing atmosphere.

I'd left the Rosicrucians before then, after five years. Certain people were always allowed to sit at the front, and I was never one of them. And when I was really in a state with my over-sensitivity and came to them for help, all they did was tell me to eat kidney beans. So suddenly I found the whole thing a dead loss. After that I went to see a clairvoyant, and she put me on completely the wrong track. She said there was a hole in my aura. I didn't even know what that meant. I thought: how am I going to mend it? Where's the hospital? She also told me: you're surrounded by a host of dead people, but don't worry about it. That really pushed me to the brink. I had horrendous nightmares, really horrific ... So I trained myself to stay awake, and to do things that needed concentration. Because I had the feeling that I was completely lost, as if I was losing my body. I started working at a day-care centre, from nine in the morning till six in the evening. And those children gave me something to hold onto. I got on really well with some of them. There was a very difficult little boy there, they said: you can't do a thing with him. Well, right from the start we were mad about each other. If he got there before me in the morning, he'd keep a chair for me. He actually kept me going — maybe I kept him going as well. He was so open, so innocent ... and very musical, a real little angel. And yet his parents were so distant; they even forgot to collect him sometimes. When they moved house, I lost him. So I left there as well.

At that time I was convinced I had no sensation in my legs, and that I had no foothold in the world. I even started wondering whether I was already dead, whether I was already in the underworld. Meanwhile I was constantly trying to put up a façade for other people, because I didn't want them to see what was going on. After all, I'd studied psychology and experienced all kinds of things; it would be a humiliation, I was supposed to know all about it. But I simply didn't know anything any more. I went to my doctor, because I had no feeling in my legs and was suffering from anxiety. He was really horrified and said I should ring him at night if anything was wrong. But that didn't help either. Then I tried various psychologists, including somebody at the RIAGG (Regional Institute for Mental Welfare) but she didn't understand a damn thing. First she said, 'You need to talk about your father.' But that was the last thing I wanted to talk about! And I could see her thinking: she's just going a bit round the bend. Then she said: you should get yourself admitted to a therapeutic centre for four years or so, that would do you good. I was furious. Absolutely furious! I definitely didn't want to be packed off to some institution or other, and certainly not by someone who didn't know what I was talking about. She missed our next appointment through illness, and I never heard any more from her after that. By this time I was convinced I was mad, but I thought: in an institution I'd go stark raving mad, and then I'd never get out. That was my worst fear. Because they wouldn't understand me there either, and what's more, I'd start empathising with all the other people there. And then I wouldn't just be mad on my own account, but through all the mad people around me! I was determined not to let that happen.

I also thought it might be worth trying the Christian perspective after all. So I went to one of those crisis centres and talked to a priest, who said, 'I can see you're having a very difficult time, but you'll survive.' I could sense his compassion, although he didn't understand much of my story. But it came from the heart, and I thought, maybe he's right. Of course, he had all those junkies coming in and he'd probably developed a good eye. I went to another psychologist as well, who said, 'These experiences of yours, they're not that serious.' That reassured me a bit, though it didn't help in the slightest. But she was honest, she said, 'I don't really know either, you'll just have to keep on searching.' So then I went to a haptonomist. She stroked my back and said, 'Can you feel this, can you feel that?' That was no problem. My whole idea of not being able to feel my body any more turned out to be wrong. But after eight sessions she said there was nothing more she could do. So I was still none the wiser. I thought, if I have to walk around with this another year, I'll end it all. And I can still see myself, sitting on the edge of the bed and thinking, now I really have to make a plan. Because I might believe I was ending it all, but maybe it goes on after you're dead. So that wasn't an option either. I felt completely trapped. And it struck me, the only thing I still had was the fact that I could breathe. That went on inside me after all, and that was my only certainty: I'm breathing. And my next thought was: I have to decide for myself. I have to come up with something here. I have no idea what's going on, but I'm going to see what I can do about it. So that gave me a sort of self-awareness. Then I thought, I have to find a way of getting rid of all my ideas. All my ideas, everything that occurs to me. If I can get rid of them, I can always see whether I still want to end it all. And the only way I could think of to do that was simply to go and do really healthy work. Then I remembered something about farms run along anthroposophical lines, where they look after you and you can work. That seemed like a good idea. They always need masses of people, because they don't use pesticides and stuff. So I got the telephone book and starting ringing round, and then I wrote to the farm that was furthest away. They accepted me within three weeks. I even managed to make my way up north. I saw a bus and thought, I'd better put a spurt on because I have to get that bus. I really had to push myself.

So I arrived there, and then I became a farm labourer. There were five other lunatics there who'd all gone off the rails one way or another. I felt at home with them straight away. One woman had been on drink and drugs, for example, she'd been abused by her parents and no rehab centre could cope with her, but she managed at the farm. I got on well with her. There was also a severely autistic girl who'd never spoken during her whole life, but she'd begun to talk there. She even blossomed, she turned out to be very musical. And a very likeable guy who'd studied medicine, turned out to be gay and couldn't cope with it, and started drinking. Very different types, all people who were hoping to find peace there. When I heard their stories, bit by bit, and realised why they were there, I felt an immediate bond with them. So I felt something for my fellow human beings again; the contact between us was real, all in all it was extraordinary. And there were all kinds of crazy things into the bargain. We used to make jokes about it. There were sheep a few fields away and if I heard a sheep cough, I'd say, 'Pardon me.' And then, 'Oh, I thought that was me.' I really thought so! We'd have a good laugh about that.

We also got some treatment, a talk once a week and a bit of therapy; it was a joke but it was healthy. We worked six and a half days a week, we only had Sunday afternoons off. Up at six in the morning, then singing, work meeting, then you were packed off to the fields. Till ten o'clock at night. Outside every day, in all weathers. All market gardening, plus a few chickens and pigs, you had to get up early on Sunday mornings for them. And one week per month you did the housekeeping with someone else, which meant cooking every day for twenty-four people.

But it was fun as well, working on the tractor and lugging heavy crates. I could lift crates with seventy kilos of sugar beet onto the cart, honestly, I had huge muscles. Besides us there were four families, we worked with the men and the women looked after the children. There were about ten children, and there were big celebrations for all those birthdays, that was fun as well of course. Riding on the hay wagon and then having pancakes with all those children in the hayfield a bit further on. Quite idyllic, actually. But there were always too many orders, so you were always working under stress. That meant there was a really peculiar working atmosphere, they were always grumbling that we didn't work hard enough. We used to sabotage that a bit, of course, but everyone lived under that pressure all the time. My father came on a visit once and he said, 'Wow, it's like a Japanese POW camp here.' But at least you had no time left to let your mind wander. And true enough, after nine months there wasn't a single thought left; I had no thoughts at all. Just, 'Now I'll do the leeks, then I'll do the carrots.'

I'd given myself a time limit of a year. I thought, if I don't see any improvement after a year, I'll find another solution. And that's how it went. Roughly a year later it was autumn and a whole lot of people got ill. I was almost the last one still on their feet, and went around looking after everyone else. The work started to pile up, it was like a hospital. Then I thought, my year is nearly up, what am I doing? I came here for myself, I don't want to work any more, I'm going to go to bed as well. So I went to bed and then I got a fever, and the fever wouldn't go, and I never really got well again. An anthroposophical doctor came to see me, he told me to take a bath every three days with some sort of herbal remedy. Apart from that, they shoved a plate of food in my room at regular intervals and that was that. For three months I lay in bed with fever. I wasn't all that ill, but I felt no desire to get better. And I had to start thinking for myself again. For two months I wrote almost non-stop, and thought about what I'd lived for. And I ended up with God again after all. And I saw that in fact the whole world consists of nothing but love. That's all there is. The rest is just clumsy expressions and misunderstandings. Then someone said I needed injections in my belly, but I didn't want that, and I thought, I've got to get out of here. Because I'd got my brain working again, I started to visualise the next ten years of my life. I definitely wanted to be independent, and then I thought over my domestic situation. I wanted to go back to my home town, I wanted to become a music teacher, I had an image of the sort of house I wanted, with a garden, and I wanted to do something with the Rudolph Steiner School, something in the anthroposophical line. So I'd conjured up the whole picture, and then it was winter, it was Christmas, it was snowing, and everyone had gone home. I thought, now I've got to get out of here. I was completely exhausted, of course, so I rang and told my mother to come and pick me up. I said I'd be staying with her for three months, and she'd just have to put up with it. And that's what happened. Two days later the superintendent came to our door to collect me, because I wasn't allowed to go off just like that. That just wasn't permitted in that group, there was that much pressure, you were disrupting things in the system. After that they used to ring up a lot, and everyone was furious, but of course I never went back.

Sure enough, those ten years turned out as I'd imagined. I started playing music again, then I was asked to teach at the Rudolph Steiner School, and I'm still there now. Everything I wanted to create for myself came my way within a week. I found my house within three months. I knew what it should look like, but not where to find it. I was walking down a street one day and there it was. I went in, the landlord himself was there and the last tenant had just left; I was able to rent it the same day. It was just the same with meeting people. I used to get a strong feeling that I was going to meet a certain person, but no idea who or where. So I'd let it go and then it would happen of its own accord, sometimes so incredibly that I didn't understand myself how it was possible. Before my time on the farm, all sorts of things that I saw as negative used to happen. I was living under great pressure, and when I went to the bathroom during the night, every light bulb on the way would go phut. Not just once, but week after week. And my alarm clocks wouldn't work any more, that really frightened me. But after that time I thought: you mustn't be afraid of this, just create something beautiful.

After that illness I felt really ecstatic for a while. I overflowed, I was so glad to be alive! I had really opted for my own life, and everything was love. God exists, and you can be part of it. I realised then for the first time that life is actually a gift. That it's not a mere case of just getting on with it. It's simply incredibly wonderful. Relationships and so on, that's often very complicated, but life itself is simply fantastic. There's always room for improvement, but everything you need is there. And a lot more besides. Of course I wanted to tell everyone about it. But that meant putting so much energy into helping other people that I thought better of it. I began to see more and more how I was falling back into my old habits, especially with my father. When he died I thought: now he's found his own solution. It was enormously liberating, for him too. But there was also something inside me that said: God, what on earth was I fighting for all those years? Suddenly it was all so pointless. I'd invested a lot of energy in it as well, trying to solve that conflict, because I kept coming across the same thing with other men. And suddenly he vanished from the face of the earth; suddenly it was all meaningless. And the fact that he'd always said I was mad — even that whole business no longer applied. It had created highs and lows in my life, and then eventually it just disappeared. I still don't really know what to think about it. But it also helped me understand what I always wanted to find out long ago. I know now for sure that nobody knows. So they can't pull the wool over my eyes any more.

After a while I got rid of all my books. I intended never to read a book again, and for four years or so I couldn't have done it anyway. Then someone I knew when I was a child, who was also from the Rosicrucians, came to my house and brought a book: *Ik ben* ('I am that'), by Sri Nisirgadatta.[3] He said, you have to read this. The title really appealed to me because 'I am', had been the only thing I had to hang on to. I've been in heaven and in hell, but I am still here. For me that was really the only thing that existed: I am. So I had a look at the book and it was quite a shock, because I understood everything in it. It's the only book you need in the house, because everything's in it. So I felt very grateful to Nisirgadatta that I'd been able to read at least one more book. And then it came about that at the same time I lost my father, I was initiated by a Dutch teacher who was a pupil of Nisirgadatta. The two coincided. It's as if one merged into the other. My father died suddenly, and the same week I told the story of my life to that teacher. As a matter of fact, they have the same first name.

Through a friend I went to a study group for Adi Da's students for a while, plus all sorts of courses, and I stayed in the ashram in South Limburg.[4] I'd also have liked to go to the Fiji islands where he lives, but of course that costs tons of money. I'd sit there all the time, but inside I felt that I already knew it all. The people around me were still searching, while I had already found it; I just wanted to understand it better. Searching also gets in the way, of finding, of being. Between the ages of thirty-five and forty-five my whole life was about finding, that was really good, I really lived without ties, really detached. That feeling of being cut off, and always looking for the answer in relationships, yes, I recognised that in myself during the past few years. I still get totally absorbed by relationships. I don't go in search of that telepathic thing any more, but it crops up every now and again, especially with men. I still don't quite know how to place it.

Nisirgadatta and Adi Da put everything on the map for me. Nisirgadatta says quite clearly in that book: you are consciousness, and all that thinking and feeling is something that appears in that consciousness. But it comes and goes, so don't cling on to it, because it's not what you are. No-one told me that during the whole psychology course, so this goes much further, and that's what I wanted as well. It made everything fall into place. I also started to sense his presence very strongly within me when I was so intensively involved with it. For example I became fantastically clear-headed, I felt almost as if I was him — yes, here we go again! I had the same thing later on with my own teacher. I was once in a concert hall and I thought I saw him. I didn't do anything about it, I didn't think for a moment I was going mad again. I realised that I lived in a much larger space than people around me. I always used to think that they lived in such a space as well, but I was always proved wrong. I used to find that odd, not about myself, though, because I'd always been bigger. I did my utmost in all sorts of ways to help them experience that space for themselves. Well, what more can you do? I've now reached a point where I really don't know any more. For a while I put everything into love, because it's always going somewhere. It's now a lot more equal than it used to be, because in the past I was always on top. Now I realise that we are exactly the same, it's just that the other person doesn't see or hasn't experienced a whole lot of things. The fact that I can see them doesn't mean that the other person can pick them up. And if I see that it's going to cost me too much energy again, and that I can literally feel myself shrinking to fit the other person's space, I quit. So now, after twenty-six relationships or so, I don't need that any more. What I do want, what purpose it will serve, that I don't know. For the moment I'm completely worn out by it all, I don't want those dramas any more, I don't want to cause another divorce. I'd really love to live in that way, but then with someone who also understands it. But before you know, it gets all tense and turns into something completely different. Advaita helps me to see it better, but I have a sort of instinctive disillusion that it hasn't really taken shape yet. That I can't really channel it yet.

During that mad period peculiar things happened all the time. For example, I'd decide: I should get a job in a shop. Then I'd walk in somewhere and be taken on the same day. Or I'd think: I'd like to get in touch with so-and-so, next thing, there they are right in front of me. Or: I'd like to have a car again. A week later someone gives me a car, it's mine to use for a while. Or: a computer would be nice. Then along comes someone with a computer. After my time on the farm I no longer thought twice about it, but before that it used to drive me mad. I tried to understand it, and I became afraid of myself. Because I thought: if I think something and then it happens, I ought to think really positive things. Because that's scary! And then I got frightened and scary things really started happening. Somewhere inside me I knew that was how it worked, but when you're overcome by fear, you're at your wits' end. The fear constricts you, and then you get more and more afraid. In the end I was really running away from myself. And if there'd been anyone around then who could have told me something about it, maybe I would have got over it a bit sooner. That's being wise after the event in my case, because I know about it now. But still, it's good to bear in mind that this is how you make your own reality. Then you realise that you're not an island, that you live in a much bigger and more infinite mystery, or source or universe, whatever you want to call *that*—God. And that's where your understanding always falls short.

Chapter Two

The Scientific View
Ego as the Measure of all Things

This chapter gives a broad outline of how the scientific outlook in general, and that of psychology in particular, relates to the experiences elsewhere in this book. Because a historical overview would not provide the most lucid beginning, we shall begin as close to home as possible, at a very elementary level, with the subjective experience which occupies pride of place in the book as a whole. Human behaviour gives rise to many questions, and western psychology provides many answers to them, but one of the most essential questions we can ask ourself remains: who are we? This question can be applied to human beings per se, as phenomena, as inhabitants of this planet, but also to ourselves as individuals. Other people usually do that for us: 'Who are you?' As a rule we come up with the name that we use in the social sphere. Or with a function that we fulfil, and which is relevant at that moment. 'I'm the owner of the bicycle that man just raced away on', 'I'm the mother of the girl who sang the school concert solo last night', or, if your name is Anita Roddick, 'I'm the founder of the Body Shop.' In this way we define ourself as an element in a social context. And if we need to explain something about ourself to someone else: 'I'm the sort of person who likes to get up really early', 'I'm the sort of person who is easily influenced by other people', 'I'm more of a Stones person than a Beatles person.' That we are a person is obvious: it is the recurring message in all of these statements. And all psychological schools and movements are concerned essentially with that basic principle. The kind of person we are differs from individual to individual, and every psychological branch has its own line of approach and methods for determining the gradations in colour common to all. But that each of us is a person is the cornerstone of the perspective. This idea was not produced out of thin air, we also experience ourself as a person. Of course I'm a person! What else could I be?

1 The dimensions of a cornerstone

In the context of this book, however, it would be interesting to dislodge that basic principle a little, to leave it less firmly wedged into its corner. Not because it is worthless, or because it is not true, but because it is relevant to see it for what it is: the cornerstone of a perspective. This insight enables us, for example, to trace consequences which would normally remain out of sight. The current idea-that-we-are-a-person may not be the last word about who we are, and will also come to stand in a new light elsewhere in this book. There is enough scope within the scientific tradition itself in fact to formulate specific hypotheses about this. But such a step would be more productive when we have found answers to the questions facing us now. What does the current basic principle consist of, anyway? What are the precise contours of the usual perspective, of the idea-that-we-are-a-person? And are we still a person when we sleep, for example, or is that a different kettle of fish?

These are the sort of questions that anyone might ask himself every day without coming up with an immediate answer. What does it mean to be a person? We can pinpoint several elementary aspects straight away. It is clear, for example, that we are ourself, and not someone else. Another person is other, someone we cannot be, and vice versa; we ourself are a different person from every other. Even if we once shared the same gene pool, the same womb and the same mother's milk, we are still different from our brothers or sisters: they remain other. There is a difference between ourself and the other, a space between, a division. Except, of course, when we are madly in love. Then things get out of hand, the boundaries dissolve as though they had never been. Then we are the other and the other is us, then we are the whole world, then everything is fluid and vivid and radiant and we would like things to remain so for ever — which is very rarely the case.

It is precisely because normally speaking we are not another person that such things as relationships exist. However we regard a relationship, it takes two to tango. Different relationships are possible with every other person, and without relationships, pleasant or otherwise, life would be hard to imagine — which is putting it mildly.

We are also a person because we have a body. We are all the more aware of that when our body is surrounded by other bodies, or if another body touches or ignores ours when we want it to do otherwise. Or when we are somewhere we don't want to be, and vice versa. This is not to say that we are our bodies, period. Sometimes we are intensely aware that we are *more* than our bodies alone. But would we still be a person if we had no body?

In addition, we see ourself as someone who functions in a particular way. Though it may not always amount to much, we are always busy doing something. Even when we do nothing, we are 'resting'. Of course, the leaves fall from the trees without any exertion on our part, but we know that because we can see it happening, and to see is also to do something. Even if we keep our eyes closed, we are keeping our eyes closed. And hearing, we do that all the time, because where can you find complete silence? And even if we do manage to end up in a deathly quiet place, where not a leaf or a breeze or a mouse is stirring, we can still hear a ringing or a murmur in one or both ears, so then we're doing that as well. Besides which, we're always breathing, although luckily that happens automatically. So we can't get around the fact, we are a person who is always doing something.

To summarise: we are a person, we are ourself and not someone else, we have relationships with other people, we have a body, and we function. And there you have the psychologist's sphere of activity: identity, relationships, perception, thought, action. The place occupied by consciousness is a thorny problem. As we shall see later, it is still far from clear what consciousness actually is. Is consciousness something that we possess? And if so, what? Psychology up to now has made do with a sort of derivative: cognition. This is a manageable concept, because it comprises the power of perception, plus countless ways in which that power produces its effects, physically, emotionally and mentally. Cognition thus as a collective term for how and what we know and understand and perceive and recognise. Without cognition we would not even know that we were someone, that other people exist, how a relationship works, that we have a body, or how we are supposed to function. In short, the plight of a newborn baby.

And that is exactly where the story of psychology begins. By now it is beyond dispute that an unborn baby experiences all kinds of things in the womb, but the general consensus is that psychological development begins only at birth. And from that moment on, all kinds of processes and phenomena are perceptible as we pass through the phases of infancy, childhood, adolescence and adulthood. The entire developmental process has been described in extensive detail; one theorist emphasises this phase, another emphasises that, one follows lines, another considers aspects, one makes a distinction where another merges, one draws conclusions where another raises questions. All kinds of things can go wrong however on the journey into adulthood, and this may also be reflected in the professional field. Psychology has in fact specialised in the mental glitches of human beings, justifying its existence socially by using its acquired insights to optimise the development of individuals. It does this in medical terms through care and prevention: intervening in problems and preventing them. A gigantic field, in short, difficult to view comprehensively, which has developed in the course of a mere 150 years, and which, aided by increasingly sophisticated technology, continues to expand. In that respect the field is certainly not static in practice. Scans of the living brain are now a mere matter of pushing the right buttons, and the development of medicine is proceeding at a large-scale industrial rate. The whole medical and paramedical circuit is switching over to evidence-based practice, with leading roles for chemistry, technology, statistics and the operation of the open market — a challenging operation, which aims to apply current psychological knowledge in a contemporary way.

2 Godfathers of the psychological self-image

Setting aside all details for the moment, the field of psychology reflects a number of foundations from an earlier date. The most important of these are the trails blazed by René Descartes, Isaac Newton and Sigmund Freud, all great innovative architects of our image of humanity and the world. Besides these, Charles Darwin exerted himself in the field of biology, and contributions were made by the fields of sociology and economy, but a glance at the first three will be enough to make us see our psychological self-image less as an obvious and absolute fact, and to some extent as the product of time and culture.

The legacy of Descartes (1596–1650) consists first and foremost of his credo: 'I think, therefore I am.' An historic proclamation in which he condensed his more elaborate proposition that gave modern western philosophy its foundation in dualism: reality consists of two essentially different 'substances' or components, i.e., the thinking mind (*res cogitans*) and physical matter (*res extensa*). And so, *cogito ergo sum* implies that, as thinking subjects, we can make no irrefutable statements about the verity of the material world, because our perception of it does not as such constitute firm evidence for it; all we can prove by thinking is the very fact that we think. The irreconcilable nature of mind versus matter is typically reflected in the scientific tradition, which evolved from the 'sacred' prin-

ciple that whatever we consider knowledge must be objectively measurable and verifiable. In Cartesian terms that is as much as to say that the
result of any physical experiment must be produced without interference
from the observer's state of mind. It is the litmus test *par excellence* which
determines whether or not acquired knowledge may be called objective
and scientific.

Descartes' watershed also has a number of consequences for psychology. Body and mind are placed on opposite shores, and never the twain
shall meet. Nevertheless, or perhaps for that very reason, one of the great
eternal questions is how they might relate to each other. First of all, we
will find that the relationship is not symmetrical, because by and large the
body plays first fiddle while the mind is regarded as secondary. Moreover
'the mind' is seen as a 'thing', like a body, but ineffable and diffuse: essentially different therefore from somatic reality. Thirdly, physical reality is
often used as a criterion; everything that cannot be classed in terms of the
body is relegated to the mind. In fact we still prefer to express what we
discover about the mind in terms of the body, because we can at least
make sense of that. In earlier times, for example, the steam engine served
as model for the workings of the mind, and we still speak of psychological
mechanisms, while nowadays we use the image of a computer in our
brain, busy processing 'information' day and night. Research into the
mind also generally takes place via the body; psychology traditionally
studies the operation of the senses, movement, behaviour, language and
suchlike. The fact that psychiatry and psychology stem from a medical
background can be seen in the methods and techniques used; their suitability for research into the 'ghost in the machine' is inherent to the outlook that developed them.

Technically seen, though, Descartes' famous one-liner could be read as
an admission of weakness. The conclusion 'I am' clearly cannot stand
alone, but must draw its evidential value from the statement 'I think'. We
feel immediately that this is all well enough in practice, but that something has already slipped through our fingers. Is our capacity for thought
the essence of our humanity? But surely we have all sorts of feelings,
desires and capacities too? The possibility of existing in a thoughtless
state moreover, so clearly absent from this credo, would even bring the
whole construction down; and yet that is a common enough human experience. Thus viewed, the famous Cartesian proposition verges on something that remains unspoken; almost inaudibly it says, 'I think, therefore I
am *a person.*' At all events that is the interpretation adopted by psychology, which takes thinking and being a person as self-evident and naturally linked; they validate each other. As when we find our minds
wandering, and we say, 'Sorry, I was miles away.' And certainly, we can-

not think of ourself as nobody, because we're always left with the person who is thinking 'I am nobody'. And if we really weren't anybody, could we then truthfully say: 'I think'?

A second point of view that has made history, even in the field of psychology, derives directly from the study of moving objects: Newton's (1643–1727) mechanics. In the mechanical world view named after him, individual physical objects with their own 'dead' weight are slung back and forth by non-physical forces: the image of colliding billiard balls. Observers gradually realised that these objects actually also attracted and repelled each other. And while the whys and wherefores of all these non-material forces may remain a mystery to some extent, insoluble within mechanics, the triumphs are no less for all that. This is pre-eminently the field that gave rise to the quantification of natural phenomena. By observing the patterns revealed by the interplay of the balls, researchers learned to make minutely accurate predictions of an object's position in space at any given moment. This applied not only to objects on a common or garden scale but also to celestial bodies, and eventually even to atoms. It is the principle of separate objects and the predictability of their behaviour; hardly surprising therefore that psychology is indebted to it, consciously or otherwise. The universe as a purely mechanical clock-work device is of course long outdated, and we have to go very far back indeed, to the Homeric epics, to dig up the idea of mortals driven to their deeds as passive victims of divine caprice. In contrast, the classical trage-dies of a later date are characterised by the protagonists' inner struggle: feelings of duty, remorse, jealousy and helplessness stem from the differ-entiation of their personal will, which makes them wrestle with instinc-tive drives, and take a stand against inordinate demands or hereditary curses. It is precisely this individual will which, nowadays in psychologi-cal terms, forms the element that distinguishes humans from other crea-tures; from closely or distantly related species, and most of all from inanimate objects. From the mechanical perspective, man as a moving object is therefore a special case. He uses that extra power of his to deter-mine his own direction and speed, thus making the outcome of his behav-iour less predictable. An external observer can only deduce this factor indirectly, as long as the resulting behaviour is distinct from a 'will-less' control scenario; in order to get to know the will itself, another sort of observation is called for. In principle, however, according to the Newto-nian method, scientific observation focuses on action, movement and change, which are observable from outside. After all, little can be learned from a screen which displays nothing but a homogenous haze, or a gauge which shows no deflection; we need separate, individual objects and per-ceptible motions. Hence the result of a well-designed experiment is the measurable change of an isolated variable. Provided that the remaining circumstances are controlled (the principle of 'ceteris paribus'), this change can then help quantify its relationship with the known variable that caused it. In psychological research, too, the subject must therefore be dynamic, and must always concern an aspect of human behaviour. Originally that meant visible behaviour, but today this also includes emotional activity and the oscillation within various brain areas. And so, aided by our technologically sharpened vision, the image of the human being in all his favourable or less favourable aspects is becoming more and more complete, at all levels of observation. We can speak justifiably therefore of a psychology of action, which focuses on the movements of various 'objects'.

A third ineradicable influence was of course the work of Sigmund Freud (1856–1939), who discovered principles in the inner motivation of human beings. By bringing the subconscious to the surface he showed how unfree our thoughts, feelings and behaviour actually are; right down to the level of our verbal slips we are driven by unconscious forces, all of which prove furthermore to be an integral part of ourself. Freud pointed out, for example, how the ego is jammed in-between our instinctive desires on the one hand and pressure from our social environment on the other. On this basis he composed a picture in which the human being rounds off his own development by managing the balance in that individual field of influence, in order to function successfully in the world. In that picture the ego is the central and active entity, which embodies the psychological idea of the 'self'. This idea of the self incidentally superseded the idea of the soul, the Greek 'psyche'. Long interpreted in religious terms, the soul fell into disfavour when science finally gained the upper hand. For in order to function, the human being had absolutely no need of a soul, and following the super-sharp guideline of 'Ockham's razor', which states that a theory should not be more complex than strictly necessary, the soul accordingly did not exist.[1] The self was then free to ascend the vacant throne. There it presides as the psychological concept for the subjectively experienced 'someone' that we take ourself to be. It is the self that proposes and disposes, and it is the self whose resulting behaviour, and nowadays also whose inner motivation, is studied by psychology. The general consensus here is that the individual self is not present at birth, but goes on developing until adulthood. The behaviour of the self occupies a central place in psychology, which makes it all the more surprising that the actual nature of the self rarely comes under discussion, if at all, but lies untouched on the philosophical plate. For example, in a textbook on clinical psychology, more than 900 pages thick, definition of the term is left to the school of self-psychology. They state as follows:

Self-psychologists give various definitions of the concept 'Self'. In general the Self is a designation for the aggregate of physical and psychological aspects of the person. In the 1970s a fierce discussion arose within psychoanalysis about the definition of the Self and the place of this concept in the formation of psychoanalytical theory. This discussion is still raging today. A 'healthy' Self is a differentiated but cohesive whole. Pathology can occur if developmental disorders prevent the Self from developing into a cohesive whole that can be clearly differentiated from others. In such a case the Self is not experienced as a whole. It is also possible that the Self does initially develop into a coherent structure, but later disintegrates. Self-psychologists have published work particularly on the development and treatment of narcissistic personality structures and the borderline personality.[2]

We must make do with this, though the main part of this depiction concerns the 'unhealthy' self. Considering the clinical focus of the publication this is perhaps unsurprising, but no more precise definition is forthcoming than that it concerns a cohesive structure. Or we must seek it within the context of the humanist psychology of Carl Rogers (1902–1987): 'In accordance with the general characteristics of the humanist body of thought, Rogers attaches great value to the way in which the individual experiences himself as an organised, unique and separate whole. Rogers designates this by the "I" or else the "self".'[3] In general therefore, while psychopathology makes many statements about the sickness of the self, it has no detailed concept of the healthy self. In the context of this present book, in which the familiar self will prove to be considerably less self-evident, this is far from satisfactory.

The above-mentioned three points of view form the pillars of the psychological paradigm as we know it. In psychological research and methodology their influence can be felt up to the present day. Firstly, attention is paid to the physical dimension of psychological symptoms, and to the correlations between them. Secondly, research focuses on symptoms and variables that can be observed from outside, and can preferably be measured. As a third point we may note that in psychology the autonomously acting individual is the predominant object of study. He or she is the microcosm who must hold his own in the macrocosm, and who reveals himself particularly in the context of psychopathology as the centre of a field of influence, various aspects of which fail to function as they should.

Although criticism of this whole perspective differs greatly, there is unanimous agreement that it is reductionist, because its traditional spokesmen basically explain all (problematic) mental symptoms in terms of the body. Over the centuries the specific focus of physical interpretation has evolved considerably: from the classic doctrine of humours, concerning the various bodily fluids, via theories on hysteria (caused by the womb rotting through lack of fertilisation), to hypotheses, more acceptable today, on hormonal disorders and neurological deviation. Genetics represents the most recent variant of this physical Pandora's box. Its devotees hope in due course to localise the coded keys to the mind. The debate on this hegemony of physical factors is already showing its age, and is not always conducted with much finesse; it is much more given to polarisation. An orthodox splinter group from what we might call the reductionist camp has proudly adopted the title of 'sceptics', and joined in battle with the 'soft' group which dares to claim that anything other than hard scientific fact could possibly be of real value. The term 'all-in-the-mind brigade' on the other hand refers to rigid devotees of the opposite idea: those who interpret physical ailments as the direct product of sick thinking patterns. The Cartesian division in public debate, it would seem, is alive and well.

3 Cognition under the microscope

For many years external observation was the predominant method in most psychological research. The behaviourist tendency basically rejected anything with even the slightest whiff of inner experience, believing that positivist science was the only true one, being able to focus exclusively on objectively measurable events. And during its heyday in the first half of the twentieth century, that applied only to visible behaviour. What went on inside laboratory animals was in theory ignored, but their behaviour and reactions to various stimuli were used to deduce the cause of their inner conditioning. After Pavlov's salivating dogs, it was pecking pigeons and bewildered rats that were subjected to the dynamic laws of reaction to pain and pleasure, all in the attempt to discover the ideal way to bring up humanity. In this perspective, the 'someone' as subject of study most closely resembles an object that is under the influence of external forces, and can thus be controlled externally. One might reasonably regard the 'Little Albert' experiment of 1920 as the ultimate symbol of psychological testing in this tradition. In this classic experiment in 'classic conditioning' supervised by John B. Watson (1878–1958), founder of behaviourism, researchers scared the living daylights out of Albert, an uninhibited little boy of eleven months, after which he displayed a generalised fear of objects which he associated with the original stimulus. How he got on in later life is unknown, as his family left the area not long afterwards.[4] Apart from the considerable ethical objections which have prevented such experiments since then, the relationship between tester and laboratory animal is an incontrovertible case of an objective, external observation, in which there is no question of human contact.

From the 1950s onwards, partly due to critical voices from the professional field itself, the cognitive approach was next in vogue. This school focused to such an extent on 'inner workings' that it gradually promoted the processing of mental information to visible measurable 'behaviour'. Breakthroughs in how we learn, understand and use language in particular brought new cognitive methods into play, and the whole can be justly regarded as a revolution, which mapped out our thinking structures more thoroughly. In this concept, the 'person' has evolved to an object or organism with a will of his own, interacting with and operating within his environment through making choices. This expansion of interest also had an effect on psychopathology. For example, the time-honoured concept of schizophrenia — the archetypal mental illness — assumes that the disease is caused by a faulty or damaged brain; even today this concept has not been totally rejected. For many years a fundamental distinction was also made between psychoses and neuroses, partly based on the assumption that the former had an organic cause, while the latter was a question of defective psychological development. Parallel to this of course is the apparently eternal dichotomy between nature and nurture so widespread in the human sciences. At all events, with the emergence of the cognitive line of approach, psychology developed a sharper eye for the image that people construct of themselves and the world, and for the problems that this may cause. Through this means people began to examine their inner world in a systematic way. The therapies which stemmed from this are accordingly more a question of 'talking' than 'taking pills'. It is not so long ago that the two trails began to merge in practice. Even without a watertight theoretical model, the practical care and nursing services often provide fertile ground for innovation. The tangible fruits of the cognitive tree are now being plucked, for example, in therapies for people suffering from the 'classic' symptoms of schizophrenia. Contrary to long held views, their hallucinations, voices and delusions do in fact respond to psychological attention of a cognitive nature. This means, at least in practice, that the strict division between body and soul dissolves even further.[5] From the cognitive viewpoint our inner life is also less of a 'black box', about which we can only draw indirect conclusions from the outside.

With that, the inner world also gained a voice in the whole process of diagnosis and treatment. Moreover, people with mental ailments nowadays are not merely passive objects, labelled by others as sick or disturbed and carted off to an institution; they come of their own accord in large numbers to the doctor's or psychotherapist's consulting room. And surely, their input on how they feel and what is going on inside them is the *raison d'être* for most of these professional fields (see also 2.6). The more refined schools of psychotherapy moreover illustrate in a profound way how the interaction between client and counsellor is hardly just a matter of exchanging information. Rather, it can make for a truly intersubjective experience, which supports the healing of personal trauma, and beyond that, potentially heartens both parties to embody their own humanity even more. Such psychological richness however is less apparent in another, significant corner which draws on the participation of peoples' inner experience — the psychological test industry. In the most appropriate research methodology for the cognitive school at large, the main emphasis lies on gathering information at second hand, through interviews, tests and questionnaires, for example. The personal experiences of the individual are thus transformed into data in a larger collection, which is then processed as a whole. The statistics involved in both constructing and completing such tests cannot be produced without abstractions and categorisations. The pre-eminent tool for this purpose is the 1-5 Likert Scale, which has now become indispensable to psychological research. For every item of a questionnaire it offers a scale of 1 to 5 degrees, representing subsequent answers like 'in total disagreement', 'in some disagreement', 'neutral', 'in some agreement', and 'in total agreement' in relation to a statement, or a similar range from 'never', 'sometimes', 'regularly', 'often' to 'always' in response to a question about certain behaviour or experience. Simple to design and adapt, the Likert Scale as a model has even popularised to become the standard tool for large-scale surveys featuring in magazines and on websites, where they enable readers and users to measure anything from their knack for Turkish cuisine to their disposition for bachelorhood, or to classify them according to anything from their political mindset to their gardening style. Typically, the Likert Scale originated in the field of business management. It essentially converts qualitative variables as if by magic into quantitative data, thus making it possible to process them at a collective level.[6] In the psychological context this then means that the significance of individual experiences produced by this approach is necessarily in terms of the whole, and is expressed in averages and deviations from those averages. This can result, for example, in a more or less distinct picture of a symptom in sufficiently large groups of individuals, at which level we can eventually make predictions. This, in broad outline, is a sketch of the current developmental phase in the field.

4 Freud's taboo and totem

Obviously, the paradigm of the psyche which underlies all such developments also sports Freud's signature. More than anything else, his pioneering work lay in lending credibility to the influence of the subconscious on our daily actions. In so doing he simultaneously charted a particular stratification of the psyche. In those days his scientific entry into the dark side of the mind was anything but a matter of course; the Enlightenment, after all, regarded the mind as free because it was rational. Freud's early interest in hypnosis, the interpretation of dreams and mythology referred rather to the dark side of life which had so stirred the emotions during the preceding Romantic era, and that was surely the domain of such irrational and highly unscientific affairs as literature and the visual arts. The inner conflicts between the drives and the social package of demands in daily life were however unmistakable, and Freud's systematisation of the therapeutic trade actually brought about a virtual revolution. High-profile characters such as he, of course, do not go uncontested, and all those bookshelves loaded with refutations, supplements and reinterpretations of his work lend some weight to the idea of a Freudological science. The relevant factor here is that, drawing on his legacy, the various layers of the psyche are always described in terms of the ego. On the one hand the instinctive drives of the original *id*—off with the pain and on with the fun—form the primal forces which the ego must manage to control—while on the other hand the internalised voices of our parents and peers form the moral beacons of the superego, within which the ego must manage to operate. In this way all inner experience is packed into one box, that of the conditioned personality. Seen through Freudian spectacles, the ego is accordingly the measure of all things. It is what we see as ourself, formed by our personal history and saddled with a unique, individual combination of preferences and aversions, strengths and weaknesses, inclinations and habits. We derive our personal identity from it, further assuming that the whole thing will change little beyond a certain point; once grown up we are more or less 'finished'. After that our character remains recognisable; it represents our essence, both for ourself and for others. If the character of someone we have known for years is changed by an accident or neurological disease, we are really shaken: 'He's not himself any more.' The 'self' that the person in question used to be was apparently the only real one. It implies the degree to which someone *is* essentially his personal character to those around him. Now there is nothing wrong with that for everyday use, it is all highly suitable for that purpose. But to apply conclusions about ego functionality directly to every dimension within a human being's scope—including that of *being*—this step is surely too sweeping. At all events, the result of this is that from Freud's point of view, the ineradicable human interest in religion and religious experience in particular comes off extremely badly. He considered such tendencies to be undeniable symptoms of varying degrees of neurosis, and in one of his works devoted to religion, *Totem und Tabu: Einige Übereinstimmungen im Seelenleben der Wilden und der Neurotiker* (Totem and Taboo: Resemblances Between the Mental Lives of Savages and Neurotics), he dismisses them in no uncertain terms as the products of unresolved, deeply primitive conflicts.[7] According to Freud the mentally healthy person would suffer nothing more serious than a light neurosis, but he categorically rejected the possibility of healthy forms of religious feeling and spirituality. This thorny problem did certainly not go unnoticed, and his initial crown prince Carl Jung (1875–1961) was not alone in rejecting the great master on this account. To illustrate this point, a recent article describes how Freud's many sayings about religion, examined by his own psychoanalytical methods, provide a highly significant depiction of his possible motives.[8] Misunderstood and vulnerable as a child, envious as an adult of 'oceanic' experiences which he had never known, and unable to live up to his parents' ideal, he seems to have directed his scorn at the illusion of the divine Father. Freud knew the work of his contemporary William James, author of the bestseller *The Varieties of Religious Experience*, a frequent visitor to Europe who also attracted much interest; not once did he refer to this work however.[9] Not that the question of religion ever lost its hold on him; on the contrary, in his old age he continued to struggle with it all the more.

5 Nuances and amendments

There has been much tinkering with Freud's model of humanity over the years, and many have made their names with specific revisions and additions. Of comparatively recent date are the system-oriented approaches, which attribute a less atomistic and autonomous existence to the individual, and interpret identity rather as a social construction. System-therapy methods therefore include the social environment—parents, siblings, children, partners, peers—of a primary client to actively participate in seeking clarification and improved contact. The interventions of Karen Horney (1885–1952), a German psychoanalyst who emigrated to America in 1930, were of an earlier date. Far from happy with the Freudian theory of sexuality, she counteracted his concept of penis envy in the female with womb envy in the male. In addition she saw that besides our idealised self, which we try our utmost to realise, we also have an 'actual' self: that which we actually are. According to her, this true self can emerge in therapy if we succeed in peeling off our defence mechanisms, and do not keep trying to become a 'better' ego. The idea of a non-conditioned, authentic self has since then cropped up in the work of various authors, and has been developed particularly by the British psychologist Donald Winnicott (1896–1971). As paediatrician and children's analyst he introduced the concepts of the 'true self' and the 'false self' to the object relation theory. The first develops in a young child in response to empathetic mothering—offered by a 'good-enough mother': the second in response to the lack of such mothering. In formal textbook terms this false self

> can be understood as an extreme form of adjustment to the environment. The child ... loses contact with his 'true self', his own wishes and desires. The 'true self' hides behind the 'false self', a mask of social adjustment. Such a 'false self' admittedly leads to adjustment, but not to a satisfying existence. This serious pathology is often difficult to recognise, because the person seems to function normally.[10]

It is interesting within the present framework to see how the false self is thus explicited as a serious disorder. On some level, to be sure, it would seem that each and everyone of us is suffering from it to some degree, because we all carry some level of our earlier conditioning as 'a mask of social adjustment'. In fact, experiencing oneself without such a mask, and seeing other people without theirs, makes for part of the shock and disorientation that marks some of the spiritual crises reported in this book. Philosophically speaking, it's a challenge to consider what this would mean for the standards of 'normalcy' versus 'pathology', much as the 'psychiatric survivors movement' suggested in the seventies. As formulated above, however, we seem to be dealing with a hitherto unnoticed complaint which therefore has not yet been named as a category or syndrome. Now Winnicott himself was clearly one of the testators of psychological genealogy who went about his work in an intuitive way, and he sensed that the true selves of the children he encountered were something extremely precious. Judging by this standard, the functional but highly adjusted self was thus a form of perversion. And yet Winnicott expounded his theories in a balanced way. He regarded the false self moreover as an aspect of the true self, for which it acts as a protector. That is why the true self does not take part in the reaction to the environment, and deteriorates unnoticed, because it fails to gain experience. It does however retain 'continuity of being' at all times.[11] Though Winnicott's playfulness and empathetic voice were not intended for academic psychology, they have influenced the practice of therapy throughout the world.

The notion of a genuine self subsequently hovered on the fringe of the professional field, forming the focus of interest for only a few psychologists. One odd-man-out in that company was the Polish psychiatrist Kazimierz Dabrowski (1902–1980), who elaborated his theory of 'positive disintegration'. The Second World War and its aftermath slowed the spread of his work, as did the fact that he wrote in Polish, translated into French and Spanish, and only learned English as his last language. His concept is nevertheless distinctly valuable. By 'positive disintegration' he meant a non-linear human development, which actually begins where Freud left off. At the level at which we normally function we are simply surviving, driven by instincts and inhibited by social norms. To Dabrowski, the difference between averagely functioning people on the one hand and criminals on the other is only a question of degree. We are little troubled by inner conflicts, because whatever we do fulfils either our own needs, or else other people's expectations. A crisis of some sort, however, may smash the balance to smithereens, leaving us suddenly in a phase of confusion. Then our whole constructed image of ourself and the world may gradually start to totter. If we cannot get through the despair caused by this, we drop back to our earlier level and dig ourself in; otherwise we come to a bad end—Dabrowski mentioned suicide or psychosis. The third option offered by this disintegration however is the proverbial opportunity: if we allow our true self to take over, we gain contact with our authentic potential. Once we catch a glimpse of that, there is no going back, because we have had enough of our former existence. The only alternative then is to steer by our own compass and learn to opt for the higher aims that we discover in ourself. In so doing we are taking responsibility not only for our own lives, but for those around us too. Eventually we can then attain a new level of integration, where creative expression and unconventional good works represent the highest in mankind.[12]

Dabrowski's concept is reminiscent of the work of Abraham Maslow (1908–1970), who became known to the public at large through his pyramid of needs and his research into peak experiences. Each propagated his own model of human development and potential that, judged by the prevalent Freudian template, went far beyond the limits. Dabrowski however developed his model still further. He stated, for example, that neurosis can play a key role in development into a complete person. Not for nothing was one of his books entitled: *Psychoneurosis is not an Illness*.[13]

These ideas refer to a landscape that Freud at all events has left uncharted. And that raises the question of whether a psychological perspective such as that of Dabrowski does not rest on other foundations than those familiar to us in any case. Whether this field of psychology is not akin to physical and metaphysical formulae quite different from those of Descartes and Newton. This issue will be further discussed in Chapter 4.

6 Pathology in the second person singular

The shift from the observation of exclusively external behaviour to the cognitive zone has already generated completely new insights in psychiatry. For many years abnormal behaviour and bizarre statements in themselves formed the evidence of mental illness, and it was assumed that to dispel these symptoms constituted a form of cure. Now, however, the work of a number of pioneers has inspired psychologists to look — and listen — more deeply. The point of view has thus shifted to the second person singular. In a revealing illustration of this in the Netherlands in the mid-1980s, the social-psychiatrist Marius Romme (b. 1936), at the insistence of a female voice-hearer in his practice, began to listen to the kind of things 'her' voices had to say. This proved to be more than the random salvos of commands and threats normally classed as the products of a deranged mind, and which by definition ought to be suppressed.[14] And so an area of research came into being in which the idea of 'auditory delusions' as the final word was largely superseded (see also Chapter 4, 'The self in creative chaos'). For one thing, it was established — beyond being mere common knowledge — that psychiatric patients are hardly the only ones to hear voices. Other than for instance artists and innovators however, who take guidance from various kinds of inner whisperings, people who find themselves in mental health care clearly have difficulty in coping with their voices. New therapeutic approaches started to evolve from this kind of challenging evidence, which enables such patients to get through life with less anxiety and in less isolation. Beyond that, it gave people a handle to gaining new insights about themselves, because it began to look as if the voices were linked to their life history, and formed an adjustment to unprocessed traumas in the past. The consequences of this line of thinking were considerable, and not only in terms of the new possibilities for everyone directly or indirectly concerned with delusions and hallucinations.

Firstly, the value of this exploratory operation for voice-hearers was quickly reflected in the revolutionary growth of self-help groups, which consequently began to take off internationally. Secondly, this break-through in the existing paradigm implied that, from close by, the idea of a specific 'mental illness' as a separate entity loses its meaning. From a safe distance, an external observer can view certain symptoms as a particular package, and point out how one package differs from another. But the same observer who knocks on the door, gets invited in and then engages directly with the tenant of the house, is unlikely to find a distinct disease; instead he will be filled in on a range of subjective experiences, perceptions, views, as well as their consequences. By stepping inside like this, psychiatry leaves the familiar home base of the external observation post, which is why alarm bells go off here and there. Its position as a science is felt to be at issue. This is awkward, of course, but only insofar as psychiatry wishes to continue seeing itself as a natural science; the social sciences, after all, operate from a role and position in which they do not view themselves as alien to the object of their study. It is remarkable at any rate that the psychiatric profession should want to continue camping on the physical bank of the Cartesian landscape, while its declared aim is to heal the mind.

Listening to a person with psychological difficulties, however, does not necessarily mean that the perspective shifts from the third to the second person singular. Psychoanalysis also had as its aim to get to the core of the pathology, and distinguished itself explicitly from the later dominant behaviourism by focusing its attention on the inner life of the person on the sofa. However, the therapist who sat next to this person—and originally out of sight behind him—did not necessarily listen with open ears, kept interaction to a minimum, and generally made use of a rather rigid interpretive framework. In this sense classical analysis is neither more nor less than a third-person perspective, although it pays attention to the inner world. Most current psychotherapeutic approaches however use a second-person perspective. While some schools, such as those based on attachment theory, represent a more sophisticated end of the spectrum, the perspective as such emerges as soon as there is real contact between client and practitioner.[15] From a strictly objective-scientific viewpoint therefore there is something fishy about therapeutic practice, while the former typically carries a label of alienation. The antipsychiatry canon provides a striking anecdote about this divergence. In a biography of one noted and notorious representative of this movement, the Scottish psychiatrist R. D. Laing, the following was recorded during his active period.[16]

> While still in Chicago, Laing was invited by some doctors to examine
> a young girl diagnosed as schizophrenic. The girl was locked into a

padded cell in a special hospital, and sat there naked. She usually spent the whole day rocking to and fro. The doctors asked Laing for his opinion. What would he do about her? Unexpectedly, Laing stripped off naked himself and entered her cell. There he sat with her, rocking in time to her rhythm. After about twenty minutes she started speaking, something she had not done for several months. The doctors were amazed. 'Did it never occur to you to do that?' Laing commented to them later, with feigned innocence.

It is no coincidence that the continuing discussion on the structure of the DSM was sparked off by practitioners and their direct contact with clients; it represents the same shift in perspective. A recurring point of criticism is precisely the classical division of the handbook into categories of diseases and disorders. Faced with these explicitly defined entities, the user has no choice but to fill in a 'yes' or 'no' here and there, and in practice that quite often causes friction, to put it mildly. According to the complainants, the categorical structure is too much of a theoretical artefact, which does not sufficiently reflect reality. As an alternative, the idea of a dimensional classification has been circulating for years now. This kind of structure is more akin to the Likert Scale. The diagnostician uses it to allot each client a score on a sliding scale with regard to particular dimensions — such as anxiety, introversion, compulsiveness, emotional stability. A type of disorder can then be characterised through a combination of certain dimensions. This approach has by now gained so much support that a dimensional section for personality disorders is in the making for the DSM-V, which is planned for 2011.

A recent study on psychosis reveals the points of interest which crop up when the second-person perspective is adopted from beginning to end. In *Psychose ohne Psychiatrie* (Psychosis without Psychiatry), German researcher Thomas Bock breathed new life into the body of thought on this subject by immersing himself in the lives of people with disorders, who went without treatment either completely, largely or for a long period.[17] For this purpose Bock did more than cross-examine dozens of people with psychotic experiences who had managed somehow to survive outside of the psychiatric circuit: he did so within the context of thorough research into countless aspects of the psychotic universe, without losing sight of their interrelationships, which is quite an achievement. For example, he reviews the various theories about the nature of psychosis: psychosis as development, as disorder in the perception of reality, as autistic withdrawal, as split personality, as expression of the unconscious, as expression of a conflict, as regression, as expression of the destruction of everyday reality, as token of vulnerability, as a problem of interpretation, and as a personal crisis. All in all, an impressive spectrum of explanations, that demonstrates at least that there is little in the way of unanimity, and at the same time suggests that this wealth of factors is inherent to the material. In one fell swoop Bock also puts the various methods of research under the microscope, analyses the strengths and weaknesses of specific quantitative and qualitative methods, and ponders their interrelationships to certain research questions. His work certainly emphasises the growing insight that, in practice, a category of illness such as schizophrenia is as good as meaningless, if only because seventy-two variations of the course of the disease have been distinguished up to now. For that reason the social services now focus more on recuperation from specific difficulties. Furthermore, all sorts of earlier reflections on thera-peutic possibilities, which had been elbowed aside by pharmaceutical advances in the course of the last century, now appear to be strikingly top-ical. Bock unearthed a number of now obscure authors and practitioners who had had sensible and encouraging things to say in their day, and cer-tainly deserve more attention in the further fleshing out of the practice of care and counselling. By focusing on people who get through life as far as possible without a pathological label, moreover, the dimension of psy-chotic subjectivity in Bock's work comes prominently to the fore. In the clinical environment the availability of effective medicines puts a stop to this as quickly as possible; it is forbidden territory. This approach, how-ever, puts further insight out of reach, and for this reason too Bock's research group is of great importance. Although his study is not the first to deal with the psychotic experience, he focuses attention on new aspects of it, and in greater breadth and depth. Within the philosophical tradition of the *Daseinanalyse*, for example, he points out that the break with 'real-ity' is not absolute in psychosis, and suggests that 'psychiatric research should be focused on the perception of the self, the self image and the independent recovery of the schizophrenic person'.[18] Not only do his findings offer leads for social policy and forms of care and intervention, therefore, they also open the doors to the interior of the psychotic reality in particular. What does the subjective experience look like, how does it develop, how does someone experience himself before, during and after a psychosis, how does he manage all that time? How does someone find meaning in her experiences, what role does the body play in all of this, what is the role of language, of religion? Questions which cannot be answered from the outside, while it would seem to be too soon for a Likert Scale graduation. Bock ends his impressive book with a 'plea for an anthropology of psychotic perception', an original and committed expla-nation of the multi-coloured complexity which constitutes life with psy-chotic experiences, and the points of departure available to the second person singular: social worker, family, acquaintances — society.

7 Madness from the inside

One step further along the way from exterior to interior lies the perspective of the first person singular — the place where experience happens. In science itself this perspective is, for obvious reasons, the most difficult to use. The most explicit sources for an impression of 'madness from the inside' are to be found, apart perhaps in our own experience, in the artistic and literary traditions, where it is certainly no unfamiliar theme. In various classical works the mental suffering or derangement of the main and subsidiary characters is a far from marginal phenomenon; think for example of widely differing authors such as Virginia Woolf, Leo Tolstoy and Guy de Maupassant. On their own terms they turn their Via Dolorosa inside out, so that the reader can be a witness to it. The fact that the suffering interior world can thus lead to artistic excellence is in itself an object of study. Specific mental disorders are increasingly often connected to literary and other artistic achievements of consequence, and art naturally offers the scope and means to provide the *condition humaine* with powers of expression, even under unfortunate circumstances. We are also familiar with psychiatrists who write novels and poetry; in the Netherlands this subgroup includes among others Frederik van Eeden, Vasalis, and Rutger Kopland. The study of manic-depression in great artists offers a specific variant: it is a speciality of the psychiatrist Kay Redfield Jamison, who suffers from this disorder herself. Her book *Touched with Fire* explicitly built a bridge between the cultural and the medical spheres surrounding bipolar disorder.[19] Before that it was the neurologist Oliver Sachs in particular who opened the gates of abnormal perception to a wide public, while allowing those he described to retain their human dignity. A close neighbour to this genre is the autobiography of a madman. As regards numbers, this is still quite scarce; from a literary angle these works are not easily accessible, and as non-fiction they meet with the traditional objections in medical respects. In that context their subjectivity is precisely the obstacle, especially since Freud unmasked our subconscious, yet continual and subtle self-deception, and left us little to rely on. That does not necessarily make these writings any less fascinating, however. From manic-depressive quarters especially, testimonies of the inner world appear with a certain regularity, in which the 'hands-on' expert reports not only on the abysmally heavy lowest points but also the unparalleled intense, creative and euphoric moments; a title such as Patty Duke's *A Brilliant Madness* speaks volumes in that respect.[20] For a broader spectrum of 'insanity' altogether, Bert Kaplan's 1964 collection *The Inner World of Mental Illness* can be seen as a classic.[21] It contains chapters on mental sufferers and 'lunatics', both famous and obscure; the writers do not spare themselves when sharing their concepts of right and wrong with the reader, *en passant* providing insights derived from their unusual point of view. The question of which perspective the reader can or should hereby adopt is not easy to answer. It is obvious that current frameworks are unable to fully comprehend the experience, and it even seems that it might be better to put the whole idea of a perspective on hold.

Although religion and religious feeling are well-known ingredients in the psychopathological experience, they have never constituted a distinct category of illness. Diagnosis takes more account of the form, rather than the content, of symptoms; a religiously tinted delusion is seen as a delusion, and the clinical environment further ignores the content of this delusion as far as possible. Underlying this attitude is the idea that such attention would only intensify the delusion, and thus make the chance of recovery even more remote. There is however little, if any, evidence to support this attitude. Most recent studies which elucidate this subject originate from Britain. For example, Mike Jackson and Bill Fulford selected accounts from an extensive database of religious experiences, which contained 'psychotic' phenomena such as apparent delusions or hallucinations, and compared those with reports from people 'who had recovered from major psychoses but nonetheless interpreted their experiences in strongly spiritual terms'.[22] Although there were differences in intensity, they found no basis for distinguishing between such symptoms qua form or content, nor via correlations with other pathological symptoms or causes, or via more modern, descriptive criteria for mental illnesses. The authors concluded that the evaluation of such experiences is linked to the cognitive system of values and convictions of those concerned. Moreover, some people managed to integrate their inner experiences into a religious life, while in the case of others a sort of paralysis occurred, resulting in a pathological condition. That religious and spiritual experiences are common among the public at large has often been demonstrated (see also Chapter 3, 'Fathers of introspection').[23, 24] It is therefore conceivable that the religious feeling of psychiatric patients is linked to their failure to integrate such unusual mental experiences, or more generally, to attempts to find meaning in experiences which are not, or not completely, understood. More on this in Chapter 4, 'Perennial philosophy'.

8 Doubt, scepticism and transparency

In spite of all modifications and expansions of psychological orthodoxy since Freud, the self-image that he bequeathed us is alive and kicking. This may have little to do with the man himself; perhaps his account of things made such a lasting impression just because it happened to provide the subtitles for western man's experience of himself. At all events, spirituality has not yet been cleared of the charges brought against it by Freud. Basically, it may be harmless enough for people of sound mind, but they obviously have little to do with the mental health services anyway. According to a recent article in the *Tijdschrift voor Psychiatrie* (Journal of Psychiatry), there is some space for religious practices, if they appear to help individuals to work through their problems and build therapeutic relationships.[25] Even so, spiritual experience leaves the theory of the psyche completely nonplussed, and in this context gets treated as an 'S-word', an inheritor of the Freudian taboo. Consider once again the public domain of literature, offering its wealth of experience, reflection and meaning, its wide horizons, heights and depths: how infinitely bleak the official image of the psyche appears in comparison! We need the vision of someone like Thomas Kuhn to show us that this stiffness is simply inherent in the status of the prevalent scientific paradigm.

It would be too easy, however, to ignore the resistance of convention to the wider perspective that is evolving. We may well learn something by zooming in on the friction, while sooner or later debate on this subject is inevitable. And it would be better to conduct it as lucidly as possible – if only to cut costs for everyone in the long run. For that reason, in anticipation of further modification and fine-tuning in the context of the transpersonal viewpoint, I will throw some light here on the contraction of the scientific framework to a predictable tunnel vision. Psychiatry as a discipline is of course a human invention. It is therefore by definition not immune from such unsavoury matters as ideological manipulation; in the worst case, this is revealed by abuse within past and present totalitarian power structures. Fortunately we are far removed from such tragedies in the Netherlands, and democratisation has not passed the sector by, but it is just as unsavoury when certain experiences, to which human beings throughout all ages and from all corners of the earth continue to bear witness, are dismissed out of hand as impossible or absurd. At this point, more fundamental questions are at stake than the most effective treatment for a particular mental disorder. The psychology of action has a weighty responsibility, but can it live up to this as long as its primary portrayal of mankind remains disconnnected from other sources, views and realities? In mental health care, sometimes real patients and clients look nothing like the psychologist's image of them, and even beyond the sector, 'healthy' people experience all kinds of things about which the prevailing paradigm is silent. Ergo: it is time for change. Once we agree on that, an engrossing quest awaits us. Visible steps are being taken; the dimensional line of approach for the new DSM-edition is a clear example of that. And at some point the quest may become more comprehensive, and actually pro-active, as we admit that the shelf-life of an essentially reductionist paradigm appears to have expired. For now, the way in which this paradigm sometimes appears to need defending is perhaps revealing enough. Its morbid growths are not only anti-scientific, they can cause an open dialogue to mutate into a mud-slinging match, and sow confusion where transparency is most needed.

As quoted above, groups which describe themselves as 'sceptical' regularly make their voices heard. An interesting fact, as they associate themselves in name with ancient philosophical lines of thinking. 'Scepticism' is a fine thing; the original Greek term means research, study, consideration. It means that we do not believe a thing too readily, and want to rummage around in it first; an indispensable point of departure for the practice of science. But in the course of time the meaning has changed. According to the Van Dale dictionary, for example, it means 'doubt'. Yet anyone who immerses himself in contemporary 'sceptical' debate is forced to conclude that some writers have passed far beyond that stage. The opening bid appears to be: don't believe anything they tell you unless there is cast-iron scientific proof for it. A modern-day echo of the godfather of philosophers, Epicurus (c. 341–271 BC), whose viewpoint was extremely materialistic. In his view, everything consisted of atoms flying around in empty space, and our physical senses alone could tell us anything about the world. His particular creed can be heard these days in both popular and more scholarly publications, but in both the authentic spirit of research appears to have died out.

The statements of modern-day sceptics have their use, of course, as part of a debate; by their own admission, their pronouncements often are a signal. It is clear for example that they are allergic to assertions about hitherto difficult to explain phenomena, and particularly to claims from the popular quarter based on half-understood science. Now obviously, such claims can be far from accurate, and when wishful thinking takes over, the 'objective discovery of truth' is indeed abandoned. But in the first place, scientific objectivity at all levels is an illusion. It is an illusion, by the way, which, if recognised, would not slam the door on scientific practice per se; on the contrary, it would ideally lead to a living science in which authentic *scepsis* would be one of the driving forces. A second point is however, that popular 'sceptical' reactions are themselves seldom shining examples of a fresh, objective look at the riddles with which existence continually confronts us. They sometimes exude the bias of an epicurean unbelief, and considering that unbelief is also a belief, tribal warfare is never far away. Actively unbelieving authors do not raise themselves by definition above the level of 'woolly statements from the alternative quarter'. For example, the line 'unproved = untrue' is a tried and tested sceptical strategy; it is like pulling one case out of the hat as an argument against a similar case. Conclusions then take the form: 'all paranormal claims are nonsense, because one particular medium turned out to be a con-man'. And 'even' eminent scientific circles seem to take up such an attitude. Well-known figures take part in what passes for dialogue, but is more reminiscent of an academic round of 'oh yes it is! – oh no it isn't!' An illustration – not a proof – of such sceptical erudition is to be found in the recent compilation *Science and Religion – Are they Compatible?*, which contains contributions from a number of researchers of renown.[26] A 366-page book at that, with portraits of Galileo, Einstein and Darwin on the cover: all icons of a visionary, pioneering science, who hardly made their names by reinforcing the established mindset of their day. The book contains a section entitled, 'The scientific investigation of paranatural claims', comprising five pages, all told, devoted to near-death experiences. The author and philosopher Antony Flew devotes half a page to making mincemeat of an American claim from the medical sector, concerning one case of near-death experience that proved to be badly documented. He then passes on to an evidently shaky bit of British research, quoting an editor of the journal *Skeptic*, also British, who relates that four of the sixty-three heart-attack survivors interviewed had reported something like a near-death experience, which was of course 'not much to write home to mother about, really!'[27] For Flew – apparently unaware of the existence of the article by Pim van Lommel's team in the authoritative journal *The Lancet* two years previously[28] – this was enough hard evidence to conclude triumphantly with a quotation from Susan Blackmore. The latter had once, while on drugs, had a near-death experience herself and carried out parapsychological research for years, only to adopt a sceptical position later on.[29] In her own words that means that she is uncertain and does not wish to draw big conclusions, but Flew lets her end with: 'The more we look into the workings of the brain the less it looks like a machine run by a conscious self and the more it seems capable of getting on without one.'[30]

Now, Blackmore made this very statement in an article outlining why she gave up her parapsychological research into the reality of paranormal phenomena such as telepathy and psychokinesis, and more specifically, in a passage where she argued that even if these phenomena could be scientifically verified, they would still not teach us anything about consciousness. Therefore, for Flew to borrow that statement and use it out of context as a kind of last word on the impossibility of an entirely different category of experience, is confusing at best. As for the notion that the brain does not need a self in order to function, interestingly enough this leads different people to very different conclusions about the nature of consciousness, and not necessarily to Flew's square rejection of anything beyond the brain. See also chapters 3, 'Being and non-being' and 4, 'Quantum speculations'.

9 The big question

Sceptical or otherwise, we cannot expect much progress from substandard science such as this. With regard to content, we now come to the most ticklish subject in the area of knowledge of the psyche. The question is a very old one, and science has long avoided it, regarding it as impossible to examine: how does our consciousness work? After the avoidance tactics of the last century, however, it is once more under discussion. The body has been looked at from every angle, the workings of the mind are under scrutiny—how do they really relate to each other? And what is the role of consciousness in all of this?

Blackmore's above-mentioned statement is strongly reminiscent of ideas that Eugen Bleuler (1857–1939), godfather of the concept of schizophrenia, committed to writing in 1894.

> Consciousness in our opinion is not a requisite condition for thinking; reasoning and thinking are both unconscious and conscious phenomena. That is not to say that consciousness is an epiphenomenon, that has no direct connection with the rest of the psychological occurrences. One cannot compare it with a clock's (incidental) striking of the hour, but with its ticking. Consciousness is the necessary result of the organisation of the brain. Because this is connected in a particular way with the senses, because all processes that take place inside it are preserved in the form of dynamic traces which can be brought to life again and can link up with one another according to particular rules, for that reason a consciousness exists inside it. It is conceivable that a clock that does not tick could be constructed. Up to now however this

has not been done. Practically speaking therefore at this moment the ticking is a necessary by-product of the functional clock. In the same way one could theoretically construct a being capable of action, without consciousness; our brains are simply so designed that part of the activity that takes place within them must be connected with the phenomena that we call consciousness.[31]

Now that non-ticking clocks have pushed their mechanical predecessors half-way to the museum, the time is right for this position. Bleuler's statement dates from more than a century ago, but apart from the clock metaphor it is not essentially outdated, going by the statement in 2003 by the American 'positive psychologist' Mihaly Csikszentmihalyi, the most prominent spokesman of the peak-like *flow* experience. Even the experience of *flow*, the mental state in which we function at our best, in which we feel ourselves to be completely absorbed in what we are doing, in which we abandon all control and nevertheless manage to do everything effortlessly, is according to Csikszentmihalyi neither more nor less than a by-product of our brains. With great assurance he writes:

> To begin with, and just to clear the air of any suspicion that in talking about consciousness we are referring to some mysterious process, we should recognize that, like every other dimension of human behavior, it is the result of biological processes. It exists only because of the incredibly complex architecture of our nervous system, which in turn is built up according to instructions contained in the protein molecules of our chromosomes. At the same time, we should also recognize that the way in which consciousness works is not entirely controlled by its biological programming — in many important respects [...] it is self-directed. In other words, consciousness has developed the ability to override its genetic instructions and to set its own independent course of action.[32]

This explanation for all subjective experience is far from satisfying, and also hardly less 'mysterious' than the alternative explanations to which it refers. Csikszentmihalyi wrote this at a time when 'not a single branch of science was directly concerned with consciousness'.[33] Of course he could get away with that in 1999, even though the *Association for the Scientific Study of Consciousness* for example was founded in 1997, but in the later 2003 edition his excuse is out of date. By then David Chalmers (b. 1966) at all events had outlined the rationale of consciousness studies quite lucidly, as in his article *Facing Up to the Problem of Consciousness*.[34] This Australian computer expert, philosopher of the mind and representative of a younger generation of colleagues in the same field, stated in this work that there is an 'easy problem' to begin with, to wit, to find answers to all questions concerning the cognitive powers and functions of the brain: the capacity to make distinctions, to categorise, to react to stimuli in the environment, to integrate information, to give an account of mental states, to focus attention, control behaviour, to wake up and to go to sleep. Chalmers worked on the assumption that in due course answers to all these questions would be supplied in terms of neuronal processes. For an author such as Csikzentmihalyi this probably settles the consciousness problem once and for all. For Chalmers however a 'hard question' still remains: subjective experience. For when our senses register signals, and our neural networks succeed in channelling them, in translating and circulating them, why is there still such a thing as subjective experience? How is it that we experience what we experience, when we walk through a field of flowering rape? And how is that different from the impact of a field of red poppies? And why is it that Pergolesi's *Stabat Mater* seems to expand our mind space in particular, while Gershwin's *Rhapsody in Blue* strikes the heart with an effervescent sense of joy and liberty, and the Kinks' *Lola* leaves you with an insolent sort of vulnerability in the pit of the stomach? Why does the smell of mixed spices take you back in time to the happiest or most miserable Christmas of your childhood? How is it that, then and now, we can feel anything at all, happy or miserable or whatever, even apart from such stimuli?

Chalmers also came up with 'a being which acts, without consciousness', such as Bleuler had imagined. He presented the 'philosophical zombie' as a conceptual experiment concerning a being identical to a human in its thoughts and actions, but incapable of conscious experience. It's an idea that also caught on in popular culture. Since the Million Dollar Man in the 1970s, one cyborg (short for *cybernetic organism*) after another has stalked across the screen. Arnold Schwarzenegger has been particularly successful as a hyper-advanced robot that resembles humans in every respect and can calculate figures, reason, catch villains, and save or threaten entire planets, but lacks every sort of inner experience. Sometimes the main point of this genre is that real people who encounter the cyborg realise that it is precisely in that inner life that their own humanity lies—while the cyborg is sort of saddened at realising his lack, except that he is not actually capable of any such feeling. Cyborgs also seem to be the playthings of many a professor of artificial intelligence, who happens to have a weakness for supercomputers. Some believe that robots will take over from humans sooner or later, simply because they would operate more efficiently in every way. Now, even if we assume for a minute that that were true, we would still be left with a Big Question: what on earth would be the point of such a project? Assuming that—ultimately, and aside from considerable distractions—the human world is all about healthy food, clean water, clean air, a roof over our heads, spending our time meaningfully, good company, perhaps intellectual growth, but above all happiness in some shape or form—how would the life of a world population of robots make any sense? This question however seems less intriguing to those quarters than Chalmers' riddle is to students of consciousness. Parallel to Blackmore's conclusion quoted above, his theoretical exercise suggests for example that consciousness as such is not a *conditio sine qua non* for an ability to function. And there's the rub: why on earth is there such a thing as precious as subjective experience, in that case? Or are we deluding ourself about that after all?

10 The subject and the methodology

At all events, subjective experience up to now amounts to little more than the Cinderella of psychology and psychiatry. And yet initially psychology took great interest in this section, and not only as a mere source of data on functionality. The two originators of psychological research, William James (1842–1910) in America and Wilhelm Wundt (1832–1920) in Germany, placed the unshared subjective experience at the top of their list, and sought to use it as a scientific base—see Chapter 3, 'Fathers of introspection'. A similar note was sounded in the Netherlands too, and an echo of that would certainly be appropriate here. The speaker is Henricus Cornelius Rümke (1893–1967), who was famous both as a 'phenomenological' and as a 'psychological' psychiatrist. His interest in phenomenology was clearly contrary to the spirit of the age within his field, when neurology still had the upper hand. Rümke had a very eclectic conception of psychology, the value of which he held to lie in its clinical applicability. In the now defunct journal *Psychiatrie en Maatschappij* (Psychiatry and Society), psychologist of religion Jacob van Belzen quoted from Rümke's reiterated holistic arguments: 'Psychiatry would flourish indeed, and would not be endangered nor endanger other people, if all the old and new were integrated in one large-scale conception of the healthy and sick person. At the moment that is only rarely the case.'[35] Rümke, it is true, must have believed in the traditional categorisation of mental illness, but blamed its difficulty of application on the 'crudeness of the psychology in which psychological syndromes are sketched. There is no language, there are no fixed psychological concepts, full of subtle but sharply differentiated nuances, which one can use in describing a clinical picture.'[36] His response was to adopt 'subjective psychology' in his own practice, which he propagated in his capacity as professor. Under that heading he included both psychoanalysis and phenomenology, and he was no doubt extremely competent in both. To him, the skill lay in 'observing, exploring, and describing well, and particularly in not interpreting too hastily what has been observed'.[37] The clinician who masters these skills would really be able to achieve 'through-knowing' — a *dia-gnosis*. Rümke's favoured concept of phenomenology, by the way, was that of the German philosopher and psychiatrist Karl Jaspers (1883–1969), whose concept of delusions and hallucinations meanwhile has been belied by recent cognitive breakthroughs, such as findings by the British clinical psychologist and philosopher Richard Bentall (b.1956).[38] Rümke's impassioned plea for the application of phenomenological methodology, because of its greater subtlety and the insight into the process that it would afford, was then heard no more. Within the context of the latest cognitive research, however, it would seem to be the very candidate for a new lease of life. In the past, psychotic symptoms were regarded as the predominant hallmark of a much larger complex of illnesses. Yet they appear to be receptive to finely attuned attention after all, once we are prepared to reopen and explore a cavern which had been hastily closed off by conventional medical means. Phenomenology therefore surely provides ingredients for the recipe book of future generations of psychologists and psychiatrists. To say that there is still a great lack of tested methodology is an understatement, however. Some would see that as a reason to persist in regarding the theme of subjectivity as unsuitable, while others on the contrary are attracted by the challenge to develop adequate methods. An obvious example of this is the American psychologist Russell Hurlburt (b.1945), who added the bleep-experience to the meagre set of instruments for introspection.[39] For twenty years now he has been equipping experimental subjects, diagnosed schizophrenics or otherwise, with a bleeper which goes off at random moments. This is the signal for participants to reach for pen and paper and write down what is going on at that moment in their experience. After a given number of bleeps they are interviewed by Hurlburt, who cross-examines them about their notes, in order to flesh these out as precisely as possible, down to the last detail. His technique and results make short work of the doubt that subjective experiences as such are not accessible to examination. Hurlburt is mainly interested in different thinking processes, and while his rough material consists of descriptions, he uses no less than sixteen separate distinguishing marks of regularly recurring experiences:

Inner speech (IS)

Partially Worded Speech (PWS)

Unworded Speech (UWS)

Worded Thinking (W)

Image (I)

Imageless Seeing (XI)

Unsymbolized Thinking (U)

Inner Hearing (IH)

Feeling (F)

Sensory Awareness (SA)

Just Doing (JD)

Just Talking (JT)

Just Listening (JL)

Just Reading (JR)

Just Watching TV(JW)

Multiple Awareness (M)

The data of his DES methodology—Descriptive Experience Sampling—which he developed over the years from this technique, rapidly produced new perspectives on schizophrenic versus 'normal' thinking processes. An import aspect of this methodology is that the bleepers are carried by subjects in their everyday life, thus ensuring the least possible laboratory influence. Another aspect is that with a bit of practice, participants can easily increase their observation and recording skills. This increases accuracy after a short time—a fundamental advantage with regard to a single or random experience which is reported after the event.[40] It further suggests that in general we are rather poor at remembering the details of our subjective experience. Which also means that there is a lot to be gained. Innovative approaches such as this meanwhile are emerging from various quarters, and via these 'gates of perception', to put it briefly, we are entering a new level of intimacy with the psychological and sometimes psychotic reality within. A level of intimacy that the religious experience had already attained.

Frans (1941)

Even as a small boy I was interested in religion. I was very susceptible to what the parish priest said, I'd sit there open-mouthed and drink it all in. And yes, it was all about guilt and punishment and hell and damnation, I took it all very seriously. Until I realised that they'd taken me for a ride. At one point I saw the hypocrisy of all those people in church, and I found it so unjust that they let me go around as a small boy with that whole burden of mortal sin and that sort of thing! I felt they'd done something terrible to me. I was seventeen or so then, and I threw it all in. That had a devastating effect on the people around me. My parents were at their wits' end, they honestly thought: he'll go to hell. They got priests to try and talk me round, but they didn't get anywhere.

That went on for ten years or so, and then I began to think: I've thrown out the baby with the bathwater. I'd confused religion with the Church, with the institution. So my interest began to revive a bit, but yoga was all the rage at the time, and oriental philosophy and religion, so I was completely focused on that. Of course my parents were worried to death about it, because oriental stuff, well, they didn't think much of that! Anyway, in the early seventies I read something by Wolter Keers for the first time, about advaita vedanta.[1] I didn't understand a thing about it, yet somehow I knew what it was about. A sort of inner knowledge. And for a long time I had the same thing with Krishnamurti. I was also with the Bhagwan for one and a half years, in a red frock and all, the only one in the village! Well, okay then, not a frock, but red clothes. I went to that houseboat on the Prins Hendrikkade in Amsterdam once, for a whole weekend. And the following Monday I stayed off work and walked all the way round Zwanenwater lake, that was an amazing experience. I had several ecstatic moments during that time, very brief ones — well, what do you call brief? When you can't keep track of time any more, one minute, a couple of minutes, ten minutes? Real bliss. And realising at the same time: Christ, it's as simple as that. This is so simple, it would be harder not to experience it. Just for a moment I could see it all clearly. But as soon as I became aware of that, it was gone, it was just a memory.

I had a very good time there, but I didn't really feel at home. That was because of the whole group thing, and because there were so many freaked-out characters walking around, Christ! I know plenty of people who didn't see it like that, but I found some people so over-the-top. Cut it out, I'd think. They really went to extremes, worshipping Bhagwan. And something happened that really upset me. Bhagwan had said, 'Death is something to celebrate, you shouldn't be sad.' And not long afterwards a baby of three or four months died in the Amsterdam commune. And the parents were really sad, but everyone around them was supposedly celebrating. And that really upset me! Because Bhagwan had said you should celebrate, they ignored their own pain. I thought, oh God, this is madness. Then that whole story about Sheela came out and I thought, get me out of here.[2] I didn't want to be associated with it, with the whole con trick. That had something to do with it.

At one point I had to go to hospital for a hernia operation, nothing very complicated. I'd asked for an epidural, but it didn't work. They injected my back three times and then they told me: it's not working. That was really tough, because the pain kept coming back. In the end I had to have a general anaesthetic, but by that time they've pumped so much morphine into your body to dull the pain that you'd agree to anything. And then I had a cardiac arrest, and I was clinically dead for a while. They revived me with an atropine injection in my heart. There was me thinking: I want as little poison as possible in my body, just give me a jab in the spine. But I got a lot more than I could handle. On the ward they thought, he's only had an anaesthetic, and they treated me accordingly. So they let me go to the toilet by myself, but when I stood up I got a tremendous headache, I didn't know what to do with myself. So, straight back to bed. I was okay when I was horizontal. Then they discovered that my spine was leaking subcutaneously, from the jabs of course, and then my brain pressure dropped. So I had to lie flat at all costs. But if I sat up for a minute, to have a drink or something—my wife said later, 'You were absolutely green with pain.' The only pleasant thing about it was that I was lying there hallucinating like mad! I don't know where I got it all from, but I saw all the temples in the world. I saw Chinese pagodas for example, big and small, in detail, really clear images, it all unrolled before me. That was all very nice, of course. I was aware that I was hallucinating and that I was in hospital. It happened another couple of times, and it went on a bit longer once I was back at home.

After that whole business I felt well enough physically, but one way or another things were a bit strange. With hindsight I would say: I didn't feel at home in my body. My own reconstruction is that I was brought back too quickly by that atropine injection, and didn't fit back into my body properly after that. What that means exactly I don't know, I was gone and then came back. I didn't have an amazing tunnel experience or anything, I just remember coming round. But later I heard that I'd slipped over the edge for a minute. Anyway, after a year I thought: I must be suffering from tension or something. So I stayed off work, the company medical officer sent me to a psychiatrist at the RIAGG, and after a couple of months I thought, I'm well enough to go back to work.

Meanwhile I'd come into contact with Avatar and I thought, I'll do one of those courses first.[3] Alexander Smit was also going to give one.[4] I'd been to a few lectures by him and they'd really made an impression on me. So I decided to do a course with him. And then something happened there. We learned an exercise to dissolve any convictions you might have about yourself. What I remember is that you rolled up a conviction about yourself into a sort of ball, in your consciousness, then threw it away as it were, and then you could replace it with a different conviction. You could play with it like that. And I was doing that shortly after the course, on my own at home. But I found that throwing convictions away was a lot easier than adopting new ones! Because I sort of felt, why get a new conviction, then you'll just be lumbered with another conviction. Because I began to realise, these convictions are usually just a load of hot air. And that had such a deep effect, at one point I'd lost everything, even the conviction that I was a person or whatever. With the result that I ended up in a sort of void. And actually it was that void that made me realise afterwards: that's what this is all about. But I suddenly had the most horrific anxiety, it was such an anxious experience! ... The first time it happened I sat dead still from nine in the morning till five in the afternoon, hardly daring to breathe, because with every breath I thought: there I go. Or something like that. I also literally said aloud, 'My God, why have you forsaken me?' That's what Jesus said on the cross. I was very very anxious. And I was caught in a sort of dilemma: I couldn't live, but I couldn't die either, they were equally frightening. So I was completely trapped. And meanwhile I was in a cold sweat. By about 5 o'clock I could move again, so I rang my neighbour, and he came round straight away. He's a really good guy, and he's also interested in spirituality, but still, he didn't know what was going on here either. So he went into the garden and got a stone for me. Frans, he said, take a hold of this. To ground yourself. Well, that was a good idea in itself, but I was already feeling a bit better. Then I rang my wife, she was staying with her sister, and I even collected her from the station.

After that it kept coming back. Sometimes it would last five minutes, sometimes a couple of hours. Then I'd feel that fear again. Fear of that hole. I used to call it the black hole. From what I'd read I knew in my mind: now I have to surrender. But I couldn't do it. And at the same time I was just hindering myself, because I was trying to do it. Something like: okay, smartass, you're only doing it to get rid of that rotten feeling. That ambivalent attitude was always there, I was driven mad by my own thoughts! And I was absolutely terrified. Because I was really dissolving, I felt, there'll be nothing left of me. During that state of fear I was actually very clear-sighted, so I saw it all happening, it was terrifically frustrating! And I could get into that state again just like that, I was always dreadfully afraid of that. I could be watching television for example, and suddenly, through some image or other, I was right in there. And I had that once with one of those 3-D pictures. You have to look at them really intently and then after a while you see the third dimension appearing. So I was doing that, suddenly I saw the third dimension and whoops, I sank right into it. That lasted three years or so, all told. I felt anxious for a while on each occasion, only the intensity became less, and the frequency as well.

A week after the first time I rang Alexander Smit, but I couldn't get hold of him. Eventually my wife got one of his employees on the line, a woman, who said, 'That's impossible.' So she didn't take any notice of it. Two weeks after that I went to Amsterdam, I rang Alexander's doorbell, he was at home, and he spoke to me via one of those intercom things and said he didn't have time. It made me feel awful. I did manage to get through to him later on the phone, and to my utter amazement he said, 'But you knew I was in a silent period.' I didn't know that, and I could tell my story after all. Then all he said was that I should do another exercise, one where you expand your consciousness completely, so that you fill the whole of space to begin with, and then you can make it infinitely bigger. But I didn't dare to do it at all, actually I could have done it just like that, but then I would have lost myself completely.

I slept fine during that period, but I always felt horrible when I woke up. Dog-tired, and I'd think: what on earth have I been up to? I also remembered dreams, really horrific ones, now and then. And when I woke up I always felt a bit nauseous, with a stomach ache. That gradually disappeared over the next seven years. After a month a friend came to collect me, he had a handyman's business and he said, 'You should just come and work with us.' Really decent. But it wasn't always so easy, sometimes it was terrible. I could talk to him about it as well, incidentally: he's a freemason. Apart from that, I could tell hardly anyone that I'd fallen into this void through Avatar. In the end I claimed it was the result of the operation. I remember that one of the neighbours down the street dropped in and I heard her say to my wife, 'And how is Frans these days?' I really had to laugh at that. I talked to the man next door about it sometimes, he reads Krishnamurti and so on as well. And my wife and children, they were all worried as well, but they knew I wasn't mad. It was just as bad for my wife as for me, actually, because she couldn't do a thing. I always used to say, 'It's enough that you're just there.' That was true as well. I felt calmer when she was at home. I was very dependent at that time, though I didn't say so, otherwise she felt completely tied down.

I was a teacher at the local technical school, and the company doctor saw that it was pretty serious and sent me back to the RIAGG. I was already seeing that psychiatrist there, and I had to inform him that I'd really flipped, but I didn't dare add that it was presumably because of that Avatar group. He would probably have found that ridiculous, because I was already a bit unstable then, yet I went and did a course like that! He was a really nice guy, but I couldn't get far with him, he wanted to fill me full of pills straight away. At one point he mentioned depersonalisation—well, that made sense, naturally! But I refused the medication. He thought that was really stupid. For more than a year I had a weekly session with him where I had to talk, and after an hour: right, your time's up. And at a certain stage I had nothing left to tell, didn't find it very interesting any more. And I gradually became depressed. After one of those anxiety attacks everything seemed pointless, the whole world was completely meaningless. So I went from being anxious to being depressed. All that time I really couldn't work. And after one year I was declared unfit to work. It took three years anyway before I could cope a bit. Before that I would think, I'll do some decorating, and I'd be standing on the ladder, brush in hand, and I just couldn't do it. And I thought, this is it, then. I'll just have to live with it.

I went to one more lecture by Alexander Smit, a year or two later, and I went up to him afterwards and told him the whole story. I remember him saying, 'I'm a lot nicer than I used to be, really.' He asked whether I wanted to come and do a week's course with him, but I didn't take him up on it, and I didn't go any more after that. I had nothing against him, though plenty of other people did, but I know that one way or another he was concerned with the essentials. It was too late by then anyway, he should have supervised me at the time. In fact he just let me fend for myself, and I still don't understand that: why didn't he do anything? But that's apparently how it had to be. And the fact that I went back was a sort of experiment for me: can I cope with this? Because I'd become a bit afraid of him. But it went all right, and after that I wanted nothing more to do with advaita vedanta for the time being, it was dangerous ground for me.

So I let it alone. But one day I came across an article in *Onkruid* magazine by Jan van Delden, and he mentioned that horrific void.[5] And I recognised so much in it, I thought, hey, that's it. Because all that time I'd been doubting, was it really that void, or did I have a psychosis, or was it caused by the operation? Then I rang him up and he said, come and see me. But I didn't have the nerve. And I didn't dare tell my wife either, she would have thought, what on earth are you getting into this time? But one day I took the plunge. And then I went to do a week's course with him in France, seven years after the event. He collected me from the station and he started chatting straight away in the car, I was shitting myself! I was really nervous and I thought, God, what am I getting into? But after a day or two everything fell into place. He described it exactly. He made it very recognisable, what that void meant, and that you had to go through it. That figures in one of Castaneda's books as well, he has to jump into a ravine, only there's no ravine there at all. If you jump all the same, you find that you're already standing at the bottom. He also has to get through a crack, and he can't do it. And I couldn't do it either, then. I tried to do something on my own. Even though I knew it wasn't possible. I was always thinking about it. Until then I'd looked into the void as Frans, and then it was whoooah ... And somehow or other he managed to twist it around, so that I could look at Frans, as the void. And then I only needed to observe, I didn't need to make any judgments about what Frans was doing. Because I was a judgmental sort of person! After that second day I rang my wife and told her everything was okay; she'd been a bundle of nerves. Later I realised: wow, that anxiety won't be coming back. Since that time it's never come back. Something had evidently happened. I don't experience that void any more as anxiety, more as something logical, it can't be otherwise. And a lot of things have become clear to me. I used to think it was all about me. That there was something that Frans as a person ought to do, that he ought to live a life that left him open to enlightenment. And I was also very critical of myself, I had to become a better person. I don't mean that I can now accept myself as I am at every moment, but I don't need to keep tinkering with myself any more either. And that's really good! Jan uses the story of Odysseus. When he comes home after years of tribulations, a host of suitors have moved in with his wife. And he has to kill them before he can regain his own place. All of those suitors are part of you — the tight-fisted Frans, say, the good Frans, the sad Frans — and the object is to disarm yourself, to remove the sting. Then you can be what you are once more.

Jan's main exercise is what he calls 'ringology'. I don't have that, but apparently a lot of people have a sort of ringing in their ears. And he says, focus your attention on that, because it arises from silence, and it's best to experience everything from within that void. You mustn't repress your emotions, but if your attention wanders in that direction, you'll be swallowed up by them. And if you stay with the silence, the emotion's there all the same, whether it's sadness, pleasure or whatever, but you can just observe it and it fulfils a different function. And if you stay inside this silence, it's just a process going on inside of you, that's all. You're looking at a film. You can see it as a free mantra that you have with you, you can use it to look for the silence behind everything. If I remember rightly, Jan experienced that void himself, but he was a student of Wolter Keers, who took him by the scruff of the neck as it were and dragged him through it. He doesn't talk much about it otherwise. I've also done his follow-up courses meanwhile, and now and then I help out as a volunteer. My wife has also been there, and my oldest child, and I think that my youngest intends to try it sometime. They thought it was fantastic that it turned things around for me. I lived in doubt for so long, about whether it was caused by the operation or not. And I wouldn't rule out the possibility that that had something to do with it, that I would have been more stable otherwise. I kept a diary for a while, by the way, but I must admit that I couldn't put into words what actually happened. I'm telling it from memory now, but in fact you can't describe what happened. That critical point, you just dissolve. And I suspect that things would have gone better if I'd been supervised at the time.

The whole episode certainly brought about a shift in my life. First of all in my work life, but also with regard to my relationship, my children, you name it. I didn't think it could bother me any more, but these memories bring back emotions, very faintly. And yet I'm finished with it, one way or another. It might sound a bit irritating, going on like this all the time, but it's really all due to Jan, through his story, I can't help it! When so much became clear, I felt, it's finished. That's obviously how it was meant to be. It might sound a bit like Jesus-in-your-heart, but that's how it is. To gain a bit of wisdom, maybe! I can now take things as they are much better. Before, I wanted what I didn't have, and I didn't want what I did have. And that has changed now. I still get fed up now and then, but it's all much easier. I'm not waiting for death or anything. Let me put it this way: I'm not afraid of it, but I'll be sad to take leave of my children and my grandchildren and my wife, etc. I think that's more or less how it is at the moment. During that period I really came very close to death, and I know now that that's something I don't have to be afraid of, just like that void.

Sandra (1973)

I had a pretty traumatic childhood, incest and that sort of thing. I come from a very criminal area. My mother only bothered with that sort of people, hard-core criminals, sick people. She's anti-social, she can't empathise with other people. That's why one of my little sisters is no longer alive. She didn't live beyond six months, I was two then. I've still got the newspaper cuttings in a box somewhere. There were all kinds of investigations, it was apparently caused by malnutrition and neglect, but what was going on exactly ... the social workers had lost track of it all as well. My real father was a gypsy, he had nine more children by another woman, after me and my brother. I have seventeen brothers and sisters. The first two years we mainly moved around, living in vans and so on, but later on we lived in a house. My stepfather moved in with my mother when I was one year old. He abused me as well.

I had spiritual experiences even as a child, I found that quite normal, but other people thought it weird. I had no sense of time, for example, and I grasped things really quickly. I'd sit and look at my hand, for example, and think, oh yes, cells. Every cell is a world in itself, and my body is completely made up of cells. I was seven or so then, and I was completely absorbed by that, with nature and all that. My parents said I was mad. And at school I told stories that my classmates couldn't make head or tail of. So I withdrew more and more. I chose loneliness. That was probably my salvation. I saw that other people didn't seem to experience things like that, there was no validation, so I just kept my mouth shut.

From the age of thirteen I had contact with a social worker at school, I used to talk to her. She noticed that I behaved differently from the rest. I dreamt a lot as well, and she realised that I felt very isolated about that, and couldn't make any friends. They thought I was weird. I wasn't bullied or anything, something about me warned them off: leave me alone. And if anyone had a go at me anyway, all the teachers would be down on them like a ton of bricks. Very odd. Because I was a loner, but the teachers really liked me. Because I was quite grown up for my age; too grown up, actually, that's what I was always told. I knew too much, I saw too much, and of course I'd been through all sorts of things, that's another reason why I happen to see a lot. When I was fourteen the child protection people put me into care. I couldn't get on with my first foster mother, and nearly all foster families want small children, not adolescents. So I ended up in a home. When I was sixteen I got myself a rented room, the juvenile court gave me permission, because I was very independent. But I ended up in a village all on my own, and I became isolated. I got depressed. No one realised at the time, everyone thought it was just puberty. So I looked for a place in a halfway house and I really blossomed there, there were more people around. I was the only one allowed to have a cat, I really looked after it. Meanwhile all the social workers were always focused on traumas, while I was interested in completely different things. I used to have really philosophical discussions at school, not just with the other pupils but with the teachers as well, about Nietsche and Freud and that sort of thing. I'd read Alice Miller's *The Drama of the Gifted Child*. But you couldn't come out with that at an ordinary secondary school, because people my age didn't understand a damn thing about me. I met with so much opposition, no one could make me out at all. That's what brought on an identity crisis.

I went to live in a rented room while I was being supervised by a psychologist from the RIAGG. I found it really hard to talk at first, because I was always used to opposition. Then he got me to write letters to help me express my feelings more, and eventually I managed to do that during the sessions as well. I developed a lot of faith in him, too much in fact, because I had no faith in myself any more. And on one occasion I felt the ground give way beneath my feet, that was at school. I saw people change, I went out of my own body, that's called derealisation. So he thought, that girl's in a bad way, and he prescribed pills for me. The first thing I got was Haldol.[1] But if there's one thing you shouldn't give people it's Haldol. You become a robot, you walk around drooling, you're good for nothing. All you can do is think, because nothing else works any more. I still had those sessions but of course nothing much came out, I was completely trapped in my own feelings and experiences. You do become calmer physically, but your mind keeps going. I tried to understand it all. And I went on observing everything. Because I experienced different realities, not just the one we're in; there happen to be more than that. One way or another I pick up a lot of information from people. I grasp everything quickly, I can also take in someone's personality very quickly. The fact that other people can't do that, I can't help that, but you meet with opposition all the time, because people don't like to be seen through. And then I started to believe that I was mad myself. Kinks in my brain. I suffered from hallucinations, voices, and that really terrified me. In the end I had voices that I could see as well, they weren't very pleasant voices. Sometimes they threatened me, but they also told me things, about other people, that afterwards turned out to be true. But I was afraid of them, and through all the medication I couldn't express myself any more. I couldn't get out, I couldn't stay in, I was completely trapped. And then when I was nineteen I was admitted to the Vincent van Gogh clinic, in Venray, with a psychosis. And that's where my ten-year career in psychiatric care began. Till four years ago.

I told them right from the start: this medication is making me even more ill. Nobody took me up on it. They still can't really place my psychoses, but I had such a traumatic childhood, that was the cause of it all. They were completely fixated on my past, not on my spiritual experiences. Even though I told them, my past doesn't bother me. But in their eyes I was psychotic, and therefore a danger to myself. When my first boyfriend committed suicide they said, 'You might go and do the same thing, you won't be able to cope.' Instead of just letting me come to terms with it, like a normal person. I used to talk to him as well, because I experienced those other realities. So that was put down to a dissociative disorder, a derealisation disorder. It's very hard to get out of a situation like that. I've been in all sorts of places, in a different group every time, and I was given one diagnosis after another. Because they didn't have the slightest idea. I got a different psychiatrist every time, and he always thought: I know what it is. I had eleven of them altogether. So I was diagnosed with everything from schizophrenia to borderline to manic-depression, dissociation and even MPD.[2] My traumas have apparently made me more sensitive, which just makes me understand and see and feel things more. I was also very good at getting under the psychiatrist's skin, and going for his sensitive points; that often earned me the isolation cell.

But I became hypermanic; as I saw it I had divine experiences. And when I felt really good, I legged it. I've had the police after me. They didn't find me straight away, but it never took them longer than a couple of days. So I had some freedom for a while. I think I ran away from the closed ward seven or eight times. That gave me strength, because I knew I was right. In the beginning especially I had lucid periods and I'd just stop taking the medication. When they found out they started enforcing it. Like, having to swallow it with somebody standing over you, or getting a jab in your backside, for two or three or four weeks. At one point I was taking anti-psychotic drugs, anti-depressives, sedatives, and Akineton to counteract the side-effects, all at the same time.[3] You're not up to activities in that state, so I went off on my own a lot. I lay on my bed or sat in front of the TV. I didn't do any painting in those ten years, for example, I couldn't do it. Or anything like gym, psychomotoric therapy, they call that. Try that with a stiff body, walking along a beam when you haven't got any sense of balance left at all. But I wanted to keep a line open to the outside world, so at one point I started to do voluntary work. That was very unusual in psychiatric hospitals. I succeeded in persuading the judge how essential it was for me, so I was brought from the secure unit to my work. I was the activities leader at a day centre, from the age of twenty-two or so. I used to save up Akinetons and take them before I went to work, so that I'd have as little trouble as possible from side-effects. Afterwards I would have huge problems with it, cramp and so on, muscle spasms, drooling, grinding my teeth, walking stiffly, just like a robot. And very tired. I tried it three times a week; sometimes it just didn't work at all, but I tried. That was in various institutions, for a longer period. I looked for places myself every time; I was just being honest then, this is the only thing that works. And people could see that as well: she's under medication but she doesn't seem mad to me. They saw that I just got on with my work with complete dedication, and that I was doing my very best.

I kept on having more and more spiritual experiences, only they became purer. I don't really know how else to put it. Real love! I didn't dare to believe that they were right, but I started having more and more of them. That's why my diagnosis was cranked up to manic-depressive. Yet I didn't go round saying I was God, or religious, or whatever. Because I wasn't. Only, I became strong. I believed in life completely. At those moments I was with God, that's how I felt. Simply one with other people; they can see it in you as well, they react quite differently. I had those experiences even as a child, only that was sporadic. It feels as though you've got absolutely no personality, you could call my name as often as you like,

I wouldn't react. It's a very pleasant experience, and I began to have more and more of them. It would arrive all of a sudden. Sometimes I would consciously evoke it, I could get into one of those states with a certain sort of music. Only there was no balance to it, I couldn't handle it, so I'd go too far. That could last for months sometimes. But I continued to resist, and that made me more and more isolated.

Until years later when I was living in sheltered accommodation and met an SPV nurse who was highly sensitive himself, and who had more idea about what was going on.[4] He started to steer me in the right direction a step at a time, and it resulted in a really good friendship. He worked with a psychiatrist who said something along the lines of, well, it seems more like manic-depression, so, not the dissociative disorder I'd had previously. And he let me try reducing the number of medicines, because I was having them administered by force. So I kept trying to whittle it down a bit more, I'd just ask, 'Can I take a bit less?' And that worked, they could see that as well. I could think things through a lot better, which meant I didn't go beyond my own boundaries and drown in my own experiences. When I could think clearly I realised: I just have to keep my mouth shut if I want to get out of here, don't kick against the traces so much. And I began to realise that the responsibility lies in myself: if I want to take charge of my own life, I have to take everything into my own hands. Because it's a home in a way, it's safe, you're looked after. But then I thought: have you got the nerve to leave altogether? Because it was literally a whole new world, I was tremendously institutionalised, I hadn't even had a break. But I thought, now it's finished, now is the right time. Ten years is long enough. I really thought that: ten years, that's a good time to go, out! Move! I didn't even care where I ended up. I had faith in my SPV nurse, and especially in my experiences. He didn't label them as disturbed. It was just part of me. He used to talk about the divine and all that sort of thing now and then, but I found everything to do with spirituality scary, so he stopped mentioning things like that to me.

I slowly cut out all my medication, until I eventually got permission to stop the lithium; it had damaged my kidneys. They let me go because they had faith in me. At a certain point you get your discharge papers, you have to draw up an emergency plan, all that sort of thing. You gradually warm up to it. I also began to paint; I did a painting for my previous psychiatrist at that time. And when I left he said, 'You've taught me something. You don't realise it, but you've taught me to trust the patient to make her own choices.' I found that so fantastic! He does that with other patients now. And he has an important position there in the mental health service.

First of all I went to a crisis centre. Usually of course they're there to keep people off the streets. I had a lot of trouble getting accepted, because they don't take mental patients as a rule. Well, most of the people there were more disturbed than I was and they just took advantage of the social workers, while I kept them at a distance. I did everything off my own bat, I just went along to a housing association. I told them, 'I'm applying for an urgency certificate. I know that it's very difficult but I'm asking anyway, so that I can start a new life at last.' And it worked. I was the only one who managed to get somewhere to live within such a short time. By being honest. It was a very run-down house, but I fell completely in love with it. In a very nice quiet neighbourhood. It took me a year to finish it. I cut off all contact with my parents in that time, I had myself sterilised, and I started a training course in Education Social Work. They shouldn't really have accepted me there, again because of my mental health history. But I had all the knowledge and the skills, through that voluntary work, that was my salvation! Because I just kept going. I also met with opposition from the social services; they refused to give me settling-in expenses, because the tester had once had a row with a mental patient. But other people didn't agree, so then I got my settling-in expenses; I was supposed to pay it back after three years, and I thought that was fair enough. When the time came I still wasn't earning, because I was doing an unpaid placement. I told them everything I'd achieved and they sent me a letter. The tester had left, and they thought I'd fought so hard for everything that I didn't have to pay the money back at all. You feel really blessed when that happens. Every time you conquer another barrier. It's the same with this work. Because of course I'd had a gap of ten years, but I just applied and said, 'Yes, I've been in a mental home, but it was far from clear what was wrong with me.' Just see it as a strength, I told them. They took me and they still don't want to lose me. So all that opposition had made me stronger in myself. I believe in myself a lot more now as well, I just know I was in the right. As regards the spiritual experiences as well. At the training course they had trouble getting used to me. When I wanted to be in a divine state, I gave a really weird impression. We had a philosopher there with a theological background, I used to e-mail with him a lot. Because he noticed that I had mystical experiences, that's what he called them. And he tried to explain to the other students what mysticism was. Those were really good discussions, that was really fantastic. I'm still in touch with him, by the way. Six months ago I got my diploma and I went back to my psychiatrist and told him everything I'd achieved. That I wanted to learn to ride a motor bike, that I worked as an editor. You should have seen his face! That was really fantastic! And he said, you're going to do something with writing, you're going to achieve even more. Wonderful to hear. He had faith in me.

I didn't always get on well, but I was better off than in the mental home. Then two years ago I came across a website about hypersensitivity, and I started writing for their forum. About my experiences, and also about loneliness, and the physical ailments I had. My thyroid stopped working all of a sudden, though that wasn't caused by lithium. The doctors suspected Hashimoto's disease, but then it started working again, so I had to have a new series of tests.[5] And I had rheumatic symptoms that they couldn't explain; they disappeared in one go as well. Then somebody wrote in: it looks to me as if you're in some kind of Kundalini process. Now I don't know the first thing about spirituality, so terms like that are lost on me. But then I read a pamphlet about it and I recognised a lot of the physical symptoms, and a lot of mental experiences as well. Via the editorial office where I was working I came across an article by Peter Kampschuur. He's a psychologist, so I thought he must be okay, because I found spirituality scary. I told him my story, and I sent him a couple of drawings, and he said I should come and see him. Well, he lived quite a distance away in those days, and I was still on a low budget, but I decided to go there once a month, for a private session. I'm still doing that. He taught me meditative exercises and breathing exercises, to stay more in balance during my hypo episodes.[6] He had experience with people with Kundalini energy, and he'd also had such experiences himself. He's also been in a mental home, but that was different for him because he's a psychologist. I started doing the exercises, and that's how he found out that I actually perceive much more than you're supposed to. Also as regards energies, that sort of thing. He really knows a lot about it, and he started counselling me. We e-mail a lot, and he just wants to know what I experience, what I see, perceive. And I draw as well, because you can capture these experiences best in images. They are the same experiences as at the beginning, but now I can deal with them without losing sight of reality. And I don't call them manic or hypomanic any more, I just call them divine. To most people they're meditative states. They come very easy to me, because it turns out that there really is something different about my brain, only it's not a mental problem.

I found out about that through someone who works as a neurofeedback therapist.[7] He asked, 'Can I give you a neuroscan? Because you have certain experiences and I'd just like to know what's going on in your brain.' So I said, 'Okay, go ahead and scan me.' They never did that sort of thing in the mental hospital, they all go by the DSM. The scan results showed that I make delta waves, which normally only happens during deep sleep.[8] In my case there's a peak there, while other frequencies of my brain are at a lower level, because those peaks use up an awful lot of energy. That figures as well, I have to rest an awful lot. And it seems that I can sense fine vibrations. But because I produce a peak, they see that as a pathological deviation. According to this therapist, these experiences could be explained by the delta waves. I had those in the mental home as well, in spite of the medication. I kept on perceiving. In my case at any rate the anti-psychotic drugs had no effect on that score. Scientists still don't know why we make delta waves. Well, he invented the most incredible explanations for that, but I completely lost the plot. After that I gave him more and more of a wide berth, he was too fixated on my delta waves, he's desperately searching for enlightenment himself. And he was attached to the Monroe Institute, they do out-of-body experiences there, and I have an tremendous aversion to that, simply because it isn't good for me. But people really want to escape from their minds. He asked me recently if I wanted to illustrate all sorts of books. But I said no, because they're about those out-of-body experiences. I found it hard to refuse, because it's flattering to your ego to be asked something like that!

I did my first paintings when I was still taken up with my house, and with surviving; with decorating and studying and working, and trying to keep my balance, lots of rest, and walking. Because I wasn't on medication any more and I still flew off the handle now and then. I still had those hypomanic experiences as well, only I tried to regulate them myself. That's why I started painting, as a means of regulating them. To express myself, and get my feet firmly on the ground. I've never had painting lessons and I could only save for professional materials later on. I paint an image that I see and finish it in two hours. That's how I write my e-mails and texts as well, without thinking about it. I have no idea where I get it from. I'm as dyslexic as they come, but my dream is to be a writer. I felt really lucky when the editorial office let me go to a conference in Tallinn, with psychiatrists and social workers from twenty different countries. I was discovered by chance at a conference in Utrecht. I worked in the editorial office for a year, but then I left because I thought they were encouraging people to take advantage of their illness. In an issue on re-assessment, I thought there was too much about how to stay on disability allowance. But if you ask me, people need a good kick up the ass, because everybody needs structure, mental patients most of all. It doesn't have to be a permanent job, as long as they do something. And that doesn't happen; not even voluntary work. In my opinion, people settle into the invalid's role too easily. That's obviously their way, not mine, but that's why I got out at a certain point. No hard feelings. I still have contact with various people in the social services.

Later on I moved to the province of Brabant, I let go of everything all over again. I left my house, that was really difficult. I've never put down roots, I'm not dependent on people, family, friends or whatever, so I can go anywhere, I could even go abroad. I got work, I did two days as a trial period and it appealed to me even then. During those two days I was

offered four other positions, to come for an interview. I was quite embarrassed, because other colleagues have been applying for jobs for ages. I
now work in an institution for mentally handicapped people. It's changing now, because they want to bring in ex-patients from criminal mental
hospitals. I work in the old convent, there's a really lovely convent garden
there, that's why I wanted to work there. They really appreciate me,
because they see I have a different way of treating the residents. That's
why they sometimes call me slightly eccentric, they called me that at my
last place of work as well. Before that I'd only worked with autistic teen-
agers. Autists also perceive more, all kinds of other things, and I can easily
respond to that. They're aware of that here as well, that I can read information from things, and that they could too, if they were open to it. There
are some residents with very difficult behaviour, who everybody has
problems with, except me. Aggression. Not only verbal, but physical as
well. But I've never had residents being aggressive to me. They become
really calm with me.

I've got a string of Christian names, but I wasn't brought up religiously
at all. We'd go to church at Christmas sometimes. And there were nuns at
primary school, we still had them in my day. We read the children's Bible
every morning, and I always liked singing. And I always had a lot of questions about the Bible, what about this then, and what about that? They
always sent me to stand outside in the corridor when I did that, so I developed an aversion to the word 'God'. Until last year I always felt this aversion. Always. But I didn't understand until now what it all means. Only
recently I bought some books on the Gospel of Thomas and that sort of
thing, I find that really interesting now. It's really not about the words in
the Bible at all, it's about the spiritual experience as such. And Jesus was
just an enlightened man! He was just an HSP type who was enlightened.[9]
That's all! And everyone gets so reverent about it, but they've got the
same thing themselves! Only they don't realise it.

When I sit at the computer, I only have to focus my mind and I know
how so-and-so is, or what that person's doing, that sort of thing. I often
used to send personal e-mails, about how that particular person was feeling at the time. Not always particularly nice e-mails, I can be very outspo-
ken. Someone told me not long ago that I'm often spot-on. People get a
shock, and that's why I get pretty violent reactions. But I shouldn't give
attention to that sort of thing at all, I should keep to my own concerns. I
got to know my boyfriend through the forum for high sensitivity. The first
time we had contact, through the internet forum, we had an argument.
But a year later we had contact again, and that blossomed into love. He
started talking about advaita, I recognised a lot of things in that, but I'm
not much of a reader. He kept urging me: you should really do something

with your story. You could learn something, but you've also got something to offer. I want to concentrate more on painting and writing. I don't want to work full time either. I work twenty-four hours a week at the moment, and I'm going to start doing twenty-eight hours. I can easily live from that.

I call that whole mental hospital period a hibernation period. But during a hibernation period you come to terms with things as well. I know now how egos work, I know now how systems work, I know now where my strength lies, and that I'm not mad! That I really am all right. All I've done in fact is to experience, experience, experience, and in theory that can be a good thing, not to possess any knowledge. When that happens, I thought, I'll really be disturbed. And I gave too much responsibility to other people, I didn't take it on myself. I believed other people too easily. That was my naïve trustfulness. I still have that, but I have more faith in my own intuition. So I drop people more quickly if they're not good for me. I tried for a long time to reflect on what it all meant, and I was the wiser for it. You learn a lot from it, I'm becoming more and more aware of that.

My last psychiatrist wrote in his diagnosis, and I quote: if I had to put her in a pigeon-hole, it would be manic-depressive. I've never had either phase, really, but they have to put my experiences in some sort of framework. So it's bipolar-II, I've never gone further than hypomania; I don't recognise mania.[10] There are people who glorify psychoses and mania, and I'm dead against that. They're using spirituality as a diversionary tactic for their disease. I've had arguments on the forum about that. Some of the things I see, I think, Jesus! They're completely obsessed by India and that sort of thing. They're not necessarily a different sort of experience, some of them actually make sense. Only some people glorify the psychosis, and that's not right. They also try to force them. But a psychosis is not a spiritual experience. In a psychosis you're too far gone already. Then you've got nothing left to hold onto in this reality. You can't reason properly any more, and you're enormously taken up with your own egoism. You're only concerned with yourself then, with your own little world. Generally speaking you have no compassion, they're actually ego-experiences. I think it's good that people don't just look at what's been conditioned into them, but it needs to be more integrated into psychiatry. It's beginning very slowly, and there are now institutions where psychiatrists give their clients meditation exercises. I find that amazing enough in itself. In my case, I wasn't concerned with spirituality at all during those ten years, but other people were always told they shouldn't do anything with it, because it would only make things worse. The younger generation is becoming more and more open, they go their own way more and more. And my last counsellor was younger than I was.

Karin (1955)

I come from a Catholic background. My father was dead against the Church, while my mother went along with it all, but not from any real inner conviction. Our primary school was run by nuns. I really liked it there, I often stayed behind to help them. There was a little church round the corner from us, we children could go in and out as we liked, and they let us play the organ, I loved doing that. And I was really gripped by the character of Jesus. When I made my first communion I fainted, it was so overwhelming. To think of receiving the body of Christ inside me, I couldn't grasp it. Deep down, my father was a very religious man, I believe. But people's attitude to their faith, he was so disillusioned about that, he was always fulminating about it. We often talked about that, never about our own experience.

I was the odd one out in our family. I've got two younger sisters who have a completely different way of seeing and experiencing life. Much more placid, you might say. They were easily satisfied with everything, while I always wanted to know how things work, how life works, why people act and think and feel as they do, etcetera. Of course, I was pulled up short because nobody knew the answers! So you learn to keep your mouth shut. My parents wanted me to go to the secondary modern so that I could become a primary school teacher, but the nuns at school said, this girl should go to the grammar school, she's very intelligent. So I went to the grammar school in another town, and I made friends there whose parents were much more intelligent than mine. I often went to their houses, and I found them a breath of fresh air. They had ideas of their own, my parents didn't. My father was self-educated, he did white-collar work, but his father had been a day-labourer. And my mother's parents were farmers. Wealthy farmers, it's true, and more devout and open to spiritual ideas, but in a weird sort of way, because of their religion. I used to stay with them in the school holidays. I could play to my heart's content and I had lots of cousins, so I was very happy there. I had an unmarried aunt living there as well, among all those country estates, she took a bit of an interest in me and she had very clear ideas of her own, I really liked that. So I was really very self-willed, an odd sort of child that went her own way. At home I was the only one who wanted to know the ins and outs of everything, but I wasn't happy there, so I only went home to eat and sleep and watch television, and went elsewhere for everything else!

I enjoyed going to church until I went to secondary school, then I finished with all that. I was pretty wild as a teenager. Even at fifteen I often didn't go home at night. I had boyfriends and I'd be smoking hash, drinking a lot, and after my final exams I couldn't get away from home quick enough. So I went to Amsterdam and really cut loose! I was a law unto myself. My studies were pointless, I thought, because I was a quick learner and always managed to scrape by. The rest of the time I messed around, pub crawling. My boyfriend at that time was keen on bird-watching, so we often went into the countryside, it was a real vagabond existence. And we had a old banger so we'd jump in it and drive to the Pyrenees, and his father had a house in France, so we'd go and work on the house in France. I had a student grant, you see. But I was as miserable as sin. I thought, if this is what life is all about ... I really couldn't settle down, I'd totally lost myself as well. I was studying teaching methods, because I really wanted to understand it from the intellectual point of view, but all you got was this scientific stuff. What with the critical schools from Germany and all those discussions and statistics, I was so disillusioned! I thought, if this is life then I don't want to go on. And I didn't complete my course.

After that I married someone in our circle of friends. But that wasn't a good marriage, because there was no love. We took care of each other and were good companions, but there was no real love bond. I'd stopped feeling that sort of love during my adolescence. That whole effervescent thing I'd had as a child had also gone. In my student days I'd started hyperventilating, and then I got toxoplasmosis, and I just couldn't get over it. In short, I became so unhappy that I started to look at myself for the first time. But I didn't want to go to a psychiatrist, I started co-counseling, and that really opened my eyes about myself. I discovered that I wasn't mad, whereas before I'd always had my doubts about that. And I learned that whatever happened in my life happened for a reason. I believed that in a way already, but this confirmed it. I also ended my marriage at that point. When I started co-counselling I thought: I'll find answers here. And in no time I was the leader's assistant, because I had such a knack for it, so I thought, I'd like to do this professionally. So I ended up at the ITIP, and I found even more searching answers there.[1] First of all I worked for a year at a criminal psychiatric clinic, and from there I went on to start my own practice. Only it didn't go very well, I was tired all the time. During that time I met my second husband, and three months later I turned out to have a serious form of cancer.

There was a strong likelihood that it would spread, my prospects of survival were pretty low, 35% after five years. As a result of all that, my boundaries and frames of reference and my hold on life disappeared. I discovered that I'd been living inside some sort of intellectual concept and now it was all falling apart. I thought, I have no idea whether I'll even be here next year or not. The only time I have is this moment, now. That was the beginning. So the diagnosis gave me a tremendous shove. I knew it already somehow, but that came more from external ideas, or from a vague, deep feeling that it was true. But in one fell swoop it became a very major personal experience. Suddenly something had been ripped open.

A year later my husband was diagnosed with a fatal heart disease. That really made us live for the moment, of course, it never occurred to us to make plans for the future, about anything. This was now, and whatever happened tomorrow, that was tomorrow! So our life together was completely coloured by illness and death. He was a very philosophical man, and this situation helped us to find more depth in our lives. When we met, all kinds of things had happened that tore away the façade, so we lived continually in a heightened state of awareness. Being aware that we should take each day as it comes, that the point is the quality of your day, and the extent to which you're honest with yourself, with each other, and with those around you. And we lived at the peak of our existence, it was really on the edge. We also had lots of rows, because everything came to the surface and we wouldn't stand any nonsense from each other. And we had to work through the fear we felt. Those seven years were very hectic and also very fulfilling, we became very close. And just when we thought we'd worked it all out, he died.

We did have a frame of reference. I'd done my training at the ITIP, that's very much to do with clarity and thinking clearly. My husband was good at that, but he soon moved over to the Sufi side, that's much more to do with the heart. He was much more a man of the heart, and he had something wrong with his heart. That caused the usual conflict between us, because although I think Sufism is a wonderful thing, I did have some comments to make about that group, so that's what the conflict was about. As he became increasingly ill, he was more often in hospital, in intensive care, than out of it, and we thought he was going to die on several occasions. Because of all the turbulence between us he decided to go and live in the Sufi centre. They were very keen to have him as a member of staff as well, because he made a very valuable contribution. He lived there for a year, I'd go at weekends, then we'd fight and I'd go home completely shattered. After a year I wasn't allowed to visit any more, because we had so many rows, and then the scales fell from his eyes and he left. But in hindsight it was a very good year for him, and he also made a really important change, a heartfelt change. He'd been on the list for a heart transplant, and through what happened to him in that year he decided to take his name off the list. He said, people talk so airily about heart transplants, as if it's only a pump. He didn't want to lose his own heart. That was a big decision. I thought it was so good of him. Then we went on a retreat, and the day after we had worked with the heart chakra, he was gone. He had a heart attack. That was unexpected, because he was reasonably well, so we thought. When I looked at photos later I could see that things hadn't been going as well as I'd projected. He died in my arms.

And with that death of his, something happened to me. Everything opened up more, and the whole dimension of form disappeared for me. I could also feel the connection with him for a very long time, and I didn't want to lose him either, I went part of the way with him. But when I did that, everything that had any form for me melted away! And that left me with an enormous sense of loneliness. Because I saw and felt and experienced in so many ways that everything is connected to everything else. That was really wonderful. Besides all the sorrow I felt, which was growing all the time. And the more I let that sorrow in, the more I remained in that oneness. That was fantastic, and at the same time it was all so raw and so painful. It was the most intense living that you can experience. I thought, if I die now: I have lived. I have seen everything that can be experienced and seen and felt and known and learned in life. So that was fantastic.

For six months I was permanently ecstatic. At the same time I couldn't even cook during those first months, because I was everywhere and nowhere. I got up every morning with no plans, it was always very open. And every day was a new gift, I felt the value of the smallest things, and I was very open and very receptive. I couldn't do much, I couldn't do my own administration for example, but that no longer interested me anyway. I thought, I could just as well go and be a tramp because I'm happy anyway! I didn't give a damn any more, about anything. It was all one. True enough, I was really well embedded, I had a lot of people around me. So I went out to eat everywhere, and a lot of people came and looked after me. I also had a boyfriend in that period, somebody I'd known earlier, he virtually became my carer. He cooked for me and took me out, he saw to the social observances, he was that sort of person. And I let it all happen. I did everything according to what I saw and felt. I rediscovered things like shopping at a certain point. But I was with people all the time. Just being with people was enough for me. Or I went for a nice walk, or I rang someone up. And people were concerned about me, so I could tell my story everywhere and people found that really interesting. That's how I got along in life!

After six months I had to go back to work, because I'd run out of money. I'd done coaching and training with my husband, but I couldn't do that any more. So I went to work in welfare organisations as deputy-manager, I was mainly concerned with personnel, all sorts of training and so on. There was also someone whose child was dying, and at a human level I was a real tower of strength at that moment, because I felt everything! So in that respect I was very valuable. But organising and being a manager, I really wasn't up to that. Because my logical thinking processes had stopped. At one point I had to do something logistical, and it was as if the fuses had been taken out. In the past I could think very clearly, that's beginning to come back now, it's a different form of clarity, you might say. But then it had completely vanished. Yet I wasn't going around with my head in the clouds. I was tremendously connected to the earth, and I felt so much strength in my belly, I could really move mountains! And I've never felt the strength of my legs so much as in that period. I used to go into the countryside a lot with this boyfriend, he was a biologist and a birdwatcher, which was fantastic because I felt such a bond with nature. Whereas normally I wasn't that keen on it. But this boyfriend thought I was a bit mad. So we clashed. We clashed more and more. Our relationship was more a case of complementing each other's shortcomings anyway, rather than a love match. That wouldn't have been possible anyway, I'd decided never to do that again. After that loss I thought, I will never go through this in my life again. After a while I went to live on my own again. Then I managed to get back into shape after that year, and things calmed down a bit. That was also a relief, because it was so limitless. I was swamped by love, continually, and my system just couldn't cope with it. Not physically, nor mentally either. I kept thinking: how on earth are you supposed to do this? But I didn't know the answer. At the time I never thought that I wasn't quite right in the head. Never! That only came later. It was a tremendous feeling of love, I could feel so much love, for absolutely everything, for ugly things as well. Everything had a right to exist, but somehow it began to cause friction. I felt trapped inside, because I couldn't cope with it.

A year after the death of my husband I started to feel pain in my body. I thought, I have to do something about this, because it's a real breeding ground for tumours. The family doctor referred me to a haptonomist, and that helped me to get back to the here and now. It was also time to come to terms with everything, to admit the pain, and to get to the rawness. That brought me real peace inside. Then I ended the relationship altogether, and for the first time I had to actually stand on my own two feet again. And that's where I lost my way. Because during that year I'd known what it was to feel a bond with my own basis, but now I began to doubt again.

About my own basis. About my own truth. And though deep inside I knew that it was true, I lacked the strength. And I lost my way in that.

I met another man that my heart opened up to completely, as it had to my husband. But this one couldn't be trusted. I put my trust in him all the same though, as was my custom, because I didn't trust my own basis, but he was a liar. And he was really scared of this tremendous love, he did everything in his power not to be a part of it. And that really confused me! When I spoke to him I used to get a really strange sensation in the head. Sometimes I would become completely dissociated. I'd just feel it coming on. Even if I just thought about him sometimes it was as if I was falling into a huge pit. I didn't see anything in particular when this happened, it was all to do with energy. I lost my way mentally, I didn't know any more who I was. And people would see me and to them I'd just be Karin, but deep inside I wasn't. Maybe it was a psychosis, I don't know. A sort of repressed psychosis or something. One time I had it, it was my birthday and I had a house full of guests, but I simply wasn't there! And when everyone had gone home it was as if I'd suddenly flopped back into my body. Then I realised, I didn't say goodbye to so-and-so, or such-and-such, how did that happen? I'd just been absent. I talked to my boyfriend about it, but he didn't understand. I rang my women friends as well, and they said, 'Oh, we just thought you were a bit drunk.'

In a way I was very needy, because I couldn't manage to find my feet, or my own basis. Once I was talking to my boyfriend on the phone, I put the phone down and then suddenly it was two hours later. I'd just been absent, lost. Other times as well, I'd been thinking about certain things then, but it was like a dream, so vague. I'd been in some sort of abyss, then suddenly I was back, and I had a really displaced feeling. As if my whole sense of self had been disconnected. My mind was gone and I had absolutely no control over it. That dissociation made life hell. I also had moments when it seemed as if I was possessed by something else, and I had really evil thoughts. I'd worked in criminal mental health care, and that made me think, oh, this is what it's like when someone is of unsound mind. This is it. Something inhabits you, it's as if evil demons suddenly take possession of you. I felt that on two occasions. I had Hell inside of me then. Of course that felt different from the feeling of being absent, but the unpleasant impact was exactly the same. That period lasted nine months, after that the sensation of losing myself happened about seven more times, and it often hovered in the background. I couldn't do anything about it, I couldn't stop it, I could only wait until it was over. And I realised that. I talked to a few people about it, they understood me and that helped me to go on seeing it as a phase in my life. I didn't really panic, either, I never thought, oh God, now I'm going mad or something. Didn't try to get help either, I thought, not if I can help it. I'm not going to a psychiatrist, oh no! He'd just give me pills. As if a psychiatrist would understand! I had worked in child psychiatry myself, and I'd had clients in my practice who were seeing psychiatrists and who also came to me because they felt the humane aspect with me, and not with them. I also have a lot of people around me who coach and do counselling, so I managed pretty well with their help.

Besides which, I couldn't share that intense experience with anyone! That feeling of oneness. I did tell people about that, and people who don't know about it find it interesting, but this is something else altogether. One day I came across advaita. And I thought, oh, but these people know about it! They know all about it! I was constantly trying to fathom out what on earth was happening to me, losing myself like that. A friend of mine had had a cerebral haemorrhage, she'd written a book, and she knew about it, so I felt that affinity with her as well. She sent me the magazine *InZicht*, and she put me in contact with Susan Frank.[2] So I went to see her, and I realised straight away, she understands. And with that everything fell into place. Not that it was over, but I was able to round it off then. What I was mainly looking for was someone who knew the profundity of that sense of oneness, when all your frames of reference have faded away. After that I didn't want to go to the ITIP any more, because that's a frame of reference and I didn't want to be enclosed within any frame of reference again. With Susan there were no frames of reference, but there is a deep line all the same which is really intensely present. And I was always searching for a way to achieve that, of living without frames of reference while completely existing as a channel. I found that in my contact with her. She said various things, that you need strong legs, and that you have to build that up a step at a time. That's what I was doing already, and I felt so affirmed by it that it strengthened my sense of self as well. And that stopped that feeling of being mentally lost.

Apart from that I did nothing with advaita, I just went there and let it take its course. It was really good because you can go there, you don't have to do anything, and you just go home again. It gave me a lot of relaxation, and my sense of self was able to take root and grow there. I went there for the first time eighteen months ago, and I still go now and then. At first I thought I ought to become a pupil of hers, but I dropped the idea after a while. I started doing it all on my own. At the same time I was very depressed for a couple of months. I just lay around on the sofa and really didn't want to go on living. I got through that as well, simply by staying with it. Now I think that during the depression all my impulses had faded away. And I really had to go through it to get back my vitality, as I did with that mentally fading away. Otherwise there's still a layer left hanging over it. It's about the pain of life, about accepting that life can be very hard and painful, and about all your strategies in order not to feel that. If you want to achieve the full force of your life — and not everyone wants to — then you have to live through it. And the openness to let it all happen, to go on observing, and not to worry about it, that's very much a part of me. Everything that happened, also the fact that I'd been diagnosed with cancer, helped me to stay with it. And I know that's good. I started working with people in terminal care afterwards, and I was able to use it to help a friend who was on the verge of a psychosis. I could help her to take the panic out of it. Because the thoughts that cause the panic, they're only thoughts. You can also experience it in another way.

When I was working on my own grief, I thought, now I know why I'm alive. Because this is what I can pass on to other people. Last year I regained my strength and then I developed a discussion group for a funeral services company: 'Living in the light of death'. For people who have been touched by death at some time. After that I got involved with a new method of bringing up autistic children, *Son-rise*. The basic principle is unconditional love. I was so taken with it because it's about rejecting your frames of reference and making contact with the child from within your essential being. Meanwhile I also had contact with an autistic boy, we got on like a house on fire because we'd found each other mentally straight away! And then you can just start playing. Some people are very much on the didactic development side, but for me it's all about trust. With both the child and the mother. So I have a lot of scope, I let things happen as they will. Then I get an impulse and follow it, and different things happen with each child. But what happens is always contact. And it always leads to something lively, to a game. They're children, and I like that! I'm counselling three children at the moment, that's quite enough, and it also helps me find my structure again. Besides this I'm working with an organisation that counsels cancer patients, and I'm in contact with a hospice. I also get telephone calls, and I help people here at home to cope with bereavement and loss. Because that is definitely something that I can contribute from the inside out. To help people to let go of their frames of reference, because I know that so well myself. That's the real reward.

As I speak completely from my own experience, it really gets across. In theory it's a very difficult journey, because I have nothing to hold onto. If I don't work, I have no income. But if you dare to simply relax and trust, there's nothing to worry about. Then things go smoothly. Now and then I don't believe it myself, then even I get anxious! But it all works out in the end, I see it happen every time. Sometimes I also do coaching for companies, then I'm paid a very high hourly rate. I always have enough. I drive a very old car, and I wouldn't mind buying a new one but I haven't enough money for that. Still I always manage.

My health has been good up to now. That can always change. I had a tumour in my large intestine, they removed a bit of it, and they found cancer cells in my lymph tissue, so it could start spreading. Later on I had restless cells in my cervix, and a spot on my back, so there's always something the matter. After the operation on my cervix I woke up and knew that the cancer had left my body. My doctor also works with bioresonance, and he keeps a close eye on my immune system.[3] It's fine at the moment, only last time he said that I have to make sure that I get enough rest. So now I have a little nap on the sofa every afternoon!

I've really been through the absolute depths. A friend of mine is an astrologist, and she could see that in my stars; I'm now coming to the tail end of that. Personally I think that something in me will soon be complete. And maybe I'll die then. But maybe I'll stop working and start travelling, I've no idea! But at any rate this whole story will be finished then. Life for me is a training school, an inner development. So that when I die I'll have done something in my life to create more light. It's really all about light, now, in this life. Everything I've experienced has opened me up more, to let the light in. That's really how I experience it. And whenever I still act out of self-interest because I want to steer things in a different direction, I block the light. All the horrors on my path help me to let go. This summer I turned fifty, and I did something with a poem by Rumi, the Sufi mystic.[4] It's about peas jumping out of the pan because they don't want to be cooked. And the cook throws them straight back in, because then they become nice and tasty! We keep jumping out of the pan, that's our nature as human beings. And then along comes something in your life that throws you back in, so that you can be cooked through and through! All you think about is getting out, but that's quite impossible, so you just have to stay put.

During the last years of his life my husband opened up more and more, and he really brought light in that way. In his dying I also saw how quickly he went to the light. The first two years after his death he was still very much present, I also got signals from him. In my mind's eye he sat on the edge of my bed every night, and he also talked to me. Over the years that became fainter and fainter, and now it's gone. Very occasionally I sense him again. At those times I feel very connected to him in my heart. Then I come home and I have the feeling that I had when he was still alive and living here. I have no control over that myself. When he was gone, I had to start doing things under my own steam, so that was a good thing.

The last few months I've become suddenly aware again that I have a Christian background. That those are my roots. The suffering of humanity, and wanting to bring light to it, that touches me these days. When those frames of reference faded away, that faded as well. It's present in advaita, but it's not linked to anything. I feel more connected now to how I experienced that as a child, and I see the figure of Jesus every time, with those hands. Those burning hands. Those giving hands. And that heart—I feel that now in my heart. My heart had to break and break every time, I had to dare to let my heart be broken, so that it could become ever more open. That got through to my life force, and I felt that in all its glory after the death of my husband. But actually I found life worthless when I was younger, I wasn't bothered about going on. In that family where everyone was so different from me, I was always doubting, am I mad or are they? I see that as well in autistic children, they don't want to go on. They also say, 'Oh, if this is all there is, no way.' It's still a compromise for me sometimes. But I can accept much more how things are, including the pain and the stings. Luckily I know several people who have gone through something similar, people who came across my path in the process, and I know that they live at the same intensity. I have those people, thank God. Otherwise maybe I'd be in an institution! Recently I was thinking, what a full life I have, what a lot I've experienced. And I can really say from the bottom of my heart: it might not always seem so, but life is good. Believe me.

Window on the God-experience
Beyond the Precincts of the Church

Besides the scientific viewpoint—and partly also opposed to it—there is a religious window to investigate, concerning the sort of accounts given elsewhere in this book. This window too forms a framework with its own structure and history, and this chapter will therefore explore the way in which the religious outlook examines and structures such experiences. Again, this will require a selective and wide-meshed approach, as the concept of 'religion' covers a whole battery of variants. Furthermore, the dividing line between science and religion, which is constantly emphasised in this book for the sake of clarity, will be just as clearly transgressed in this chapter. After all, religion as a field of study has also led to various scientific (sub)disciplines, which provide relevant sources: these are naturally derived from the social, rather than the hard brand of science.

To begin close to home once more, let us first of all explore the terminology. When we talk about a religious framework we are in fact using a pleonasm, since 'religion' itself implies a certain framework. In this sense it is distinguished here from 'spirituality', and this differentiation is important across the board, precisely because we explicitly focus on the space between the experience as such and the way we frame it. Spirituality and spiritual experience here concern the dimension of the experience itself, which can occur both within and beyond a religious framework. This accords with the meaning that spiritual terminology has acquired in common parlance too, and that fact in itself indicates the resurgence of older human impulses. I will not embark on a definition of religion or spirituality here, however; too many others have burned their fingers in the attempt. This is borne out for example by the publication *The Pragmatics of Defining Religion: Contexts, Concepts & Contests*, which includes a chapter headed: *To Define or Not to Define: The Problem of the Definition of Religion.*[1] A serious attempt within this limited compass therefore would inevitably come to grief. Furthermore, it would entail the use of a broad concept such as 'supernatural', to avoid the exclusion of particular religious systems from the outset. Yet such a term comes with the fundamental objection that it defines only what something is *not*. For that reason we will simply have to assume the reader's tacit agreement to make what follows meaningful.

1 Mystical empiricism

Religious feeling and spirituality appear to be natural to humanity in general, but the experiences of individual historical figures always form the foundation of specific systems. The doctrines of such systems also refer explicitly to these experiences, and in some cases are largely centred on them. In a religion's basic story, its mythology, these experiences are linked to each other, and to the present-day life of the believers. Those of local shamanic cultures differ markedly from those of the organised world churches, and are sometimes regarded more as historical events than as a real possibility for the monks and nuns of today, but they have a place in principle. That is why religious traditions have made them the object of the requisite study and reflection—and will continue to do so. Now within the spectrum of religious empiricism there seems to be one experience *par excellence*, and that is the mystical experience. While in pagan times the term 'mystical', derived from Greek, applied to the rituals and doctrines of secret ceremonies, and in the Christian era to the divine mystery, from the fifteenth century onwards it was used to describe an inner experience. By a mystical experience we mean the ultimate feeling of oneness with the divine. The similarities of countless first-hand descriptions from all eras and corners of the globe are so striking that we may generally assume that we are dealing with one and the same type of experience. All of these writings, moreover, bear witness to an experience so different from everyday life that it occupies a category of its own. This profound strangeness is also explicit in these accounts, as in this fragment from the work of the Flemish priest and ascetic mystic John of Ruysbroeck (1293–1381), translated from Middle Dutch:

> Raise then your eyes above reason and above all practice of the virtues and behold with a loving spirit the living life that is the origin and the cause of all life. Regard it as the glorious abyss of God's richness and the living spring in which we feel ourselves united with God. There we must abide, undivided, empty and without perception. There, in

not-knowing and in darkness, is nothing other than a fathomless seeing: what we see, that is what we are, and what we are, we see.[2]

As the language used in Christian sources is relatively accessible to
most readers, this book will continue to draw from them. An impression
of the similarity of accounts from quite different quarters, however, is in
order here. We read in verses 4–7 of the Isha Upanishad, translated from
the original Sanskrit by Swami Nikhilananda:

> The Self is one. Unmoving, it moves swifter than thought. The senses
> do not overtake it, for always it goes before. Remaining still, it out-
> strips all that run. Without the Self, there is no life.
>
> To the ignorant the Self appears to move — yet it moves not. From
> the ignorant it is far distant — yet it is near. It is within all, and it is
> without all.
>
> He who sees all beings in the Self, and the Self in all beings, hates
> none.
>
> To the illumined soul, the Self is all. For him who sees everywhere
> oneness, how can there be illusion or grief?[3]

A crucial hallmark of the mystical experience, though, is that it cannot
be captured in words, and a mystical testimony is accordingly at most a
paraphrase, never a direct description. That empirical fact underlies for
example the Jewish doctrine that the name of the One is unutterable, and
within such a tradition as Taoism, in the dance of words around the
simultaneous being and non-being of things. The Carmelite John of the
Cross (1542–1591) explained the situation further:

> Fancy a man seeing a certain kind of thing for the first time in his life.
> He can understand it, use and enjoy it, but he cannot apply a name to
> it, nor communicate any idea of it, even though all the while it be a
> mere thing of sense. How much greater will be his powerlessness
> when it goes beyond the senses! This is the peculiarity of the divine
> language. The more infused, intimate, spiritual and supersensible it
> is, the more does it exceed the senses, both inner and outer, and
> impose silence upon them ... The soul then feels as if placed in a vast
> and profound solitude, to which no created thing has access, in an
> immense and boundless desert, desert the more delicious the more
> solitary it is. There, in this abyss of wisdom, the soul grows by what it
> drinks in from the well-springs of the comprehension of love ... and
> recognizes, however sublime and learned may be the terms we
> employ, how utterly vile, insignificant and improper they are, when
> we seek to discourse of divine things by their means.[4]

The characteristic 'unutterability' of the mystical moment has never
prevented those interested from sifting through the matter further.
Whereas Christian theology focused on how the content of experiences
related to Holy Writ, the psychology of religion — of which more later
— immerses itself in the whole phenomenon of the experience itself, and

of the person who undergoes it. One of the great Dutch scholars in this field was Gerard van der Leeuw (1890–1950). Before he introduced his own version of religious phenomenology in his main work in later years, in 1924 he began his monograph, entitled simply *Mystiek* (Mysticism), with the following statement:[5]

> There is scarcely any word which is used so haphazardly, with so many different meanings as 'mysticism'. Though it is sometimes used as a positive antithesis to dogmatism or formalism, it is just as often, if not more often, used to refer to phenomena which in fact could be described perfectly satisfactorily by the related word 'mysterious', and to movements which display a tendency to the occult. And yet mysticism is an extremely clearly delineated and distinctively marked phenomenon in the history of religion. We do not wish to venture on a definition which is too easy, nor on conclusions from the etymology of the word, which says nothing after all about the phenomenon itself. But we will try to sketch that phenomenon as it appears to us, in order eventually to briefly trace its relationship to Christianity.

> In so doing we shall need to devote much attention to the radical forms of mysticism. Just as, by studying abnormal 'verzerrte' complexes which verge on the insane, the psychologist often gains insight into the workings of the normal mind, in the same way we can best become acquainted with mysticism when we see it in its extreme consequences, sometimes bordering on insanity: we must of course never forget thereby that for the final judgement on the phenomenon, we must bear in mind the average at least as much.[6]

2 Describing the ineffable

The Flemish Jesuit Rob Faesen (b. 1958) elaborated on the fundamental difference between the experience itself and how it is described. He distinguished different forms of accounts of experiences, each one a further quantum leap away from the original experience. With regard to the experience itself, we have seen that mystics invariably report that every description falls short, but at the first level from that we find the spiritual journal. The foremost testimony is written shortly after the experience by the person in question, and is generally meant for his own eyes only, not for publication. Faesen gives as example the scrap of paper on which the mathematician and physicist Blaise Pascal (1623–1662) scribbled directly after an intense experience:

> In the year ... 1654. Monday, 23 November ... From about half-past
> ten in the evening until half-past twelve. FIRE! God of Abraham, God
> of Isaac. God of Jacob, not the God of philosophers and scholars. Cer-
> titude. Certitude. Emotion. Joy. Peace. God of Jesus Christ. Your God
> shall be my God. Forgetfulness of the world, and everything, except
> God ... The greatness of the human soul ... Joy, joy, joy, tears of joy ...
> May I never be separated from Him.[7]

Pascal, who was in poor physical health, suffered from severe headaches
and was hardly the most cheerful of souls, sewed the paper into his
clothes and wore it always. He promptly left science to its own devices
and threw himself into philosophy and theology. After his premature
death his testimony was accidentally found by a servant.

The next level of reporting is that of memoirs written by mystics; in
these they look back on their lives, drawing from their experiences.
Faesen states that while these are indeed accounts of experiences, they are
written from a reflective distance and function as elements in a story — the
'narrative perspective'. Next, he distinguishes letters or discourses in
which the mystic gives an account to others, clears up misunderstandings
and offers instruction to those who are unfamiliar with the experience.
The ignorance of (part of) the reading public again creates further distance from the original experience. And in an even more distant outer
zone there is the biography, written by someone other than the mystic
himself. This forms the most difficult genre for those who wish to learn
more of the experience, since the writer by definition conveys something
different from what the mystic would have done.

3 Visions in many senses

In contrast to the mystical experience which — in more than one sense — is
pre-eminently so unequivocal, visionary experiences are strikingly multi-
form. If we characterise the mystical experience as 'empty' in terms of
structure and form, visions on the contrary are typically 'full', and some
religious traditions are crammed with metaphorical stories which speak
to the hearer in parables and symbols. The Old Testament, for example,
would be unimaginable without its mythological revelation by means of
visions, dreams, apparitions, promptings, revelations, commands and
insights granted to individuals, who used them to give explicit direction
to the course of the Jewish people in its special bond with the one true
God. Traditions such as Hinduism and Tibetan Buddhism have even

developed the use of imagery and visual symbolism into an extremely differentiated constituent of religious practice. Something similar applies to the collection of shamanic systems and cultures, in which the imaginative powers of the central seers and healers constitute an indispensable element of their stock-in-trade.[8] In Sufism the forms of allegory, music and dance have a place of honour.

An impression of a visionary experience of the 'seer' and composer Hildegard of Bingen (1089–1179), from her work *Scivias* (Know the ways of the Lord'):

> Suddenly I saw something like an enormously wide, high, iron-coloured massive rock of stone. And on top of it was a gleaming white cloud. Above that was a circular royal throne on which sat a living Being, that glittered in marvellous radiance. It shone with such radiance that I could not look closely at it. In its breast it had something that resembled a dirty black clod of earth, as big as the heart of a full-grown man. This clod of earth was girt with precious stones and pearls. And from He who sat on the throne there came a great golden aureole, like the red morning sky. I could not measure its extent at all.[9]

Quite apart from the celestial music which she revealed to humanity, Hildegard had dozens of visions to deal with in the course of her life. In the most intricate detail she recorded her inner visions of angelic hosts, legions of heavenly spirits, human forms, paradisiacal gardens and sacred buildings. These descriptions were so vivid that others painted miniatures of them, and these in turn served as illustrations in her books. It was no unmixed pleasure, however, to be used as a conduit in this way, and Hildegard is known for example to have suffered from severe, migraine-type headaches.

In a condensed second-hand account, we read of the experiences of another Christian mystic, the thirteenth-century beguine, Hadewych:

> Hadewych found herself in a state of burning desire, so that she trembled and shivered throughout her whole body. It was as if all her limbs threatened to burst asunder. For she desired to possess the Beloved completely, to be united with Him in his Humanity, to absorb Him completely and become strong in Him, to suffer much without fainting; this she longed for, so that even his Divinity would be closely united with her, complete and perfect, in order to be able to satisfy Him in all suffering; what she had continually desired most, to be made divine. From the altar an eagle comes flying to her, telling her that she must prepare to become one. The eagle flies back and asks the God-man to reveal himself to her. Jesus appears to her, first as a child; then He brings her communion, as a man, wearing the garment that He wore at the Last Supper. She receives His Body and Blood. Then she is united with His Humanity; and for a moment she has the strength to bear this. Little by little the beautiful man disappears: she

feels one with Him. This was as the pleasure of Lovers. After she had
felt herself to be one with Him, it was as if she had merged into him.[10]

4 Love and mania

Religious experience is thus far from being a question of ready-made
notions based on biblical texts. This account of Hadewych's seventh
vision involves not only the inner eye and ear, but the total involvement of
the senses. Other than one might generally expect in a religious context,
the subject matter of many traditions outside of Christianity is also markedly erotic. Imagery and language express the all-encompassing love
which awaits the man or woman who surrenders to the divine. The low
countries were no exception to this, producing a separate school of medieval literature. Following in the footsteps of Hadewych in particular, we
have the *'minnesong'* genre, which sang of man's fundamental love for the
divine. Even so, the said *'minne'* or love does not grant its favours at every
moment, and when the beloved is not to be found, his absence makes itself
painfully felt. It can drive the believer 'distracted with love', like John of
the Cross in his 'dark night of the soul'. In those who have once known
love and are now bereft of it, such a great and intense desire flares up that
it seems capable of driving the soul even to madness. Hadewych used the
word *'orewoet'*, related to *'woede'* or anger, to describe a sort of religious
rage of love, which also lashes out in other languages and cultures. For the
most famous western example, though, let us turn to Plato. In his *Phaedrus*
he has his mentor Socrates say that the greatest blessings of all come to us
in the form of madness — if their origin is divine. And that from the pen
which wrote above all in rationalistic terms … ! For such 'divine madness'
Plato used the ancient term *mania*, distinguishing no less than four different forms: prophetic, ritual, musical and poetic, and last but not least:
erotic. These divine powers of love clearly compel us to go through hell
and high water — whether our desire is aroused by the innocence of beautiful youths or by that of our own souls. In this spirit, religious poetry
from far and near also allows the flames to flare up, as symbol of these
supreme desires.[11]

> Deep, deep down,
> in the total darkness of the Cave,
> is a Flame,
> a solitary Flame!
> Who will ever tell the secret

which the Flame
hides at its heart?
He alone will learn the secret
a secret he can never share
who, once fallen into that Flame,
and swallowed up, remains henceforth
nothing but Flame!

The fact that most religious systems have taken measures to at least temper this fire is therefore hardly surprising.

5 Divine madness

If the order of the day in most churches is chiefly piety and moderation, the spectrum of religious experience itself is infinitely wider and richer. In religious poetry of all ages and from all corners of the earth we can sense something of this dazzling, multidimensional, kaleidoscopic universe—and yet this is no more than a mere reflection, which we must accept at second hand. And like the language of love that it contains, crossing all moral and intellectual boundaries, gibberish also narrowly escapes the obligatory code of behaviour. Virtually all traditions include forms of belief and devotion that strike us as foolish or idiotic, and are often also referred to as such. Insanity and holiness are sometimes closely interwoven, and not within the bounds of religious institutions alone. Closer to home, for example, this phenomenon is rooted in the English word 'fool', which means among other things 'One who subverts convention or orthodoxy or varies from social conformity in order to reveal spiritual or moral truth.'[12] Erasmus' famous work In Praise of Folly, in which he satirises Catholic piety in particular, is not far removed from this reading.[13] In Europe too, until the Enlightenment, the 'holy fool' who wandered about singing, dancing and proclaiming unintelligible profundities was a familiar feature of the social landscape. In what Michel Foucault called 'the Big Lockup', the streets were only swept clean from the seventeenth century onwards, thus removing all sorts of troublemakers and eccentrics from the view of decent citizens.[14] Although western Christianity also numbered odd characters among its flock, the archetype of the holy fool has practically disappeared from it. Except perhaps in America where, thanks to the presence of countless charismatic churches and sects, you can go far as a street prophet with a bible in your hand and foam around your mouth. But in many non-western traditions, saintly fools or foolish saints go on living their wondrous lives. Sometimes such men and women are actually recognised as wise, enabling them to teach and inspire followers, while at other times they fulfil a ritual role as fool or jester. The power of this archetypal figure is that it unites and embodies opposites; it reflects the undivided primal principle, beyond all morality and division. The Lakota shaman Lame Deer explains: 'A clown in our language is called a *heyoka*. He is an upside-down, backward-forward, yes-and-no man, a contrarywise.'[15]

In Jewish, Islamic, animist, Buddhist and Hindu cultures especially we encounter them, these frenetic, wise lunatics. In June McDaniel's well thought-out study, *The Madness of the Saints*, she shows the vigour of living religious traditions in Bengal. On the grounds of both traditional writings as well as interviews with ecstatic leaders and their followers she creates a picture of — to put it mildly — a fascinating and colourful landscape of divine madness in this part of India. The range of the subject can be sampled in a poem such as the following:[16]

> God's Idiots
> Mumbling and prattling the many names ...
> while onlookers say, 'They're crazy'
> entering and not entering cities
> standing still or swaying
> before a laughing world
> they dance, they leap
> undone by feeling
> And the gods
> bow down before them.

The Bengali ecstatic tradition comprises various sects, regions and ethnic groups, involving countless divinities, ritual practices and expressions of devotion. Here, the rigid Indian system of social organisation according to caste and gender allows remarkable scope, considering the frenzied, chaotic and anarchistic behaviour of the gurus and saints concerned. Insanity, far from occupying a marginal position, is in fact the central principle here, and the system has accordingly developed ways of assessing ecstatic phenomena. Other than we might expect, these methods are more often employed to distinguish divine inspiration from trickery than from disturbed behaviour. There are detailed typologies of physical symptoms during trance states, and ecstatic expressions are tested for authenticity in recognised ways. Some of these are rather violent and akin to exorcism, while others focus more on gentle ayurvedic techniques for removing energy blocks or strengthening the nervous system — which has quite a lot to put up with under divine high tension. A further, generic criterion is that the ecstatic's private life should be in harmony with his or her teaching.

In addition, ecstatics may also pose as idiots in a pathological sense, as a deliberate means of avoiding the status of sainthood. For them, undergoing the contempt which falls to the lot of the 'real' lunatic forms the true exercise in humility and detachment. Take St Simeon Salus, for example, who achieved a recognised place as an icon of holy foolishness in the eastern orthodox wing of Christianity.[17] On the way back from a visit to Jerusalem this Syrian and his childhood friend renounced the worldly life of the sixth century and entered a monastery on the fringe of the Jordanian desert. The detachment practised there did not go far enough for them, however, and not long afterwards they made their home in the neighbouring wilderness, where they lived for years as ascetics. When Simeon felt that he had completed his spiritual journey, he decided to return to the inhabited world, in order to share his inner riches with his fellow-men. His friend did not dare to come with him, however, so he set off alone, determined to keep his true spiritual condition hidden, and at the same time to expose the madness of the world. And he certainly succeeded in his aim, by behaving as a half-wit for the rest of his life. On a dunghill by the city gate of Emesa he found a dead dog. He tied the cadaver to his belt and when he dragged it behind him into the city he was immediately jeered and spat at, and his reputation was established. The following Sunday he went to church with the devout population, but once inside he blew out all the candles, ran up into the pulpit and started throwing nuts at the women below. When people finally managed to get hold of him and bundle him out of the church, he knocked over the bakers' stalls outside, whereupon the bystanders beat him up. Nor was that the end of it. Simeon worked on his reputation as a village idiot on the loose by grabbing the dancing girls in the circus and whirling them around the circus ring, by eating meat on fast-days in the middle of the town square, by running stark naked through the women's section of the bath-house, and when left in charge of a market stall, by eating copious amounts of beans and then farting prodigiously, and by furthermore aping everyone he met, limping about like a stage cripple. Meanwhile no one knew about the miracles and cures that he performed, and if anything threatened to leak out, he was quick to retaliate with a practical joke. Only after his death was the secret side of his life revealed. Simeon had devoted the second half of his existence to putting into practice chapter 1, verse 27 from St Paul's first letter to the Corinthians: 'But God hath chosen the foolish things of the world to confound the wise.'

In the Russian Orthodox tradition from time immemorial there were dozens of such *yurodivy*, cultural figures which also feature in the great Russian literature of the nineteenth and twentieth centuries. The cathedral on Red Square, for example, is named after St Basil the Blessed, a

popular *yurodivy* of the sixteenth century — who reduced no less a person
than his contemporary Ivan the Terrible to fear and trembling — while
Dostoevsky's *The Idiot* tells the story of Prince Mishkin, the epileptic who
is too good for this world. In pre-Christian western sources too, references
to spiritual madness are to be found. The Celtic tradition, for example,
included the crazy visionary and poet who has come down to us as the
sorcerer Merlin.[18] And while the schlemiel appears to be a somewhat
naïve relation within the Jewish tradition, the stories in which Sufism is
wont to express its wise lessons teem with mad mullahs.[19] The works of
the Sufi author Idries Shah include the book *Wisdom of the Idiots*, the title of
which refers to the real human being whose wisdom cuts right through all
intellectual pedantry.[20] Stories and satirical poems about a certain Abu l-
Fath of Alexandria, in which he features variously as hero, sly beggar,
brilliant poet, charlatan, hypocritical leader and gibbering idiot, were put
into verse by Al-Hamadhani (d. 1008 AD) and published in German
under the title: *Vernunft is nichts als Narretei* (Reason is nothng but Folly).[21]
The Persian poet Jalaludin Rumi summarised this paradoxical congenial-
ity as follows: 'I have tried caution and forethought; from now on I will
make myself mad.'[22] Poetically, this state of consciousness was often portrayed as drunkenness, and Rumi himself conjured up hundreds of verses
with images of the tavern as the home of real wisdom, and of wine as the
nectar in which we drown our inhibited selves — and of which we cannot
get enough. Taking pride of place in this tradition is the prototype
Nasruddin, who as the Til Uilenspiegel of the Middle East constantly
made a fool of bystanders and followers. The American David Leeming
testified in his article 'The Hodja' (The Wise One) how alive this mythical
figure still was in the 1960s.[23] When he started teaching in Istanbul, aim-
ing to instil western rationality into Turkish schoolchildren, he was
embarrassed by the stream of jokes and anecdotes about Nasruddin's
inimitable carryings-on which he was treated to in his classes. Incidentally, the riddles which this originally Persian character posed to everyone, are akin to the *koan* of Zen Buddhism. Zen pupils break their logical
teeth on their master's *koans*, and can only find the solution when they
give up thinking out of sheer desperation and receive a flash of direct,
essential insight. In this wordless dimension they make a gesture to their
master, to show that they have seen behind the problem. This tradition
underlines the paradox as correspondence between wisdom and folly,
incomprehensible to the linear intellect. Finally there is a category of spiritual teachers who set about their work in a way which has 'crazy wisdom'
as its hallmark. The title of George Feuerstein's book on this subject is significant: *Holy Madness: The Shock Tactics and Radical Teachings of Crazy-wise
Adepts, Holy Fools, and Rascal Gurus*.[24] These figures are found within the

context of various specific traditions, but in their behaviour they form a pre-eminently idiosyncratic phenomenon. In essence, adepts are stripped of all intellectual frameworks; eventually they never know where they are with their teacher, and all attempts to approach the spiritual path through intellect end in frustration. Feuerstein also specifies a number of recognised psychopathological syndromes which are reminiscent of the behaviour of some *crazy wisdom* teachers and saints. Certain deep meditative trances resemble catatonic states, while the ecstatic chatter about heavenly bliss and the venting of obscenities and sexual puns for which some are notorious, sound like the ravings of schizophrenics historically classified as 'hebephrenic'. It goes without saying that the working methods of these teachers are surrounded by controversy. Although this paradoxical approach may enable people to make leaps of consciousness and learn to look behind linear reality, the main problem is that human judgement is bound to fall short on the way to—hypothetical—ultimate knowledge. This makes it difficult to recognise potentially false or criminal variants, while excesses in the spiritual field of action demonstrate with some regularity that it is in no way absurd to wish to distinguish between the genuine and the fake.[25] One good piece of advice, emphasised by Lee Lozowick (1943), who is himself a 'crazy wisdom' teacher who has remained untainted by scandal: look at the pupils, and look at how the teacher treats them.[26]

6 Conversion and classification

Of quite another order than the mystical and visionary experience is a category which is even more closely linked to religious frameworks: the conversion experience. There is no more high-profile example of this than the about-turn in which Saul became Paul. As an orthodox Jew with a priestly *carte blanche* for hunting down Christians in Damascus, he was bowled over by a divine light and likewise divine voice in the year AD 36. After several days of confusion, he staggered to his feet once more as an equally passionate champion of the new doctrine of salvation, and went on to become a founder of the Christian church. God had addressed him in person, demanding why he was persecuting Christ, and what man would be proof against that? His case was naturally a dramatic one, and while it therefore speaks to us vividly, conversion does not always take place in such a way. In fact, it is often more of a gradual process, sometimes evolving over many years. In the Netherlands, for example, conversion plays a crucial role within certain orthodox sections of the Dutch Reformed Church. Recent research by Nicolette Hijweege throws light on the process in these circles, and she is the first to approach this from a psychological rather than a theological angle.[27] Conversion in the so-called *bevindelijke* or experiential wing of the Reformed community is one of the five types she distinguishes in her theory. Besides the believers who transfer their allegiance to a new church, or to another faith, there are those who lapse completely, as well as those who are new to all religious belief. The brand of conversion in these particular circles, however, implies an intensification of an existing faith, which reinforces the believer's identity, while anchoring their membership of the same community more strongly. The person who arrives at perfect faith through his own experience of God (*bevinding*) lives another life than he who is still travelling towards it, full of doubt and without a firm relationship with God. In successful cases this leads to the use of the *'Tale Kanaäns'* — 'language of Canaan' — by initiates. In this somewhat archaic jargon, a sort of Authorised Version Dutch, the latter give expression to their experience of God, and their newly acquired insights — and status.

Some time ago the theologian and pastoral psychologist Ruard Ganzevoort briefly brought up the subject of conversion in the context of his doctoral thesis on crisis and faith.[28] Psychologically speaking, he makes a distinction between conversion as an avenue to faith and conversion via religious socialisation, which most believers acquire in the course of their upbringing. In this context, too, conversion emerges as a gradual process, in which social interaction plays a prominent role. One group — namely, the family — is exchanged for another — a new community of faith — while in a parallel shift a new system of interpretation is established in the individual. This differs from many of the stories related in this book, although technically speaking a number of these crises could be regarded as conversions. While social shifts certainly make up part of the 'new' life after the crisis, these are secondary. Of primary importance are the inner experience and its significance for the individual and his or her own existence. And their collected stories precisely reflect how those involved design their further lives according to their own lights, often deliberately without any existent framework or model. Therefore, there is nothing to speak of in the sense of a conversion-to-something because there *is* no such 'something'.

On the theological bookshelf, the phenomenon of conversion features more as a kind of evidence in a successful scientific experiment. The framework of theology gives meaning to experiences that take place in a religious context, and when those experiences unfold along theological lines, they accordingly emphasise the truth of the latter. But this does not cut much ice with those who do not identify with the framework in question. Not surprisingly, this is where a sharp dividing line between — to put it briefly — believers and non-believers comes into focus. Staking out a 'religious' territory in the limitless potential of human experience is almost certain to cause friction — and it does so to this day. At one level, this friction occurs between the actuality of individual experiences and the conceptual nature of a collective doctrine. The more vital the doctrine, the more open it will be to the perceptions of both believers and non-believers. For both groups to be able to structure and understand their experiences, a doctrine must offer concepts that are appropriate, or can be made so. And this structuring begins with the initial conceptualisation of the raw material of experience, in the use of words to approach and capture it. Now with the best will in the world, if words had no generally accepted significance, the use of language would not get us very far. A meaning, however, unlike a physical object, is not a 'thing', and only when misunderstandings appear on the horizon do we discuss the question of what precedes the language we use — the underlying experience we wish to convey, or the lenses which allow us to see what others do not — and vice versa. One might wonder how well people understand each other in daily life anyway, never mind in the context of phenomena that are so explicitly outside the usual scope of language. Mystical experiences and their proverbial ineffability are of course a particularly clear example of this. Now as a means of expression, religious language does not have to form a stumbling-block, even to non-believers; in the end it is just a language like any other language, a system of references. Yet when this solidifies into a 'thing' which then takes on a life of its own, independent of the experience, the danger zone looms in sight. There, language no longer forms a bridge but rather deepens an existing chasm. No term illustrates that better than the name of the unnameable.

7 The G-word

As we have just seen, after the mystical union of the soul with its own divine essence, nothing remains as it was. In a fragment from the writings of the Spanish Carmelite Teresa of Avila (1515–1582) we read:

> God establishes himself in the interior of this soul in such a way, that when she returns to herself, it is wholly impossible for her to doubt

that she has been in God, and God in her. This truth remains so
strongly impressed on her that, even though many years should pass
without the condition returning, she can neither forget the favour she
received, nor doubt of its reality. [...] But how, you will repeat, can
one have such certainty in respect to what one does not see? This
question I am powerless to answer. These are secrets of God's omnip-
otence which it does not appertain to me to penetrate. All that I know
is that I tell the truth; and I shall never believe that any soul who does
not possess this certainty has ever been really united to God.[29]

In Teresa's experience, therefore, there is no arguing with the immediate certainty that takes root in this way. Moreover, no one faced with her
testimony can get around the fact that 'God' here signifies something
essentially different from any abstract morality, let alone from the kind of
anthropomorphic image — bearded or otherwise — which is generally
associated with religion. One of the numerous sayings of Meister Eckhart
(c. 1260–1328), the Dominican from the Rhineland, also suggests a relationship — if we can call it such — between the individual and God that is
very different from what is accepted as doctrinally correct: 'Das Auge, mit
dem mich Gott sieht, ist das Auge, mit dem ich ihn sehe, mein Auge und
sein Auge ist eins.' [30] (The eye with which God sees me is the eye with
which I see him, my eye and his eye are one.)

Now Eckhart was ranked as a heretic precisely because his views presented subtleties which did not conform to the rules. At all events such
revelations remind us that there is a life-sized gap between 'God' as the
unfathomable yet perceptible essence, as the full Void or the empty All,
and 'God' as an all-seeing arbitrator, who rubs mankind's nose day and
night in its inevitable guilt and the innocence of his own murdered son.
And that discrepancy is the cause of many a non-believer's or ex-
believer's allergy to the whole religious caboodle; a case of the baby and
the bathwater. Not because they are not interested in spiritual experiences, but because in many cases the concept of God in itself has undergone a transformation, like someone driving the wrong way down the
mystic road. From unutterably undifferentiated and ever-changing to a
deathly, rigid construction with certain political leanings. We are dealing
with a categorical error; a confusion between the category of subjective
experience with that of social morality. All religious institutions run the
same risk in that regard: of allowing their identity to become fused with
the form that once held the living flame. And all traditions struggle with
the tension between the rules and the actual game, between the wisdom of
yesterday and the truth of today, even without taking the content of their
revelations or doctrines into account. Most readers though are rather
more familiar with the Christian framework, and this confusion can be
adequately illustrated therefore through developments in that field of

influence. However painful or uncomfortable, a sketch of the historical tension between individual revelation and the institutional framework may give some insight into how to avoid such developments, and what difference that would make if it were possible. In addition, this approach emphasises once more the importance of the power of discernment in the whole subject matter.

8 Gnosis and orthodoxy

The philosophy of Plato provides more than one suitable starting point for a glance at the history of western culture. Here too his name irrevocably crops up, although he was not the only philosopher in the pre-Christian tradition, nor did he fail to inspire followers. In his most famous allegory he contrasts a man who has always been chained inside a cave and derives his only awareness of reality from moving shadows on the wall with a man who lives out in the open and knows the sun to be the only true origin of all separate phenomena, including shadows. However relevant it might be for profound questions, we shall not further explore Plato's works here, but simply follow the line of direct knowledge that he captured in that image. The direct, intuitive knowledge of the true nature of things became known to history under the Greek name *gnosis*. For centuries the quest for gnosis was central to movements that nowadays come under the academic heading of western esotericism. Gnosis was traditionally known as 'the knowledge of the heart', which suggests that it is something other than the product of rational thinking processes. In a classical definition, it is the redeeming knowledge of 'who we were, what we have become, where we were, whither we have sunk, whither we hasten, whence we are redeemed, what is birth is and what rebirth'.[31]

The quest for this most profound knowledge was not restricted to the Gnostics, but this early Christian movement is naturally connected in name. Until the year 1945 the most that was known about it originated paradoxically enough from the early Church Fathers, who had done their best to suppress it. The discovery of the Nag Hammadi scriptures suddenly threw new light on the phenomenon. What Plato saw as the direct knowledge of the Good was regarded by gnosticism, flourishing in the first two centuries of our era, as the only way to escape from the reality of this earthly vale of tears to the true, divine state. Originating in Jewish circles which could not identify with priestly authority in spiritual matters, the doctrine on personal revelation took shape in ascetic communities — presumably all-male — which favoured life in the desert. Strictly celibate and cut off from the world, they devoted themselves completely to their programme of fasting, prayer and meditation. For them this was the only logical answer to their view that this world had not — as in the Platonic outlook — sunk into Evil through experience, but had itself been brought forth from Evil. For the world was not in fact created by the Most High, but by the Demiurge, a sort of divine sidekick with ambition. Only gnosis could bring redemption from the essentially evil, tainted and treacherous nature of reality, through inner revelation to the individual by the One. Now by the time Jesus appeared on the scene, the power of the gods of the Hellenistic pantheon and the old philosophical world views was already fading. There was confusion, and there was also hunger for a new 'big story'. With Jesus' coming the existent idea of imprisonment and redemption accordingly gained a new dimension; his deeds were regarded as the fulfilment of ancient Jewish and Greek prophecies. In the Nag Hammadi scriptures, which contain gospels which were never absorbed into the official Christian canon, the Gnostic content of Jesus' sayings is striking, as in verse 2 of the gospel of Thomas: Jesus said, 'Those who seek should not stop seeking until they find. When they find, they will be disturbed. When they are disturbed, they will marvel, and will reign over all. And after they have reigned they will rest.'[32] Or in verse 67: Jesus said: 'Those who know all, but are lacking in themselves, are utterly lacking.'[33]

Now in the first century of our era the Roman empire was swarming with spiritual cliques, all trying in their own way to fathom the meaning of the events surrounding Jesus' life and death. The early Christians got on the wrong side of the Romans because they refused to sacrifice to their gods, and could not accept the emperor as a divinity. Initially it was mainly slaves and the poor who eagerly embraced the idea of personal redemption, and its great power of attraction in the form of gnosticism was a factor in its downfall. As the example of Jesus' condemnation had already demonstrated, the consequences of the radical idea that true knowledge is a question of individual revelation were quite simply intolerable to secular power structures. Once again this was translated into intolerance, and so the relative religious freedom under the Romans virtually came to an end, when one faction declared itself the one true Christian church. By specifying where orthodoxy stopped and heathenish false doctrines began, the church fathers themselves brought the idea of heresy into the world. As their successors, the ecclesiastical institutions went on to select from the available writings on Jesus' teaching and life, thus compiling the New Testament, which has called the tune since then. Once this movement had become identified with the Roman political authorities, there was no stopping it. Where formerly there was a *distinction* between different views and movements — and no doubt a fair amount of interpersonal tension and intrigue — this combination of a clearly defined doctrine with secular power brought about an actual *division*. This, as we know, had consequences which went further than a bit of squabbling among dissenters. Within the new institution of orthodoxy the central place once occupied by the quest for gnosis gradually shifted to the margin. In the place of direct revelation of true knowledge to the individual, with Christ as inspiring example, revelation from then on was channelled exclusively through his representative on earth, the church, and after all manner of schisms, the Roman Catholic church. Those who considered themselves quite capable of striving for gnosis without such mediation had to be shown the error of their ways. It is well known that in the course of western history few means of doing so were eschewed. Hardly a pleasant story, and who would not prefer it to have been otherwise? Nevertheless, there is no denying that the history of the tradition that bears the name of Christ contains a number of pitch-black pages. Those who sought for gnosis had to carry on their activities underground. Gnosticism as such did not in fact survive, and when one thousand years later a similar spiritual orientation emerged in the south of France in the form of Catharism and spread successfully, it too called an orthodox counter-movement into being. For the Cathars this ended at the stake, to which according to tradition they allowed themselves to be dragged singing, confident that the truth they carried in their hearts would survive the flames. It was not only gnostically inclined factions that took the rap in the process, essentially everyone who did not buy into the strict ecclesiastical belief system could expect that knock on the door. God's work on earth appeared to entail that the eventual unity of existence should manifest in the created world, by making everything perfectly unequivocal, uniform and unanimous. That led to the virtual extinction of magical and mythical world views and practices, sometimes of great antiquity, and is why, on balance, we are perched on the ruins of a gutted European culture. The intellectually and artistically rich renaissance, it must be noted, sprang directly from the rediscovery of earlier cultural substrata, and even during this period it was advisable to tread carefully. The practitioners of hermetic philosophy and its branches were to feel the Roman Catholic church breathing down their necks for some time to come. Only after another symbolic low point, the burning alive in 1600 of the brilliant, magic-erotic freethinker Giordano Bruno, on the Campo de' Fiori in the Holy City, could these undercurrents slowly begin to break free, and compose themselves into what in later centuries would evolve into science. Of course the individ-

ual quest for true knowledge did not cease with the physical downfall of
Gnostics and witches. In the shadow of the dominant religious history
this took many forms; these together make up the rich tradition of western
esotericism, which has only recently begun to find recognition. Incidentally, similar safety valves were needed as an alternative to organised
Protestantism which, as reaction to Roman Catholic excesses, promoted a
return to the letter of the Scriptures. That however was hardly the frequency on which gnosis could be found; the seeker must be attuned to the
spirit of God's word. The Reformation also failed therefore to resolve the
tension between truth-seekers and religious establishments. For example,
the successful persecution of the Anabaptists in the sixteenth and seventeenth century by Protestant authorities throughout Europe illustrates the
continued lack of freedom suffered by recalcitrant spiritual groups under
early Protestant rule.[34]

9 The God affair

Times have changed, but the fact remains that this whole disgraceful
history underlies the mistrust of present-day non-believers and non-
churchgoers when it comes to a certain three-letter word. Even so, this is
not to say that the Christian context per definition has no nourishment or
family affection to offer the authentic seeker after knowledge of the heart.
This is borne out by the many historical figures who have been directly
inspired by the life of Christ, and who have devoted their own lives to imi-
tating it; it is mostly in their legacy to us that we find the now classic
descriptions of mystical insights and spiritual transformation. The fact
that Catholicism in particular is being given rather a hard time these days,
more so than most other religions, is hardly innovative or trendy, and the
rationale for it is also rather outdated. Perhaps the angle of approach
which is most appropriate in the context of this book will modify the picture somewhat after all. It shows how the church herself provoked such
resistance, because she is the most objectified of all religious institutions;
the way to Roman Catholic deification is pre-eminently one of reification.
As a purely spiritual way Catholicism is in a position to inspire people or
otherwise, but as an institutional monolith with an agenda, the church
must be prepared for repercussions. While not the only tradition with a
highly-organised hierarchy, she also possesses a representative of divine
authority on earth, the only genuine one in her opinion. But the Roman

Catholic church distinguishes herself most from all other religious systems in her historical ambition to maintain the good old connection with secular power, and to play a role in world politics. The throne of God stands in the Vatican, possessing among other privileges the formal status of permanent observer at the United Nations, including the right to vote at various conferences. The original revelation, via the intermediate step of religious ethics, has thus solidified further into ideological merchandise. And this certainly does not help believers to distinguish between the truth of their own experience and the interpretation provided by such a sanctified environment.

It is no easy task to make such a distinction, in any religion or church. It is even more difficult, however, for the overwrought believer who can no longer automatically steer by the old compass. His or her personal crisis may be brought about not only by the 'ordinary' hurdles and pitfalls of life – loss through redundancy, illness, bereavement – but also by the disruption stemming from unusual mental or emotional experiences. The person who turns in desperation to a familiar religious framework hopes for answers to sometimes urgent questions. And it makes a world of difference if these are then met by a dogmatic lecture or a listening ear – by a morality that claims to reflect the truth like an abstract object, or by a human being who feels and thinks with the sufferer from within his own situation. At such moments the pastoral worker is the real mediator between the believer and his Creator. Even an 'ordinary' crisis demands an advanced handling of the framework in question, and this obviously goes much further than self-evident piety. Speaking from within the Reformed context, Ganzevoort stated that 'in a period of crisis the essential questions come under discussion', and that 'these fundamental questions are profoundly religious in nature'.[35] When faith helps to give meaning to critical events and allows one to emerge purged, a crisis can have a 'positive' effect on one's faith. That is the sort of effect to which Anton Boisen (1876–1965) referred, even in cases of such severe crises and psychoses that admission to a mental hospital was unavoidable. Boisen, who went through five psychotic episodes in his own life, did pioneering work for the pastoral care unit of Worcester State Hospital, MA, and through this, for the entire field of hospital chaplaincy and clinical pastoral education. In his perspective, psychiatric patients had arrived at a confrontation with ultimate reality, in which both creative and destructive forces were unleashed. He saw furthermore how the existential wrestling of the soul could result in personal maturation – if the person concerned could summon up the necessary willpower and responsibility. From a standpoint which is admittedly rooted more in the practice of psychotherapy than in pastoral care, Dutch scholar Agneta Schreurs showed that, in the hands of a skilled social worker, a framework such as that of Christian middle orthodoxy can provide a rich source for aid to believers in spiritual need.[36] When used in this way, the religious framework embodies not a fossilised doctrine, but a living context in which the believer can undergo a meaningful interaction. Of course it only becomes really interesting when the believer comes up with questions or problems about which the doctrine concerned speaks in contradictory terms, or even keeps a resounding silence. That may occur in the case of unusual states or experiences of consciousness, such as reported in a number of places in this book. Such experiences can knock the believer's world view so off balance that it creates great tension with long-held convictions. Faith may suddenly appear to be something quite different from knowledge; see Chapter 4, 'Crises of knowing', on this subject too. Now religious movements tend to solve ineradicable internal differences by schisms and splinter groups, but when these differences persist, an individual believer usually tends to loosen his ties with the institution, or even radically depart from it.

As we have said, the tendency to reification or *Verdinglichung* is innate in all human beings, and in all human institutions, including churches. And yet the degree of solidification such as that of the church of Rome also has specific western traits. Just as science primarily represents a particle perspective, treating physical matter as the firstborn of the Cartesian twins, the Book of Revelation in western Christianity is first and foremost condensed to the solid form of a morality. As with other Abrahamitic bloodlines, of course, this is closely linked with a story indisputably recorded in writing. Although they have always been subject to various interpretations, the gospels in principle remain unchangeable. They possess moreover a status which no other frame of reference can possibly equal, so that the moral of that particular story is regarded accordingly as the highest norm of human goodness. As a yardstick by which believers can assess their own inner struggle, they can certainly offer them the structure that spiritual growth requires. Meanwhile however, we have become accustomed to the universal use of excerpts from holy books as weapons, and to the little good and considerable misery that results from such improper use. Frankly, this situation is simply unimaginable without an underlying faith in the eventual truth of form as form. In comparison to this, for example, Buddhist doctrine is centred on seeing through the transience of all forms, both material and spiritual, and of the illusion of autonomous personality. A difference such as that of a chair and the space that it occupies. Two anecdotes as illustration. On the film set of Bernardo Bertolucci's *Little Buddha*, reincarnation was not only the subject of the production, but also of discussion between the Americans and Tibetans present. For most of the

Americans, the subject was interesting but seemed unreal to them; it was something you could choose to believe in or not, and their position was that they did not. After much discussion, Tibetan lama Sogyal Rinpoche, who featured in the film, pointed out that it makes no difference whether someone believes in it or not, only whether or not it is true. And years before that, when the Dalai Lama was making one of his first journeys to the west, one of the American Buddhists on the plane did his utmost to explain the nature of self-hatred, and the pain and difficulty of struggling with it. The interpreters had a hard time of it, as Tibetan has no word for this frame of mind so common in the west. However, after an hour or so it finally began to dawn on the spiritual leader. And the last thing he said, from the depths of his being: 'But why?'

There is a difference in orientation between west and east, just as religion for members of a religious order differs from that of the man in the street, and churches further differ from each other. The Latin church offers interested parties the cloistered life as exclusive context for a truly spiritual life, while lay churchgoers follow a subsidiary programme of belief in established doctrine. For a long time believers were even actively discouraged from acquiring knowledge on their own initiative. Their self-knowledge accordingly stuck at the level of the prescribed penance, and their individual experience was thematically defined in advance. Beyond that framework however there are all manner of things to experience, while within it, the starring role of the Supreme Being is taken over by the institution and its functionaries. Perhaps it is for that reason that such a thing exists as the proverbial, relatively carefree Roman Catholic life, in which church membership may consist largely of external forms, Catholic identity may be a matter of cultural flavour, and church and pub are found side by side. The Protestant universe in comparison provides very little in the way of escape clauses, while it safeguards morality in the relative seclusion of the individual's inner world. Here, the relationship with the Creator is one-to-one, while all experience is known to Him, and judged according to His Word. Coloured by moderate or orthodox tendencies, a highly personal alchemy of experience and significance takes place, from within which the believer deals with the world.

From a bird's-eye view we can distinguish a third variant in the charismatic quarter. For a century now the Pentecostal movement has been growing, firstly in Protestant and later in Catholic circles too. Although the bible asserts its unassailable authority here, and is taken rather literally, its significance is understood to lie not in morality but in personal experience. Specifically, the essential point for an individual is to experience the descent of the Holy Spirit directly. This gracious event however is generally a collective occurrence, in the often motley community of adherents who form the appropriate context for it. Generally well attended services provide the setting which assists the participants — with fife and drum — in the reception of the healing touch, and thereby takes them under its protection. And that is just as well, because the extravagant tableaux to which the infectious Pentecostal fire gives rise would evoke very different reactions outside of this context. Their seventeenth-century forerunners, the Quakers, Shakers and Ranters, owed their originally derisory names to their characteristic expressions; in the same way, this 'speaking in tongues', singing, crying, laughing, shouting with joy, waving, praying, shaking, laying on of hands, dancing, leaping, falling, rising, kneeling, crawling, and racing through the corridors would provoke mainly frowning glances in outsiders, and no doubt the odd emergency call.

10 Psychology of religion

At the end of the nineteenth century a new framework for insight into the religious life of mankind emerged: the psychology of religion. It was one of the earliest sub-disciplines of psychology as such. The latter was for a long time the poor relation of philosophical tradition, which was dominated by the German speculative idealism of Kant, Fichte and Hegel. This sector plumed itself on its exclusive use of 'pure reason'; others hinted increasingly that it simply demonstrated a categorical lack of empirical grounds for making statements on the inner world of mankind. At a time when the success of methodology in classical physics could no long be denied, the growing dissatisfaction resulted in the empirical study of the psyche. Probably no one embodied this development more than the American William James. His pioneering spirit, on which more later, not only hovered over psychology as a field of study in general, but also got the psychology of religion in particular off the ground. After his starting signal around 1900, great academic enthusiasm for this subject welled up not only in the United States but also in Germany and France. In all cases however this was of short duration. How different from in the Netherlands! In this country the new field was approached initially with great reserve by the theological establishment, but in the course of the twentieth century support for it grew significantly. So much so that the Netherlands today boasts perhaps the greatest number of university chairs of religious psychology in the world.

In fact the academic interest in religion in the Netherlands had had a broader base in the past. In 1860 Cornelis Petrus Tiele (1830–1902) embarked on his struggle to completely remould theology into the new field of religious science. In 1876 his wish was granted in a political sense, when parliament approved the new Higher Education bill, and he was able to go and teach both the history and the philosophy of religion in Leiden.[37, 38] In Tiele's view these two angles were fundamental to the study of religion: the manifest forms of individual religions and the essence of the phenomenon of religion as such. This division runs parallel with the esoteric and exoteric dimensions of religion, that is to say the inner and outer dimensions. The latter comprises the forms by which we recognise a system — its customs, rituals, symbolism and doctrine. Social and cultural phenomena which stem directly from the religious participation of a community can be included among these. In contrast, the esoteric dimension is centred on the inner experience of the individual in his religious practice, quest and faith. This latter dimension has somehow acquired a shady reputation, with the result that to many ears it sounds like voodoo and hocus-pocus. In Tiele's days there would certainly have been individuals who were sore afraid that the renewed religious sciences were going to study precisely that — and in fact they were not altogether mistaken. For curiosity was focused mainly on the religious systems of non-European cultures. This interest had been felt earlier in the nineteenth century, and concerned among others the traditions of the Indian subcontinent. This of course reflected the colonial relationships of western Europe to parts of Asia. In this dramatic expansion of the academic field of vision, the Hindu world alone formed a veritable universe. It proved to be a vivid, highly sophisticated and many-sided system, with ramifications from philosophy via kinetics up to and including medicine, all of it furthermore being of a scientific calibre. Moreover, various aspects were also of impressive antiquity, making Christianity appear rather paltry by comparison. The encounter with the wisdom embodied by this universe would historically open the door to a new level of intellectual involvement with religion. There proved to be a whole spectrum in existence of human etiquette in relation to 'higher powers', and the study of this subject is generally designated as 'comparative religious science'. Just as explorers in former centuries had blazed their way to the sources of exotic rivers, within the space of half a century this new family of academics, some of Dutch origin, assembled an enormous quantity of knowledge about religious catchment areas, some of which appeared to be extremely strange, and operated according to mysterious principles. Discoveries about Islamic, Hindu, Buddhist, Taoist, shamanic and countless other, mainly smaller, systems stretched our image of mankind and the psyche as never before, thereby also enriching our old familiar ways of thinking. Like a mighty intake of breath this wave reached far further than academe itself, and dating from before 1900, formed the greatest innovative influence on western philosophy and literature in Europe and beyond.

Meanwhile, the advancing secularisation of the western world inevitably went hand in hand with a fundamental cultural relativity. Within this, all cultural and religious interpretive systems formed their own truth and value, which consequently made them impossible to measure by any absolute or universal standard. Finally however a certain paralysis set in, because more of the same was being served up increasingly within the field of study. More and more descriptions in ever increasing detail of exotic rituals and symbolic systems of communities who lived cut off from the world, voluntarily or otherwise, as the original inhabitants of forests, mountains, deserts and morasses, or as distant descendants of shipwrecked mariners, adventurers, runaway slaves or missionaries, and all of whom increasingly wrestled with the reality of globalisation. Interest in the subject from a scientific point of view simply began to fade. More recently however, the pendulum has been set in motion again and questions on the essence of religion are heard once more. Following the interest in the broad spectrum of the subject, it is now the turn of Tiele's philosophy of religion to fathom the depths, in search of the significance of all those diverse manifestations. What makes a religion a religion, what motivates a religious person, what does he seek or experience in religion, why does he construct religious systems? Research into these matters focuses on the ontological dimension, the essence of the religious impulse and activity, which is assumed to belong to all eras. And, by chance or otherwise, the revival of this field of study coincides with topical global problems about religion, its values and truths. By putting social and political emphasis on external differences, individual religious traditions increasingly resemble monolithic, atomistic entities. From these, believers manage to derive an identity which has something absolute, and seems irreconcilable with other systems. This development has come to form an everyday problem worldwide, which prompts many people, including those outside the fields of science and religion, to wonder what religion actually is. What actuates the human being within it? What is 'true' religion, since different traditions claim that honour, while excluding all others? If these questions initially occupied philosophers and psychologists of religion, current events give every inducement to look at them in a new light.

The psychology of religion is no rose without a thorn, that much is obvious. In the Netherlands, as in the rest of Europe, this field of study first developed within a Protestant theological context, and later within its Catholic counterpart. And even today its practitioners are almost invariably to be found among theologians, not among psychologists. To be sure, its hybrid origin is still reflected in two sensitive areas. On the one hand, the gospel will cast its shadow over the authentic scientific quest as long as the former is regarded as ultimate yardstick for the validity of any discovery whatever. On the other hand the current psychological framework cannot possibly make any pronouncements on supernatural matters. Accordingly such a theme as transcendence, that would seem essential for theistic religious empiricism at least, is ruled out in advance. No wonder that the discipline on the whole displays little cohesiveness at an international level too.

11 Sanctity

As regards content, the work of Rudolf Otto (1869–1937) has exerted great influence on this academic field. His study *Das Heilige*, which has never been out of print since 1917, is centred on the idea of the divine as the 'numinous': a non-rational, non-sensory experience or feeling, of which the primary and immediate object exists outside of the self. For Otto this was the *mysterium tremendum et fascinans*. For an impression:

> As horrific and frightful as the demonic-divine can appear to the mind, it is just as alluring and enthralling at the same time. And the creature that trembles before the numen, flinching most humbly, always feels in himself at the same time the urge to approach, indeed in a manner to appropriate it. The mysterium is to him not only the wondrous, but the wonderful.[39]

Otto thus established the status of the divine as a separate category, which in an academic sense too could not be reduced to anything else. Now in the second half of the last century the idea of a separate divine category found little support, but more recently, with the above-mentioned shift towards the essential problems of religion, this notion has come back into favour. One constant point of discussion is where this divinity might be found. Is it transcendent, and thus beyond the reality we know, or is it immanent, present in the here and now? Religions differ as to their inclination to one or the other theory, but as long as they primarily offer a moral framework for the devout masses, that is not really important. In mystical empiricism however this is a relevant point. In general the monotheistic religions localise the divine above and beyond man and matter. The hereafter too is a transcendent idea, and whoever seeks a direct encounter with the divine would therefore need to go beyond the limits and transcend the here and now. In the immanent viewpoint on the other hand the divine expresses itself in the immediacy of all existing forms —'dead' or 'alive'. Unmistakable immanent traits are found in eastern traditions, and in shamanic and animist systems. Even so, it is quite impossible to draw a clear line on this basis. Every individual tradition always has both dimensions anyway, which appear to merge with each other in mystical cross-currents or undercurrents.

12 The journeying soul

In all experiences of the divine we encountered earlier, the soul itself is the subject. The soul as the deepest, most essential part of the individual person, as the immaterial antenna capable of receiving divine transmissions. The soul also as wax in the divine hand, which leaves an imprint at every encounter. A deeply felt religious life progresses through such blessed moments, and according to the tradition in question and the qualities it ascribes to the true, complete human being, the soul's powers and sensitivities mature in the attention devoted to it. Charity and humility in a Christian timbre, wisdom and compassion of Buddhist growth—and, it would seem, intimacy with a dash of humour as in the Islamic recipe.[40]

> The Vegetables
> Tonight the vegetables
> would like to be cut
> by someone singing God's name.
> How could Hafiz
> know such top secret information?
> Because once we were all tomatoes,
> potatoes, onions or zucchini.

The English writer Evelyn Underhill (1875–1941) worked through piles of mystical Christian literature and distilled their essence in her standard work *Mysticism: A Study in the Nature and Development of Spiritual Consciousness*.[41] Here she describes in detail the various stages of the mystical way, and the gradual development of the mystic as human being. In successive order she names the phases of awakening, purification, enlightenment (with phenomena such as voices and visions, ecstasy and rapture), the dark night of the soul, and of living in undivided oneness. More recently, the Eastern Orthodox author John Chirban saw the mystical way beginning with the potential of the human being, and progressing further via intention to dedication, purification, enlightenment, and *theosis* or deification.[42] Sin, that traditional stumbling block, seems to play no role of importance in these movements apart from in the purification stage. In Zen Buddhism, the path to enlightenment is traditionally portrayed by a series of ten pictures in which the spiritual seeker is shown discovering a wild ox—symbol of man's true nature—gradually learning to tend it, finally becoming completely one with it. Other traditions proffer different ladders, with different steps. But as Van der Leeuw had written earlier:

> We do not wish to name all the variations which tend to come in stages when classifying the way; they are always different and yet always the same; whether it is a division into seven steps, from contrition through abstinence, renunciation, poverty, patience, faith in God, to fulfilment (Sufi mysticism), or into four steps: dedication, calm and quietude, psychological indifference to incompletely conquered feelings of lust, and physical immobility during psychological decease (Buddhism), or into six: touchement divin, illumination, elevation, union divine, quietude, and, very characteristically, sommeil (Labadie), it is always the way of being and non-being, of the hollow fullness of life to the sublime void of dying in God.[43, 44]

Such an image could be justly regarded as one of the fruits of the psychology of religion: behold the human being in his inner development on the religious way. William James, who fathered the field of study, left no room for doubt whatsoever as to the empirical object of his interest, in *The Varieties of Religious Experience*:

> Religion, therefore, as I now ask you arbitrarily to take it, shall mean for us the feelings, acts, and experiences of individual men in their solitude, so far as they apprehend themselves to stand in relation to what they may consider the divine. Since the relation may be either moral, physical or ritual, it is evident that out of religion in the sense in which we take it, theologies, philosophies, and ecclesiastical organizations may secondarily grow. In these lectures, however, as I have already said, the immediate personal experiences will amply fill our time, and we shall hardly consider theology or ecclesiasticism at all.[45]

A devout man himself, he emphasises once more in his pioneering work:

> I speak not now of your ordinary religious believer, who follows the conventional observances of his country, whether it be Buddhist, Christian or Mohammedan. His religion has been made for him by others, communicated to him by tradition, determined to fixed forms by imitation, and retained by habit. It would profit us little to study this second-hand religious life. We must make search rather for the original experiences which were the pattern-setters to all this mass of suggested feeling and imitated conduct.[46]

In the above-mentioned work James ventured on both higher and lower levels of consciousness, and in the process posed questions, which have yet to be answered, on the relationships between psychopathology and spiritual experience.

13 Fathers of introspection

Whether James, son of a theologian, was the first person in the world to embark on psychological experiments, or whether that honour could be claimed by his European counterpart, the German minister's son Wilhelm Wundt, is less important than the fact that both opened their laboratories to study human experience, doing so directly and from within, through the subject of the experience himself. In their observational tests, moreover, they explored the old problems about the relationship between body and soul in a new, systematic way. On the basis of that pioneering work each produced a hefty tome; Wundt published his *Grundzüge der Physiologischen Psychologie* (Principles of Physiological Psychology) in 1874, comprising 879 pages,[47] and in 1890 James produced *The Principles of Psychology*, all 1200 pages of it.[48] According to estimates Wundt's complete oeuvre amounts to roughly 53,000 pages, yet most of it has never been translated from the German and is thus unknown to the international community.[49] In the meantime scholars have realised that Wundt approached inner experience in an infinitely more sophisticated way than had been supposed for many years. His students and other researchers were strictly trained; he made a fundamental distinction, for example, between sensory or emotional experiences, and the processes of perception and interpretation. He analysed sensory experiences further in terms of mood, quality, intensity and duration, and emotions in terms of pleasant-unpleasant, tense-not tense, and active-passive. Wundt tried in this way to grasp the elementary processes of the inner experience, while continuing to observe the underlying connection. The latter fact prompted his followers after his death to dub his work *Ganzheit psychologie* (Wholeness Psychology). Altogether, the scope of his publications as regards both physical size and content cries out for a chance to breathe new life at last into the study of the psyche. Meanwhile James focused on the mechanism of habit forming, developing a theory that the conditioning process wears 'pathways' in the brain, as organic basis for the mental 'grooves' along which our behaviour is structured. He had a similar dynamic vision of the development of emotional patterns in the individual, and of the whole of human consciousness besides. He saw our way of thinking for example not as an accumulation of separate ideas but as a continuous stream, which he compared to water that is constantly moving and continually merging with streams flowing in from outside. This stream of consciousness also included the vague connections and fleeting intuitions ignored by others, and he further recognised a rhythm in this stream; movements set in motion by external stimuli alternate in this rhythm with rest periods, which set in as soon as we have found a name and significance for something. As richly as he wrote about this subject, and about self-consciousness, will and emotion, so laboriously did *The Principles of Psychology* come into being. After working twelve full years on it, he at last handed the manuscript to his publisher with the words that it was a 'loathsome, distended, tumefied, bloated, dropsical mass, testifying to nothing but two facts: 1st, that there is no such thing as a *science* of psychology, and 2nd, that W. J. is an incapable'.[50]

James' disconcertingly negative self-image no doubt reflected the severe bouts of depression from which he suffered now and then. When he wrote *The Varieties of Religious Experience* years later, it was accordingly as an expert in the dark recesses of consciousness. His interest in religion, or to be more precise, in religious experience, stemmed from his unremitting interest in the complete history of the human being. For James it went without saying that religious experience was the pre-eminent field of research to which psychology ought to devote itself. The *Varieties*, as they are often affectionately called, appeared in 1902 with the subtitle '*A Study in Human Nature*', and form a monument that marked the beginning of the psychology of religion.[51] James compiled this work on the basis of twenty or so lectures delivered in 1901 and 1902 on the invitation of Edinburgh university, under the umbrella of the *Gifford Lectures*, as one of the prominent scientists who had appeared there since 1887. The subject of the readings was given as 'natural religion'. He studied this primarily from within, by examining what occurs in individual consciousness, how this occurs, the ensuing effect; how it influences the way in which someone sees himself and develops, and how he sees the world and deals with that. The phenomena that reached him through this open visor were therefore not restricted to the sort of ecstatic heights that Richard Bucke, following in the steps of countless historical mystics, had marked out—see Chapter 4, 'Perennial philosophy'.[52] Whether the dark side of the soul in this whole subject should come under discussion was beyond question for him; this was part of the religious experience. At the end of the chapter 'The Sick Soul' he included an excerpt from his own life, under a pseudonym:

> Whilst in this state of philosophic pessimism and general depression of spirits about my prospects, I went one evening into a dress-

ing-room in the twilight to procure some article that was there; when suddenly there fell upon me without any warning, just as if it came out of the darkness, a horrible fear of my own existence. Simultaneously there arose in my mind the image of an epileptic patient whom I had seen in the asylum, a black-haired youth with greenish skin, entirely idiotic, who used to sit all day on one of the benches, or rather shelves against the wall, with his knees drawn up against his chin, and the coarse gray undershirt, which was his only garment, drawn over them inclosing his entire figure. He sat there like a sort of sculptured Egyptian cat or Peruvian mummy, moving nothing but his black eyes and looking absolutely non-human. This image and my fear entered into a species of combination with each other. That shape am I, I felt, potentially. Nothing that I possess can defend me against that fate, if the hour for it should strike for me as it struck for him. There was such a horror of him, and such a perception of my own merely momentary discrepancy from him, that it was as if something hitherto solid within my breast gave way entirely, and I became a mass of quivering fear. [...] It was like a revelation; and although the immediate feelings passed away, the experience has made me sympathetic with the morbid feelings of others ever since. It gradually faded, but for months I was unable to go out into the dark alone.

In general I dreaded to be left alone. I remember wondering how other people could live, how I myself had ever lived, so unconscious of that pit of insecurity beneath the surface of life. 'I have always thought that this experience of melancholia of mine had a religious bearing.'[53]

And to clarify that last remark:

I mean that the fear was so invasive and powerful that if I had not clung to scripture-texts like 'The eternal God is my refuge,' etc., 'Come unto me, all ye that labour and are heavy-laden', etc., 'I am the resurrection and the life,' etc., I think I should have grown really insane.[54]

Anyone with even the most rudimentary acquaintance with the writings of St John of the Cross knows that the mystic way is no primrose path. The image of 'the dark night of the soul', personified by him, indicates that a man feeling his way to the light is liable to encounter other remote corners of the inner life. The literary classic the *Divine Comedy* of Dante Alighieri (1265–1321) bears this out, as do the life stories of all authentic seekers and finders. And the great names which speak here from the past — those with pen and paper to hand — did not just go round in ecstatic circles, but ploughed resolutely through their inner mud and barbed wire. Sometimes with the support and advice of others, often with that of sacred texts, but always trusting in the end to their own compass.

It is always easy to talk with hindsight, but on balance it is not so surprising that James' quest met with approbation, but no immediate following. There is at least one methodological and one intrinsic reason why subjective approaches still form a largely underdeveloped area. As regards methodology: throughout his work James employed what he called 'introspection'. He defined this quite simply as 'looking into our own minds and reporting what we there discover'.[55] This prompted Wundt, who at the time passionately but vainly defended his own systematic approach of *Selbstbeobachtung*, to describe the *Varieties* as 'literature'; 'it is beautiful, but it is not psychology'. And indeed, it is interesting to think that Wundt and James gave the kick-off to psychological science by beginning at the very beginning: the closest and most direct individual consciousness, observed moment by moment. However, the necessary instruments for this sort of research still largely had to be invented, and besides, both pioneering approaches were somewhat idiosyncratic, which did not make them easy to reproduce. At that time the objective scientific approach to the psyche was just beginning to build up steam, partly through James' own work, and the subjective opening moves of both scholars were easily swept off the table by the advance of neurology. This latter field produced highly applicable insights which evidently found favour, particularly in pragmatic America. Thus, psychology developed successfully in the course of the century into a form of social statistics, in which we can bombard every human characteristic with a battery of tests. For James, however, the human experience, like a stream of water, could not be split into a perceiving entity and a completely separate experience. Only with reflection on our experiences do concepts come into being, with a certain objectivity; in his view however these by definition cannot possess the originality of the experience itself.

The wintry years of the psychology of religion however did produce a number of surveys that attempted to fathom religious experience beyond the walls of religious institutions. Once more, the point of departure for these was the phenomenon of mysticism. The science of comparative religion by this time had shown that mystical experience is not linked to any specific religious system. Different forms were encountered in different systems, so much so that one could speak of different 'mysticisms'. Now the term 'mystical' is derived from the Greek *muo*, meaning 'to hide', and it is thus related to 'mystery'. For that reason we often find the term used popularly in the sense of enigmatic, shadowy or arcane. It is striking however that in the actual sources the mystical experience itself has absolutely nothing dark, impenetrable or woolly about it. Anything but, it is an outstanding case of complete transparency, in which everything is shown as it essentially is, in its utmost simplicity. On that note, the later discredited church father Clement of Alexandria, who lived around the year AD 200, wrote in a report on the Great Mysteries of the Greek Eleusis, the elaborate annual act of worship in honour of Demeter and her daughter: 'Here all education is at an end, things are seen for what they are; and nature and the nature of things become facts to be understood.'[56] It seems inevitable however that the man in the street would interpret a phenomenon associated with mysteries in more than one way. This is borne out by those few, roughly contemporary surveys carried out among the general population. Through their very rarity they crop up in all sorts of places as a reference—and here too they fulfil this role. In the USA in 1974 two American researchers, the critical Catholic and priest-sociologist, Andrew Greeley and population researcher William McCready, succeeded in incorporating a couple of questions on mystical experiences in a national poll on 'ultimate values'.[57] They did so out of sheer curiosity about the frequency of this phenomenon among the general public, as opposed to the traditional environment of the monastery or convent. To their utter amazement, of the 1500 people interviewed, roughly 600 answered that they had had a mystical experience at least once in their lives, of which 300 several times, and seventy-five often. That implied 36% of Americans.

A comparable score was produced several years later by a British survey, carried out in 1978 by David Hay, a zoologist with an interest in religion, attached to the Religious Experience Research Unit (RERU) at Oxford, and Ann Morisy, a sociologist.[58] They assessed the religious experiences of 1865 individuals, and also carried out in-depth interviews with a random sample of inhabitants of the Nottingham region. This also produced a result of 36%. In both cases this unexpectedly high score caused a fair amount of excitement. Looking back, the pivotal point of this startling conclusion was probably that so many years after Nietzsche had proclaimed the death of God, modern man had not in fact rejected the idea that there is more to existence than what meets the eye. Greeley and McCready published their striking findings in the *New York Times*, among other places, in the article: *Are We a Nation of Mystics?*[59] A good question, apparently, but it has not produced an answer yet, as it seems to have become bogged down at that stage; since then virtually nothing along the lines of this sort of broad-based survey has been done. This, incidentally, is in marked contrast to a certain tradition, mainly in America, of studying the influence of religious belief on physical and mental health—see Chapter 3, 'Risks and faulty measurements'.

Through both their pioneering status and their modest scale the above surveys had such a global character as it was that their conclusions remained vague, and in fact rather gratuitous. Both studies were centred on one question, which served as prelude for a possible specification of frequency and content. The American survey centred on the 'Greeley

Question': 'Have you ever felt as though you were very close to a powerful, spiritual force that seemed to lift you out of yourself?'

The 'Alistair Hardy Question' in the British survey runs as follows: 'Have
you ever been aware of or influenced by a presence or power, whether you
call it God or not, which is different from your everyday world?'

What strikes one in the answers—here too—is the multiplicity of the
reported experiences. This however did not stop the researchers from
lumping them all together in one job lot labelled 'mystical'. In fact, this
move would have largely reflected the prevalent lack of consensus on the
nature of these various experiences, their implications, and how to make
the best use of the terminology. At all events, someone with the authority
of a Teresa of Avila would have insisted on the need for discernment (see
Chapter 3, 'The G-word'). And bearing in mind the profound impact of
the mystical variant of experience in particular, we may start to wonder
how all of those new-found mystics' lives had succeeded in bearing the
fruit of ultimate knowledge, while we remained in collective oblivion
about it. Attempts to provide more clarity in these matters can in fact be
traced back to the end of the nineteenth century, when a small number of
authors started to immerse themselves in the nature of mystical experiences, using various religious, cultural and historical sources. Based on
their findings, Thomas and Cooper used distinct criteria in an authoritative survey of 302 individual reports of the above kind of generic spiritual
experience. They concluded that 2% of these could actually be regarded as
mystical.[60] This finding too has little statistical power, but it does support
James' hypothesis that the mystical experience forms the archetypical
spiritual experience, the 'core experience', of which all other variants are
less complete manifestations. The more we come to know and understand
about these phenomena, the more we can fathom their significance for
mankind. It seems that if we wish to achieve this, we still have a long way
to go to develop the appropriate tools.

14 Risks and faulty measurements

By developing along objective lines, the mainstream of psychology has at
least succeeded in detaching itself from the inherited theological framework. In principle this means that an intrinsic obstacle for future successors to James' agnostic curiosity has been removed from the path. Still, we
need not be surprised that the separation within the psychology of reli-

gion has never been fully realised. True enough, the reputation of the great pioneer rubs off on the present generations of religious psychologists, but judging from much of his inheritors' work his eclectic outlook has not been a dominant trait. The situation recently provoked an eminent Dutch author to wonder bluntly whether anything of importance had happened since 1902.[61] The interweaving of religious themes with the outlook of their traditional guardians, prevalent in those days, is not too difficult to recognise in contemporary studies, albeit in modern guise. To illustrate the sort of smugness which would appal the 'real' scientist, let us choose something from the well-filled quantitative box. Its contents reflect the development over the last decades of methodical testing into merchandise on the world market, parallel to which the 'measurement' of religion and spirituality became a veritable psychological industry. In modern-day tests and questionnaires, we can just about trace James' multicoloured spectrum, now narrowed down to a handful of variables. Yet an even greater problem is that little distinction is made between religion and spirituality. The critical reader can see how the methods used lead to conclusions which leave much to be desired. An example of such a biased measuring instrument is the much used *Spiritual Well-Being Scale*.[62] This was designed, as the title makes clear, to measure the spiritual well-being of individuals. Now the first ten questions of this test concern the subject's experienced closeness to God and his degree of satisfaction with this, while the next ten points are about well-being and general happiness. This makes it obvious that those who enjoy life without a relationship with a personal god emerge on this scale as only half as happy as those who lead a traditional theistic-religious life. And in other ways too, the present-day discipline of psychology of religion can be caught out in a certain evangelistic, or at least theistic complacency. Those who wish to see a plot in this can even find the necessary arguments: financial support for research, the composition of editorial groups and commissions, the nature of research material. With regard to subject matter, it is striking in the American context that the (positive) relationship between religion on the one hand and physical and mental health on the other is given abundant attention. 'Religion' is hereby—probably needless to say—conceived of along conventional, if not fundamentalist, lines. As if the possible relationships between strict dogma and psychological rigidity, between awareness of sin and depression, between belief in Evil and social intolerance were not also interesting, and highly topical, themes. All things considered, it would probably have been unreasonable, even a century ago, to expect anyone to follow James' path of an inspired, humanistic sensitivity to the spiritual potentialities of mankind, and do so under the heading of religion. If we wish nevertheless to proceed further in this field, we shall badly need at least one faculty from the scientific arsenal: the power of discernment. To be able to see the difference between 'healthy' and 'unhealthy' forms of religious feeling, for example; to know, when we measure something, what it is we are measuring; to be clear-sighted about the assumptions that prowl around this complex and delicate terrain; and to make sure that qualitative methods in their way also deliver results that can be deemed accurate.

Qualitative and accurate—can they really go together? In order to approach the subject matter as closely as possible, a researcher must as it were 'get right inside the experience'. The salient discipline concerned with this type of technique is phenomenology. If we label this as the discipline of perception, we can kill two birds with one stone. Discipline—an agreed procedure as well as a practised attitude; perception—attention as well as depth of field. Is this enough for accurate, qualitative research? Phenomenology developed historically from various fields of study: psychoanalysis—in which the first-person perspective at least had a place; existential philosophy—which examined subjective existence; and anti-psychiatry—which emancipated the experienced reality of patients. Sociology has also made various contributions, as has gestalt psychology, which even as a European invention found acceptance in American practice, where it helped to get humanist psychology off the ground. All in all, a many-headed creation, that has survived on the margins of science. It will probably be given another opportunity to develop its own power, because interest in methods of introspection is unmistakably growing. In the same way as the psychiatric context encourages this development, and the vision of old hands such as Rümke and Van der Leeuw is still full of insight for the future—see Chapter 2, 'The subject and the methodology'—James' intrinsic empathy and Wundt's methodological exactness are no less worth dusting off. There is no satisfactory package of methods on hand as yet, but work is being done on that in various places, particularly by representatives of multidisciplinary consciousness research—see Chapter 4, 'Quantum speculations'.

15 Being and non-being

A detailed look at experiences occurring within a religious framework yields a number of essential insights. For one thing, it turns out that there is much to be discovered about the mere concept of 'being' in itself. As earlier stated, the soul, which in the Christian religious tradition automatically takes central place, was abolished by science long ago. Its existence was not necessary to explain how human beings function, and if it existed at all, it would have to be as a 'thing', and that 'thing' was nowhere to be found. On this point the two paradigms are diametrically opposed; the innermost essence of the religious person versus a thing that has no scientific existence. In comparison to eastern traditions, western Christianity in its turn does in fact adopt a 'thing-like' position. Buddhist philosophy for example regards all perceivable 'things' in the end as illusions, with no permanent or autonomous existence. In addition the Buddhist concept of 'emptiness' for the true state of reality is an over-simplified translation of the Sanskrit term *shunyata*. Judging by western concepts *shunyata* does indeed look tremendously empty, but only from the perspective that reality consists of what has been created; of 'things' that exist, and take up space. 'To be' for us accordingly means: to be 'something', to be 'someone'. And if there is no 'something' or 'someone', then that makes for emptiness. But for the Buddhist, 'to be' means: 'to be there', 'to be present', 'to be connected', 'to be everywhere'. Like the nature of space itself. Originally *shunyata* signified a state of 'total openness and pure relationship'.[63] A separate thing such as the soul therefore definitively does not exist. The same applies to the existence of God. As a theistic religion, of course, Christianity is centred on God, and in everyday practice — and also quite far beyond that — God figures as a 'someone', a personality; a bit like a human being, but different. Admittedly the official doctrine makes a distinction between the respective members of the Blessed Trinity — the Father, Son and Holy Spirit — but they are explicitly named 'persons'. All the same, we mainly opt for God as one entity and one personality, and in common parlance we attribute certain qualities to him: of the male gender, loving, all-seeing, almighty, sometimes compassionate, sometimes vengeful, strict but just, etcetera. And often when we banish our anthropomorphic images of the Supreme Being, that same old beard is quick to show up, even when we're busy pointing out that it is no longer in the picture. Now according to the accounts, during the mystical experience the human being — as soul — is absorbed into God: through this it becomes one with God, and itself divine. But in that case, what about the category of holiness which is God's exclusive domain? How can a human being, who is so essentially different, achieve equality with God? From a Buddhist perspective, he can't, at least as long as soul and God are two separate 'objects' — two billiard balls. Now for a long time, scientists regarded matter at the simplest level as consisting of hard atoms. Then on closer inspection — quite literally — atoms turned out to be infinitely 'empty': they revealed themselves as wide open space. This space then turned out to be full of 'vibration', and later on it was discovered that this emanated from an omnipresent potential. And yet the discovery of this space does not undermine the reality of the billiard balls, because at their own level these continue to do what they were already doing. At the same time, we can no longer extrapolate them to the subatomic scale; the reality of space, vibration and potential which characterises that level, applies permanently. It applies even if it reveals itself explicitly only in certain conditions, which can be stage-managed. Something similar probably applies in the spiritual dimension. The believer functions as a separate object, with relationships to all other possible objects, and these also include a divine entity. These things however do not rule out the fact that in essence, at a deeper level, they probably consist of the same 'material', of space, vibration and potential.

In Buddhism, questions about the soul and God do not exist. The human being differs in no respect from the Buddha nature, and as a spiritual traveller one learns to recognise this in oneself. At the same time the fundamental connection with all other phenomena gradually reveals itself. Now, since the middle of the last century a strong bond has been established between contemplative Catholics on the one hand and Zen Buddhists, mainly from Japan, on the other. Each side immerses itself in the other's theory and practice, and this appears to be productive for both parties. It is agreed that both traditions form an authentic way to the ultimate secret of existence. And yet the differences are enormous. How can we explain that? The Flemish Ruysbroeck scholar and Jesuit, Paul Mommaers (b. 1935) focused on this problem, together with a compatriot, the theologian Jan van Bragt (b. 1928), who taught for many years at the university of Nagoya and still lives in Japan. In this context they point out that the west is only familiar with an atypical 'cut flower' of Buddhism.[64] After all, the general public's acquaintance with Buddhism only began after the Second World War with the emigration of a number of Japanese Zen masters to America, and by now we are accordingly more familiar with what is after all the most formal and radical movement within Buddhism. Its doctrine is represented here by monks who live in monasteries cut off from everyday life, and who by definition regard all everyday human phenomena—worries, memories, fears, desires, preferences, ambitions, surprises, disappointments etcetera—as irrelevant. All personal attachment to earthly things, and every expression of personal differentiation is regarded within their framework as *samsara*,[65] an obstacle on the way to nirvana. A personal God, or a relationship with Him—the very idea! A sort of blasphemy, and proof of ignorance. That this strict variant of Buddhism, spiced with a historical cult of swashbuckling samurai, and under the pressure of political changes, could also lead to shockingly morbid ideological growths, was shown by Brian Victoria's book *Zen at War*, published in 1997. In the dark years of the twentieth century the formidably no-nonsense spirit of Zen entered into the service of an arrogant, militaristic nationalism, and was one of the inspirations for Japanese war ambitions.[66]

Nevertheless, the 'ordinary people' in Buddhist countries have a different place in the tradition. Zazen, the traditional meditation, is practised mainly in monasteries, while the 'ordinary' lay Buddhist performs rituals, honours his ancestors, worships 'Lord Buddha' and the various families of bodhisattvas, sacrifices to their images and seeks support for his everyday problems in the temple, just as 'ordinary' Christians are encouraged to practice their faith: through a personal relationship to a divine figure. Mommaers and Van Bragt suggest accordingly that Zen Buddhism is not vitally human enough at a mystical level — too much ethereal detachment and formlessness, too little soul. In the domain of the daily shopping, without which there would actually be little monastery life, people simply function as personalities, who have lives to live. What they are taught about the true state of affairs — *shunyata* — does not necessarily harmonise with this. But the Zen Buddhist who does not arise from the one Absolute as a man of flesh and blood, takes no part in the experience of a life in the world as a person, who after a stiff climb feels exaltation at the view, who knows the depth of heartfelt sorrow at the death of a loved one, and the immanence of a fit of the giggles with a group of friends, should it so happen. In their turn, ordinary believers in Christianity learn that salvation and blessing await them, because they are God's children and made in His image. In practice, however, in the sublunary world, they are regarded as made of (sinful) flesh, which they will never completely transcend. They can pray and do good all they like, but they will never achieve more than the forgiveness of their sins: holiness is 'other'. The Christian who hangs on to her self-image as an autonomous soul who can never be good enough, can therefore never be truly God-like, even though the divine fire burns in her heart and the living light opens her eyes. And at the moment that this self-image gives way after all, and the believer is prompted to testify: I am the truth, God is no other than I — then the break with tradition has occurred. The present-day advance of charismatic movements presumably make it possible after all to take part in the divine without a middleman, as in Biblical times. An image of Christendom then arises that reveals a three-fold path of personal relationship: through the Roman Catholic church with the Father, through the Protestant church with the Son, and through the charismatic movement with the Holy Spirit. Perhaps western man has satisfied his hunger for transcendence by first departing from the accepted religious frameworks, and now finds himself, secularised in a technical sense, refocusing on the original, universal, eternal, single creative principle: the 'something' that has appeared once more between heaven and earth.

Theo (1961)

I wasn't brought up in a religious way; nor as an atheist either, really, that means actively not believing, my parents just didn't believe anything. I was a bit nihilistic as a teenager, I read Willem Frederik Hermans and he said that the world had no meaning, because the world was out there on its own, and anything that has meaning always has meaning for something else.[1] The world is pointless, I thought that was fantastic, so you see, I was really negative. At one time I shared a flat with my brother; I was about twenty-two, I reckon, he's a year older. He'd discovered Krishnamurti and urged me to try it, after all, I could always reconsider. I said I was afraid of talking myself into all sorts of illusions, only to discover at the end of my life that Hermans had been right all along. But one day I tried it anyway, and I changed my mind straight away. I started reading the *Tao te Ching* and all sorts of spiritual books.[2] It had to do with the gestalt therapy I was having. I was a very rational teenager, but that therapy put me in close touch with my feelings. And that also made me open to spirituality. The therapist had the *Tao te Ching* lying around, I believe, and I bought a copy for myself. I could see the wisdom in it straight away, and it took off from there. I saw that a lot of these books talked about the universe, or the universal spirit, or the universal will and so on. New age beliefs usually avoid using the word 'God', because of its associations with our Christian tradition. I discovered that new age as a movement — apart from a whole lot of eyewash that comes along with it — is in fact searching for ancient, esoteric wisdom, for timeless truths. Which it then presents in a new form. But to me it was clear: what they mean is God. And I had no problem with that because I wasn't brought up that way. I could take it on board without all the old connotations. After a while I accepted that there were such things as chakras, and auras, and I could well believe in the existence of angels, so there was plenty of room for God.[3]

At one point my brother became psychotic. I found it dreadful. I felt tremendous compassion for him, and I was afraid of going mad myself. It also had to do with what he was reading. In a way he'd always had it in him, as a child he was almost autistic, pretty withdrawn. He'd been interested in spiritual things from an early age, and he wanted to put the world to rights. My father was a very down-to-earth man, he said, 'In that case you'd do better to study economy rather than theology, because economy makes the world go round.' My brother had a lot of faith in my father so he went and studied economy, but he didn't like it and then he started reading Krishnamurti. That prompted him to claim his freedom, so he dropped out of college. He was home a lot after that and started throwing the *I Ching*, and at one point he started having delusions of reference.[4] When you throw the *I Ching* you assume the existence of meaningful chance, because you're asking a higher source for an answer. The answer comes, but because your ego gets in the way you can't be sure whether you're hearing the source properly. So you use a personal medium such as the *I Ching*, which assumes that it's not a matter of chance. And my brother applied the *I Ching* texts to himself. Which is the whole idea, of course, but he took it further and further and further, and at one point he just flipped. I think that was partly to do with a heavy load of repressed emotions and problems caused by the way we were brought up, and partly because he was trying to develop spiritually too early. It always makes me think of that song by Pink Floyd: '*You reached for the secret too soon*', they sing somewhere. And they say that someone who becomes enlightened ends up in the same ocean as the psychotic, but that one swims while the other drowns.

I had a breakthrough myself in a workshop run by Paul Solomon, a spiritual teacher from America. It really got through to me, and it was to be a turning point. His philosophy was that in the end there are only two forces, two sources that everything comes from, namely fear and love, and that all negative emotions come from fear, and all the positive ones from love. I was deeply affected by it. He also said that if love wells up inside you, fear comes along with it, because it puts up resistance. But love wins because in the end fear doesn't really exist. He compared love with light and fear with darkness, and darkness is the absence of light, but it isn't something that exists independently. If you shine a light in the darkness, you see that it isn't there. And while he was saying all this, the very thing he was describing happened to me. I felt love welling up inside me, literally from the base of my spine. And it felt like a ball, a sort of fireball with enormous force, which I felt was greater than I was, greater than I could control. Something like life itself. An enormous energy welled up, but out of a sort of trust in him I let it all happen, and it literally welled up inside me. And true enough, somewhere around my chest there was a sort of turning point, then the fear fell away and I reached the very centre of my heart. That lasted for one and a half days. My whole way of seeing things was changed. I saw the world differently. Not in the sense of seeing different things, and there was nothing crazy about it, it was nothing but good. I had a much more benign way of seeing things. I felt completely connected, I found everyone I met really kind and likeable, things were more friendly, I was also really grateful for everything. That was very strong. When I came home from the workshop and went to bed, I felt tremendously safe. I was grateful for the wood my bed was made of; I could see God in everything, I think. It slowly faded away, and all in all it was a good experience.

One of the things that Solomon mentioned now and then was *A Course in Miracles.*[5] Some time later I saw it in a bookshop, and it appealed to me because it talked about healing your brother. The *Course in Miracles* uses very Christian terminology, terms like Holy Spirit, Son of God, Christ, your brothers and so on, but it's really radical philosophy, not like the Bible. Because of our Christian heritage we have all sorts of unconscious associations with them, but if you keep on reading, they acquire different meanings. But 'heal your brother', I took that quite literally. It made me think of my brother straight away, and I thought: if I succeed in this, I can pull him through it. Something like that. He was in a mental home by this stage. I'd just gone through a difficult period myself at the time. I had my problems with the past in any case, but I was also having trouble at work. I'd built up a very good career as a journalist, working for several magazines, then I was asked to become editor of a magazine. I was flattered and wanted to live up to expectations, but I was actually too young for that, I just couldn't manage it. So I failed and they sacked me. After that I started doing temporary work through an agency for a while, that gave me some freedom, which I really craved, but it was barely enough to pay my mortgage. That's when I discovered *budo*, that's a collective name for Japanese fighting sports: judo, karate, taekwondo and so on. You can take it up just for the throws and exercises and so on, but it's also a spiritual path, an active meditation. I got to know a guy who was a *budo* teacher. He was tremendously inspired and also very inspiring, and I was deeply impressed by him. He was looking for space for a *dojo* but he had no money, and it sounds crazy, but I offered him my downstairs flat.[6] It had a nice wooden floor, and it was already painted white and everything, and I went and lived upstairs. But after a while we didn't get on so well, and then I was left with the feeling that I had an interloper in the house. I had trouble getting him out, but I managed in the end, because the neighbours complained about the noise, but I felt a bit humiliated, and a bit of a sucker for letting somebody else live in my house. When he left I'd just bought the *Course in Miracles.* And I had a new job that I liked, and then I decided to do the course in earnest.

When I was younger I'd also had problems with addiction. Between the ages of nineteen and twenty-five I'd been addicted to cannabis, and I'd got over that by going to the CAD.[7] Actually they didn't help me at all, in those days it was seen as harmless and not recognised as an addiction. I felt that it would be stupid to ask for help and keep on using the stuff, so I stopped, just through going there. But what I did do was drink, for comfort, for something to hold onto, it took the rough edges off my mind. So I'd drink four or five beers every night, never during the day; that would get me off to sleep. And when I started doing that course, it felt so good that I stopped drinking, which was quite a step for me.

Paul Solomon had said to me, 'Don't do that course on your own,' but I brushed it aside. I couldn't imagine how else I could do it, anyway, it's quite a book. It consists of a philosophical section of about 600 pages, which explains the whole system of belief, and a work book with 365 exercises. I started with the work book, and from the very first exercise I found it fantastic. They're ideas that you repeat quietly to yourself, and I'd sit there on my mat every morning, meditating on one of these exercises. In between times I'd read the text. For me, it was a real tower of strength, having that course. It just gave me safety, security, support. It really was like that. I had really beautiful religious experiences and I started seeing a sort of light around things, just by doing those exercises. So it had a really powerful effect on me. On the one hand it did me a tremendous amount of good and proved that it's true, that God is real, and that you can turn to God; you can make that choice and that will bring peace. I experienced it myself. On the other hand I went about it the wrong way, because I also used it as an escape. And I used the exercises to get rid of all kinds of unpleasant feelings. One of these exercises for example is: God is in everything I see. Or: God is in everything I see, because God is in my soul. Forgiveness gives me everything I want. Forgiveness is the key to happiness. I don't need anything but the truth. So you repeat one of those thoughts to yourself, every morning and every evening, first for less than a minute and later on for five minutes. But I used to do it for a lot longer than that, I became really obsessive about it.

In the book it talks about God and the Son of God, they're a single entity. There's no point where one stops and the other begins. The only difference is that God is the creator and God's Son is the creation. God is something like ever-expanding love. And the original situation is one of knowledge, but beyond perception. So there's nobody who thinks: God is there and I am here. There's no subject and object, it's a state of knowledge, of unity, of being. And it takes place beyond time, but if for the sake of convenience you want to place it in time, you could say that we used to be one with God, and then we lost it. Because according to the story, it all went wrong because the Son thought that he wanted something impossible, or had trouble with the fact that God had created him and not the other way round, something like that. Anyway, he did something that created guilt, arising from the idea that he had turned his back on love. That guilt is then projected, and that gives rise to an ego, a separate 'I', that feels guilty and expects God to punish it. Separation. And that separation went further and further and further, but essentially it never took place. It was all one big dream. It's a tremendous hallucination, a guilt trip. So in essence we all have the same identity, that's Christ, but we identify with our ego and that makes us feel cut off. So the way back is to see that and to realise that you're one with other people. And the way to that is forgiveness, because we're burdened with a huge amount of guilt because of the separation, and we project it outside of ourselves. But in fact you forgive yourself, and the more you forgive, the more you can accept your own innocence. And so you come back again.

So I was constantly learning: I can identify with my ego or I can listen to the Holy Spirit. The Holy Spirit is God's answer to that separation, it was an immediate response. It's something like the bridge to God, it's also called the voice of God, something that reminds you of your origin. I experienced how it all worked, I often felt very moved and grateful and felt a lot of love for people. So much so that if someone came to see me, they disrupted the contact I had with them before they came! Because that person would be in his ego-identification stage, and come with all sorts of mundane chat, while just previously I'd maybe felt connected to him at a very high level. Crazy things like that. I used to get confused as well, because I knew the feeling was right, but I was sitting there judging the world. It was very tricky, I was afraid of losing my serenity, because when I did my exercises properly, I felt tremendously serene. Besides which I suffered a lot from guilt feelings, all the time, that was also my main motivation for going to work. I wouldn't feel safe if I didn't do it. And by doing exercises like that I gained such a strong realisation of innocence that my motivation for going to work faded away. Because I realised that I only did it in order to do the right thing. But now I had such a strong sense of my right to exist, I felt happy and at peace and I felt continually so loved by God that I no longer needed any confirmation from the world. And I often got to work much too late. And there I was, faithfully doing my exercises, I used to go to the toilet once an hour to do them. I remember doing the exercise 'God is in everything I see', and looking at a tile and realising: God is in that tile. And because I thought it with so much respect and took it so seriously, I became more and more serene and suddenly my hand reached out to the tile. And when I touched it, the tears spurted out of my eyes! There was such an enormous amount of love, and it made sense, it wasn't madness, because that's how it is, God is in everything. You can ignore that or you can grasp it.

So I had really beautiful experiences, and especially a lot of gratitude, and there was a period when I saw the forgiven world, as it's called in the course. I was walking through a really pleasant town and saw the lights in a different way; my perception had changed because the guilt had vanished from everything. So that all made sense in theory, but I handled it in a peculiar way. Because at the same time I used these exercises to affirm my feelings of anxiety and discontent out of existence. I thought that was the whole idea, in fact, because every morning you began straight away with the thought for the day. And when I woke up, I usually felt really awful, with a ball of guilt and anxiety in my belly, so I'd start to affirm it out of existence. And that made sense in some ways, because then I'd snap out of it and feel happy again, but I made an increasingly strong distinction between the perfect peace of God and my consciousness of my own innocence and a friendly world and everything in order on the one hand, and that anxiety and guilt on the other. And I started feeling it more and more strongly. What Paul Solomon had talked about, love or fear, I could see nothing in between, while at the same time I felt more and more that I owed it to Jesus, as the author of the book, to become enlightened, to make it. Because it became more and more clear: there's nothing wrong, no separation ever took place. So there's no such thing as sin and guilt. You learn to read the story of the crucifixion, for example: he rose again and went on living, for we're not our bodies. In this way Jesus showed us: you cannot kill me. But I began to feel guilty about my lack of faith, because although by now I knew it all so well and received all that love, I still sided with my own ego. So I wanted to get rid of that ego. And I thought, if I was enlightened I could help people.

In the end it all went wrong when I did a particular exercise *'in my defencelessness my safety lies'*. That had a tremendously strong effect on me. I was sitting on the sofa one evening and I was becoming more and more tranquil by repeating the exercise, and it worked. I let my defences down, the everyday defences you walk around with. And sure enough, nothing but love came flowing in. As soon as you start to feel that, you let go of things more easily, and so I arrived at total serenity. A really profound peace. And I kept on slowly thinking the exercise. I felt that I didn't have to protect or arm myself against anything, and because this peace became deeper and deeper and my soul became more and more serene, I began as it were to see my soul. I began to see that there was a core somewhere where thoughts still came trickling out. As if I was being shown that ego. And I saw: this is what keeps me separate. And driven by a feeling of being under an obligation, or the idea that this would be a way of showing my loyalty or something, I opened up completely. I still get frightened when I think about it, because I then felt something crack open on top of my head, and a really horrible .... ugh ... I felt my fontanel open, and the room was filled with a blinding light. Pssst, just like that, and I thought of the course, because it mentions a *blazing light* when the moment comes. I was scared to death. So much light, everything white with light, the whole room. I was scared to death and went out running, to distract myself, and it kept on coming, and I felt such a pressure here on top. That's where the pituitary gland is, under your crown, and it almost hurt because there was so much light. I just didn't know what to do any more, and sometimes I thought, now you're resisting, now you're siding with the ego, and it's probably happening now so just grin and bear it, but you haven't got the guts for that. That was the mad thing about it. But because I couldn't see a way out, I thought, I'll just have to give in to it. So I sat down again and that light came back again. Because as soon as I relaxed all that light came back. And I thought, that makes sense, because the exercises mention this relaxation, and I was resisting it, so I thought, I need to relax again. But every time I relaxed all that light came flooding back, and in the end it simply made my head ache! So then I felt: this can't be right! So that was an enormous conflict. I ran into the street thinking, this body, I have to ground myself, I have to go running. And there on the street I finally realised that I had flipped, because I started reading advertising slogans on billboards and thinking they were all about me. All through that despair. It was so bad, I was just craving for help. Then I bought some beer and started drinking, I thought, I have to do all the earthly things. Somehow or other I got to sleep later that night. And as soon as I woke up, I started doing the next exercise. It was that deeply rooted. I still found it too difficult to quit doing the course altogether, I wasn't ready for that. And then it started coming from down below, the kundalini came back, but it all went wrong. I was really frightened, I was in shock as well. I had trouble just letting it happen, it took over my whole body, because it's such a superior force. So it went wrong from two sides.

A friend of mine sensed the next morning that there was something wrong, he rang up and then came to collect me. He and his wife helped me, but my struggle went on there as well. I withdrew a couple of times, with the idea, I'll just let it happen. But at one stage the pain became so intense that I decided: there's something wrong here, I mustn't let this happen. That's how bad it had to get. So I sided with my own ego, which meant the whole course was for nothing, because I knew that the light would come back otherwise. So I couldn't be doing with God and spirituality for a while, it wasn't healthy for me at that time. That also destroyed the security I'd had. And I had to ground myself, and go running and eat meat, everything, I was desperate to ground myself. After two weeks my friends decided, it's time for you to go home now, you're a bit better and you need to learn that you can cope. That was a good thing, and then I started working like mad and distracting myself. For a long time I'd work late into the night, just to find some distraction and to justify my existence again. Very gradually I was able to relax into it. For a long time I was afraid that the top of my head would burst open again. But it was only after I married that I was healed even more, because there was an inner child inside me that was miserable. All that security, all that love of God, suddenly it didn't exist any more. And there I was, saddled with a crying child, scared out of its wits. But with her, another person, that side of me could open up again, and so recover.

I considered getting professional help, but I didn't know how. I thought, you've got two worlds: the normal world where I'm regarded as mad, and where people don't understand that other bit, and the spiritual world, where they're too much under the sway of enlightenment to understand that you might actually be afraid of that. And that it's not always the right time for enlightenment. That's why I didn't dare to call on Paul Solomon again. What I needed then was some sort of institution that understood what was happening, but I didn't know of any. At the time that I flipped, I was training as a gestalt therapist, but I no longer fitted in there either. And they didn't do much for me there either, it was beyond their powers.

A long time afterwards I took up the course again. I'd always had the feeling I ought to do it sometime. That's the odd thing, I have every reason to be scared to death of it, but at the same time I know that it's love, and it's not the course that caused it, I caused it myself through my weird ideas about it. That was ten years later. I'd written a children's book based on the course, though, and I had to give a talk on it in a spiritual centre here in town. There were some people there who'd formed a group to follow the course, and they invited me to join. So I thought, maybe that would be all right, not much can go wrong in a group like that. From there I formed a new group with two other people, and it's still going strong. With completely new people, that's true, but the group has continued, and that's a tremendous help. It makes everything more easy-going and less strict. You learn a lot. We meet every week or fortnight, we read the text and discuss it, and besides that everyone brings their own themes and the things that are bothering them, relationship problems or whatever. So we sort of look at those in the light of the course. That works really well. I sort of lead it in a practical sense, by saying a prayer at the beginning, and doing some rituals during the meeting, but in fact everything happens of its own accord. When I work with someone else it all takes a bit longer, and of course we explain things a bit more to new people.

I also started using the handbook again, but in a much more easy-going way. I have a family now, there are continual distractions, and then you automatically shoot back into your ego because someone irritates you, or you get angry or stressed, that's just how things are. During that last period I could stay right out of the storm, but if you're out of the storm, it's easy. Among other people, in the world, that's where the real teaching material is, of course. Having grievances against your wife and child, and forgiving them. I decided to take two years to do the handbook, and if it didn't feel right, I'd stop. I was a bit less intense about it as well, and it all went fine. It was a bit scary when I got to that particular exercise, but I got through that as well.

What I learned from that episode is that you have to do things gradually on this path. The whole path is tricky. Even if you believe that you've found the truth, even if the course is the whole truth, it still doesn't mean that everyone has to do it. If there is a God, he is loving enough to think, maybe it would be better if this person didn't believe in me, and that person did. And you don't have to believe in God in order to grow. I still believe that it's a good path, and in the end there's no other way than the spiritual way, the religious way, but you have to do it properly. I used to condemn myself for having an ego, while the whole point is that there's nothing wrong with that. I thought I had to go away in order to come back to God. But it's precisely that little bundle of misery that finds it so hard to get through life that needs love. In the book it says that if you approach God out of love, you'll kindle nothing but love. But if you're stuck in your ego, or in fear, and you still come face to face with God, it arouses panic! That's all it says about it in the book. I know what went wrong, I forced something. And I ended up somewhere I wasn't ready for, I was a toddler at university.

I think that I was psychotic during that time, but I don't know for certain. Psychotic is the word I use for when it goes really wrong, and in a certain way I was mad. I remember looking at a hedge and seeing the face of Christ in it. Something that wasn't there, just a figment of my imagination, but not a very pleasant one, no, that was terrifying. Not to mention all that kundalini that was racing through me. I walked down the street and it felt as if my leg had given way beneath me. It really was a different world. That idea about the ocean, that mystics and psychotics are both in the same one, I could well imagine that, but I just don't know that much about it. My brother became psychotic during a spiritual quest, but maybe other people become psychotic for quite different reasons. It seems to me like a further step in separation, in that idea of separate people, of separate bodies that have nothing to do with each other. Like splitting the smallest atom even further. Perhaps it's also an escape, when there's too much emotional pain that you don't want to feel. Sometimes you have to go and confront your own existential pain, without stepping aside. And perhaps a psychotic is someone with his back to the wall, facing all his misery, who then starts fantasising that there's a door in the wall that he can get through.

I've got no problem as such with the fact that the world is often cynical about spirituality. I have my fears, and to some extent they're justified! But there should be something like an institution that knows about these things, somewhere you can go. I think it would be a huge spiritual under-taking in itself to set something like that up, something that takes time, but really important, because so many people are searching for it. And actually everyone ought to know anyway that you can flip along the way, and that it might be better to do it gradually.

I married the woman whose house I stayed in for those two weeks. So she and her ex-husband know about my crisis, but my parents only know the basic fact that I flipped while doing that course. They were worried enough as it was, they thought it was dangerous, going about it as obses-sively as I was doing. I've mentioned it in the course group as well, a bit at a time, and I've told some friends. And my brother. He gets almost angry at books like that, he gets angry about gurus who present us with all sorts of wonderful religious paths that can make you flip. He had a really bad time at first. He's officially paranoid-schizophrenic, has always been under heavy medication, has also made suicide attempts. He hanged him-self and the rope broke, he tried to buy a pistol in Belgium, and lots more attempts besides. Very gradually things improved, which was actually all his own doing. At first it was dreadful to see how different he is from how he used to be. Now he's actually doing very well, partly through some new medication. He's also gained quite a lot of wisdom, now and then I'm impressed by what he says, but some of his ideas don't make sense. After dithering for ages he bought another copy of the I Ching, he was afraid of that of course, that was how the delusion of reference began. One day he was leafing through it in a shop and read: ten horses cannot hold him back. So he bought it! He lived in a commune at first but now he's living on his own in a sort of sheltered project. He watches a lot of MTV, uses the computer, throws the I Ching, lays tarot cards, reads spiritual books, he goes to the odd lecture, and visits our parents now and then. He does very little, is very sensitive to stress, but he enjoys life now. My most loving relationship is with him. I love him to bits. During the time that every-thing was going so badly I felt a tremendous amount of sorrow and com-passion, and did exercises. I feel really good as well when I'm with him. I only told him about my experiences very recently, it would have been too much for him at that time. For a while I was afraid of going mad again myself. I also used to obsess about contamination, I'd wash my hands after contact with him, when I was going through a very sensitive period. I used to sense something hanging over him, maybe that was a delusion, but it's all very different now. It's in this relationship that I feel the most love, and the purest. There's very little distance.

The most help and support came from my marriage, in the first place, that's the most important thing to me. It gives me security, it gives me safety, it gives me normality, I think I've got a very normal wife! Very grounded and very loving. My daughter, and having a family, that's also support. And I've got a good job again. I was a freelancer for a long time, you do everything on your own at home, and now I work for a really normal magazine in a really friendly editorial team, that really helps. And so does the course group. So what happened, that's really in the past.

I'm not afraid of death, just of dying. For me that's the point at which you confront everything that you haven't dealt with. And the more you're at peace with yourself, the better your deathbed probably is. So I wouldn't have a very good deathbed at the moment, not yet! Of course it's the ego that dies, and that wants to keep control. If that's attacked, it feels literally life-threatening, simply because you identify with that. And that's what happened to me. I think that an enlightened person is someone who has died in that sense before his death. You need a tremendous amount of surrender and courage to die anyway. I do think that after the ego there comes a state of oneness with everything, but it's no longer personal. And that is love.

I'm open to other sorts of spirituality, but it's all about the same truth after all, and you choose the form that suits you best. I wear a cross around my neck, people associate that with all sorts of Catholic things, but that's not what it means to me. Hardly anyone around me is religious, but I had a need to stand up for my faith. Also felt a bit embarrassed about wearing a cross like that, then my wife gave me one as a present. It touches me to say that now, and that makes me realise once again how important she is to me. The personal love between two people, that's so important. As a spiritual seeker you're concerned with abstract love, of course, vertical contact, not horizontal. But it was my wife who saved me. That's what it comes down to. She's not so interested in spirituality herself, but she understood me at the time. It's not the intellect that understands these things, it's love.

Leonor (1957)

As a child I had very early memories of lying in bed as a toddler and inde-
scribable images coming into my mind between waking and sleeping.
That really frightened me, but it fascinated me as well. There were two
kinds of images, something that evoked a really unpleasant feeling, a
dreadful loneliness, with shifting flesh-coloured images. When I experienced this as a child, I knew that it was something from the past. But there
was also something really beautiful, I can't really describe it, but a sort of
veil came over me covered with all sorts of really lovely sparkling things,
and there was a sound that went with it. That evoked a really pleasant
feeling. And as a toddler I knew that that was a memory as well, one that
went back further than the other one. Later on when I was pregnant I
could place it. I interpret those lovely experiences as memories of my own
time in the womb, and the others as around the time of my birth. All
purely intuitively. But it raised questions in my mind at an early age. I
didn't have any answers to these, because I grew up in a very atheistic
family. Father was Catholic, mother was Protestant, there were objections
to the marriage, the usual story, and then you get a very defensive attitude. Faith was for the ignorant, that's what was always dinned into me.
So I always kept that sort of question very much to myself.

I just went on exploring it, and then one day I met my husband. He was
Catholic and he didn't bother about his faith much, but he thought it would
be nice if I was Catholic too. Some time later I met a Jesuit and I used to have
discussions with him, nothing to do with religion at all, but about a portrait
of Teresa of Avila on the wall, for example. About what we saw in it, that
sort of thing. And because I recognised that religious feeling was something I'd had all my life, I became a Catholic. But when I went to church I
was put off immediately because honestly, the stuff I heard from the pulpit,
that didn't appeal to me, it was so dogmatic. That's why I kept on searching, and then one day I came across Jung's views on eastern religions. And
that appealed to me enormously, I recognised my own way of thinking in
it. I always used to think, that world is so foreign to me, and then it turned
out to be a whole perception of the world according to eastern religions. I
started to go into it further, Taoism, Buddhism, all very intellectual. All
very intuitively linked, but not in the sense of: I'll take up a religion,
because religion itself, with all those rules and regulations, that's just not

for me. Then one day I had a dream that I still remember vividly. I dreamt that I was an old man in some sort of primitive village, and I was being carried out of the village on a bier because I was going to die. And I could see the people around me, brown, very healthy people, all with long, shoulder-length black hair — really weird, all those details. I could see the village with all these thatched roofs, and rolling hills covered with grass that swayed in the wind, with trees dotted here and there. I was actually saying farewell, and I was thinking of the ritual that was about to take place. Outside the village they laid the bier on the grass, and everyone sat around it. And I felt the grass with my hands — I can still feel it — and the grains of sand between it, the roughness of the grass, and suddenly my arms seemed to have merged with the whole world. It was an experience of oneness, oneness with the grass, with everything I saw. Then I lifted up my hands again, towards the people who sat behind me, and I felt an enormous kinship with them, with all humanity, with everything around me. It made no difference whether you were close or not. As if death were no separation; it's difficult to put into words, because it's interpreting what you experience. Suddenly a veil fell over my hands, and then there was a sort of feeling of completion. Then I knew, now that moment is coming; that is what they always said in that community. You had to put your hands above your head, and then you would be taken up into the other world. There was a moment of fear, because okay, I'd always heard it said, but I didn't know if it would really happen. But after a while I put my arms above my head anyway and then, much sooner than I had expected, there was suddenly a tremendous light, a tremendous heat and my hands were grasped, and then everything faded away ... Everything was absorbed into that light. And then I woke up.

That dream has always stayed with me, and it brought about a certain shift in my life. I could also see the similarity to mystical experiences I'd read about, and that made me a more self-assured person. No longer afraid of death or whatever. But at the same time I had the feeling: I cannot do anything with this. That made me feel very isolated. It was years before I told anyone about it. I went on studying on my own, read an awful lot, and then I began to write as well, for my own pleasure, I enjoyed doing that. At first I didn't dare show it to a soul, but then I entered a competition, and I won. And that had to do with that experience. Some time later we got a new parish priest here and he was open to everything, and I thought, there must be a place for me as well, then. At the same time someone asked me to write a play for the church, and so I got involved with the parish, and I found it a very open community. Next I did a two-year course on exploring your faith, given by a Dominican, it was all very open and to me it was like coming home. On one occasion we were discussing the story of Solomon, who received a command from God in a dream.[1] The general attitude was that it was very noble of Solomon to have responded to the dream, to have taken that decision. But as usual I was the odd one out who said: if you have a dream like that there's simply nothing else you *can* do! And suddenly the two course leaders turned to me—that moment is engraved in my memory—and said, 'It was only a *dream*!' And at that point something snapped. I had a flash-back of my own dream. I burst into tears and walked out; they actually thought I was moved by the music!

I cried for days after that, and sat at the computer trying to write it out of my system. That dream had given me such insight, such a reason for living, I couldn't let go of it. I could only place it outside of my self a little, to get it down on paper. I got very little sleep, I hardly functioned at all, and I felt myself going stark raving mad! I thought, this must be lunacy! I'd always been a rational sort of person, I could not place it at all, I thought, am I becoming a religious maniac or what? It made me think of people with those hallelujah experiences, with their 'Look at me!' attitudes. I didn't want to be seen like that. So it was very isolating. Eventually the tears stopped. I explained it away in the group, but I naturally felt let down. Some time later we were discussing the meaning of the word God, and everyone started coming out with really emotional stories, so I just told them about that dream of mine, I didn't care any more. Once again I got into a state, but this Jesuit handled it really well. He said, 'What you describe, I have experienced something a bit like that.' He went on to describe one of those light experiences, also very personal, which gave me a bit of affirmation. Books alone don't take you very far, there comes a time when you need another human being. Of course the usual reaction is: nice story, you should do something with that—along those lines. That's what the rest of the group said as well: nice. Enough to drive you mad! Later on he took me aside and said, 'Don't talk about it, just let it be.' That was a terrific moment for me, I was glad that I'd mentioned it after all. But it was good advice all the same. You have to let it grow within you, you should allow it to find expression in your way of life, rather than run around telling everyone about it. He also made it clear that I could talk to him about it if I wanted, but I had the impression that he didn't really want to. It was a camouflaged sort of affirmation. And maybe I was too shy about it, but I didn't do it again at any rate. So I continued to search for that; for other people with these experiences.

I went further into eastern religions on my own initiative, and then took up meditation in order to get away from the books. First the Japanese form, Zen meditation; that also gave me a bit of affirmation. My teacher really concentrated on the form, on learning to sit. From the first session that went really well, quite literally: it sat well with me straight away! Later I realised: yes, but I am not a complete beginner, meditation is something I have been doing all my life. From the time I lay in bed as a child and drifted into that in-between state of consciousness, and tried to concentrate, to combat my fears. That was actually meditation. When the lessons came to an end I did it at home on my own at first, but later I felt the need of some supervision after all. Two of my children were keen on karate, and their teacher was really inspiring, it was very much a way of life. I started doing Tibetan meditation with him, and that did me good straight away, to experience some input from other people again. And once when I was the only one in class, I told him about the dream. And then he told me a lot about himself, he really teaches from his own experience. Suddenly there was a feeling that that was possible, and that was really good for me. Later on I went to a lecture by the Friends of Buddhism society, in that Chinese Buddhist temple in the Warmoesstraat in Amsterdam. I once studied architecture and I was quite curious about that building. Then I saw the incredible sugariness of the temple, and I felt: well, I'm not about to exchange Christianity for Buddhism, that's for sure! The lecture was by a Dutch Zen teacher, and when he began I became completely … I really thought I was going mad! He spoke about the temple, which is dedicated to Kuan Yin, the *bodhisattva*, and about the myth of Kuan Yin, who achieved such a high level of consciousness that she was permitted to enter nirvana.[2, 3] And on the threshold of nirvana she turned back, and made a vow that she would never enter it unless she could take every single living creature with her. And … then I was overcome by all sorts of emotions at once. I felt an intense identification, not just: what a fascinating story, no, I really discovered my own essence in it, my own *raison d'être*. That was the crazy thing about it. And I felt embarrassed by all those emotions of mine, all those reactions. This teacher also drew from his own experience, and he quoted a Russian philosopher who'd really had an impact on him, Shestov, I wrote the name down. He also talked about Dostoevsky's wall, one of those archetypal images of a wall constructed of laws and rules, where everyone says, 'Thus far and no further.' I'd also kept walking into that all the time. Not that I recognised the image of a wall, but if there is a wall, I want to get through it, and I'll always try to as well!

I opened right up emotionally, and once again I felt: I cannot tell anyone about this, I am stark raving mad! And that's not how I want to be seen. So I walked back to the station with tears in my eyes, and the first thing I said was, 'And that bloody lot of ours, all up there in heaven!' I found that so ridiculous, I had to laugh at myself, what are you going on about? It was always what I argued with other people about, that Christianity means caring for your fellow man, while Buddhism is so aloof. And here I was, seething with irritation and anger! Because Christianity's only about getting yourself a place in heaven, while Buddhism on the other hand tries to achieve self-realisation in order to include others! It was just one big mess, which makes it difficult to talk about, everything gets tangled up. It was a total surprise attack by every possible emotion, even though I knew: this is about my whole existence. And suddenly it began to dawn on me why I thought in a certain way, why I am going through a process of development, why I was fascinated by some things without knowing why. So I just started going through the same process: sitting down and trying to put on paper exactly what had happened. Trying to grasp it somehow. But I got absolutely nowhere! I gave myself a year and it still didn't work out. As I saw it, there was nothing more I could do, I did what I had to, the minimum, and the writing was a dead loss. That story about Kuan Yin was always in my mind, but every time I tried to put it into words, I'd end up crying my eyes out again! I'd always tried to find my own way, I felt at home with Buddhism intellectually, but culturally speaking I felt part of Christianity. Actually, I was fooling myself there as well, those were only boundaries for the outside world. But I kept trying to find something to hold onto, because to surrender so completely, that was scary, frightening, it was maddening. I thought, I would be mad to leave things like this!

It really made me afraid that I *was* mad. I sometimes considered talking to the parish priest; he is a fantastic man who dares to go his own way. But in Christianity the focus is not on guiding you on your spiritual journey. It's a faith of consolation. And I really didn't need consolation; I needed guidance. So I started reading books again, that's my escape route. I also started looking for Shestov's work in antiquarian bookshops, but I couldn't find it. And after a year I thought, okay, now I really have to do something. First of all I wanted to do a *sesshin* with this Zen teacher, but you have to book that a long time in advance.[4] So I went on a weekend course in the province of Drenthe, led by Jiun Hogen Roshi, the only Dutch Zen matriarch, which was also a good idea because I'm always complaining that women have no authority in the Church. I remember, I went in and there was such a positive atmosphere, it radiated tremendous vitality. The weekend is always in silence, but you can talk a bit beforehand. There was one man there in a Harley T-shirt and I asked him, 'Did you come on your motorbike?' No, he'd sold it, because he lived here, he was a monk! And I thought, wow, fantastic! Then came the introductions. I was used to the Christian sphere, where if one person starts on his personal problems, you get interminable stories from everyone, but here someone started by saying, 'Well, what can I say, I'm fine.' And the next one, 'Actually, I'm fine as well,' and the next one, 'Everything's going fantastically well for me.' That sort of reaction, it was such a wonderful atmosphere! And so I broke away from all that sombreness, all that wallowing in suffering, glorifying it. And male and female monks all together. And the roshi said, 'Well, we're all Buddhas together here — oh, there's another one on the phone.' What an atmosphere, what a difference! So I meditated there, I also had a talk with Jiun Hogen Roshi, I was having such a conflict of loyalty with Christianity, because although I have such a good community and circle of friends at home, I still break free from them. She said to me: what are you worrying about? If you wonder every time you say something: what am I basing this on, and why am I saying it — what difference does it make whether it's Buddhist or Christian? It was such an obvious thing, but for me it was the helping hand I needed at the time.

After a year doing nothing I suddenly started to get busy. I went on with the meditation, without all those Tibetan frills, mainly using visualisation, plus other forms of meditation such as Zen, and a bit of Chi Kung.[5] But the teacher taught purely from his own experience, and that's the most important thing to me; that he's very direct and doesn't push some theory or other. If that man taught French knitting he'd manage to make it interesting. I went to another lecture by my first teacher, then I talked to him and said that I'd been very moved the first time, and was still looking for material on Shestov. He sent me some stuff about him, and I managed to find a book in a second-hand bookshop, then I came across a whole website with all of Shestov's work. I could really identify with that. The most important thing was that he stated that there are no truths. And he must have experienced something like that as well, it shows in everything. Imagine having such an approach to life ... Someone from the turn of the nineteenth century, early twentieth century, but with such a vivid way of expressing himself, anything but old-fashioned! His great crusade was against reason as the be-all and end-all, against the constant formulation of all those truisms. For Shestov the only truth was personal truth, and even that was a product of its time. I could see that for myself in everything around me. When do I find people attractive? When they speak from their innermost being. They may refer to something they have seen in someone else, or something they have read, but only with regard to how they experienced it themselves. Through that, I suddenly made a huge leap forward. I could see it in my own writing as well. So I wrote a play, about Mary Magdalene. I began with another idea that came from a dream, that was the creepy thing about it. I've been indignant for a long time about women's position in the Church, and there has been the odd sermon about it in my own parish, but no one does much about it. But now it doesn't matter to me any more whether it fits into a system, if I feel that something is right, I ought to be able to say so! For my play I used all sorts of gospels which only came to light during the last century, and I took on a director who gave me the leading role! I was very happy about that, because I wasn't really playing a part, I was playing myself. And the reactions it got, people were moved to tears! They talked to me as if I were Mary Magdalene. That is really something; you speak from your own truth, your own feeling, and you touch other people. People even started hawking it around, to show it to other people. So writing is my safety valve, my way of communicating with the outside world. I don't want to veil my real self any more, I couldn't do it anyway.

Through that play I was also taking my leave, in a manner of speaking. Here I stand, this is how I am — a bit like Luther! I was confused because I felt very involved in that community, I was very creative within the church — arranging exhibitions, working out annual themes and so on — while I no longer felt like a Catholic and definitely not like a Christian. So I wrote the parish priest a letter and told him the whole story later. I had the impression that he didn't really understand what my religious ideas actually were, but he couldn't see any problem. Which actually pushed me even further away at the time. And maybe I will leave one day, I'll see how it goes. At the moment I just feel religious, I didn't officially become a Buddhist either. Maybe I will one day, I don't know. Apart from that, writing plays is my basis. I can channel it all through that.

Later on I finally had a *sesshin* with the Zen teacher, in a Christian monastery; we could take part in all the prayer cycles as well as our own meditation. At first I was very obstinate about it, oh no, I'm not doing that, but I did go to communion on Sunday morning. So after three days of intense meditation, after almost complete silence, eating and everything in a meditative state, suddenly there I was in church and everything seemed so superficial! It all seemed so phony to me! There was a monk from our group there as well, but I thought: I don't belong here. But I couldn't get away. And then came the sermon, and Vocation Sunday had just come and gone, so it was all about dwindling congregations and the new priests that would be needed.[6] In short, it was our Christian duty to force the message of the liberation of Christ on other people. Well, that was quite a liberation for me! Suddenly I could distance myself completely from that community, in a completely open way ... I didn't join in anything, I didn't sing with the rest, it wasn't my way any more, absolutely not! But then the time came for the 'kiss of peace', when you shake hands with everyone and wish each other peace. And I could do that with such intense feeling ... I was completely free, and I could wish the other person the same freedom. I went on to complete the meditation, and went home jubilant! That was a really odd experience as well, that euphoria, I kept thinking: have I gone mad? One of the priests here is also a Zen master, as it happens. What always strikes me about that is that Zen is being used here as a means of deepening insight, and as a way of opening dogmatic questions to discussion, but it still takes place within the confines of Christianity. Whereas for me, Zen is about throwing everything wide open, being limitless. So I am in the process of withdrawing from the dogmatic, organisational side, but that community means a lot to me. Partly because of that experience.

Through my parents' atheism, religion actually became a very important subject. It was never a topic of conversation though, you sense that as a child. My sister studied Hebrew and became a Jew, a liberal Jew, and she's very taken up with rituals. My parents found that tremendously hard to accept. She used to talk about it a lot, while I was more inclined to keep quiet about what I was doing. But they found my becoming a Catholic totally unacceptable as well, they kept going on about that. To them it was ignorance, there was something absolutely ridiculous about religious faith. But their idea of it was sheer caricature: science is a sort of religion to them, and religion is superstition. Actually they'd always thought my sister was crazy, for being interested in religion at all. And when I tried to tell them something about it, that for me it wasn't about dogma, it was a way of life, their expressions said it all: oh lord, she's completely round the bend!

When I was going through that crisis there was nowhere I could turn. During that time my oldest son, ten years old, told me that he had been toying with thoughts of suicide for a year, but didn't have the nerve to do it. He finally told me about it after a really terrifying dream, and I probed further. We went to see a psychologist about what my son had told me, but he brushed it aside completely. That's why I was so sure later on: there would be no point in going to him, because he'd put me down as mad! I've also read about people who had religious experiences and ended up in an institution. I had doubts myself sometimes, when I was being bombarded by all those emotions at the same time, but I didn't want to be mad at any rate! I also went to the RIAGG with my other son. He thinks in images, which is also what I do apparently, but he had a lot of problems with it; he became depressed. In fact I had to counsel him myself, because those places have their particular methods, and if you don't fit into those, there must be something wrong with you! Whereas this is quite separate from limits and methods.

The most important thing to me is the experience of limitlessness; the limits that people set up no longer apply. The experience of openness, of being able to accept other people completely, and also to accept things that I just find difficult, such as my relationship with my parents. Our lives have completely diverged, but how should I handle that? I don't make plans any more. That comes from Zen meditation of course: a sort of alertness to the things that happen, and taking things from there. For me that is an important way, just meditating every week with a group, personal contact is also important. I really want to make sure that that will always be there. Apart from that, I am sifting everything: what matters and what doesn't? What sort of things do I do because other people want me to do them, even though they no longer tally with what interests me? I throw them out. I am now developing through drama, I also find that in acting, in letting go of yourself. And not playing another person, but just being able to *be*. As for my religious development, well, I just play it by ear. Sometimes I see a course somewhere and I think, wow, that's really cut out for me. Then I go and do it, and that kind of thing happens all the time. During that first period I was very reserved. Now I am much more open to everything, and I try out all sorts of things. As regards my personality I have changed a lot. Also become much more emotional; I can express it all better and that's really important to me.

Jeroen (1931)

During my time as abbot I introduced Zen into the monastery. Why? Because when I discovered Zen I was immediately reminded of the crisis I had been through, and of how I came through it.

I was born in Goes, in a Catholic family, but religion meant little to me as a boy.[1] I was brought up as a Catholic, but never felt the urge to become a priest or anything of that nature. I must have been a difficult child, I think. I have vivid memories of sitting fidgetting beside my father in church. We said the family rosary at home and I loathed it, I used to fidget all the time and my mother found me a real handful. When I went to secondary school I opted for grammar school. As there was no Catholic grammar school in Goes I was sent to boarding school. So I spent the years between fourteen and nineteen at boarding school, first a year in Rolduc, then four years in Sittard. My last vestiges of religious feeling were completely wiped out there. During my final year at grammar school we had a sort of obligatory retreat with the Jesuits in Spaubeek. That did not appeal to me, so I went armed with a novel by Bordewijk and the poems of Slauerhoff. Then I came across a book by Chesterton, *Orthodoxy*, and that started me thinking. I read the book and was struck by the sentence: 'The Catholic religion is the harmony of opposites'. That made a deep impres-

sion. I started searching and opening up to things. Later that year a religious instruction teacher gave a talk on the Carthusians, and I was
thunderstruck by it. Suddenly I knew what I wanted to be. Because until
then I had had no idea, I was still searching, and I had always found life
rather incomprehensible, rather vague. Somewhere deep inside I was
always wondering: do I really exist? Do I really exist? As a sort of fundamental question. And I had no idea what I wanted to be. Until that
moment. So then I started searching and eventually I ended up at the
abbey. For a few months I studied classical languages in Nijmegen, living
in lodgings, then in May 1951 I entered the trappist monastery.

Through reading that book of Chesterton's I made a choice for the
Catholic faith. That gradually opened me up to a sort of oceanic sense of
God. I started reading *The Imitation of Christ*, I started reading the Bible,
especially the New Testament; something inside me opened out when I
made the Stations of the Cross and said the rosary.[2] I had heard about that,
but now I was experiencing it for myself. Gradually I arrived at an oceanic
sense of God, and I allowed myself to be guided by that. In the monastery,
of course, that expanded and deepened. I lived in that state for the first
couple of years.

Then philosophy came up on the training programme. I did it reluc-
tantly at first, it was all too rational for me. But after a while metaphysics
began to get through to me, and I started to go further into it. I had no one
to teach me about it properly; it was largely my own quest and my own
experience. Then one day I read a book by De Raeymaeker.[3] Every thing is
what it is — a chair or table, for example — but it would be just as true to say:
every thing *is*. An insight that at one point became an experience. A real
enlightenment experience. That was very beautiful, very powerful and
profound, but threatening at the same time. I felt very disorientated and
torn, because in that case, what was my body for? I thought, I do have a
body, after all, so this enlightenment experience, how does it all fit
together? I could not reconcile the two, because the experience was purely
intellectual. The idea of infinity frightened me, I could not place it. There
was no one I could talk to either. So I suppressed the enlightenment
experience.

Then came February 1954. I had already taken my provisional vows,
but all the time I had been thinking: I will go ahead, and somewhere
inside me I actually want to, but I am not sure what I am doing. Then
something undermining happened — I remember the exact moment. I had
just done my first refectory reading. In a monastic community there are
certain things that have to be done — the washing-up for example! — and
reading aloud during meals is one of them. So there I stood, reading
aloud, and suddenly I thought: I am going mad, I am going completely

mad! I kept on reading, but I felt: I am going mad. That was really shatter-
ing. I mean, what was I supposed to do? I was still a novice, so I went to
the master of novices. Humanly speaking I had quite a good relationship
with him, at a cultural level for example, but that was as far as it went. I
went to see him and said, 'I think I'm having a bit of a breakdown.' I
touched on the subject very carefully. His reaction was: oh, I'm sure it
won't come to that. So the subject was immediately brushed aside. And I
was all on my own.

How on earth was I supposed to cope with it? I never considered for a
moment going to a psychiatrist, or anything like that. I thought: I need to
sort this out myself. I found a way to do that by telling myself: don't make
any judgements about yourself. It was like a text from the gospel: 'judge
not'. I took the text literally. I said to myself, 'What I am experiencing is
true, of course—I feel as if I am going mad.' The feeling amounted to:
everything is becoming confused, and I will end up in a madhouse in no
time. That was the experience. Of course, when I look back on it I have my
own views about it now, but at the time it was quite an experience. And
that gave me the feeling: I have failed. My whole life is a failure. In order
to cope with that I said to myself: I do not know who I am. I have had that
experience and I do not deny that, but those are just fragments on the outside. What I am in my innermost being, that I do not know.

I drew on my stock of spiritual experience, of course, but what I was
going through now was a completely new process. Looking back, I managed to carry on like that for several months. That was pretty difficult, living in the consciousness of not-knowing; not reconciling myself to the idea
that I was mad. Because 'I'm going mad', that might not be very pleasant,
but it would give you some certainty, at least you would have something
definite. What I did, time after time, was to ward off the judgment 'I am
going mad'. That was really very hard. Like being on a steep slope between
a yawning chasm and the unattainable summit. Later on I recognised that
in Zen. In fact, that is the fundamental experience in Zen: entering the
dimension of 'not-knowing', of the mystery of your innermost being,
within your own consciousness. I functioned like that in the community for
several months, but I had the feeling that everything was slipping past me.
To all appearances I conformed and did what I had to do, but a completely
different process was going on inside me. It was a very painful business. I
interpreted it in terms of Christ. Christ, who took human suffering on himself. I felt: the suffering I am going through is part of that.

Suddenly, a couple of months later, in May or June, something burst
violently through to me. Light ... light! Something quite unbelievable. I
remember exactly where it happened. We were walking from the church
to the refectory. I went outside and *saw* for the first time. For the first time I

saw the grass and the trees and the shrubs. And there was … light! Light! And above all the realisation: God loves me.

Looking back, that is exactly what is called an enlightenment experience in Zen. For me, that experience contained an inner certainty: now I know that I exist. I had always had the underlying doubt: do I really exist? That experience of going mad was connected with this doubt. What burst on me then was: now I know that I exist. God loves me.

That went on for three days or so, after which I had the feeling that I had to go back. I empathised with the Biblical images of Moses on the mountain, who was allowed to see God. That is how it felt: I have been on the mountain but now I must go down again and return to everyday life. The experience of happiness through expanded consciousness faded, but the certainty remained and was expressed in the realisation: now I know that I exist! A knowledge that has never left me since. Then came the question: what should I do now with this new certainty? The answer was obvious: I should approach the life I lead with great awareness.

When I look back, my personality had never been able to develop through making choices. As a boy I had never made a choice, because I had never had occasion to in my life. I had always existed in a sort of vagueness. I sometimes think that I was really a soul that did not want to become a human being. I did make the decision to enter the monastery, because I felt that I had been called by God. But I had never made a concrete human choice, because the inner uncertainty had persisted. When that was destroyed by the enlightenment experience I also acquired the power to focus on something. And what was on offer was life in the abbey, with work and study.

So how were things different from in the past? Previously of course my spiritual activity had been focused on my relationship with God, in that oceanic feeling. But during this intellectual enlightenment experience I was thrown back on myself; that is a completely different sort of experience altogether. I had not managed to integrate this experience into my personality, and that certainly contributed to the crisis. In the journey towards enlightenment and in the enlightenment experience itself I discovered who I really was. That was possible because I had consciously chosen to remain in a state of not-knowing. I had a relationship with God in so far as I accepted the painfulness of that process. And so I could finally accomplish something that I had never been able to do as a boy: to make a choice.

For a long time I could not talk about it. Once the uncertainty had faded away there was a sort of end, but also a new beginning. My human existence, my human relationships still had to be realised. As trappists we had an intensive communal life, but there was no such thing as personal

interchange in those days, because of the vow of silence. We did everything together, there were no separate cells, just a dormitory with
curtained-off cubicles; very open, you could hear everything that everyone did. The reading room was communal, everyone had his own desk,
but you all sat there together. A radical community, but without the
slightest personal interchange. We talked about work and so on, but that
was so simple in those days that there was very little to say about it.
Everyone was alone, in his relationship with God.

It was not until 1958 that I could talk about these things for the first
time. That was with a fellow-student I was friendly with, during our studies in Rome. I told him about my experience, the crisis and the enlightenment, and he recognised its authenticity. His affirmation was a significant
moment for me, of course, since back in the abbey I had not found anyone
willing to listen. I remember very clearly how and where and when that
happened. Something deep inside me found recognition with a fellow
human being, and that helped me to integrate those experiences better.
But it was only through the discovery of Zen that I understood them fully.

Around the same time I found out about yoga, through a book, and I
began to practise it myself. The good thing about that was that it taught
me to accept my own body. In monastic training and the atmosphere of
monastic life the body exists only to suffer. And through doing those yoga
exercises I perceived: God creates me through my body. I came home to
my body. Once again, it was something personal that I discovered. I tried
to go further into the background of yoga and Hinduism, but I found it too
complicated; I could not quite handle it.

That changed when I discovered Zen. Firstly through the books of
Von Dürckheim and later via those of Lasalle.[4, 5] The simplicity of Zen
appealed to me tremendously, and I immediately recognised in it what I
had gone through myself. I was already familiar with forms of meditation
and inner prayer, of course, but Zen penetrated much further. In 1970 I
went to see Von Dürckheim. The first Zen session in the abbey was given
by Gerta Ital, Von Dürckheim came in 1972, and from 1973 onwards
Father Lasalle came almost every year.[6] Over the years I have kept switching between the two; a bit of Zen, then back to Christianity, then a bit of
Zen again. Each has its own place: Zen for exploring the depths of existence, Christianity as the experience of the relationship with God. I have
succeeded in uniting the two within myself.

In the meantime I have been to India several times to see Ama Samy, an
Indian Jesuit who trained as Zen master at the Sanbo Kyodan school in
Japan. Back in India he founded a Zen centre. I have been there several
times, mainly in order to work with kôans. I had never had the chance to
do that before, and it really does something special. The relationship of

kôans to my crisis is that they confront you with questions that you cannot solve through your intellect, only through a direct insight that you lack. Kôans are a sort of riddle. 'Stop the sound of the temple bell from a distance', for example. You can hear the bell tolling at a distance: how do you stop the sound? The inclination is to start thinking about it, but you have to let it sink in straight away and give an intuitive response in the form of a gesture. Not with words, but with a gesture that expresses the insight. You show the master the gesture and he assesses whether you have gained the insight. There is no right response, but a master can see from a gesture whether or not someone has gained insight.

In the late sixties there was a powerful movement towards horizontalisation in church and monastery life. Human interaction came to the fore. Of course, that was good in itself, but I felt that something of the mystical and transcendent dimension was being lost in the process. I believed that Zen could restore this to the church in a new way. Asia and the western world experience the transcendent differently, and I think that the connection between them is very important. When you look around, you see how the concept of God is simply slipping away over here. In the western world we must explore the depths of our own existence in order to prevent it from dying out.

In 2001 I resigned my position as abbot. I was so busy that I was verging on a burn-out, so I resigned. I took a sabbatical year and went to India. On my return, I found that the model of monastic life had lost its meaning for me. It had slipped off me like a jacket. Nowadays I experience the essence in the silence of a hut, in the grounds of the abbey, apart from the community. The crux of the matter is: how do you apply your enlightenment experience to everyday reality? The western Christian tradition doesn't really recognise that as such, but it is much more alive in Zen. Zen simplified my life. I see it now as my mission in life to be a meditation teacher.

Chapter Four

The Transpersonal Perspective
The Psychology of Being

If we ask: what is the world? — we embark on the traditional outward journey of science, to earthly phenomena, to the furthest horizons of the physical universe. If we ask: what is a human being? — the way leads inwards, through the inner cosmos, on the religious quest. These are great enterprises; they reflect great expectations, demand great investment, and are sometimes abundantly fruitful. And they are all too human enterprises; not always well planned in all respects, not always skilfully carried out, nor honestly rounded off. But one thing leads to another; just as a river constantly changes its course. And philosophy is everywhere. It holds things together, seeks for what remains when the form is gone, and raises questions about the raising of questions. Albert Einstein once said: 'My religion consists of a humble admiration of the illimitable superior spirit who reveals himself in the slight details we are able to perceive with our frail and feeble mind.'[1]

Which branch of knowledge is concerned here? Science, religion, philosophy? Or perhaps intelligent design *avant–la–lettre*? There is a catchment area where the tried–and–tested ways of knowledge converge; it forms a tradition of research in the widest and deepest sense. Aldous Huxley's *Perennial Philosophy*, published in 1945, indicated the renewed interest in this subject at that time.

1 Perennial philosophy

Huxley (1894–1963) adopted the concept of *philosophia perennis* from the German polymath Gottfried Leibnitz (1646–1716), whose philosophy drew largely from mathematics. Leibnitz encountered the idea of 'perennial philosophy' in the work of Augustinus Steuchius, a sixteenth-century theologian and Vatican librarian.[2] The basic idea goes back even further than that, to Plato and Aristotle. Huxley breathed new life into this ancient line of thought by proposing an eclectic mixture of western and eastern ideas as the spiritual food of modern man. In his view this was a philosophy that dealt with 'a divine Reality substantial to the world of things and lives and minds.'[3] Such a philosophy of philosophies, of course, forms an immensely rich treasury for everything concerning mankind and human existence. The sheer multiplicity of such themes, however, makes their predictability all the more striking. One inevitable notion is that man cannot know this one reality through his intellectual powers, but only through immediate experience. To know is to experience, to know is to exist. We have met with this notion before, in the context of mystical experience. Now Huxley used the word 'divine' in his description, and that of course rings a religious bell. And yet, more than anything, his impulse represented a vision of reality which has not been encapsulated by any particular religious framework. In fact, the 'divine' in this case signifies something that no one group or ideology can incorporate or claim, and though its exclusive association with belief and the church is historically understandable, at times very subtle, and inevitably rooted in language, it is nevertheless unjust. By definition there is a gap between the immediacy of our knowing and how we reflect on it afterwards. It is precisely here that we can pick up the thread of that immediate knowledge once again. In order to distinguish this theme from the field of religion, I will mainly use the terminology of spirituality and spiritual experience here, which since it designates the experience of essential and inner realities, will be quite adequate for this purpose. And in order to illustrate *perennial philosophy*, let us take one particular spiritual experience which revived interest in the subject. In 1872 the Canadian doctor and psychologist Richard Maurice Bucke (1837-1902) was visiting England, where he had an experience which affected him for the rest of his life. His account was as follows:

> I had spent the evening in a great city, with two friends, reading and discussing poetry and philosophy. We parted at midnight. I had a long drive to my lodgings. My mind, deeply under the influence of the ideas, images, and emotions called up by the reading and talk, was calm and peaceful. I was in a state of quiet, even passive enjoyment, not actually thinking, but letting ideas, images, and emotions flow of themselves, as it were, through my mind. All at once, without warning of any kind, I found myself wrapped in a flame-coloured cloud. For an instant I thought of fire, an immense conflagration somewhere close by in that great city; the next instant I knew that the fire was in

myself. Directly afterwards there came upon me a sense of exultation, of immense joyousness, accompanied or immediately followed by an intellectual illumination impossible to describe. Among other things, I did not merely come to believe, I saw that the universe is not composed of dead matter, but is, on the contrary, a living Presence; I became conscious in myself of eternal life. It was not a conviction that I would have eternal life, but a consciousness that I possessed eternal life then; I saw that all men are immortal; that the cosmic order is such that without any peradventure all things work together for the good of each and all; that the foundation principle of the world, of all the worlds, is what we call love, and that the happiness of each and all is in the long run certain. The vision lasted a few seconds and was gone; but the memory of it and the sense of the reality of it has remained during the quarter of a century which has since elapsed. I knew that what the vision showed was true. I had attained to a point of view from which I saw that it must be *true*. That view, that conviction, I may say that consciousness, has never, even during the periods of the deepest depression, been lost.[4]

In response to this experience, Bucke gave a reading entitled *Cosmic Consciousness* at the American Medico-Psychological Association in Philadelphia, and published his book of the same title in 1901.[5] Bucke, the innovative director of a psychiatric hospital, thus anticipated what would later become transpersonal psychology. Subtitled *A Study in the Evolution of the Human Mind*, the book introduced his theory on the development of consciousness. The phases that he distinguished here were: simple, animal consciousness; self-consciousness, such as that of humans with their reason and imagination; and cosmic consciousness—a great human potential, though realised only by a tiny number of great minds. Besides Jesus, Mohammed and Buddha, these include Dante, Balzac and the poet Walt Whitman, a personal friend of Bucke.

William James, who delivered his *Varieties* lectures in Scotland (see Chapter 3, 'Fathers of introspection') during the same period, wrote in a letter to Bucke shortly after the publication of *Cosmic Consciousness*: 'I believe that you have brought this kind of consciousness "home" to the attention of students of human nature in a way so definite and inescapable that it will be impossible henceforward to overlook it or ignore it.'[6]

This was very optimistic of James. Although psychoanalysis was charting the unconscious, and physics was making its leap to quantum reality, it would be some time before Bucke's 'superconsciousness' was adopted as a subject of study. Now experiences such as his appear not only to reveal something about the qualities of a 'higher' consciousness, but also to provide new insight into the nature of consciousness as such. As a result, the age–old interest in the immediate knowledge of reality has focused since then on consciousness, and spiritual experiences form a prominent theme in current research into *'consciousness as such'*.

2 Secular mysticism

As a prelude to this, publications on spiritual experiences that explicitly cast aside existing religious and therapeutic interpretive frameworks appeared in the course of the last century. Huxley's book breathed new life into the concept of *perennial philosophy*, which holds that divergent cultures are merely different expressions of one and the same vision on the nature of reality. Marghanita Laski placed secular before religious experiences in the subtitle of her main work *Ecstasy*, and Abraham Maslow coined his own terminology for the peak experience.[7, 8] Walter Stace was one of those who saw mysticism in a broader framework, and gave an account of this in his *Mysticism and Philosophy*, while the Dutchman Frits Staal made an unequivocal plea for research into mysticism, detached from any religious or psychological dogma whatsoever, in his *Exploring Mysticism: A Methodological Essay*.[9, 10]

In the 1960s curiosity about the inner world of consciousness spread like wildfire, from a few scattered academics to large regions of the western world. The impetus given by the emergence of psychedelic drugs, and the counterculture as the place to use them, was historic. Many an author would later refer, bashfully or boldly, to the fact that earlier psychedelic experiences had helped to redirect his or her course to the secrets of the inner cosmos. One outstanding example of this was the Czech psychoanalyst Stanislav Grof (b. 1931). As a young researcher in Prague, he started testing the effectiveness of a new medicine for the treatment of psychotics. The powerful consciousness-expanding effect of this substance had been discovered by chance in 1943 by its maker, Albert Hofmann (1906–2008), a chemist at the Sandoz laboratory in Basel. After becoming acquainted with this drug, lysergic acid diethylamide or LSD for short, Grof supervised its use in 4,000 or so psychotherapeutic sessions. This work formed the basis of his revolutionary view of consciousness itself, and thus of the need for a proportionately more liberal psychology than that in which he had been trained.[11] 2000 or so scientific articles were published on the therapeutic blessings of LSD, before the substance stepped out of the lab onto the street and made history there as a recreational drug. Using it out of context and without supervision was bound to lead to accidents, however, and the drug was finally banned in 1966. This did not diminish Grof's curiosity in the slightest. He was able to continue his work in the

US for a number of years at the John Hopkins School of Medicine in Balti-more, Maryland, but even the end of his official research there did not extinguish scientific interest. The 100th anniversary of Hofmann's birth was celebrated in Basel with a symposium on LSD, and many a pharma-cologist and psychiatrist took the stage as speaker.

3 A model of expanded consciousness

The pre–eminent academic podium for psychological insight into extraor-dinary inner experiences is now roughly thirty-five years old. Through the participation of Abraham Maslow, among others, the *Journal of Transpersonal Psychology* was founded in 1969, the Association of Transpersonal Psychology in 1972, the Institute of Transpersonal Psy-chology in 1975, and the International Transpersonal Association in 1977. In the 1980s transpersonal organisations sprang up in one European country after another, and the whole movement thus acquired its place on the map as the fourth school of psychology, after the psychoanalytical, behaviourist and humanist schools. Transpersonal psychology bears a particular resemblance to the humanist school, but has always differed from it in its focus on experiences that are 'beyond' those of everyday consciousness.

This idea of experiences beyond some particular boundary marker in our consciousness is certainly not new. Psychoanalysis divided the psy-che into different compartments, mysticism has its transcendence and immanence, and for general use we imply dividing lines—even if very faint ones—between health and sickness, virtue and vice. Originally the term 'transpersonal' referred to potential experiences that transcend the individual, conditioned personality. Carl Jung (1875–1961) was the first to use it, namely as an alternative to 'collective' in designating his concept of the subconscious.[12] This concept made Jung's preliminary work extremely relevant for both humanist and transpersonal psychology. Even though his own analytical school achieved only secondary impor-tance, he structurally expanded the image of what a healthy person might encounter within his consciousness, thereby exerting much more social influence. For example, he tangibly and ineradicably introduced the con-cept of archetypes to our cultural template. Overall he was less strong the-oretically, however, which is where transpersonal psychology takes over. Where Jung continued to relegate all non–personal experiences to the collective unconscious, as if it were one vast teeming ocean, transpersonal psychology fills in the map of our consciousness as completely as possible. It was the Italian psychiatrist Roberto Assagioli (1888–1974) who expanded earlier versions at crucial points. Though trained in psychoanalysis, he became convinced that human beings needed more than that to become truly whole, and he developed that idea into psycho*synthesis*. Besides the traditional layers of the subconscious and ego consciousness in the normal waking state, he distinguished a higher consciousness. Initially, the self takes up only a fraction of waking consciousness; through therapy, insight and practice it expands both 'downwards' and 'upwards'. In this way a much broader and transpersonal self gradually develops, and the latter touches on the collective unconscious that everyone shares.[13] Since Assagioli, transpersonal theory has been further refined and developed. Developmental models are becoming increasingly less linear and structural than in the psychoanalytical era, evolving beyond the more spatial-dynamic views of Jung and Assagioli, and becoming distinctly ontological-holographic in appearance. One contributor to this field, Kuwait-born Hameed Ali (b. 1944), who writes under the name of A. H. Almaas, takes up the thread of the 'true' self from Horney and Winnicott (see Chapter 2, 'Nuances and amendments').[14] In his terminology, the 'true nature' of the self is Essence, which is both intangible and substantial. Paradoxical or not, as the most vital part of a human being, it is Essence that is directly perceptible. Essential experience however is subdued and distorted by the ego structure, which results from the conditioning of both the mind and the nervous system. The development of personal consciousness involves, among other things, the exercise of proprioception and the refinement of inner perception. This amplifies the felt experience in the moment, so that it can be examined more closely. In combination with the intellectual understanding of one's historic patterns of conditioning, the individual then increasingly clears the way for the manifestation of the pure qualities.[15] For even though Essence as a 'primal substance' forms a single source, in human experience it is perceived not in a uniform but in an extremely differentiated way, like the colours produced by the splitting of a beam of white light when it encounters matter. At a psychological level these essential qualities are perceived as the various 'hues' and 'flavours' of emotional affect. As the hold of the past weakens, the charged subjective experience gives way to the corresponding frequencies on the original spectrum. Thus for example the inauthentic, reactive rage of the ego transforms into essential strength, a quality of the true self. The 'true' person then develops as a creature of flesh and blood, one that functions in the world while drawing freely on all his authentic qualities and powers. In his extensive spiritual psychology, Almaas regards the soul as the essential individual, and as the organ of universal holographic consciousness—see also Chapter 4, 'Quantum speculations'.

4 The world according to Ken Wilber

The further refinement of consciousness models is a recurring theme in transpersonal psychology. No one has made a greater contribution to this field than the American Ken Wilber (b. 1949), and no outline of transpersonal psychology, however concise, would be complete without mentioning his work. An almost frighteningly productive thinker and writer, who, under the heading of transpersonal psychology, in fact mapped out the entire inner and outer world of human beings, and in particular made the idea of a vast spectrum of consciousness socially acceptable in many different circles. To this end Wilber browsed virtually every accessible source and tradition—old, new, eastern, western, physical, metaphysical—and set about integrating them. From these he distilled a layered model in which the individual potentially evolves from birth to the highest consciousness of what in western and eastern mysticism is called, among other things, the One, the Absolute, Brahman or the *Ungrund*. The most simple classification into different states of consciousness is into waking, dreaming and sleeping, in which we perceive realities which are respectively material/gross physical, subtle/fine physical, and causal/formless. The first naturally forms our everyday frame of reference; it is filled with 'things' of the world, and is so normal that more often than not it is landed with the role of the *real* world or reality. The subtle department represents the reality of non–gross forms: coherent patterns of varying complexity, which manifest themselves as images, ideas, stories, metaphors, archetypes and so on. Causal reality consists quite simply of a sort of formless space, in which everything is present in potential, without any differentiation having taken place, comparable with white light in which no separate colours can be distinguished. Within each of these main divisions Wilber distinguished further specific layers, which correspond in part to the various cognitive functions familiar to western psychology. The contribution of eastern traditions lies primarily in the many higher rungs on the ladder to the absolute One, in which it is no longer possible to distinguish anything and pure consciousness alone exists. The transitions between the different levels are also part of the model;

they reflect, among other things, familiar insights from developmental psychology.

From another angle, Wilber characterised our human potential in terms of successive levels of logic. This development ranges from archaic, magical, mythical, rational, psychological, subtle and causal to non-dual. This has proved a meaningful frame of reference in transpersonal practice. Later on he arrived at a classification within the various means of perception: the eye of the flesh, the eye of reason and the eye of the spirit. With the aid of such a lens, Wilber put so much flesh on the bones of what had been dismissed all too often as 'vague' and 'woolly' by those outside the circle of self-confessed adherents, that everyone with the slightest interest in consciousness is indebted to him. This perspective, of course, also forms a theoretical foundation for the ways in which psychological problems develop, and, complementary to this, for possible treatment. In Wilber's view, we develop a normal ego by repeatedly identifying with a part of ourselves and splitting off the rest, at successive levels. If we wish to realise our full potential, we must enter at the relevant level, and manage to reclaim what we have lost. In this way his map also shows how different therapeutic movements have specialised at particular levels of consciousness. As small children we are unfragmented and experience the world through our bodies, which we inhabit completely. But then we start to draw the boundaries; what is pleasant becomes 'self', what is painful becomes 'non–self'. We gradually do the same thing with our emotions, which we suppress selectively, and with our thoughts, part of which we alienate ourselves from. Hence, by a certain stage we have *become* our self-image, we drag our bodies along with us and are subject to a manageable repertoire of emotions. (Incidentally, at least in theory, the reverse is also conceivable—that we are just bodies, with no self–image, besieged by unfamiliar emotions and controlled by a mind with its own agenda. It sounds very tedious, and is perhaps valuable as a concept of forms of psychopathology.) At all events, progression to the next level is normally only possible when the two halves are reunited. At the mental level of the persona we regain our shadow; here we are reminded of Jung's work with animus and anima, or the division between male and female qualities. At the affective level, we reclaim our territory by digesting our stored–up emotions, and if we wish to be on friendly terms with our bodies again, we'd better engage ourselves with full awareness in healthy eating, sports, exercise, body work, walking, dancing, lovemaking. By becoming whole at all these levels we gain command of our organism's full array of personal powers. At yet higher levels of integration in Wilber's model we focus more, for example, on reconnection to other people and the world, to the higher self, to the collective unconscious, to the basis of existence.

Far from restricting himself to this extensive interior world, Wilber focused his gaze, in parallel, on the exterior cosmos. This is similarly constructed as successive levels of increasing complexity. He named the cosmic building blocks *holons*, units which form an entire system in themselves but which in their turn form part of a holon at a higher level, which then displays new characteristics. The degrees of complexity and power range from atoms via molecules, organelles, cells, tissues, organs, organisms, species and eco–systems to planetary totality, and beyond. His description of earthly phenomena draws from every conceivable science and outlook, and places physical and social, individual and collective, 'feminine' and 'masculine' variables and phenomena in functional relationships with each other on diverse multidimensional chessboards. It is clear, Ken Wilber is the great cartographer, and his work is, to put it mildly, impressive. There is little in life for which he has no perspective, and anyone who wishes to go further into his work will have his hands full for some time. Wilber's Dutch translator Frank Visser opens the door to this universe in the making in his own book *Ken Wilber, Thought as Passion*.[16] Wilber naturally comes in for the usual criticism, however. This comes not so much from conventional sources, which largely — and quite unjustly — ignore his work. Critics in transpersonal circles complain for example that it is all a bit too schematic and categorical, that everything is rather more 'fluid' in reality, and that a dimensional model would be more appropriate. His later work accordingly reflects this more, but he has now parted company with various people in the meantime, and calls his outlook and practice 'integral psychology'.

5 Transpersonal health

The consciousness spectrum outlined here can be applied in many ways, but the field of mental health is the most obvious candidate. Accordingly, the transpersonal approach to healthy development and its associated problems is well represented. Recurring themes in research and literature include the relationship between mysticism and pathology, psychological problems on the spiritual path, therapeutic applications of meditation, and Buddhist views on mental health. The contribution of Stanislav Grof to the development of theory and practice follows similar lines. His works include a model of the psyche, in which he distinguishes between three levels of experience. The first level concerns the reliving of emotionally relevant memories, to which classic psychological approaches can be applied. The second, 'perinatal' level is about reliving one's own birth, and the existential confrontation with death. At the third, transpersonal level, human consciousness unfolds independently of time and space. Grof makes no bones about the fact that we humans, both individually and collectively, would derive most benefit from exploring our own consciousness in all its heights and depths. The concrete transformation of individual consciousness takes place mainly during what he calls 'holotropic' experiences. In these, all the registers of experience are opened wide—physical, sensory, emotional, mental, energetic, intuitive—and consciousness is given the opportunity to exercise its self–healing powers. Grof fleshed out this theory in an intensive, therapeutic working method. This combines specific techniques for relax-ation and breathing with personal counselling, music and a secure environment.

Grof is also the man behind the concept of 'spiritual emergency'. This term signifies a mental crisis with a spiritual component, which under favourable conditions can lead to further growth and development. As a concept it forms a crucial framework for the experiences in this book. Firstly, it assumes the possibility of a spiritual dimension in human experience. Secondly, it approaches a crisis as a phase in further development, and thirdly, it pro-vides points of departure for counselling in practice. With his wife Christina, Grof developed the concept in two of his books, *Spiritual Emergency: When Personal Transformation Becomes A Crisis* and *The Stormy Search For The Self: A Guide To Personal Growth Through Transformative Crisis*.[17, 18]

The spiritual crisis in this sense is also the sort of experience referred to by the originally proposed article for the DSM-IV (see Introduction). One way or another, such crises involve confusing and frightening situations, during and after spiritual experiences which may be very positive and pleasant in themselves, but so profound or intense that it may be long before they can be integrated into everyday life. Those who have been through such an ordeal will be presumably less inclined to panic in future, owing to their greater awareness of spiritual dimensions. And a counsellor, official or otherwise, who can fathom a crisis situation from a transpersonal angle, will be better able to recognise these dimensions. In practice, such a counsellor is likely to be more receptive to expressions and processes which another would feel obliged to suppress. This much is clear: the power of discernment is indispensable here, as is knowledge of the greatest possible part of the human spectrum of experience: the heights and the depths, the wide expanses and narrow straits, the calms and the chaos. When someone's panic triggers our own, we may try to make them get rid of their fear as soon as possible, which is not necessarily helpful, nor is applauding someone's mania out of our belief that it represents some greater truth. The more familiar and comfortable we are with what may be unusual inner territories, the more we have to offer those who seem to have become stranded in them. Over the years David Lukoff, one of the authors of the DSM-IV article, has explicitly concentrated on giving mental health workers extra training in this field. In the courses that he develops, participants work on increasing their 'spiritual competence'. By also making these available on the internet, academic certificates and all, he reaches a specific group of interested parties, thus enabling them to expand and refresh their field of work.[19]

As the concept of spiritual emergency and crisis implies, mental states that we associate with pathology need not be purely unfavourable, but may form a developmental phase resulting in a more than satisfactory outcome. This idea is not the mere fantasy of the odd quacksalver, as is shown by the surprised comment of Karl Menninger (1893–1990), one of the leading men of modern American psychiatry. 'Some patients have a mental illness and then get well and then they get weller! I mean they get better than they ever were … This is an extraordinary and little–realized truth.'[20] Other references to such unorthodox or anomalous yet encouraging psychological processes, apart from Dabrowski's 'positive disintegration'[21] (see Chapter 2, 'Nuances and amendments') and Grof's 'spiritual emergency',[22] are found in Boisen's 'problem-solving schizophrenics',[23] Ellenberger's 'creative illness',[24] Laing's 'metanoic travel'[25] and Perry's 'visionary states'.[26] Over the years, it seems, all of these have indicated a perspective on mental health that transpersonal psychology meanwhile has started to elaborate.

6 Pre/trans confusion

Wilber too has something to say in this respect. He arrived at an interesting application by condensing his entire spectrum into three basic developmental levels: prepersonal, personal, and transpersonal. In the first two or three years of our lives we are at the prepersonal stage, before our personal ego–structure develops. Basically, as long as a toddler talks about herself in the third person—'Fransje walk'—she is prepersonal. We are personal when we see ourself as a distinct personality, as an ego with a body, as the centre of our world, from which we control ourself by will-power and operate purposefully, and to which we refer as ourself. We are transpersonal when we abandon that identification, define ourself less absolutely, are more open to what may happen, and display ourselves in a more qualitative way. Culturally speaking we are almost exclusively focused on the personal level, as was shown earlier; unconsciously we use the personal self therefore as the measure of all things, including the naming of this trio of developmental stages. From within this almost exclusive familiarity we tend to see the prepersonal baby and toddler as a Lilliputian version of our personal self. And from the same perspective, the prepersonal and the transpersonal resemble each other in that they are both non-personal. Endowed as we are with so little vision and depth of field for the transpersonal, we can hardly avoid describing anomalies other than as prepersonal. When, for example, we develop a certain impartiality in the course of psychological maturation, not everyone is able to fathom this. Some might even regard it as a lack of personality, of courage to adopt a definite viewpoint. According to Wilber's spectrum, this is the first categorical error. It is the failing of the strictly Freudian outlook, which classifies all transpersonality as immaturity. Subsequently Wilber refers to the second variant of this error. This version 'promotes' infantile ideas or immature behaviour to a transpersonal height. Through idealisation of the transpersonal, for example, or through fear of the personal, which involves many conflicts. But those who have never actually flown the nest in order to become an individual, and who wish to merge with each and every one in the name of universal love, are missing out on something, and are cheating themselves in the end. This second categorical confusion is the vindication of Freud: an expression of a happy-hippie atmosphere along the lines of 'actually we're all enlightened already', typical of lesser-calibre new age literature. With regard to the expansion of general spiritual competence, Wilber's 'pre/trans confusion' is another necessary and useful concept. It offers a rough handle for differentiation, which if further developed would not be out of place in a clinical context.

The first person to explicitly use the qualification 'transpersonal' in a psychotherapeutic frame of reference was, once again, Roberto Assagioli. The combination gained momentum ten or so years ago, and nowadays there are various authors able to hold forth as authorities on transpersonal psychotherapy. It is a typically eclectic appproach in which all levels of experience have their say: physical, emotional, mental, spiritual. From an interpersonal angle too the choice is widening, now that these levels are receiving more attention within system-oriented approaches. As early as 1994, the American Michael Hutton concluded that members of the international *Association of Transpersonal Psychology* also draw from the three older psychological traditions — psychoanalytical, behaviourist and humanist — and in that sense they represent a really eclectic approach.[27] Such a broad approach seems a precondition for the use of such a concept as the pre/trans confusion. Meanwhile the transpersonal school is beginning to find its way into the psychotherapeutic mainstream, via the work of author Seymour Boorstein, for example, and more recently, John Rowan.[28, 29] In the Netherlands, as elsewhere, it appears that various meditation techniques are finding their way into the regular mental health services. Removed from a purely spiritual context, the practice of different methods of meditation is proving valuable to an increasing number of mental health workers and their clients. Further application in a multitude of situations is hence to be expected.

7 Cognition and intuition

Another relevant transpersonal theme is the interaction between various modes and ways of knowing. In classical psychology several sub-schools have developed from the umbrella concept of cognition, and the cognitive human powers have accordingly achieved a well-deserved place as a phenomenon. Measurements in this field initially fell under the hegemony of the intelligence quotient, but times have changed; various scales for the measurement of emotional and social intelligence have appeared in the last ten years. Not that these have been generally accepted, and it remains to be seen whether they will ever be, but the idea that intelligence can also be conceived of in less strictly logical and intellectual ways is generally favourably received. This expansion was brought about earlier by Howard Gardner's theory of multiple intelligence, which originally distinguished seven different sorts: visual-spatial, logical-mathematical, linguistic, interpersonal, intrapersonal, bodily-kinetic and musical.[30] A more recent addition is the naturalistic variant, in which the possessor is sensitive to minimal changes or differences in natural phenomena, and recognises patterns and connections within them. Gardner is said to be working on a ninth, existentialist variant: the power of clear insight into fundamental, spiritual and philosophic questions. In all, it is a fascinating, mind-broadening way of looking at people, which was also taken up by Wilber — and which has raised a number of older eyebrows.

Compared with earlier psychological concepts of cognition, transpersonal elements crop up more and more. That can be seen mainly in connection with the idea of a direct, inner way of knowing, as also found in the *philosophia perennis*. This particular theme, long discussed in transpersonal circles, was put on the agenda by William James. When he explored mystical experience in the *Varieties*, he distinguished a number of characteristics, the two principal of which he considered sufficient to qualify an experience as mystical. These main characteristics were ineffability, and direct knowledge. He attributed the term 'noëtic quality' to the latter, thus harking back to Plato's use of the term *noësis*, one of several terms used by the ancient Greeks for different modes of knowing. Between factual knowledge and practical insight, *noësis* concerned the intuitive way of knowing, without the intervention of intellectual reasoning or mental representation. James explains the noëtic quality as follows:

> Although so similar to states of feeling, mystical states seem to those who experience them to be also states of knowledge. They are states of insight into depths of truths unplumbed by the discursive intellect. They are illuminations, revelations, full of significance and importance, all inarticulate though they remain; and as a rule they carry with them a curious sense of authority for after-time.[31]

James' nomenclature for this aspect of the mystical experience explicitly redeemed this faculty of immediate insight from oblivion, and so it arrived in the transpersonal repertoire of phenomena to be researched. Judging by his description, it most resembles a superior form of intuition; we all know what is meant by that. You know something. You get a brainwave, you wake up with an idea, you realise the deeper significance of something, yet reasoning has no part in it, either your own or that of anyone else; you don't know how you know it, but you know that you know it, because you know it. And it is not just about the price of fish, or how to keep your car-windscreen clean — although creative insight seems to be akin. What is of interest to transpersonal psychology is the entire human capacity to know and understand directly. In general, intuition is not usually included in the classic psychological repertoire, presumably because it eludes the methodology which enables the more linear thought processes to be studied. In contrast, forms of intuition have been thoroughly nosed through in philosophy and literature; the Parisian Henri Bergson (1859–1941) for one devoted original ideas to them. The mystical variant however continues to attract the most attention, as it appears to express the immediate, because unmediated, operation of consciousness.

8 Pure consciousness and participation

Beyond transpersonal circles, opinions differ fundamentally on the question of whether such immediacy is possible at all. The philosopher Steven T. Katz expressed himself very clearly on this subject. In his book *Mysticism and Philosophical Analysis* he once stated:

> There are NO pure (i.e., unmediated) experiences. Neither mystical experience nor more ordinary forms of experience give any indication, or any grounds for believing, that they are unmediated ... This epistemological fact seems to me to be true, because of the sorts of beings we are, even with regard to the experiences of those ultimate objects of concern with which the mystics have intercourse, e.g., God, Being, nirvana etc ... A proper evaluation of this fact leads to the recognition that ... the experience itself as well as the form in which it is reported is shaped by concepts which the mystic brings ... to his experience. Thus, for example, the nature of the Christian mystic's pre-mystical consciousness informs the mystical consciousness such that he experiences the mystical reality in terms of Jesus, the Trinity, or a personal God, etc., rather than in terms of the non-personal, non-everything, to be precise, Buddhist doctrine of nirvana.[32]

This position raises various objections. It is always risky to make an absolute statement that can be disproved by a single case. While genuine proof is inherently unfeasible, it is not difficult to find cases that plead against Katz' conviction. He may have based his argument on a limited range of sources, such as the sort of testimonies that emphatically confirmed certain traditions, or at least made them recognisable for him, by using familiar language and images. For in addition there are countless firsthand accounts of people with experiences that did not fit into their former religious convictions or cultural assumptions, and sometimes even tended towards heresy by comparison. This is borne out by the statements not only of historical mystics (see also Chapter 3), but also of some of those interviewed in this book. Such experiences generally trigger considerable shifts in the cognitive orientation of the person concerned; the familiar phenomenon of conversion would not exist without it. Katz' views in this respect are diametrically opposed to the authority displayed by the testimonies of Teresa of Avila (see Chapter 3, 'The G-word'). Moreover, the mystical experience usually impels an individual to a total revision of his belief systems. On this subject R. Woods, for example, wrote in the introduction to his collection of essays on mysticism: 'If anything ... a revaluation and reorganization of conceptual systems is typical of mystical experience.'[33] In addition, Katz implies that the religious and cultural context of mystical experiences is static. Now that hardly applies to the extent of a single human life, let alone to the life cycle of a culture. Even disregarding numerous less authoritative renewers of religious cultures, one must nevertheless wonder about the nature of the experiences of Jesus and Buddha; they seem at least to have experienced something for which their inherited frames of reference had no answer—hence their impetus to replace them. Lastly, with regard to Katz's decisive dismissal of the unmediated experience, his conviction that such things cannot exist 'because of the sort of beings we are' is revealing. Considering our usual image of ourselves, that is a valid enough statement; unusual experiences of consciousness, however, form the context *par excellence* that undermines it.

Transpersonal scholars do not automatically dismiss the possibility of pure consciousness experiences, but explicitly keep it open and explore it. This essentially distinguishes these circles from other psychological schools and tendencies. In its questions on this subject, therefore, transpersonal psychology stems more from the philosophical tradition; its lines of inquiry, from both west and east, do not stop short at the borders of conceptual thinking. It is not even necessary for this purpose to cross over to the radical non-dualistic east; the German philosopher Martin Heidegger (1889–1976) for example pointed out the crucial difference between rational, reasoned thought and intuitive, meditative thought.[34] In so doing he set aside the classic methodology of logical dealings with representations and abstractions, and devoted himself explicitly to contemplation, in pursuit of direct knowledge of the *Dasein*. Now language itself, as a conceptual tool, forms a considerable hindrance to the direct expression of this ontological dimension. And even if philosophers are wont to introduce their own concepts, the new linguistic paths that Heidegger entered on in the process did not make his work any more accessible. Recent authors of the transpersonal persuasion however are hard at work trying to reveal more about direct knowledge. Joan Waldron concurred with James' use of the term *noësis* when she examined the impact of profound transcendental experiences on the lives of those concerned. She used the concept of *noësis* for the 'direct apprehension of knowledge and understanding' that then takes place, and for 'a completely new understanding that comes in an instantaneous fashion' and 'transcends previous understanding'.[35, 36] In her classic study of transcendent ecstasy, Marghanita Laski distinguishes the category of 'knowledge ecstasies'. She concludes that

> knowledge of its nature incommunicable ... is felt to derive from experiences better than those in which communicable knowledge is gained. And it follows that knowledge of *all* or *everything*—a very usual claim—which can not of its nature be communicated, is derived from experiences felt to be better than those in which knowledge of *something* is gained.[37]

Precisely how we must understand the qualification 'better' is not further explained, but the distinction is clearly important.

For many years James' earlier typification of the mystical experience served as the pre-eminent reference point in transpersonal literature. In a more recent work however Kaisa Puhakka suggested refinements and alternative views. She questioned the statement that this knowing constitutes a condition or state of consciousness:

> True, everything that can be known or represented as a content of experience appears to be subject to the influence of states. Yet I had come to see that knowing itself is not essentially state–dependent. More than that, I had come to see that knowing is not a 'state' at all but rather an 'activity'.[38]

In the same book, *Transpersonal Knowing*, Jorge Ferrer put his finger on the subtle Cartesianism in present-day experience-oriented theory: the dichotomy between the person who experiences and what is experienced, or the knower versus the known. The approach he suggests is one of participation. This entails no expansion of individual consciousness, that gains access to transpersonal content in the process. Rather, he suggests, it seems to be a case of a transpersonal event, that leads in the individual to what we call a transpersonal experience. 'Thus understood, the ontological dimension of transpersonal phenomena is primary and results in the experiential one.' He regards the dimension of the experience therefore as the participation of an individual consciousness in a transpersonal event.[39]

Six and two threes, in transpersonal guise? On the grounds of witness reports this idea seems to hold enough water to function as hypothesis. A comparison with physics may clarify things. The laws that describe the behaviour of molecules have an area of validity connected with the state of the matter concerned: solid, fluid, or gaseous. In the transition from one phase to another, different values for the same variables are thrown up; when we determine place and speed of motion, the same collection of molecules produces a different overall picture. When physics arrived at the edge of the molecular area of validity however, the familiar terms lost their meaning entirely; the matrix of space and time could go back on the shelf, and we found that we needed to think in terms of *events* that *may* take place as manifestation of an already existent potential. Ferrer's participatory suggestion of events on the edge of personal consciousness bears a striking resemblance to this. The atomic entity of that consciousness ceases to exist in this form, and its place is filled by an interactive occurrence, in which the normal and essentially linear causality of cause and effect appear to be replaced by phenomena of resonance, which we describe in very different terms—such as waves, frequencies and probabilities.

In the subjective terminology of the process of experiencing Ferrer adds:

> As used in this work, participatory knowing refers to a multidimensional access to reality that includes not only the intellectual knowing of the mind, but also the emotional and emphatic knowing of the heart, the sensual and somatic knowing of the body, the visionary and intuitive knowing of the soul, as well as any other way of knowing available to human beings.[40]

The usual duality between subject/consciousness on the one hand and object/experience on the other thus ends somewhere, according to these authors. This metamorphosis into Puhakka's activity or Ferrer's participation has a parallel in everyday language. While 'knowledge' concerns an object—something we do or do not have—'to know' as a verb refers to something that is going on, and something that 'we', as bearers of consciousness, participate in. 'Knowing' actually refers to both sides at once; to the event in which our capacity to know is active, and to the knowledge that becomes available within that.

9 Crises of knowing

However fine and elevated the reflections on mystical events may be, im—mediate forms of knowing, involving no mediating stages of thought, can land us in hot water. Intuition and cognition sometimes come up with very diverse contents, which is not always easy to deal with. At the common-or-garden level, for example, we are all familiar with the continual negotiations for peace within us between both modes of knowing. We can cope with this, but there is generally no question of simply returning to business as usual after a consciousness experience which deviates sharply from the more familiar states of waking, dreaming, and deep sleep. As stated earlier, profound experiences may strip us of many of the ideas and assumptions by which we know ourselves in the world. On the other hand, our cognitive structures very seldom vanish from the scene for good. As the 'flavour' of the experienced immediacy fades, the former mental frame of reference returns to the foreground, although not usually in the same form or with the same degree of authority (see Waldron). This frame of reference then partly determines the way in which an experience is understood, accepted and integrated in the course of time. In his book *Meanings of Madness*, published in 1998, Castillo used a case study to illustrate how pronounced, even dramatic, the influence of various cognitive frameworks can be on the integration of transpersonal experiences. He compared the notion of consciousness among Indian yogis with the western concept of self, and showed how people attribute meaning to similar experiences on that basis.

> In the Hindu Yoga system ... it is assumed that both aspects of consciousness exist simultaneously, but that observing consciousness (*atman*)[41] is only experienced as a separate entity when participating consciousness (*jiva*)[42] is restrained ... The goal of yogic practice is to separate out atman from jiva, thus creating a division of consciousness in the individual.[43]

As typification of the cognitive structure among westerners, Castillo suggests that 'western psychiatry conceptualizes this type of split in consciousness between a participating self and an observing self as depersonalization'.[44] And 'in contrast to Western psychiatric patients, whose experiences of divided consciousness are characterized by panic and anxiety, the experiences of the yogis are normal and normative religious experiences characterized by ecstasy and bliss'.[45]

Three groups of participants who had all had distinctly unusual experiences of consciousness in the past—people who meditated, psychotics and epileptics—were compared in a study by the Indian clinical psychologists Komilla Thapa and Vinoda Murthy. Their results too indicated the importance of specific cognitive structures for the subsequent understanding of unusual experiences.

> The non-integrative groups (i.e., subjects experiencing the Psychotic and Epileptic ASCs) were bewildered, perplexed and confused by the imagery and perceptual-cognitive changes associated with the ASC. In the absence of a cognitive structure and social and emotional support they were unable to handle these experiences. [It has been] pointed out that mystical experiences involve a breakdown of cognitive structures, including those which help define the self. The experience was given meaning by the residual cognitive structures provided by a philosophical or religious system. Where the meditator interpreted his/her experience as achieving a higher plane of reality, others without similar benefits and anchors would view it as catastrophic, 'a plunge into nothingness'.[46]

Someone who has trouble digesting an unusual experience may find it even more difficult to communicate such things. Sometimes we are perfectly aware of what is going on within us, but find ourselves at a loss for words when in company. For example, we may be familiar with a particular physical sensation, a certain itch or cramp or pins-and-needles that we have known since childhood, but could not for the life of us explain to someone else. In the same way someone might be unable to explain to others that she simply *knows* that her crisis is about something essential, and has some particular significance. Even so, if one's private compass indicates the way, one can still try to steer by it. This is not the territory of 'classic' cognitive psychology, which is primarily about serial tasks and causal connections. Now the topic of 'consciousness' is regularly raised in that context too. Before long, however, it becomes clear that this subject is surrounded by abundant fuel for misunderstandings and a confusion of tongues. There are probably few terms liable to so many different interpretations as 'spirit', 'self' and 'consciousness'. There is also the English term 'mind', which has no direct equivalent in Dutch. These concepts are far from exact, and open to a variety of interpretations; no wonder that so many are in circulation. The term 'consciousness' in particular has essentially different meanings in different research traditions. Within cognitive psychology it signifies 'that which we are conscious of'. In the interdisciplinary work *Brein en bewustzijn* (Brain and Consciousness) for example we read: 'In fact consciousness is a state of our brain which is the exception rather than the rule. Most of what we do during the day and the information we process and the brain activity we arouse takes place in the cellars of the mind: the subconscious.'[47] Consciousness therefore as the counterpart to subconsciousness, as qualification of a part of our brain activity and of the content of our experience. Within transpersonal psychology the term is used in a completely different sense, namely as a sort of living, immaterial substance, which gives us the power to experience things in the first place—whether we are mentally and conceptually aware of it or not. These different outlooks can be summarised as a 'consciousness of things' versus a 'consciousness as potential'. Even at the level of the definite article there is an implicit distinction: '*the* consciousness' could easily refer to a thing, state or quality that can be demarcated, while 'consciousness' indicates a facilitating factor, a context or foundation. In simplified form, these outlooks can be interpreted as a western versus an eastern orientation; this is illustrated by the difference cited in Chapter 3 between the bias of Christianity towards the 'objects' that appear in consciousness, versus that of Zen Buddhism on consciousness as the location or medium in which the objects appear. In line with the classic western focus on the objects of consciousness, contemporary cognitive research focuses primarily on the content of consciousness, such as that produced by sensory perception. It thus represents a classic western perspective, which is reflected in the most recent research programmes.[48]

In a much smaller number of laboratories meanwhile, consciousness has also turned up as the basis of all perception, namely in the context of explicit interdisciplinary approaches, in part associated with views on causality, time, space and matter, that are essentially different from classic theories. An impression of this angle of approach follows in Chapter 4, 'Quantum speculations'.

10 Transpersonal phenomenology

It is clear that, with regard to methodology, there are many snags attached to research into intuitive and other direct forms of knowing, not to mention the nature of our consciousness. Scientifically speaking, the practice is still in its infancy. The equipment used to develop new ground here and there has had to be imported, and its suitability for the soil conditions of the new territory still leaves much to be desired. The case of phenomenology may serve as illustration. The perspective of the first person singular is indispensable in order to increase the depth of field here, especially when brain research into consciousness, as someone once suggested, amounts to holding a stethoscope to the outside of a football stadium in order to work out the rules of the game.[49] For research into subjective experience, as seen in Chapter 2, 'The subject and the methodology', there are points of departure in phenomenology. The best known representative of this, the school of German scientist Edmund Husserl (1859–1938), developed from the field of philosophy into a method of working which proved applicable not only to the 'lived experience' of things in the outer physical world, but equally so to that of the thoughts, images and feelings that fill our inner world. Through a clearly delineated procedure, phenomenological research strives for example to distill the essential significance of an experience from both its content and its structure. Various authors have treated subjective experiences such as of rage, of being at home, of friendship, guilt, desire, sleeplessness, and even open–heart surgery in this way.[50] Just as psychopathology increasingly typifies negative experiences in a dimensional way, it must therefore be possible, with a hefty phenomenological injection on the part of psychology, to further map out positive or healthy empiricism. This would remove all fundamental objections to themes regarded as transpersonal in one go; the starting point is neither more nor less than the experience itself, not some frame of reference which supplies meaning in advance. As ways of obtaining knowledge, there is moreover little to choose between phenomenology and objective observation. Phenomenology too naturally makes a 'strict' distinction between subject and object. What appears in our consciousness is never consciousness itself, it is always a *consciousness of something*.[51] For that reason phenomenology is fundamentally a suitable instrument for research into that which appears in consciousness. In order to create a more valuable methodology, the protocol could do with some refining, as Richard Stevens (b. 1939) among others convincingly argues, in his contribution to the compilation *Investigating Phenomenal Consciousness: New Methodologies and Maps*.[52] The views on consciousness on which the tradition is based now seem somewhat out-of-date, as can be seen for example in Ferrer's participatory point of view. The axiom of a consciousness versus the objects that it perceives is naturally related to the thesis of the philosopher Kant, who stated that we cannot know the *Ding an sich* because we can only perceive it, we cannot be it. In order therefore to describe the event in which pure consciousness, according to various sources, can manifest itself, even the existing phenomenology falls short. Psychologist Ron Valle therefore suggested a transpersonal phenomenology which omits the necessity for a consciousness *of something*.[53] Even though he does not yet address the need for a practical methodology, together with Puhakka and Ferrer he does create the theoretical space for the existence of an unmediated perception, which precedes the development of any structure, whether in the form of ideas or feelings, images or meanings.

For the methodological approach to that hypothetical, unstructured consciousness, transpersonally oriented researchers draw not only from the phenomenological tradition but also from sources that still carry an explicit 'spiritual' stamp. 'Eastern' techniques such as *mindfulness meditation* seem particularly appropriate for the exploration of the diverse manifestations of consciousness.[54] One aspect of this that also featured in Hurlburt's bleep-controlled observation of psychotic experiences (see Chapter 2, 'The subject and the methodology') is that the method allowed the 'subjects' of the survey to become increasingly skilled in perceiving and reporting their inner states. If one ascribes any credibility at all to subjective consciousness, increasing its requisite accuracy with regard to observation and representation is comparable to the refinement of any random objective means of measurement. Now since the design of psychological laboratory projects structurally ignores introspective exercise, there probably is much to be gained here. There is still an unprecedented gap between the students of Wilhelm Wundt (see Chapter 3, 'Fathers of introspection') and the traditional masters in the observation of the mind. This is not a mere supposition, but a significant, objective fact, demonstrated by the use of the 'stethoscope' on the stadium of the trained brain. Tibetan monks with decades of intense meditation to their credit agreed to be examined by means of EEG and the neuro-imaging technology of fMRI and MEG.[55] The results showed that in comparison with beginners they produced significantly more gamma waves, their brain activity was differently distributed over various areas, with a high degree of synchronisation between those areas. It was striking, moreover, that some of these differences were not only apparent during meditation. The latter fact suggests that the mind can permanently change not only the inner person, but also the physical organisation. This sort of research is extremely recent and exceptional, and while the consensus is that the mind at all events can be physically stimulated in many different ways, confirmation of an actual mind-over-matter effect would be quite a revolution. And yet, how hypothetical *is* this whole mind-over-matter business anyway, when human beings are hard at work day and night, moulding earthly and physical reality according to their ideas, ideals, aims, wishes, schedules, principles, programmes, moral laws and development plans?

11 Peak experiences before and after death

Studies of praying nuns and meditating lamas have yielded fascinating information, and continue to do so. But human consciousness, whatever our conception of it, does not operate only in convent cells or Zen centres. It also reveals itself in less everyday ways on the athletics track, between the sheets, in the desert and on the deathbed. Since the 1970s, inventories of unusual states of consciousness have been made in a number of these 'secular' territories. Americans Michael Murphy and Rhea White researched transcendental experiences in sport, and called their account of it *In the Zone*.[56] It is the term used by top stars and amateurs of every conceivable sport—baseball, basketball, golf, tennis, running, sailing, racing and so on—for those magical, mythical and mystical moments in which athletes rise above themselves and possess superhuman strength, inexhaustible energy, deadly precision and razorsharp timing. Jenny Wade collected the experiences of ordinary people who had extraordinary sexual experiences; undreamt-of experiences of fire and fireworks, magnificent nuances of light, of melting souls and timeless, spaceless Being. These are accounts of transcendence, in which lovemaking draws aside the veil of normal perception.[57] Then there are experiences in the natural world, which also featured on Maslow's list of situations in which spiritual peaks can be achieved, intentionally or otherwise. In *Wild-Animal-triggered Peak Experiences: Transpersonal Aspects*, for example, Ryan Demares and Kevin Krycka describe the deeply moving and transforming effects of personal encounters with dolphins and whales.[58] And last but certainly not least, research into near–death experiences has been going on for years now. Research that generally begins not in the psychologist's consulting room, but in the ambulance or the intensive care unit. In a hitherto undemonstrated way, the findings so far lay an empirical foundation under the transpersonal outlook, that life is more than a mere three-dimensional multiple pile-up of atoms, and consciousness more than the frictional heat of our cerebral machinery. Moreover, they correspond to ideas and proverbs about life and death that humanity has cherished throughout the world, and in all ages — knowledge which is borne out by such sources as the *Tibetan Book of the Dead*, and which has formed the foundation of the metaphysics of spiritual traditions. One Dutch pioneer in this recent field of research is cardiologist Pim van Lommel. As a result of technological developments over the years, he encountered an increasing number of people who had survived heart attacks. When it emerged that some of them had also had specific experiences after a cardiac arrest, Van Lommel and his team began to research this phenomenon. They found for example that 18% of those affected reported an experience that could be termed *near–death*. Certain elements and overall patterns recur in these accounts. These include a sense of ineffability, profound serenity and peace, an awareness of death, and an experience of leaving the body. Almost everyone reports entering the stereotypical dark tunnel with light at the end of it, and then arriving in an unearthly world, full of colour and sometimes music. There are encounters, often with familiar people who have died, and the general experience is primarily of light and love. There is a sort of life assessment, and sometimes a preview of the future. Then they perceive some kind of boundary, which cannot be crossed, and they 'return', sometimes with a sort of mission in life, but they generally end up in the painful and highly uncomfortable situation of a gravely ill patient in the intensive care unit; an environment and a state of being in stark contrast to the near-death experience. This experience is almost invariably one of undreamt-of and unprecedented bliss. It may even banish our ultimate fear, the fear of death, melting it away like snow in the sun, so that the lives of those to whom it happens, in their own words, is never the same again. While in their earlier lives these people often had little or nothing in common with each other, and represent the whole spectrum from strict orthodox to strict atheist, after their transforming experience they all devoted themselves to values and activities that can be described as religious or spiritual.

Apart from the similarities of their experiences, various things happened on site in the clinic that unsettled the familiar interpretative frames of reference. Some survivors could afterwards describe the interior of treatment rooms in detail, and report things that medical and nursing staff had done at moments when the patients registered no brain activity at all. The duration of the cardiac arrest in these cases was much longer than the fifteen seconds that experimentally marks the end of all brain activity, and thus the beginning of a 'flat' EEG. Among other cases out of the common run, the vicissitudes of a set of false teeth may achieve a lasting place in history. The teeth belonged to a comatose patient who was brought into the coronary care unit, and given artificial respiration, heart massage and defibrillation. To enable intubation, a nurse had to take out his dentures, which she then put on the 'crash cart'. After a good hour the patient was transferred to the IC unit, still deeply comatose. More than a week later, the same nurse met him again; now convalescent, he immediately said: 'Oh, that nurse knows where my dentures are'. To her surprise, he added: 'Yes, you were there when I was brought into hospital and you took my dentures out of my mouth and put them onto that cart, it had all these bottles on it and there was this sliding drawer underneath and that's where you put my teeth.'[59]

Comparable research has shown moreover that blind people, including those born blind, are capable of verifiable visual perceptions in such circumstances.[60] All physiological, neurological and psychological explanations of varying degrees of obviousness for this sort of remarkable incident were considered by Van Lommel's team, but proved to be far from explanatory. Publication in the eminent medical journal *The Lancet* followed.[61] It would not have got this far if there had been anything even slightly amiss with the methodology. The publication of the article remains remarkable in all respects because the conclusions of the article, as Van Lommel himself points out, gnaw at the prevailing medical image of the relationship between mind and brain, and in a friendly but insistent way demand a thorough re-evaluation of the conventional paradigm. In the meantime he has explored his findings in further depth, thus representing a small group of scientists who give expression to a vision of human consciousness as a reality that is essentially separate from all physicality, time and space, although it does manifest itself there in a functional way. The fact that others in his field did not exactly beat a path to his door after his publication, which caused scarcely a ripple in the medical world, must be due to the impossibility, as Thomas Kuhn puts it, of leaving the familiar paradigm for what it is. Even so, Van Lommel's work forms an unmistakable token that the heart is more than an organic pump that, when it breaks down, automatically switches off the light in the upper storey.

12 Kundalini, ecstasy and nightmare

One frequently recurring topic in transpersonal circles is the *kundalini* experience. If you search for it on the internet, you will be inundated by information. The term *kundalini*, liberally used in the present–day spiritual universe, refers to an ancient classical Hindu concept, passed on for centuries from teacher to pupil by word of mouth, so that the earliest written source dates only from the eighth century AD. In this tradition *kundalini*—Sanskrit for 'coiled' or 'writhing like a snake'—stands for the human life force that lies curled up in three and a half coils at the base of the spine. This snake can be awakened by spiritual exercise and creep upwards along the spine to the crown of the head. The energy is seen as the power that the energetic body brings to consciousness by activating the chakras on the way one by one. In this role the energy is associated with the goddess Shakti, who unites herself in the crown of the head with her consort Shiva, enriching the person concerned with the fruits of their union. Philosophically speaking, the individual self thereby realises its deepest essence as Brahman, the universal consciousness. The traditional phenomenology of this whole process is moreover extremely differentiated. Apart from as a snake, the energy can also be experienced, in the words of the formidable Indian ecstatic Ramakrishna (1836–1886), in the form of ants, fish, monkeys and birds.[62] The lore covers an infinite number of such qualitative details and subtle phenomena, each with its own exotic epithet, thus forming a science in itself. The energetic balance also plays a crucial role in the health of the whole person, as carrier of the self–healing powers for body, mind and soul. An interesting point is that the traditional western symbol of medicine, the staff of Aesculapius, portrays a snake wriggling up a rod. This again is related to the *caduceus*, a winged staff with two snakes, used mainly in America. While the Greek roots of the staff lie with the god Aesculapius, presumably a mythologised healer, the caduceus is associated with the originally Egyptian god Thoth, who as Hermes became the standard–bearer of western esoterism.

The first westerner to reveal his knowledge of 'snake power' was Sir John Woodroffe (1865–1936), a British Supreme Judge in the colony of

Bengal, whose extensive hobbies included yoga, indigenous languages and philosophy. Woodroffe's translation of two classical scriptures, *The Serpent Power*, which he wrote under the pseudonym of Arthur Avalon, made tantric wisdom permanently available to the west.[63] Virtually all later western publications draw from his work, which describes the shakti energy as a divine force that is neither physical nor mental, but the creative foundation of both. No less a person than Carl Jung held a symposium on kundalini in 1932, in which his psychology and concept of possible access to higher states of consciousness reflected the sophisticated lore of the yoga model of spiritual development. For Jung, kundalini played a crucial role in the individuation process, while also holding the keys to infinite creativity. Furthermore, he saw an analogy of the snake in the mythological dragon, as the greatest challenge that a person can encounter in life; this reflects the traditional view that kundalini, as the pure life energy of human beings, requires skilful handling. As a volatile phenomenon, it is said to potentially cause a whole range of physical, physiological and neurological ailments. Apart from a growing genre of somewhat popularised accounts, an extremely small number of scientific sources in the meantime also attest to that. In the originally self-published *Kundalini: Psychosis or Transcendence*, the American doctor Lee Sannella developed his vision of the phenomenon on the basis of both literary and clinical cases.[64] It prompted him to compare the stormy, chaotic, physiologically unsettling spiritual birth of an awakened self with the birth of a human baby: intense, sometimes bloody and violent in appearance, but natural. On the basis of diverse sources, Sannella concluded that though the kundalini lore, including all possible physical and mental side-effects of its ascent, has been developed most exhaustively in the Hindu canon, traces can be found in all cultures: from the !Kung of the Kalahari, who describe strikingly similar phenomena, to countless nuns and monks throughout Christian history. Prickling limbs, trembling muscles, rumbling intestines, rolling eyes, sensations of alternating heat and cold, itching, pain, sexual charge, sensory failure, flashes of light and visions, vivid dreams, noises, violent emotions, raving thoughts, trances, out-of-body and other remarkable states of consciousness, no account of a devout monastic life seems complete without this sort of experience.

The potential ascribed to kundalini is in fact infinite; its powers are said to be far beyond our understanding, and to be closely linked to the transformation of individual consciousness. Nevertheless, the ancient sources point out frequently enough the risks of playing with powerful forces such as these. Could Allen Bergin have been talking about the same thing, when, prompted by his research into religious lifestyles and mental health, he declared:

Some religious influences have a modest impact, whereas another portion seems like the mental equivalent of nuclear energy ... The more powerful portion can provide transcendent conviction or commitment and is sometimes manifested in dramatic personal healing or transformation.[65]

From an orthodox western perspective that might seem like a lot of nonsense, but body–oriented therapy schools take a broader view, although actual information in this area seems positively scarce. Now the idea of kundalini is strongly reminiscent of that of *orgone*, the primal energy named by psychoanalyst Wilhelm Reich (1897–1957), while the bio-energetics of his pupil Alexander Lowen (1910–2008) provides a modern language for the whole state of affairs. The fundamental tenet is that there are energy blocks all over the body. Unprocessed emotions from one's personal history leave unconscious tensions in very specific places, and as long as the snake slumbers on, we are not aware of — or troubled by — anything. Subjectively we have never known our bodies to be any different; furthermore, it is in fact through these subtle tensions, and the inner form and attitude that fits in with our self–image, that we recognise — largely subconsciously — our own bodies from within. As soon as primal energy goes into action and encounters blockages, however, things can go badly wrong. Just as subtle distortions of the spine radiate pain in the surrounding area — the daily routine of the physiotherapist — the high-voltage kundalini current is believed to start roaming around elsewhere in the body if diverted by blockages. This would also explain, for example, why, when westerners throw themselves wholeheartedly into a demanding, weeks–long meditation retreat, some of them get into such difficulties in the process; apart from long–term physical complaints, there have been reports of psychotic phenomena, which can lead to hospitalisation and medication. In an article on this subject Lois Vanderkooi described how the first generation of meditation teachers to arrive in the west straight from Asia had to adapt their approach to the reality of sturdy, unpractised western egos.[66] A small-scale exploratory survey however did not indicate that kundalini problems were being structurally interpreted as psychosis.[67] Nevertheless Jon Ossoff, a male nurse at the psychiatric clinic of Glen Oaks, New York, devoted an article to a fascinating case.[68] A Mexican woman was brought in who seemed psychotic, and who therefore received the same treatment as so many other clients who prefer crack to anti-psychotic drugs, and are fished off the street every day. Several days later she was doing remarkably well. She turned out to have no psychiatric history at all, but to have taken part in an intensive meditation training shortly before admission. When she asked whether the whole affair might be connected with *shaktipat*, the traditional transference of consciousness from teacher to pupil, Ossoff had to shift gear for a moment, to the yoga frame of reference with which he was familiar. Somewhat amazed, he began to see her earlier behaviour in a new light: all that jumping and skipping, rapid breathing, rolling eyes, bowing and elaborate gestures. Over several sessions he discussed these matters with her, and his colleagues in the clinic could not see her as a genuine psychotic either. Some time later she wrote him a clear–headed letter from Mexico, which showed that she had managed to process several emotional themes. When he told the story later to Dr Vasant Lad, *the* Indian authority on ayurveda, the latter finished Ossoff's sentences correctly now and then, so familiar was he with the phenomenon.[69]

Western clinicians are quite a different story. For one, the individual symptoms of a faulty or too rapid kundalini flow are so divergent that any specific clinical picture is virtually impossible. More fundamental of course is the fact that western medicine has no frame of reference to motivate the search for such a picture. To rational minds kundalini lore represents at best a sort of exotic superstition, a source of hilarity during the coffee break. It would take a lot of nerve to be seen to take it seriously. In Asia there is a different climate altogether, and a number of more recent publications not surprisingly come from an eastern clinical environment. Yet there are sporadic western attempts to map out this matter. The most prominent Danish medical journal, for example, once published an article on the diagnostics of kundalini problems.[70] But the most important preliminary work was by Sannella, who categorised the various physiological phenomena, and whose work was supplemented by the biomedical engineer Itzhak Bentov (1923–1979). This Slovakian Jew, who had diverse inventions such as the mobile heart catheter to his name in America, took up meditation, then went on to investigate the physics of consciousness.[71] He was one of the first to measure the process of meditation in test subjects, which yielded insights into a variety of physiological and neurological changes and connections. Among other things he discovered the wave and resonance patterns of the heart, of the skull, of brain cavities and the ear, from which he drew conclusions about the electromagnetic fields in and surrounding the head. He began for example to regard the head as an antenna that transmits its own field, and interacts with the existing magnetic field of the environment. Meditation training over a long period would eventually make it easier to synchronise wave patterns in different areas of the brain. As a result, all sorts of glands, organs and senses become more easily relaxed, and begin to feel 'more at ease with themselves'. This is something that practitioners may well recognise in their own experience. In this context moreover eastern spiritual sources refer to the incidence of *siddhis*, increasing sensitivities and 'supernatural' powers such as clairvoyance.[72] These give the practitioner more insight into the essence of all things, but may also tempt him to start regarding himself as very exceptional—thus impeding his own development. Bentov saw the whole kundalini business as a natural spring–clean of the nervous system, proceeding in a sequence that correlates with Sannella's clinical documentation. His view of what he called the *physio-kundalini syndrome* in fact implied that these shifts and their complex chains of effects can be intensely disruptive. For in the course of a human life, the nervous system receives countless impressions, probably hovering in most cases between permanent stress and traumatic impact. The urgency of the present-day need for real release and relaxation can be plainly seen in the cultural and economic interests behind the consumption of alcohol and drugs, food and sex, the obsession with danger, violence and everything that is extreme, and in the multifarious body-industry of sauna parks and healing crystals, feel–good music and elixirs, fitness, and these days wellness too. It goes without saying therefore that the parasympathetic part of the nervous system structurally receives too little attention, and does not allow itself to be switched off without protest by any kundalini awakening. In Bentov's hypothetical model this can bring about long–term and often diffuse problems. Moreover, we also come into unavoidable contact with the magnetic fields around the earth, and the turbulence within them. And, as he showed, the process may be triggered when the magnetic field surrounding the head is influenced. At all events, the said wave patterns appear to get the hiccups, as it were, before—with help—they manage to settle at a higher level of integration and resonance. Bentov's physio–kundalini model offers the sort of matrix on which there is still much research to be done; he himself made a series of suggestions at the time. These suggestions incidentally point out that the whole physiology of this complex business only concerns the physically measurable dimension. For him this runs parallel to the cognitive and psychological dimension, while the process as such originates from a non-physical basis. His own experiments were prematurely cut short by his death in an air crash. Related research however is being carried out all over the world, primarily in the context of neuro-feedback and interdisciplinary consciousness studies (see Chapter 4, 'Quantum speculation').

13 The self in creative chaos

From a psychological angle, authors of various persuasions are currently focusing on the questions: how spiritual are pathological experiences, and conversely, how pathological are spiritual experiences? Their approach begins with the observation that we still lack the ability to distinguish between the two. If we represent both categories by the type of experiences on which we have most sources, we can focus for the sake of convenience on psychotic versus mystical experiences. The British cognitive neuropsychologist Caroline Brett provided a good outline of recent insights in an article significantly entitled: *Psychotic and Mystical States of Being: Connections and Distinctions.*[73] In this work she surveys various sorts of criteria that are at all feasible. Of these, the criteria governing the particular content or structure of states of consciousness now carry little weight in theory; no sequence of imagery, for example, is inherently sick or healthy. As anthropology shows, the cultural significance of a particular delusion determines whether we see it as psychotic or mystical. It may be more fruitful to consider the effects of an experience, such as self-inflated ideas about oneself, which would point to a psychotic rather than a mystical origin. Similarly, persecution mania and self-destructive behaviour typify the first category and not the latter. Another phenomenological criterion, from the British psychologist Peter Chadwick, who has inside knowledge of psychosis, states that the mystic feels that his inspirations emanate from himself, and focuses on his place in the greater whole, while the psychotic feels that the outside world impinges on him and is generally hostile to him.[74] Cognitive studies of psychotic experiences further reveal a difference between how literally psychotics and religious people take their experiences, and how much influence these have on their daily lives. Also, we could argue that the dividing line runs between 'negative' and 'positive' experiences, but that is clearly too simplistic.[75] While we would probably class guilt feelings as negative, for example, they may constitute a lifeline to a psychotic. Next, through a glance at the structure of psychotic thinking, Brett indicates the ways in which the self becomes confused. Western philosophy provides various solid insights into this problem. Normally the self organises everything we perceive into a limited number of categories, namely:

things in the outside world, thoughts in our heads, and feelings in our bodies. The ability to keep this up virtually automatically all day long is not the product of chance, but of a successful cognitive development. In a psychotic state, however, something in that whole constellation appears to shift, so that the outside world is not perceived as fixed — and thus as separate from the subjective self. The normal categories that help us to understand ourselves and the world no longer work, and that is quite a fundamental difference. The perceptions themselves continue to function, but we can make absolutely no sense of them. Time is no longer the reliable continuous motion that we know, sounds in the outside world might just as well be our own thoughts, and our self as centre of all our perceptions and actions is no longer what it was. One Dutch publication has thoroughly explored how inaccurate it is to dismiss this situation with 'a psychotic sees things that are not really there'. As a philologist, Wouter Kusters was able to make an acute analysis of the collapse of his world of significance after his single psychotic episode. In his *Pure waanzin — een zoektocht naar de psychotische ervaring* (Sheer Madness — A Quest for the Psychotic Experience), a rare and acclaimed account in essay form, he reveals the extent of the gap between the world of 'things', that we normally regard as reality, and the psychotic world of unconceptualised, direct experience. To the psychotic, things cast off their symbolic cloak and appear not through such agreed concepts as 'violin case' or 'bus stop', but as bare manifestations with no fixed form, name or meaning. Only the psychotic himself can endow these things with meaning, but when words no longer refer one-to-one to objects, thoughts or feelings, he lacks the tried-and-tested tool of language. It goes without saying that this makes normal functioning extremely difficult.

Kusters distinguished three aspects in his psychosis, which overlap in time: the destruction of rules, ecstasy, and the construction of new rules. In the first, objects lose their symbolic value; in the second, all rules of language disappear. Kusters:

> I had achieved my aim: all limits had vanished, the dykes were breached, I stood outside of myself, I was literally in 'ek-stasis'. What happened within and beyond me became one whole. I was perplexed and bewildered. I was no longer imprisoned inside language, but could move freely in all directions.[76]

The third aspect concerns the continual attempt to reconstruct meaning from the remaining 'debris'. A fragment:

> Warsaw is war-saw in English ... so the 'war' was seen. In Poland, in the Second World War, but also now by me, because they say I am 'in de war' ('in de war' = 'confused' in Dutch). People who are 'in de war'

have to get out of 'de war'. In Poland there was one way out of the
war, via the 'spoor'(railway), the war-spoor.[77]

Another fragment shows how this search may indeed lead to coherence:

I try to work my way through the walls of the isolation cell with the
aid of the plastic knives and plates that I get at mealtimes. While I try
to scrape through the wall with the plastic plate, I feel like a worker
from head to toe. I'm wearing a sweater that goes well with this activity: grey with red stripes. This pattern is derived from constructivism,
an art form from the Soviet Union, where workers are also in power.
The red stripes of my sweater connect me to the power of the commu-
nist workers in Russia. So I'm not scraping on my own.[78]

Kusters' logic is not the usually accepted sort, in which the meaning of
one thing is attached to something else. The connections that he makes are
no longer conceptual but instances of a direct, individually experienced
resonance, via colour, sound, energy, emotion, and free association. It is
clear that this can be a very creative process, and the relationship of various forms of 'madness' to creativity and the artistic vocation has often
been pointed out. From a psychotic position it is of course quite a different
matter to function within the context of the social consensus. Further,
Kusters counts himself fortunate in that his episode was much less frightening than those of many other people. The most interesting thing here
however, as he also shows elsewhere in his book, is that most current theories on psychosis essentially fall short. The popular image of psychotics
is of people who think, talk and act completely incoherently and chaoti-
cally, and who ought to be cured of this as soon as possible. A little insight
into how we construct and exchange meaning among ourselves by means
of the symbolism of language, and at the same time communicate via a
less 'exact' system such as body language, will show however that listening to verbal text is only one level of understanding. The same applies to
our view of behaviour. It is perfectly logical to systematically avoid everything to do with screens, telephones or radios, if you are convinced that
these are beaming evil thoughts into your mind. The conclusion that the
'content' of statements or behaviour does not form the criterion for 'madness' made its appearance in psychiatry ten years or so ago. This has also
led meanwhile to a widening of the cognitive route to research and treatment. Paul Chadwick, another British clinical psychologist, is a pioneer in
cognitive therapy for schizophrenics. This is a relatively new terrain for,
since the days of Freud, the conventional view has held that, unlike common neuroses, delusions are immune to any kind of treatment or modification. In an early work, however, Chadwick and his colleagues showed
that even diagnosed delusions do repay close scrutiny.[79] They demonstrated that delusional clients can be helped to deliberate on their convic-

tions and to check them against 'hard' reality; when their cherished beliefs fail to stand up to the endorsed tests, people gain more room for manoeuvre.

Now that is valuable enough in itself, but but there is more to it. Various phenomena have begun to detach themselves from their inevitable association with schizophrenia. In this respect, British researchers in particular seem to be actively opening up new perspectives. Gordon Claridge, for example, broadened the concept of schizotypes from a sort of predisposition for psychoses and schizophrenia to a spectrum that also allows for 'healthy' forms of certain 'schizophrenic' behaviour.[80] And similarly, Chadwick's work showed that the dividing line between normal and disturbed behaviour is in fact less distinct than may be comfortable for many of us. We all have our private assumptions and ideas about reality, which we more or less consciously allow to play a role in our lives, and which we are disinclined to check, as we are really rather attached to our own version of it. Of course this does not bring a hard criterion for 'normality' any closer. This much has been illustrated by Dutch researchers Romme and Escher, who explored the experiences of patients who heard 'voices' (see Introduction, and Chapter 2, 'Pathology in the second person singular'). Traditionally, all 'auditive hallucinations' were seen as straightforward symptoms of schizophrenia, but people with no history whatever of psychiatric problems also turned out to hear such 'voices'. Some 'voice-hearers' even functioned extremely well, and their experiences were reminiscent of historical descriptions of religious, intellectual and artistic revelations. By looking at subjects with such widely different experiences, Romme and Escher gained insight into how people can give their voices meaning, so that these do not ruin their lives. Meanwhile, there is increasing evidence that hearing voices is related to traumatic life events, in particular childhood sexual abuse,[81] which needs to be recognised and accepted before such voices can be managed, banished altogether or even felt as life-enriching.[82] We must bear in mind that many of us are familiar with the internalised voices of our parents and educators, which has never meant that we are ripe for a diagnostic label and medication. And various studies have now shown that even those who do hear 'pathological' voices are not simply hearing 'voices that are not there'. As neuro–imaging technology has revealed, at the level of brain activity there is no clear difference between voices heard inside or outside the head. When voice–hearers signal that an inner voice is speaking to them, the same brain areas are seen to be active as when a real person speaks to them.[83] This finding has opened up a whole new avenue for research, bringing together a range of disciplines, and promoting experimentation with therapeutic approaches. And who knows, it may one day even throw light on an incident described by Dutch psychologist G. de Bruijn. Her young client described hearing voices which seemed to come from 'a terrifying world' that existed 'behind the ordinary, real world'. De Bruijn was not paying much attention, as her thoughts were distracted by a blazing row with a colleague she had had an hour previously. The boy was visibly afraid of what he seemed to hear inside his head, but was persuaded after some time to tell her what the voices were saying. The therapist was dumbfounded when he repeated to her, word for word, the stream of abuse that she had mentally thrown at her opponent.[84]

14 Pyschosis as immanent experience of God

In the present context Kusters' book touches on another interesting point, to wit when he mentions religious feeling. Though the stereotypic images of religious maniacs may have lost strength, the obsessiveness of many psychiatric patients about religion, spirituality and invisible 'forces' such as radiation is a well known phenomenon — see also Siddle et al. (2002).[85] Kusters offers an explanation for this from his former psychotic position: when all experience is direct and unfiltered, there is simply no transcendence. As we have seen, the conceptual reality that we would normally be able to transcend no longer exists for the psychotic. He already lives in the raw material of pure experience, everything is the *Ding an sich*. And so there is no idea or image of God, however abstract — God exists, right here, right now. There is only this direct experience of immanence. This prompted Kusters to write about a visit to church:

> The church is pretty full when we arrive, but halfway down there are still some places free for us. That's good: all likeminded people together, who are familiar with the unity of all things. The people who come here are sensitve to the power of symbols and they know about the many ways that lead to God [...] What bliss that these words and the church hymns now flow over me. But what an awkward place I have here. In order to receive the blessing from above to the best advantage, I need to go somewhere else. The energy comes from the highest point in the church and descends on us via the words of the speaker. I could go and stand by the altar to help to distribute the energy through the church. But I prefer to keep quiet. In order to absorb the energy as well as possible I'd do better to lie down and relax completely so that my body does not build up resistance to the outside world. I slip out of the pews and go and lie down on the

ground by the side wall of the church. I do yoga exercises and focus as much as possible on the church energy.

Now the nurse comes and sits down beside me. Does she actually know what the point of a religious gathering is? Of course not, she tells me off for behaving oddly and disrupting and making fun of the service. If anyone here is taking this seriously, it's me.[86]

By now we have gone beyond the beaten path, and in some places beyond mainstream western philosophy too. With Kant, this stopped more or less when it came to what we as humans can know: not the *Ding an sich*, but merely our concept of it. Kusters' direct exposure to the world of conceptless phenomena however affords us access to that other category of experience, which is compared above with psychosis. Before Brett places the mystical experience under the microscope in her article, she shows how reality looks from a Buddhist point of view. In contrast to Cartesian thinkers, Buddhists make no essential distinction between the world of things and the world of the spirit, for there is only one reality, which both inhabit. In short, the *Ding an sich* is not only unknowable, it does not essentially exist. The only abiding thing is consciousness itself, which is therefore the only thing that can serve as a sort of reference point. There is no such thing as a self, except as one of the countless mental concepts that come drifting by in consciousness. The apparent unity of our functioning self is simply produced by the human tendency to organise our perceptions. Normally speaking, we steer by a cognitive compass in order to find our way in life: familiarity with things in the world and our concepts of them are enough for that purpose. In order to get to know the naked truth, however, attention must be scaled down to perception itself, and that happens explicitly in meditation. The detailed series of states of consciousness that can be distinguished in Buddhist philosophy reflect an equal number of 'depths' at which things and concepts collectively lose their seemingly autonomous existence, and consciousness finally makes itself known as the basis of all perception. Along this track the mystical experience occurs, in which the distinction between self as subject, and things or concepts as object, also proves to be a mental construction with no essential basis of existence. And at this point the direct realisation of the underlying unity of all perception makes its appearance.

Without a separate subject and object, the structure of this experience differs radically from daily experience, but not, as we saw earlier, from the psychotic experience. Brett concludes in her article accordingly that these experiences are indeed related to each other in many respects, and certainly in comparison to the structure of the 'normal' experience. She thus subscribes among other things to the notion that crops up in popular texts on spirituality, that the psychotic and the mystic inhabit the same 'ocean' of undifferentiated consciousness, but that the former drowns while the latter swims around in it. At the same time, however, she shows that this image — presumably derived from the mythologist Joseph Campbell — is rather sweeping, and provides no insight into the difference in dynamic between the two situations. She attributes this to a difference in identification. As the mystic has theoretically trained herself to abandon her identification with a separate, subjective self, she can permanently merge with the non-dual basis of all perception, within which all phenomena are recognisable *as* phenomena. The psychotic, on the other hand, finds the loss of the normal perceiving self extremely threatening, because he identifies with it and its absence simply negates his existence. Which is why he makes every effort to restore the one reliable structure of himself as subject versus the world, while so painfully lacking the necessary tools. Inasfar as this is possible, with a self that can be perceived everywhere in the ocean, and a stock of cognitions from the past floating around, the result generally deviates so greatly from the structure employed by the outside world, that social isolation is virtually inevitable. This marginal position may become in turn an element in the psychotic structure, which consequently does not produce enough motivation to review the whole business. This also explains why psychotics develop delusions of reference; they will grasp at anything to reconstruct the missing self. It also throws light on the religious preoccupations of psychiatric patients; the inescapable, immediate presence of the *raison d'être*, and the crying need to make sense of it all. The combination of course can easily lead to religious delusions of grandeur. Richard Alpert — who writes under the name of Ram Dass — made the following observation on that phenomenon during a conference on Buddhism and psychotherapy: 'The psychotic brother thinks he is Jesus Christ and only he. I think I'm Jesus Christ, and everyone else too.'[87]

15 Mixed bathing

Of course, both 'positions', psychotic versus mystical, are simplified here for the sake of convenience, but Brett's microscopic examination relies on tried and tested theories and practices from various traditions. According to a popular idea among westerners, the eastern philosophy of *maya* implies that the reality of daily life is nothing but a grand illusion, but she suitably modifies this sketchy notion.[88] As we saw in Chapter 3, 'Being and non-being', instead of the absolute value that western materialism attributes to our daily reality, the eastern take is an essentially relational one, and Brett shows how it allows us to observe at close quarters the psychotic struggle of our perception with structured reality. One shares Brett's hope that this line of approach will shed more light on the origin of the psychotic experience, so that we can continue to search for adequate remedies in that direction too. A potential means of access for this purpose lies in the ways in which mystics prepare for their union with the pure basis of consciousness.

Various authors recognise the importance of such preparation. Kenneth Wapnick, writing about schizophrenia and mysticism in 1969, compared such preparation with training one's muscles, in the sense of a capacity to bear the experiences of the inner self. The psychotic, who has entered the inner world without preliminary training, is overwhelmed by its potential, lacks the means to cope with it, and above all the conviction that he will survive it.[89] Vanderkooi, quoted above, pointed out that in the relevant Buddhist traditions only advanced students are allowed access to the most esoteric tantric exercises. Such exercises demand supervision by a qualified teacher, plus sufficient ego-power and a firm foundation of philosophy and meditation on the part of the pupil.[90] Finally, Holger Kalweit, anthropologist and authority on shamanism, argues that shamans, through their traditional protracted training 'are able to determine their own stations in life because of mythical and cultural models. They know what awaits them, through what euphorias and torments they will have to pass.'[91]

Now such traditional practices are very far removed from the western sickbed, and the social services sector moreover is not the place for higher spiritual education. Certain principles and models however can be translated, as the work of the American psychiatrist Edward Podvoll (1936–2003) shows. He bases his theory on the origin and development of psychoses on his knowledge of Tibetan Buddhism; in his case via the Shambhala school, the legacy of the 'crazy wisdom' teacher Chögyam Trungpa. In Podvoll's most famous book *The Seduction of Madness* he argues that, even amidst the madness and the terrors, somewhere in the background there is always a watchful eye, a consciousness that observes everything.[92] And he stated that there is hope for recovery if the psychotic can manage to distinguish the 'islands of clarity' that crop up now and then, to safeguard them and to develop them within himself. Meditative and contemplative techniques from the Buddhist praxis are indispensable tools for this purpose, as a specialist form of psycho-education. In Podvoll's homecare programme *Windhorse*, for people with psychiatric problems, these techniques form an essential element of the tailor-made treatment on offer, alongside medical, psychotherapeutic and educational support and practical voluntary aid. Spiritual training and modern-day psychotherapies can further complement each other in many ways, beyond the field of emergency care. 'Training the heart' in capacities such for as Christian humility or Buddhist compassion could as it were soften up a heavily barricaded ego, and act as preventative against pride at the moment when the familiar self converges with the All. And, according to more recent insights, while spiritual traditions generally avoid physical problems by denying their existence, body-oriented forms of therapy can actually help to process emotional pain and energy blocks. General training of the capacity to 'earth' one's own ontological presence in the body, and via perception to be present at everything that manifests itself in consciousness, lessens the need to resort to a structured self when the basis of that self is lost, intentionally or otherwise.

The earlier mentioned DSM-IV article on religious and spiritual problems came into being after David Lukoff and colleagues had distinguished a number of partly overlapping zones in the spectrum of experience from psychotic to mystical. Lukoff argued, for example, that besides the two extreme poles there are also 'mystical experiences with psychotic traits' and 'psychotic experiences with mystical traits'.[93] As Kusters similarly related, something of an ecstatic nature is sometimes experienced in a psychotic episode, particularly in and around the initial phase. Moreover we know that the mystical path has deep, dark pitfalls here and there. Lukoff's distinction is relevant here, for the very reason that we appear to be talking about a continuum. The mystic—who functions as well as, and possibly better than most people—is among us, and teaches us something about ourselves; the same applies to the psychotic. For all we know, we ourselves may one day belong to one of these two groups, or to both. And the better we understand the dynamics involved, the more we can help ourselves and others. Lukoff's intermediate categories of course are also examples of spiritual crises. In addition however, according to his original proposal (see Introduction), 'purely' mystical experiences can also be psychologically unsettling. Moreover, besides more or less successful mystical adventures, there are various other sorts of episodes to distinguish. Experiences in the subtle levels of consciousness for example, where mythical and archetypical forms and images are wont to emerge (see Chapter 4, 'The world according to Ken Wilber'). Over the years a number of authors have proposed a typology of spiritual crises. The first of these was Emma Bragdon, who based her work on six different patterns observable in the inner life during a crisis, such as 'possession' and the 'shamanic journey'.[94] Stanislav and Christina Grof, and the *Spiritual Emergency Network* that they founded, produced a more elaborate typology of experiences, to which Lukoff added several more items.[95] Bragdon's 'fluid' classification of manifest patterns appears to do more justice to the nature of this sort of turbulence than a categorical division into clear–cut types. The reliable recognition of different sorts of spiritual crises however is still in its infancy, and warrants extensive field research. For that reason the priority of this book is to provide a solid introduction to the phenomenology of such crises, rather than to delimit them conceptually.

16 Quantum speculations

The psychological dynamic of the self in this sort of study is increasingly scrutinised within a broad, interdisciplinary context. The frameworks of both classical psychology and classical physics have been left behind, and the relationship between these two fields seems to be echoed in that between transpersonal psychology and quantum physics. The focus of this academic teamwork is the phenomenon of consciousness as such. The concept of a consciousness unconnected to time, space and matter, as presented for example by Van Lommel's work (see Chapter 4, 'Kundalini, ecstasy and nightmare'), is accordingly filled not with colliding molecules, but with waves and fields. This terminology is derived from the quantum field theory developed in the post-Newtonian era, which enabled the solution of a number of fundamental physics problems, in particular the behaviour of microscopic matter as particles on the one hand, and as waves on the other. Now the discovery of the wavelike nature of matter was a revolution in itself, which brought about a wave of applications from a physics standpoint, and which we can scarcely imagine life without. Insight into the reality of subatomic space, for example, has given us a considerably better view of the content of the brain, by means of the powerful lenses of PET and MRI scanners in particular. Modern neurology is no longer conceivable without those familiar coloured pictures of various levels of brain activity. Nevertheless, direct application of the quantum theory on brain research is far from common. In this field of research, matter is still regarded essentially as a conglomeration of particles, in which the movement of one directly and predictably influences another. The American semantic psychologist Bernard J. Baars, a prominent scholar in current consciousness research, formulated one of the great riddles in his field of study as follows, in the title of an article:

'How does a stream of consciousness that is relatively simple, serial and limited in capacity emerge from a brain that is largely unconscious, complex, and massively parallel?'[96] From a mechanical point of view, however extraordinarily complex it may be, the brain does indeed cut a poor figure. And yet the consequences of the quantum revolution are tremendous; in the words of the Danish physicist Niels Bohr (1885–1962): 'Those who are not shocked when they first come across quantum theory cannot possibly have understood it.'[97] One of the most astounding discoveries at the time was that, at a subatomic level, matter behaves like a particle or wave, depending on our observation. Taken further, that would mean that 'hard' logic and experiment have brought us to the point at which human consciousness would seem to form the missing link that makes reality into reality, transforming a potential into the manifestation of the same. Now at the time of this first quantum revolution, it was not yet possible to study various points at the level of everyday life; moving electrons were all very well, but a complex organ such as the brain was too much to take on. And that is more or less how it stayed in classical medical circles, who seem to share, for example, the popular idea that the memory is a sort of physical storeroom somewhere in the brain. Or of thoughts as 'things' in our head, that we have trouble keeping inside, when we are doing many things at once. Classical mechanics experts have after all succeeded in pinpointing the locations of various brain functions; for the sake of convenience, the brain—or rather, a computer model of it—was unrolled like a map. And such a model is adequate, as long as we continue to see the brain merely as one and a half kilos of thymus gland in which—mysteriously, but still—the transportation of chemical substances delivers the messages. But once we stop seeing things from a particle physics point of view and focus on the electromagnetic activity itself, not only as the product of brain cells and atoms but as a phenomenon with its own laws representing the different nature of those same atoms, we shall see something completely different. That the brain *in vivo* may be capable of things that are out of the question when it has been unrolled, for example. The classic explanation of the strikingly convoluted nature of the brain is that this saves a vast amount of space, thus ensuring that a baby's head is small enough to pass safely through the birth canal.[98] Which is true enough, but that is not the only way of looking at it. The brain seems to be an organ with a great many convolutions, but could equally well be one huge, close entwinement, a process or a state, rather than a thing with characteristics. And this convolutedness may be a *sine qua non* for electromagnetic activity—regarded as the visible working of the mind. This activity, studied and measured with supersonic instruments, may tell quite a different story altogether.

The work of Karl Pribram (b. 1919) gives us an idea of the doors that are then opened.[99] This Viennese neurosurgeon did pioneering research in the US into the cerebral cortex, the typically human layer of the brain, in which our higher cognitive functions are situated. For many years he combed through it, searching, among other things, for the organic traces of memory, which stubbornly refused to reveal themselves. The idea of a literal imprint, of the storage of information inside brain cells, was old even then, but it proved to be fundamentally at odds with research findings. Laboratory animals' brains were cut in half and even into tenths, but the memory continued to work—although in the smallest fragments it became rather vague. This demonstrated that a small part of the same material continued to do the work of the memory, and also that the memory was not connected to any particular place. Furthermore, a right–handed person can write with his left hand without much trouble, or even with his foot or his mouth—although those parts of the body have never been trained to perform that trick, and have therefore developed no direct organic connections. It was a difficult puzzle, because the particles approach was unproductive. Then came the invention of the hologram in 1947, followed by that of the laser in 1960. And then it dawned on Pribram. For the principle of the hologram is that an imprint of a physical object is recorded on a sensitive plate, not by direct light as in an ordinary photograph, but by the interference pattern of a beam of pure (laser) light which has been split in two. One ray reaches the plate via the object, while the other falls directly onto the plate, and the information about the object is recorded in the pattern of their meeting. By directly lighting the film again with the same ray, the image is revealed—this time in three dimensions. And here is the interesting thing: even a small part of the same film produces the whole image—though in the smaller fragments it becomes rather vague. This characteristic of the hologram prompted Pribram's theory that a memory trace is recorded and produced in the same way: as an imprint of interference patterns. How that would work in practice was not immediately clear to him. Meanwhile, however, the Japanese scientist Hiroomi Umezawa (1924–1995) was investigating theoretical physics, as trailblazer of the quantum field theory. As this theory describes fundamental characteristics of matter, these must inevitably apply to the physical brain as well.[100] And then it all fell into place. The interference patterns of the memory are formed by the electromagnetic waves of the brain. This view explains how such a tremendous quantity of information can fit into a sizeable handful of grey cells—a problem that cannot be solved in a linear and cybernetic way. According to the theory, these waves are produced by a permanent and universally present quantum field—the field in which 'particles' are born. Does this mean that we have finally got hold of the field of consciousness, in which memories lie dormant until they are stirred — by the beam of our attention, perhaps? Do individual brains form the fragments of a hologram that spans the universe? Such a theory will not appeal to everyone, but it deserves to be better known and explored.

As Thomas Kuhn stated, existing scientific paradigms fall into disuse when their seemingly insoluble codes are cracked by means of another language. And no doubt there is more in the pipeline regarding these innovative hypotheses. Meanwhile, recent technology has confirmed a number of Pribram's predictions. Once again, of course, it is all about the relationship between mind and body, which appears to demand human-ity's most concentrated effort. Who would have thought that in exploring the correspondence between subjective experience and electromagnetic activity in cortical cells — the level at which we have meanwhile arrived in this quest — we would find ourselves drawing on the higher mathemat-ics? Pribram — a cognitive psychologist by this time — had to borrow from one expert after another in order to arrive at his formulations. It is as clear as day to him that classical physics only applies on a microscopic scale, and even though everything there works in the dizzying terminology of wave, oscillation, frequency, interference, charge, discharge, current, feedback, algorithm and so on, insight into the workings of the brain can-not be achieved without quantum physics, which describes phenomena at a submicroscopic scale. In passing, he also notes how well spiritual expe-riences can be described in quantum physical terms, suggesting that such a model may also come to explain such phenomena. And in another aside he notes how the holographic model of consciousness, in which each indi-vidual point directly emulates the whole, offers an analogue to the ancient, mysterious mantra, that man is created in God's image.

Umezawa has since died, so it is up to others to work out the nuts and bolts: how does a quantum field manifest itself in the brain as mental activity, as cognition? It may be indeed through water molecules, which are universally present in the brain, and which he saw as the main candi-dates for a crucial role. However summary, this sketch provides enough leads for a fascinating conception of human beings and consciousness, and not merely as background for transpersonal psychology. An interpre-tation of the memory in terms of waves resonates very satisfactorily with subjective experience. 'Images' of whole situations flood in whenever something triggers them off, and certain memories are so vivid that we experience them as if the past is present right now. Waves, moreover, resemble other cognitive phenomena; emotions, for example. Fear, rage, joy, sorrow, jealousy, pride, excitement, compassion — they can deluge us, and sometimes we feel that we are drowning in them. Or insights — do they not often emerge in an unguarded moment, like a suddenly unfolding field? Thought disorders—could they be caused by badly co-ordinated undulations? Meditative states—could inner relaxation be produced by the synchronisation of brain waves with a universally present field? Paranormal phenomena—according to the current view they are all nonsense and unworthy of research, and yet people continue to report them. But if we all exist in an infinite, unbroken vibrating field, could waves from elsewhere indeed cause ripples in our own system? The death of the body—does broadcasting cease if our television breaks down? Divine experiences—are they interpretations of the direct perception of an eternally present, creative field? And experiences of non-duality, of absolute oneness, of seeing all, feeling all, knowing all, being all—could that be the immediacy of the undifferentiated quantum consciousness field itself?

Research groups, of necessity interdisciplinary, are now focusing on this sort of question. Consciousness studies form a fairly recent branch of sport in which neuroscientists, physicists, philosophers, cognitive psychologists, theologians, mathematicians, linguists, pharmacologists, IT specialists, cyberneticists and other connoisseurs together tackle what was long regarded as the unresearchable mystery of human consciousness. The truths gathered from the same number of observers are focused into a new kind of light. It is no longer possible to distinguish who or what in this light is religious, agnostic or philosophical. This melting pot of boffins comes out with remarks such as that of the German philosopher Thomas Metzinger (1958), who airily but confidently asserts: 'There is no such thing as a self, no one has ever had a self or has ever been a self, there are only phenomena in our consciousness.'[101] This roughly coincides with the wisdom from the depths of mysticism, from east to west. But what then does it mean to be self-conscious, and what does an apparently split self look like? How do those phenomena show up in our consciousness, and does the idea of synchronisation have something to do with its transformation? And what about Descartes? Are we wise to parrot what he says, because we believe so firmly in matter that we continue to lump thinking and consciousness together? Do both halves of his universe not rather form the twin principles that emerge from a more fundamental, first cause? And could this first cause hold the key to inner transformation? It is time to return to the everyday level, to the human lives in which the surging waves break now and then into whirlpools and foaming white crests.

Egmont (1962)

I always functioned well, though I was a boisterous child and had problems at home, but what you might call normal psychological problems.
Ours was a noisy, exuberant family, with lots of door-slamming, shouting
and crying, but also lots of music. All my life I've been attracted to religion, spirituality, secret places, perceptions and so on. My parents were
always aware of this, to them it was just the way I was. They didn't bring
me and my three sisters up in any particular religious tradition, but they
taught us respect for traditions, very open-minded. So if I wanted to go to
mass on Christmas day with the girls downstairs, that was fine. And later
on I visited a mosque or synagogue once or twice. As a child I felt instinctively drawn to quiet, holy places, I was evidently able to recognise them.
I can also be very unbiased about religion and find it easy to talk to religious people, but then I have no baggage, as I never had to go to church
twice a day or pray before meals. But it's more than that, it's a sensitivity
to presences and paranormal things as well. When I cycled to school the
street-lights always used to go out when I passed by. Always the same
route, and at a certain point, phut! out they went as I went by, really
weird. And later on, when I went to music college for example, I always
knew whether the tram would be waiting round the corner or not, or
when someone rang up, I'd know who it was, that sort of thing. This
whole sensitivity business is really a thing apart, so you can't fit it into any
frame of reference. That's exactly what I tried to do, of course, had myself
baptised a Catholic and so on. There was a funny little ritual attached to
that, but afterwards I was really disillusioned by the Catholic church, so it
just doesn't work like that. It's about intangible things. I've taken an
active part in a tremendous number of things. No sects, that's going too
far, but I really went in search of forms of meditation. I've seriously considered entering a Benedictine monastery, for example. I actually lived in
one for a couple of months, I was incredibly happy there, and now and
then I really yearn for that monastic life, for that profundity. I also went
through a period of Buddhist meditation, a Japanese version. That's also
sheer bliss, no trouble at all. I can really get immersed in it. And I was
taken up with Sri Chinmoy for a while.[1] I had a good feeling about that as
well, only you had to meditate in front of a photo of him sometimes. I
never liked doing that. I'm too much of an artist, you might say, to take on

the role of disciple or whatever completely. Apart from that, I got deeply involved in alchemy, through reading about it, the ancient sources, all kinds of things. About Michael Maier for example, who composed music inspired by it, during that alchemistic bubble at the end of the renaissance, beginning of the baroque era.[2] When you're deeply involved with Jung in particular, those subjects are very good for creating art, in order to crystallise it somehow in projects. And somewhere along the way my psyche became saturated with all those images and information, and started drowning. I don't feel that that's what caused those psychoses, but it had to do with great sensitivity.

Quite simply I can say that always, continually, night and day, I feel a sort of antenna. I'm constantly receiving messages, it's been like that all my life. A cosmic child. Like everybody else, of course, but some people have their antennas all folded up. But I didn't become a musician out of the blue, I was one even as a child. I have an auditive approach, I seem to make contact with the cosmos through my ears, mainly the right ear. And my attitude to life is a listening one. I can make a lot of noise, talk a lot, teach a lot, make a lot of music, but meanwhile something within me is always listening. A sort of periscope that listens in all directions. And that means I can hear at different levels. For example, when I listen to someone, it's not so much what he says but how he sounds. One person may be quieter, with another I hear much more noise. That's one level, there are a whole lot of layers of listening like that. And there is a layer that I regard as the deepest form of listening. And during that period, between 1989 and 1993, I became aware of an enormous activity. Later on several people told me that a sort of special event cosmically speaking was taking place around that time - whatever that means. Like the chaotic feelings you've had during the last couple of years, things are just not going well. I don't even mean terrorism and all that, there's just a sort of agitation. People experience this period as apocalyptic. Well, that's not without reason, when I look around me. Only I don't happen to be the sort of person who can be driven mad, and I hope that applies to most people. But there's a lot of rubbish now, and at the time I found it mostly positive, a bit like the sixties. Not just my psychoses—I don't mind calling them that these days—but just my dream, my dreams. There was absolutely a special force.

I was studying music then, and doing a course at the ITIP on the side, so I'd taken on quite a lot.[3] I was already very involved in meditation, I lived on my own, I worked on my own as composition student of course, I was intensively involved with composing, and I taught a lot. And it was almost as if, very slowly but surely, a lens was being adjusted. That made me rather euphoric. Your powers grow enormously of course once you tap that energy. It's still like that, only I can channel it better now. And you can do an awful lot, it really is like that, physically for example. I was also doing an awful lot of sport and yoga and fasting. But I don't know what was the chicken and what was the egg, it was probably the sum of a lot of circumstances all put together. Anyway, in the course of one year I had three, maybe four, serious attacks. In a hyperactive, manic form, in blocks of two, three days, with a prelude probably of weeks during which I functioned normally and went on teaching and so on. The first time it all remained reasonably within limits. It's an avalanche of impressions, such an awful lot happens in a few days. For me it was nearly all pleasant. I could tell you a hundred things about it. For example, I had a lot of plants in the house and I'd made a sort of jungle of them in my room, and I started pacing up and down inside of that in a sort of pendulum motion. Hour after hour, it felt to me like centuries, but it might have been only ten minutes. And I had to turn either to the right or the left, compulsive things like that. What all that was about I couldn't say now, but it all meant something. It must have been something magical, all my perceptions had something magical about them as well. At one point I made a robe and a crown from some sort of tinfoil, and I think I also carried a staff in my hand. It was spring, fine weather, so I went to the Vondelpark and just walked around there, couldn't hear any sound, and everything happened in slow motion. Actually I was just having a heavy trip, it was really like a sort of LSD trip. I was also convinced that music was over and done with, and from now on all communication would be through colour and light. So music, that was finished. And I went to see my father around then, to tell him something or other. That would have been one of the first attacks, because somehow I came out of it all right. Don't ask me how … well, after a while it just fades away. It's probably to do with the chemical balance in your system. In those days I didn't use drugs, I did smoke joints at one stage, like everybody else, but that was fifteen years earlier! I mean, I never went in for trips or magic mushrooms, that sort of thing, I was too scared. That was sheer intuition, realising how sensitive I was. I never went in for heavy drinking either. I have been really stoned a couple of times, but that was always with other people and good company, good food and making music, so in a good atmosphere. I don't experiment on my own, it doesn't interest me. It's really the drugs that exist in your own body. Anyway, that first attack just ebbed away of its own accord. The actual facts about what happened when, that's partly a blank, and it's quite a while ago now. My mother told me a few things about it recently, I had absolutely no idea.

But there are countless moments that I do remember. For example I started wandering around, got on the tram stark naked and so on. Those are excesses to the outside world, but it all meant something to me. One time I was standing in a street, leaning against a building, I turned round and looked over the parked cars to the other side. There was a sign with three times one. Well, that's just number 111, in the Van der Helststraat or somewhere, so it means nothing. But to me at that moment it was three times one, number three and number one. At such a moment you feel you have the answers to everything, and it was quite clear to me that it was the very last day. There were also so many hallucination-like incidents, for example I saw the clouds suddenly gathering above me, I heard thunder. I also rang people's doorbells, even at night, to warn them that the day of judgement was at hand. But they were all people I knew, and I went away again, so they didn't go ahead and ring the police. One thing I know for sure, I don't have a seriously violent nature, because I bothered people but I didn't walk round the Vondelpark with a chainsaw, and I didn't strangle people or rape them or anything. It was all out of a sort of *Begeisterung*. And an incredible concern for what was happening to the world. I was actually a sort of messenger, I do remember that. And of course at a certain stage that had something a bit desperate about it, because I couldn't get the message across, but that's not how I saw it. As if I had morphine in my body, so I didn't feel any pain. My inner world was really mythical.

There was never a moment at which I thought: this is all very peculiar. Because everything had a meaning. I did think, this is amazing, but it came from this loving feeling: what an amazing phenomenon — something like that. I also managed to keep my head above water socially, I kept on going to music college. And there was only one moment during all those psychoses when I was really frightened. I think I'd been walking all night through the streets of Amsterdam, and I believe the sun hadn't risen yet when I got to Overtoom Street. It was completely silent there, but high above me I could see a circle of sulphurous clouds. I had no idea what sulphur smelt like, but I knew it was sulphur, the actual smell of sulphur. And the earth wasn't flat, it was curved. At that moment I felt, this is another dimension, this is dangerous. Somebody went past and he was all covered with black spots or something, then I got really terrified and realised, I have to get away from here, this is not good.

The third time, I went to see the leaders of the ITIP, somewhere in Holland, at their own house. I probably went to tell them something, or bring them something, but there was a stalking element about it. That really wasn't my intention, but it must have been very scary for those people. Because of course they were involved in psychology, and then they saw one of their students completely lose it. I believe I stood there shouting in the garden. They dropped me completely after that. First with a warning, if you don't go and get help we'll have to expel you. In the euphoria of my trip I couldn't take it in. Then they threw me out, and told everyone around me not to have anything to do with me. That really hit me hard. My parents were furious, but looking back, I feel ambivalent about it myself. You could also see it as a sort of biological survival of the group, which could have made me think, wow, I'd better get well quickly so I can be part of the group again. But it was really hard at the time. Five years or so ago I composed a cantata and sent a CD of it to my former teacher, as a sort of apology. Meaning something like, I can express it best in music, and things are going well at the moment. Next Sunday incidentally I'm going to sing Bach chorales for the ITIP. So then the circle will be complete and that makes it magical all over again!

The fourth time it really went wrong. From my house you can see the motorway to Schiphol airport, and I couldn't tell you now how I got there, but I walked along the central reservation into the Schiphol tunnel. There are some sort of antenna-like constructions there, I don't know what they are but I've probably been passing them by for thirty years now. At that moment I saw them sihouetted against the skyline, and that was one more confirmation of the last day. And the world was tilting to one side again, so I had this theory, don't walk towards the west and the setting sun, because then you're walking east. And I had to get to Schiphol, because I was going to be collected and taken to New York, to see Sri Chinmoy, and I was also going to work for Prince and play in his band. It was urgent, I was in a hurry, I just had to be at the right place. And then all train services between Amsterdam and the Hague were cancelled, because there was a lunatic running around in the tunnel. Next thing I was taken off the line by the railway police or somebody, and taken to Hoofddorp. I was put in a cell there, I've only got vague memories of that, and then they put me in a straitjacket and took me to Vogelenzang asylum.[4] I remember a bit about being carried in, there was a cloakroom and all these things hanging up there, and I had a vision of Judas hanging himself. So, it all happened in a flash after that! And men in white coats are a real nuisance then, because they come and disturb your euphoria. Because even a straitjacket, it doesn't hurt and life just goes on. Until they knocked me out with sedatives, put me in a padded cell and then, zonk!

I was in Vogelenzang for six or seven weeks. That was a real jolt, after that enormous trip. A real *coming down*, as junkies call it. Back to earth, and earth is a very unpleasant place. You're not allowed outside, you get really bloated with the medication, you drink an awful lot of coffee and eat a lot of biscuits, and I had therapy which made me think, what the hell am I doing here? I can't remember what the diagnosis was exactly, there were three key words. I remember that I kept my certificate of lunacy in my desk for a long time. But I lost it, maybe I ritually burned it at one stage or something.

These days I would want to frame it! Anyway, it made out that I was a danger to myself, but that really wasn't true. I never considered self-harming for a minute, and I had no negative drives at all. Well, okay, you could see running through the Schiphol tunnel as a suicide attempt of course, but in my view I wasn't really mad. And for the rest I was pretty dopy, because that Haldol[5] and stuff, wow, that's really heavy. And a lot of people used to smoke one fag after the other, not exactly uplifting.

I remember one moment, after a week or so, I was walking down a corridor and I heard an inner voice, which said, 'Okay, Egmont, this is the very last time you'll have to go through this.' That was a sort of primal voice. And then there was a change of course, after that it was all about healing. One reason for that was that I was aware the whole time that I am a precious person. Probably a left-over from the way I was brought up, which was good in that sense. I realised, I can't let it go on like this, I deserve more than stuffing myself with biscuits while stunned with Haldol. I've got something to offer the world. And so I did, in the following years. A couple of months later in fact I was back with the conservatory choir in the Concertgebouw, with Jard van Nes, performing Mahler's second.

Of course there's a big gap between spiritual experience on the one hand and scientific observation on the other. Like the way I was treated then, it was all so terribly out-dated! I remember for example that I had to look at those ink blots.[6] And at one stage I had music therapy, well, banging on a triangle a bit; I only went to that once. At the end I played a piece from a Beethoven sonata, I thought, up yours, mate! And every morning we'd sit in a circle, mind you they're really nice people, but still, this was how it went: 'And, how are we all today? Egmont, you look a bit cross, is anything the matter?' Well, that's just not my wavelength. And yet those people do it with real love, I really believe that. But I had the feeling I was back in primary school. Maybe it's a good way of doing things, it got me out of it. I had a weekly session with a psychiatrist, I found her an awful bitch but she did hammer home to me that I had to take the medication. And it had a really quick effect on me, thank God, so I was finished with the whole bloody mess really soon.

I never felt that I needed help. My only contribution to this process was that I accepted that I had to take medication. And I still do today. At first that was pretty drastic, a sort of loss of face, or the idea: so now I'm handicapped. Looking back I think, stupid of me not to have done that earlier. I have very mild medication, Semap, half a pill per week if I'm not going through difficult times.[7] It stabilises my levels or something, it doesn't really interest me that much. In the beginning I took Orap, that's a real sledge-hammer.[8] When I was back at home it used to make me sleep an awful lot. And I was depressed, a sort of after-pain. And further, I was incredibly lucky that the conservatory kept my place open; I was half-way through my course, and they let me continue. So later on I went back to composing classes, often I couldn't do more than half an hour at a time. And my teacher, Daan Manneke, always used to say calmly, 'Okay, we'll see each other next week then.' He was really fantastic. He wrote to me in the institution as well: went off the rails, did you? I'll wait till you get back. Really warm, really special, that's a precious memory. He also kept a lesson period for me free. Nothing but praise for the musical world, also for the composers in my class. Of course they're all people of great psychological sensitivity, so they can easily imagine how it is. The artists among my friends were also the ones who stayed closest to me, they weren't in the least afraid. And the others who stayed close were people like Bep, my upstairs neighbour, who'd just wink and say: 'Oh, the leaves are falling again? Well, I've fed your cat and I'm glad you're feeling better.' Really uncomplicated, that's that. They have another frame of reference, it comes straight from the heart. But there was a whole group of people who were afraid for themselves or something like that. I don't know how I could pose a threat to them, but a lot of people vanished for a while, or for ever. Incidentally I know a musicologist who was stuck in the train between the Hague and Amsterdam, because a nutter was walking through the Schiphol tunnel. I worked with him years later and I told him, well, I could tell you a bit about that! I was quite proud, actually, I've achieved something anyway!

As soon as I was back at home I started going for walks in the neighbourhood, and swimming, really active, a bit of exercise. I also had a sort of RIAGG counselling, a weekly interview or something, I only know that it was all very pleasant, a sort of probation. It's also true that psychoses can provoke more psychoses, so it did crop up again, but I was so much on the alert and just took more medication. At a certain stage I really got the chemical balance game down to a fine art. By then I could also see how destructive the whole situation had been. Not my inner world, I didn't find that destructive, but I'd completely dislocated myself socially. It was a real shambles, it took me at least a year to sort out the financial chaos. I had all sorts of help with that, but socially speaking everything healed very slowly, that was the price of the euphoria. So when I felt it starting to happen again on the way to the gym, I just had to get off my bike. It's like being put under anaesthetic, a sort of natural force that takes over from the inside. Then I'm afraid of losing control, and in the past I just slipped into it, in a sort of daydream, and on one occasion for example I saw a tree walking up and down. But I knew this time, if I go there again, it'll be Vogelenzang for me. So the consequences are social. And then my immediate reaction was: bam, get it out of the way. These days I realise that I used to drink far too little water, that's another piece of the puzzle. I've become much calmer and more stable since I started drinking one and a half litres of water a day. I have a natural aptitude for it, it definitely has a spiritual aspect, only now I know that it can happen without me completely ending up in that dream. There's something greedy about it. It's just wanting to have too much in one go.

During these experiences I was absolutely convinced that I wasn't psychotic. There's no reflection at such moments, I'd slipped into a certain dimension—in my case that happened very gradually, as if the world gradually changed colour, and I just changed along with it. And in that dimension everything has a meaning. That's probably true as well, I'd go along with that so far. Only it's just not feasible for a normally functioning person. You have to absorb it filtered and in small portions, and it gradually becomes part of your consciousness, and the older and more mature you become, so that you're able to record it and pass it on, the more use it is to you. But if you guzzle the whole lot in one go, that just makes you drunk. That doesn't work. It's far too much.

When I see someone screaming in the street I think, take some medication, mate, then you'll be done with it. I'm very down-to-earth about it, you see. I'd be able to deal with someone on such a trip, but what on earth can the normal world do with with someone like that, barking his head off with a bible on the Leidseplein? They just can't fit in socially, so make sure you stay healthy, if necessary by using temporary measures. When I think, this is getting too much, I just take two extra pills. It's just the same as with diabetes, what difference does it make? All the people who go through this are exceptional people, that much is clear. They've got a certain gift. And the best time to communicate those gifts is when you're reasonably in your right mind. Before my psychosis I never fully realised all the abilities I had. You know, but you don't know, and it was really narcissistic. I was quite an arrogant person, of course that got damaged, I came a cropper. A sort of moral lesson that I had to go through, maybe, because of course that's a gain. I can thank my lucky stars that I could take part at all, that it happened in this era, and that I came out of it like this. And though I might consider myself exceptional in what I make and do, it's no longer based on arrogance about those abilities. I've acquired a sort of modesty, a sense of proportion about how that works. That whole episode is now something that I can look back on in a relaxed way, and also talk about easily, even joke about it, but at the time it was pretty tough. I really had to go through the depths.

My psychoses were not frightening in themselves, actually, thank God, and I think that one reason for that is that my life already had a strongly surrealistic stamp. I make dreams, shall I say. My life is so active and so creative, I go from one project to another, I do so many nice things, so many crazy things, also in my way of working with people, so much colour every day, which means one thing can naturally merge into another. At the same time there's an air of disappointment in the whole story, as I feel that I was allowed a private glimpse into something, and I can't do much with it. The vessel I communicated with, bit by bit I get the feeling that it is gradually revealing its significance. Only, up to now I find it disappointingly little. When I think what an incredible power I had then, I realise I haven't yet been able to convey that to the rest of the world. And yet I have the feeling that slowly but surely I'm expressing those experiences through my compositions. In fact that's the gift, because the actual spirituality that I see in the world is not just in music but in teaching. I have a lot of pupils, and through the contact with that dimension I've acquired a sort of authority that I didn't have before. And I can now communicate it in small doses. The mistake that a psychotic makes is that spirituality always has to remain at the level of a euphoric moment like that. But if you look at Heidegger for example, the man kept on producing steadily all his life. Or Einstein. He kept it up till old age and gave the whole world a boost. And that's an enormous gift. I'm now working very hard as it were to see how much I can get out of myself during the next sixty years! Yes, everyone lives to a great age in my family, so for all I know I might live to ninety or one hundred, having fantastic inspiration all the time, that's terrific, isn't it! It's also a solemn resolution, okay, I know that dimension exists, I was allowed to see it. In all that intensity I wasn't able to translate it, but if I can convey it in small doses, maybe very slowly, with a bit of pushing and pulling and steering, I could produce an incredible force. Maybe collectively, maybe alone. And all that by grace of the fact that I have seen that. You could compare it to St Paul, but of course there are masses of people with visions, who preach about them for the rest of their lives.

What really frightened me during the first years was that my senses were so dulled. I see that as a sort of sprained psyche, that you get such a 'doyng' that it leaves you numbed. But during the last ten years one aspect after another has reappeared, practically everything has healed. The tremendous clarity that I had before will probably never return. I mean the clarity of my childhood, I used to have an incredible power of perception, and a clarity and also a speed in composition. I could see whole pieces at a glance. Maybe it's simply growing older that changes things, but I would find it fantastic if it came back completely. At any rate I heard something not long ago that fits in with this. A piece of music that I've been listening to for eighteen months now, but a couple of weeks ago the penny finally dropped. I recognised the sound that I hear myself at the deepest level of listening, as I know it. I call that 'listening to the world', and when I perceive it I always visualise that I'm flying upwards, and then I'm in space looking down at the earth as a planet. And from a distance I listen to the sound the earth makes. A stormy sort of sound. As if six billion people are all talking at once. Well, they are talking all at once, of course, and shouting, but it's also a cosmic sound. It's actually an incredibly baroque business, with an incredible amount of colour and richness and noise. It's exceptionally pleasant for me personally, and it produces one of the highest forms of alertness that I know. It also arouses an incredible anxiety in me, as if I'm keeping watch over the whole situation. And now I've found a sound that reflects that.

It's by Brian Wilson, he was the genius of the Beach Boys; the musical leader, but also someone who listened. You can see that in the photos as well. Four of the men really enjoy being in the photo and being very famous, and there's one standing there a bit awkwardly, a bit out of place. That's him. It's the same on every photo. And in my opinion he's listening. From 1960 onwards they had more and more hits, and at a certain stage he withdrew. He was a very sensitive person, vulnerable too, and tormented and so on, not an easy customer. And at the height of his powers, when he was rounding off this project, *Smile*, he ended up in a crisis. Including psychotic situations. That project stayed on the shelf for thirty years. He ended up in a dreadful psychiatric drama, with medication that would knock out a herd of horses or whatever. He also got tremendously fat, well, one way or another he got out of it, with more modern medication and a better marriage. And then he rounded off that project with a hefty number of young musicians. It is splendid music, really glorious. But the bit I mean is not exactly that, it's in a song about the element of fire. It's called '*Mrs O'Leary's cow*', which is based on the great fire in Chicago in 1871; this was caused by a cow that kicked over an oil-lamp, which set the hay on fire.[9] Well, that's the anecdote, a sort of statement about the history of America. But for me it's about experiencing sound, that's just a short bit, and the rest is just art, you might say. Maybe he found it scary after all to put it on paper. But for me it's clear which dimension he tried to reach by doing this, and in my eyes it's a very brave and moving attempt to capture it purely accoustically. I listened to it again not long ago and I thought, my God, that's it, of course! That's the wavelength I understand. I once heard actual recordings of the planets, and the sun, simply through putting microphones in space. Those sounds, it's a sort of zoom, a sort of rattling, spluttering, interference-kind of thing. And he made an attempt, forty years later, to reconstruct that in music. That's extraordinary, of course. It made me think of Vincent van Gogh, he was a very committed and inspired man. He's bound to have sensed that dimension. So in that impulse, in that enormous activity, there's a perception of a whole lot of information at once. Someone who's not sensitive to that would experience it as total chaos. But at the time I could totally see what a state the world is actually in. Through that I feel in a way challenged, it was a sort of cry of distress from the other side, and intuitively I want to respond with something consoling. And in my experience that has something huge and all-embracing. That's in fact what I'm working on all the time. And I'm going to manage it as well, I reckon.

Mariet (1954)

I am a doctor, and I have gone through an evolution in my work. I was classically trained and started work, and all the time I felt: what am I supposed to be doing? Fighting symptoms, only treating this and that? And then I started doing acupuncture, in order to broaden my knowledge. That opened up a whole new world to me; there was more to it than mere physical symptoms. There were also such things as energy, and energy paths, and all that energy had to be in balance. From there I searched further, homeopathy, neural therapy, you name it. I applied it, and it worked. Every time I came up against boundaries, with emotional things as well. You can just watch that from the sidelines, but you're actually being stimulated in yourself. And every time I took it a step further: what shall I do next?

I remember that at some point a therapist had come to see me, for some sort of shoulder problem, and that I had a genuine and authentic feeling about that person. And while I was treating him, I began to cry. One way or another I was touched by something. And I mean, come on, Mariet—I really wasn't prepared for that. But I had to get that emotional charge out of the way before I could go any further. I knew that he'd started a group with a woman here in Belgium, the Oasis (Oase), and that it was about meaningfulness and essential significance. But I kept it at bay; it wasn't my kind of thing. All the same, with some people I could often see: that's not a medical problem, it lies much deeper than that. And then I would send them to the Oasis, to see what could be done. It's not really psychology either; I know psychologists, and that's talk talk talk, it doesn't reach the core. I kept on searching myself, I did emotional bodywork, I was at Body & Soul in the Netherlands, I studied with a teacher in Italy for several weeks, and later in Berlin as well. So I did that, but it was really an avoidance tactic. I kept coming up against boundaries in myself and then off I'd go to the next thing, and then on to the next. And I always went as a practitioner. I wanted to learn at a professional level, and I also wanted to learn something about myself, but always keeping something in reserve. It was acquiring knowledge, that was how I'd always studied. That other teacher in Italy did more energy work, and I learned to sense things there, but there was always something uncommitted about it. I could walk away whenever I felt like it. And looking back I see that I performed all of those avoidance manoeuvres in order not to go to the Oasis.

And in the end I took the plunge. At first I only went for polarity massage, that made me really calm. But that was also without commitment. I was married to an alcoholic and I stayed stuck in the marriage. I see now that I gained something from it, but I could fight and fight with him and he just kept on drinking That was a vicious circle; he didn't stop drinking and I couldn't leave the guy! And I would go back to him and get beaten up, then I'd ask myself, come on, how is this possible? I remember that I once bit him on the backside, that was the first time that I was actually really angry. Now I wanted to learn about myself, and one day I rang the Oasis. I said that I wanted to come to them, because I just didn't know what to do any more. When I talked about it there for the first time, they threw the book at me: what was my part in all of this? And I was so affronted! What, *my* part? But I felt that it was true, and kept on going to them. After a year I left my ex. I had thought: there's going to be a fight and then the decision will be made. For the last ten years I'd been considering the idea of one day leaving him, but I was convinced that I would take that step only when I couldn't cope any more, when I was sick and tired. And I remember clearly, it was a Thursday, I said, 'There's no connection here, I'm going to get a divorce.' And that was that. It took another six months or so before the break was complete, and we still had a legal battle ahead of us, but that decision was very clear.

I kept going to the Oasis every week, and later on I started a new relationship. That made me really anxious, the reverse side of all that aggression. Anyway, at the Oasis they often asked me: how are you dealing with your competitiveness? You're very competitive. But me, I didn't want to see that. Who, me, the one who always did her best! It was always somebody else's fault. And I always did my utmost for other people, I'd also adapted completely to my partner, but I didn't feel myself any more. He was so well-organised, you eat at such-and-such a time, go to bed at such-and-such at time, get up at such-and-such a time, everything all nice and tidy; well, I'm not like that! I went along with it and learned to be organised, but at the same time I was angry at myself for doing it; I had no space of my own any more. And if I turned up late for work, I got a lecture. So at the Oasis I'd go: bloody hell, that's because *he's* the way he is! It was *his* fault, *he* was the bad one. But the way I felt about myself evoked a certain energy in other people. I always wanted to brush that to one side, but the people at the Oasis kept confronting me with it. After that I started having problems with my eldest child, he went to live with his father, and I thought: that's because I'm going to the Oasis, because of that energy … And at a certain stage something inside me said, '*Nobody* is going to tell me what to do any more! Nobody! From now on *I'm* going to say what I'm going to do.' And on the one hand that created an abyss in my life, and on the other hand it was my salvation. From one moment to the next I ended up in a sort of madness, as I call it. I didn't know such things were possible. It had developed gradually, I started to function at a much higher level of consciousness, was feeling better about myself, more content, and suddenly it went … bam! I remember leaving the place, and feeling like an absolute *clochard*. I went to Liège, and it was as if I was inside a sort of glass bell jar. I had no contact with people, I couldn't make the connection any more: a *clochard*. I ended my relationship, I moved house, and in those two months I did absolutely everything to find a way out. I went to one group here, then another group there, even to a retreat run by a Christian organisation—in fact anything at the back of my mind that made me think: might be worth trying. I went back to the other teacher as well, that was awful! I couldn't break out of the isolation, that never changed.

At the Oasis I'd seen how I competed, but what it was like to be alone, that was shoved under my nose during those months. So I did a week here and a week there, working in between. And I'm usually a sound sleeper, but I couldn't sleep any more. I felt this pressure in my head, and I really thought I was going nuts. So I could understand people killing themselves, taking pills or drinking, everything. I had another drug, that was my precious books; I read Osho, and every book that had ever moved me in any way. I was constantly reading and reading, to keep it all a bit under control. Because it was enough to drive you mad! I did tell myself: I won't drink, and I won't take pills, I won't do it! That was very clear to me, I won't do it! But meanwhile: not sleeping, losing weight, not being able to eat. And the worst of all was that at work I was only capable of doing technical things. If anyone came with a problem that lay a bit deeper, I could have killed them! They were welcome if they had a pain in their knee or shoulder or neck or whatever, but woe betide them if they started complaining: Oh, I feel so … I snarled at them if they even mentioned anything like that! I remember someone who'd lost her husband, and I'd just ended a relationship; I really barked at her. I couldn't cope with it. At that moment I was on my own, so I had to make sure that the money came in, but that was really difficult.

Then I started getting this pain in my belly. Every time I rang up someone I used to know who had also been involved in personal growth, something happened in my belly. I suddenly had the feeling that I had a lump there, and it wouldn't go away. I got three lumps like that, and one day when I was coming back from a workshop I had to stop the car at the side of the road, because I had such a pain in my belly. I'd studied medicine, and I knew that it wasn't a physical pain, it was really an energy block. During my period with the group my belly had opened up, and now I felt it was getting narrower and narrower and narrower. This was something that was happening inside of me, there was nothing I could do about it. And come on, I'd always been able to stay in control of myself, so this really wasn't possible! But it got worse and worse every time ... and I knew that something in my belly was going to kill me. Something was going to happen in the long run.

So I read books, and I kept coming across things that made me realise: that's what the Oasis says as well. Then I thought: I'm looking somewhere where I can't find it. I'd really sunk very deep. And I felt such pain, in my whole body. I had been set free from everything, so to speak, but really, I was racked with pain inside. I went back to my children, but that was the same; there was no contact any more. So then I said, 'Okay, they can stay here, I'll be over there.' I felt completely detached from everything that belonged to me, but that's how it had to be. Then I remained static for a bit. I didn't go to a psychologist, quite the reverse.

Somewhere inside I felt that I had experienced something in that group, that through contact with those people I had learned something. Through that I had started to function in a certain way, and I had abandoned that in a negative way. I knew that. I talked to a lot of people who were open, but I felt like a bottomless pit. It flowed in, and flowed out again. It was as if I could never get enough, and that was enough to drive me mad. I was mad. I was really mad. I used to phone people up, which I normally never do, and then I wouldn't get off the phone, it didn't bother me what they thought about it, it was never enough. I called on someone who had once left that group, and after three years she was still affected by it. She looked for it everywhere, but she could never find it. At that point I said, 'I feel as if I've done something that wasn't good, and I'm going to carry it with me all my life. I'll die like that.'

And then there was an inquiry. In '98 a commission was set up in Belgium to investigate all sorts of groups, what you might call cults.[1] The Oasis was also investigated. As I was no longer a member, I was rung up by the judicial police. They came to see me and I just told them what there was to tell; what they do, and how that goes. And that was a turning point for me. Because I began to look at things with more common sense: what do they actually do? And what do I do? I remember that some time later I was lying in bed looking at the wall, and I said, 'All right, I might just as well die now. I could commit suicide, but then, that's my life done for. If I come back, I'll have to go through it all over again.' And I literally thought: I'm not dead yet. What is it that I'd still most like to do? And what came to me was: look into my fears. There was fear, a tremendous lot of fear, to live and to be confronted by it, but I said, 'I have to look at my own fear. I want to go back!' That took another week or so, then one morning I went and parked in front of the house. I wanted to drive away and then I saw them. I rang the doorbell and I said, 'I'm dying. I'm dying!' I felt that, quite physically, I felt I was harbouring a disease. Then I went into the house, I had to wait a bit, and I said, 'This is where my home is.' It's not about them, it was my basis I betrayed. It was betraying myself and everything I cared about.

And so I went back there, and it took two more years before the pain in my belly gradually healed. Whenever I experienced something about myself at the Oasis, I got pain in my belly again. And a lot of sadness. For me it was tremendously good training, because you're not in control of it. This is what you do and these are the consequences. Whereas for me that wasn't medically possible! But I learned to see my whole past like that, it unleashed things every time; my resentment as well, because my ex-partner was there too. I didn't know I was so jealous! I had to experience that, because I really felt my jealousy, my resentment and my hatred then! … And when I was at home or working in my garden, I really felt: I want to live in order to become unselfish. To learn to enjoy seeing someone without wanting something in return. For me, to love was to possess. I had to possess, I felt that. And slowly but surely I lived through those two years alone with myself, no visitors. When I look back now, I say, 'Thankyou.' It's like this really: I climbed the mountain, and I had to fall. My pride got in the way. I mean: I'm going to do this, I can do that — and suddenly I could do nothing any more! I had to learn that. But at that particular point I couldn't laugh about it. It was painful, it was dying. I was mad, yes, I'd say I was mad. Pride played a role in my first marriage, and in my second relationship, and it still plays a role. But I don't have to search for it anywhere else now. No more backdoors. And I've closed all the backdoors, I've shoved all my books in the garage, I won't be touching them again. For me that was a tremendous effort. Because afterwards I still had that tendency; if something needed sorting out I'd go and get a book and read about it. But that would be living in my mind again, rather than through experience.

If I'd really lived like that, day-in day-out, maybe I would have ended up sooner or later on pills or the drink, or committed suicide. I'd simply betrayed my deepest self, tossed it aside for something else. When I read about spiritual things I'd say to myself, really harshly, 'Oh, I can't do anything, I'm nothing, I'm worthless. My own experience is nothing, these writers know better.' And that goes much deeper than feelings of guilt. You can push guilt aside, but not this. And at the Oasis they sense that as well; when the people they're connected with start being dishonest with themselves, they sense it. And the more you grow in consciousness yourself, the more you'll feel that. When my partner starts being shifty, never mind what it's about, I begin to sense it.

I remember one day saying to myself, 'Now I know from the inside out what it's like: being mad.' That's a difference. You can hear it when you get a nutter in the surgery — between inverted commas, I mean; someone who's emotionally or psychologically confused. But that was really my experience. And looking back I'm glad of the experience. You can really see it in my work. I mean, people come in with bellyaches or headaches, or 'I can't see properly' or 'my mind doesn't work any more' and you can scent it, you can feel it. And if I didn't know that it wasn't me, I'd begin to doubt myself. If someone is friendly and I suddenly feel furiously angry, while I know that I'm not angry, I can place it. I put a few careful questions, and then it all comes out. Every time that I look at a problem from a strictly medical point of view, I feel that constriction again. Then my whole body contracts, my belly begins to hurt and it travels upwards, up my back, to my shoulders and then my neck. It has sometimes happened that I couldn't move my neck, my head hurt, I couldn't think any more. As if I'm standing there like a plank. Headache? I never used to have headaches. So I can't bear that. And my joy in life fades, I become anxious, that madness comes back, it resembles an acute depressive state more than anything else. Often when I lie in the bath it gets better. Or when I meditate, I have to get into a deeply relaxed state, let go, become aware. You can really become aware from the inside out, literally creep from one to the other. And definitely when I sleep — it can all be sorted out the next day. I know now that I can't do things in an uncommitted way. It's not a bit of this and a bit of that, it's one entity. I can't detach that from myself.

Tanja (1968)

Some years ago I started to look at things differently. I suddenly started to wonder: who am I really? I worked as an army psychologist, and I was sitting at my desk one day when I suddenly wrote down: who am I really? Some people think I'm this, others think I'm that, I see myself as this, then again as that. I had been searching for something like this, but always within my ego, as if to say: I'm Tanja and this is how I am. But when this question suddenly occurred to me, I thought: hey, what does it actually mean, do I have such as thing as a core? I was going on holiday shortly after that, and my father gave me a book to take with me, *Bewustzijn* (Consciousness) by Alexander Smit.[1] I read it and didn't understand the first thing about it, but still it sort of clicked. As if to say: what is this? After my holiday I went to see Smit, about six months before he died, and I went on doing that every Tuesday evening. It was mainly very amusing and great fun. I didn't understand much about it but I found it all really interesting. Then he died, but I was so fascinated that I started reading everything: by him, by Nisargadatta, everything I could get my hands on.[2]

My first real experience was when I got to know Francis Lucille, a Frenchman who was visiting the Netherlands at the time, also along the lines of advaita vedanta. Something happened with him that made me question my way of seeing things for the first time. It was just a weekend where you could ask him questions, we sat there listening to him, and at one point he looked at me, and I looked at him, for quite a long time, five or ten seconds or so. And I remember, when he looked away, he smiled at me. And then suddenly I felt so ... phew ... I felt myself turning completely transparent. I'd never experienced anything like that. I felt such an openness, as if I ... well, as if I'd become transparent, shall I say. I was sitting next to someone and he'd obviously had a revelation, it went straight through him, and I also felt ... zappp ... something going through me. I thought, what on earth is this? It made a deep impression on me. I wondered, wait a minute, is my body really me after all? Or where do I stop? Questions like that. It was very calm; nothing frightening about it. I remember ringing up my boyfriend of the time and saying, 'Some really crazy things are happening here.' So I opened up to the idea that the way I'd always seen things wasn't necessarily right, nor who I was, nor what sort of person I was, nor how all of that worked. I'd read an awful lot, but I wasn't yet prepared for the fact that such things existed. I read it all quite differently from how I would now. Alexander once said: you're the part of me that's called Tanja, and I thought, what a load of nonsense! So I couldn't grasp it at all, but it was a very calm experience.

After that weekend I felt *so* open ... it made my boyfriend nervous. I felt *very* calm. Then I took part in a week's course, it was just a get-together, you could just ask him questions, really friendly, great fun. But from that time onwards I noticed that many of my ideas about the nature of things started to change. I remember walking through Amsterdam and seeing a boat moored there. Then I suddenly wondered: when I get closer the boat gets bigger, when I'm further away it's smaller, so what's real? Is that boat really there? Does that boat have any solid reality, if it's so bound up with my perception? Things like that. Or I considered: what is time, actually? So everything became a bit unsettled, and I got completely immersed in it, I started reading everything. And then on top of that I started to feel despair. Profound despair, especially about the point of everything, significance. About the total pointlessness of everything, as I felt it at the time. I read U. G. Krishnamurti, for example, that actually made me ill.[3] On the one hand I found it fascinating and on the other I found it tremendously confrontational. It had always been just Tanja's little ego, with its own little life. But now it was: Christ, so this is it, it means nothing at all, not a damn thing. And that made me lose all interest in the world. That went in phases, they could last a couple of days or a couple of months. Sometimes I felt it really intensely, and then I'd withdraw. I'd sit on the sofa all day long, and I'd be terrified. Terrified of losing control, really intense fear. At the same time I felt that I actually *wanted* to live with this total pointlessness, this total futility. I said: this is the only way. I didn't want to reassure myself, then just go and find something nice to do. Somehow I knew that it was true, and I wanted to accept it for myself. That was always clear to me.

When everything was clear, I felt no fear at all. But when it was only half-clear, I became really afraid of going mad. I remember sitting on the sofa and looking out of the window, and nothing seemed real any more. Formerly I had felt: I'm here and there's the world, and everything was so solid, it was beyond doubt. But then that faded away and everything became transparent or half ... a sort of in-between state. Or I'd see that everything manifests itself in me, or that this chair ... And then my intellect began to intervene—that's how I put it. It wants to understand, it wants to make sense of it, or it wants to find out what it means for *me*. And then there was my fear: oh God, I have to do something because I'm just going mad! I work as a psychologist so I thought: if I tell anyone about this, they'll just put it down to a disordered perception of reality, or depersonalisation, or God knows what. So my mind started working overtime and sometimes I started having doubts. I'd think: it's all very well dreaming up things like that, but all I need is medication. In actual fact I knew that wasn't the case, but I also thought: I just have to function in this world. I always kept on working, but sometimes I needed a lot of time to myself, and I'd look for a job for two or three days a week, where I'd earn just enough. I also kept seeing my friends, but sometimes I withdrew for a while. After one of those periods there would be one of clarity, and that would make me feel better. And then the fear would come back, so it went up and down.

I was still training as a psychotherapist, so I was supervised by psychiatrists, and sometimes I'd let something slip to one of them. For example, I had a new supervisor and I thought, I'm going to be very open now, I'll just tell him how I see things. So I told him all about it, it was quite a story, no idea where it all came from. I did that once, but never again! This psychiatrist was a very nice man, and I tried to explain to him what fear was, because my ideas on that had changed as well. What exactly is fear? In some ways it's the same as a pleasant feeling, and that's what I tried to explain to him. Or take the 'self', what exactly is that? We psychologists claim to know that there is a self, and we work on that basis, that's the basis of everything. So I started arguing with him about that. Does the self exist? And what is a thought? But I couldn't get through to him *at all*. Because he saw the spiritual — or whatever you want to call it — as a way of controlling your fears. Just to make things meaningful. Anxious people often find something to hold onto in spiritual things, or in endowing things with meaning. And there was me, explaining that it was the pointlessness that attracted me! I thought, bring it on! So that didn't work. Later on I went into therapy with someone else, and that didn't work either. He didn't understand the first thing about me, and we always ended up in a sort of argument. Because the sort of fear that I used to feel, and that I felt as a child, he kept interpreting as something to do with my mother or father. And I realised: I can't go on pretending that's real. I tried to tell him: I absolutely want that fear, I want to go right into it, I just don't believe the stuff around it any more. And I want to live without anything to hold onto! When you start to see that time doesn't exist, when you start to see that *this* is all there is, where everything happens, your life-story doesn't matter any more. And if one more person starts banging on about how dreadful that must have been … I was aware the whole time that I didn't want that reassurance. So that didn't work. That was actually rather painful, because I still got quite anxious or despondent. Or that feeling of going mad, I talked to him about that as well. And I really

thought, I could put everything down to that, but if it really goes wrong ...
He was a very nice, decent, safe sort of man, and I realise that he couldn't
do a thing with me in that sense. I wasn't really looking for a psychological answer anyway. I didn't know what I did want, but I could see that I
just had to keep on searching. I talked very openly about that, and so that
came to an end.

After that I went to see a lot of people, just about everybody who came to
Amsterdam to give *satsang*, and after a while I realised that I didn't want to
do that anymore.[4] I wanted clarity, I didn't want all that claptrap around it,
and people bringing up their personal problems, that didn't interest me at
all. I was very blunt about it—all that riff-raff ... I didn't understand it
either, it was all so clear to me: free will, there's no such thing. There's
nobody here, so I wanted nothing to do with anything involving a particular way; the idea that you could actually do something, and ought to be
more open, and so on and so forth, that didn't feel right to me. So I struggled with that for some time. Then I thought: well, these are clear-sighted
people after all, and yet they say this. I felt that there was a lot of clear-sightedness with Francis Lucille too, but he also tended towards a bit of meditation, a bit of openness, and so on. And for me that didn't make sense. I also
went to see Gangaji, but I thought: oh my God, all I really want is clarity.[5]
The way she made her entrance, it was all very holy, but for me that was
completely irrelevant! Then I eventually came into contact with Tony Parsons, I thought that was wonderful![6] For me he has such clarity ... He does
talk, but that whole spiritual rigmarole around it, wearing white garments,
he doesn't go in for that at all. And he's really just a very ordinary man, you
can just ring him up. I went to one of his retreats in the Netherlands, and
another in England, and just before I went I woke up one morning and I
knew: there's nobody here. Everything happens within me, but there's no
person to whom those things happen. It's all a bit disillusioning for the
intellect, the simplicity of it, and that's how it felt to me. So I went there with
the idea that great things had to happen. I was sitting at a table with him at
one stage and I said something about it, and he said, 'You're so overthere.'
Not that you can go somewhere else, it's more that: you're already terrifically awakened, or however you want to put it. I thought: oh, great. And
what about this, and that, and the other, and all sorts of other things? But
then I felt a sort of relaxation and I thought: oh, okay, this is it then. I kind of
stopped searching, searching for something, for a mental picture of how it
should be. And I always found the contact with him really great. I don't
ring him very often, but it's nice that it's possible. And it's also nice that he
doesn't give you anything; it doesn't matter a damn how or what. I was also
with someone once who said, 'I have high hopes for you.' Well, that's really
not what I want to hear! It doesn't quite tally. And with Parsons you don't

have that at all. No carry-on, no specialness. And his attitude is: awakened or not, what difference does it make? Those retreats were also simply a lot of fun. I once asked him about that fear of mine, but I didn't get any response, he just said: oh, lovely! He doesn't go into it, it's just something that manifests itself, and well, these things happen. But I have the feeling that we talk differently now from how we did at first. Because he sees that I have that clear-sightedness and that I won't take it to be something in particular. These days we can talk about personal things, but I know that it doesn't matter.

Apart from that, I once emailed Hans Laurentius in a fit of despondency, and then went to see him.[7] One-to-one, which was really nice. I brought up my fear of going mad and my despair, and he said, 'I see so much clear-sightedness in you, you can see it.' And it's precisely when you achieve more openness that all sorts of things can surface in the mind. Or fears from the past, that need to be recognised. It has also often happened that I felt tremendously clear-sighted for a couple of days, and that this was followed by the most awful cramp! At any rate, it reassured me that it was normal, that loss of control, and madness. He also said that he himself had thought he had arrived, once he'd seen how everything works. And that he'd been wrong about that because true enough, all sorts of things happened, whap whap whap. I recognise that as well; you can keep getting ideas or a sort of arrogance, as much to say: now I see it all, and then it turns out that life is still unfolding. It has also been said, 'See the face of God and be disturbed.' I find that a beautiful saying. I can see the total impersonality of it, the neutrality, it really has nothing to do with this life. And that was quite alarming, even alienating. The absoluteness, the impersonality. The simplicity as well. That is wonderful, of course, but it takes some getting used to.

Two or three years ago I moved to a new flat and I was looking out of the window and completely without warning, whap! ... I could see so clearly how it all works. In one go. I saw what they always say: nothing ever happens. No time, nothing, I saw it! I can't explain it; there's this, and time goes through it, I could see that. It was very calm and very obvious and very clear; simply, this is how it is. And not at all frightening. Well, that happened, for a while it was very clear, and then life just went on again. And a couple of months ago I was sitting here in the living room, and suddenly it became so clear that everything manifests itself within me, and that I am everything, that it's all one. And I felt: oooh ...! Somewhere inside I knew it already: oh yes, of course, how logical! Anyway, life then goes on as usual, only now you've gained an awareness, even though you don't feel that any more. And in the last few years all sorts of concepts and ideas just kept on fading away. So I continually had the feeling: now that's been taken away as well, damn it! That you see that things are a form of thought, that there's nothing to hold on to. When I got to know my current boyfriend, I also realised so clearly that nothing is yours, that nothing has anything to give you. I thought, well, that's a cheerful thought! Because Jesus wept! On the one hand I know that's how things are, but life keeps showing you that you can't create anything. And that's still going on. On days full of clarity I can't imagine it'll ever go away, and then it does go away, and then I'm left in some sort of anxiety thing. But it is different, the other thing is more in the forefront. Those fears can also feel pretty intense, but it doesn't make that much difference. Physically I feel different then, constrained, even in my head. It's an insecure feeling, as if I'm looking for something to hold on to, or trying to locate myself somewhere, and I realise that. And that alternates, with that clarity and openness.

I still work as a therapist, I've got to earn my living after all. I started working shorter hours, and I don't want to increase them, but my way of working has changed a lot. I come in contact of course with people who have lost touch with reality, or are very anxious, or have something psychotic about them. Sometimes that's quite obvious, and if someone under some delusion or other believes that he's someone he's not, he just has to take medication, and that's that. But sometimes I meet people who may be experiencing the same kind of things, and who have no frame of reference for it. I talk differently to such clients than a psychiatrist would. I keep it very open. I also say that we don't know, so in that sense I give it a different frame of reference. Recently for example a woman came to see me, but I sent her on to a psychiatrist all the same, and he prescribed pills for her straight away. She didn't want that, it didn't feel right to her. A psychiatrist like that says, 'Ah yes, disordered perception of reality.' And then I think: well, in that case I've got that in triplicate! But I want people like that to be carefully examined. And for all that, I do in fact think that people with this sort of experience are sometimes labelled psychotic, when they may be experiencing how things actually are.

At first I found it difficult in those groups. I was all on my own there, and old psychological fears kept on surfacing. But you are actually alone, that's part of it. That one-ness also means: there are no other people! I began to see that at a certain point, and it took me a while to digest it, because well, I didn't like that! It made me feel sort of sad, as if to say: that means my sister never existed either. But I didn't say that in therapy! In that sense I chose my words carefully. Now it's less of an issue, it's lighter, I don't need others to understand it. I've never really been part of a group, I don't like them. But a good friend of mine is also very much involved in this, so she sort of understands it and that's really nice. I always had people whom I'd got to know and we'd exchange e-mails, I always really enjoyed that. But most people in my life know nothing about it. It's not a secret, and I talk about it quite openly, but we only share the pleasant things of life. My parents had books by Bhagwan and Krishnamurti in the house, and they understand it to some extent. But somehow you can't put it into words, people absorb it within their own experience. Other friends find it all very interesting, but that's as far as it goes. My boyfriend sometimes talks about me, and somebody once said: oh, she ought to stop that, it'll end in tears. Later on I once asked my parents whether they were worried about me, but it isn't a cult, so they weren't. Personally I haven't the slightest inclination to go to India, for example. I've no idea what I would do when I got there. Alexander Smit once said, 'What is here is nowhere else, and what is not here is nowhere.' I think that's brilliant. God in the sense of a person doesn't appeal to me at all, nor does the God of good and evil or whatever, but I can see God simply as life itself. If that makes sense. I've never read the bible, but nowadays I can place the sayings of Jesus. I am the light, I am the truth, and so on; it makes me think: aha …

In the past I never had this sort of experience. I was serious about finding some meaning in things, but never in this field. And I remember now that when I was about fourteen I came across a poem that ended: 'and only the very last remains: I am.' I cut it out, I didn't understand the first thing about it, but it was so reassuring, such a relief. In that sense I experienced a lot of anxiety in the past, a sort of irrational, existential anxiety. An undefined feeling of being unsafe, even when I was doing something pleasant. I'd think for example: if you kept walking straight ahead, where would the world stop? How is it possible, how does that work? It must stop somewhere. Space is weird, that sort of thing. And when I was young I always felt that I wasn't completely alive. I just felt: I'm not completely alive. And that put my life on a completely different track, it bears no resemblance now. In the past I used to think: there's someone called Tanja and her life is like this; she's going somewhere, she's playing basketball, she must behave herself, for instance. When I had my first experience I still believed in a self that had simply become transparent. And now it's totally different, because I no longer believe in that life story. At first, of course, I found it very interesting, as well as scary and depressing, and I met nice people. Then I discovered that I had a choice. But later on I realised: this is just doing its own thing, and I can't switch it off any more. I've wanted to often enough, and that made me reluctant to talk about it. I often found it horrible, and I'd think: I wish I could just believe that life has something to offer. And not all this difficult business. But in another way that wasn't so. And though it frightens me, it develops of its own accord. I've always had a sort of fierce hunger, and at a certain point that's all I did have. And things are becoming clearer and clearer, I notice that. When I saw that everything is a form of thought, it was all very arid for a time. But I've also often felt: I'm not afraid of fear, I'm afraid of love. Because I felt that love knocked you completely sideways, so that there's nothing left of you. And in this I feel that things are still developing. I wouldn't call it love, but it is a sort of *flowering*, a sort of regeneration ... The mind doesn't recognise that as love, because then you're dealing with a man and a woman and need and so on, and all that intensity. Whereas this is a completely different sort of love. Something very gentle, that you could easily overlook. A very mild sort of gentleness ... how can I put it.

At first I used to think, when you're awakened, or whatever you want to call it, there are certain things you don't feel any more. But life shows that that makes no sense at all. If you take death for example, you can react with shock, or fear that there's something wrong with the body. This body also belongs to me less, it manifests itself as it were in me, it does its own thing and moves and everything. But I'm aware of the fear that this body is going to die; I can feel that at the same time. And at the same time it feels good to talk about this, and to know that other people are struggling with it, because I've often felt so alone in this. That gives me a sort of support-ive reassurance, which is part of the story. Because there is a story, only there's no belief in it any more. I write things down as well, to express it all, and I also have this real passion to talk about it. But I don't have a mis-sion any more, and I wouldn't even contemplate leading groups and answering all those questions! Because of course I know what kind of questions might be asked, and then I think oh God! All those difficult things. Because it achieves such simplicity that in a way there's very little to say about it.

Peter (1967)

When I was twenty-six or so, I suddenly found myself in a considerable crisis. I don't really know the clinical term for it, but it was a genuine exis-tential crisis. Who am I? — that's what it was about. I didn't really want to go on living as I had been, either, because I was carrying the weight of the world on my shoulders. I'd travelled a lot, and been to college. I did an agricultural course, at the Warmonderhof Biodynamic Agricultural School; I finished it, what's more, though I always knew I didn't want to be a farmer. I did it because I thought it would always come in useful.

I come from quite a problematic family. My parents are divorced, my father was a borderline alcoholic, and he was quick to lash out. He left when I was twelve, and in the end I grew up with three sisters and my mother, so very much in a female household. Later I felt the lack of a father-figure. Later still I made up for that lack pretty well. But things didn't run smoothly as regards love either, not really. And then at a certain stage I more or less broke down. Sort of, I can't go on like this. I wasn't very happy about what was going on in my head, that's what it comes down to. I thought, I'm going mad; I couldn't live with the things I was thinking and feeling. So I thought I'd better do something about it. How — that I didn't know. In short, I withdrew for a couple of weeks, in my bedroom at my parents' house. I didn't have a place of my own at the time because I travelled so much, and of course I felt secure there.

It was all very instinctive. I didn't want to speak to anyone. Not even my mother, most of the time; I stipulated how much contact she was allowed to have with me. I shut myself in and opened up to everything that was bothering me; it was a sort of journey that I was making. I tried to get a grip on my entire emotional reality, that was the theme, as I remember. Being master of my own inner world, my thoughts, my feelings, 'master of my own mind', I called that. I lay on my bed all day long, now and then I'd take a walk in the woods nearby, and that was all I did. Apart from that I just lay on my bed for two or three weeks and shut out every single impulse from the outside world. I let everything come to the surface. So all my fears, everything that bothered me. It was as if there was a sort of authority inside me, because even as regards those fears … I evidently knew that there was something somewhere, something I could trust. I had a really strong feeling of: trust yourself, it's okay to feel yourself. Before that I would clam up with fear, of course, but this time I really wanted to be able to manage it. I ended up in a sort of madness, in which I simply admitted all my fears and instinctively magnified them, so that they could go away. I was searching for a sort of purity in myself; simplicity and purity. I asked myself: why do I think this? I really don't need to think this. Is it true or false? That was the journey, to be able to feel that all at once. If I didn't feel it, I wasn't on the right track. A lot of sadness came to the surface too, and I let it all come. I instinctively looked for the resistance to an emotion, I simply knew: I have to investigate that resistance. At times I thought, I'm going mad, I can't handle this. The world appears a certain way, and you have to live in that. But at that point I could relinquish the idea that I had anything to do with the world at all. Maybe that's the madness that you experience, that you no longer have any connection with those around you. I probably didn't have much of that in the first place, but at that point I made a very conscious choice to go on with it, and to define my life for myself. That's how I explain it now, anyway. There was something inside me that understood, that kept me focused. At the same time I was very self-centred about what I did and didn't want, and what I could cope with. Everything was very instinctive, without any sort of authority; in that respect I really had nothing at all. I wasn't very interested in the Bible, as dogma, although I'd learned something about it. My mother was quite devout, she was Catholic; my father was Protestant but he never really went to church. My mother got the parish priest involved. I said, 'Don't do it, I really don't want that!' It was useless with that man, he came up with all sorts of dogmas, and I thought, what are you talking about? Of course my mother was worried, but I have to hand it to her, she did act as a sounding board. At moments when it was all too much for me—and I did have those moments—I could let off steam with her. I'd asked her not to say anything to me, not to react, but if something exploded inside me, I could express it to her. Emotional things, about my past of course, my upbringing. Then I'd got it out of my system and I could go on. And I remember very clearly the moment that I woke up one morning and everything was light again. It was just quite simply light. I looked outside and I thought the world was wonderful. It's an ordinary residential area, houses with nothing special about them, but it was probably a bit like Jesus in the wilderness after forty days, that image.

Shortly afterwards I met a guy in the train who I knew from Warmonderhof. I told him a bit about myself and he said, you should go and see Ellen. He gave me her telephone number, I knew next to nothing about her, but I rang her up, because I was finding it very hard to place what was happening to me. It was really a sort of surrender to something I didn't have a name for. We made an appointment and I remember getting out of the train; she was waiting in her car, I got in beside her, she took it all in for a minute and said, 'You're free. You're just free!' I hadn't thought of it that way myself, but in fact that was how it was. When I look back now I get the same feeling again. But I had no one around me who could reflect that. My mother thought I'd gone mad as well. I couldn't talk to anyone about it, really, because I'd gone further than they had. Not in the hierarchy, but in an emotional sense.

So in the car she said, 'You're just free,' … but I had no idea who she was, I knew nothing at all, only what that guy had told me. Therapy wasn't completely new to me, but she was something else altogether. I had the idea that I ought to go to a therapist or a psychologist or something, but she said I didn't need to. And in a way that was my salvation, as I was looking for help because I couldn't place it at all. I feel very glad that I got what I needed so quickly. First of all we had a talk in her kitchen. She told me something that really made an impression on me. She took a sheet of paper and said, 'You're really a blank sheet of paper. If you feel this, it's very different from feeling that table.' She was very insistent on experience, and that helped me a lot. The root of the problem of course is emotional, because when you feel bad and you react to that because you don't want to feel that way, you actually consist of two people, and then you're no longer immersed in the experience itself. But if you allow yourself to be all of that, it's okay. I'd realised that myself instinctively, but by giving it a name she actually gave the experience back to me. And then she did some drumming for me, as a shaman, and that just felt really good. I didn't really have any more opinions at that point. She drummed and I sat there beside her, and that was it, really. That was the first time. When I left she said, 'Go and buy yourself a bunch of flowers. Because you're free; that's fantastic.' So that's what I did, at the station. I had felt the freedom, but I'd been unable to put a name to it like that. That was really great.

A week or two later I made another appointment with her, and it came up in conversation that I couldn't really share the experience with anyone. Or the liberation either. In response she invited me to come and live there, so that I could allow the liberation to really take root. So a couple of weeks later I went to live in that enormous house, and stayed for three months. There was another woman living there who taught Avatar courses with her, and I took part in them as well.[1] To keep myself I worked in the garden, and apart from that I went walking a lot. They also travelled a lot and then I looked after the house. The idea was to enable me to develop the freedom in a sheltered environment, where it was also recognised. Because I really was free. I noticed that it had a lot of influence. There was an awful lot of love, a tremendous amount of love. My experiences at that time are also very closely connected to silence. When I had a grip on my emotions again I was very taken up with silence. It was simply perfectly silent. I didn't have a thought in my head and merged completely with my surroundings. Like a Buddha, I could sit all day long under a tree. I had to eat or drink now and then, but apart from that I had no urge to do anything. Not out of lethargy, it was just that love was enough in itself, something like that. That's how I felt, and I still do.

I had suddenly started to see the world. That's the difficult thing about it, I started to really understand and sense why things happen as they do. And that gives rise to tremendous sadness, sheer sadness about the world. I comes over me again now as soon as I talk about it. In itself that sadness is no reason to turn away from this freedom, though, because the next minute you might be laughing at the world, it's just like a film. During my schooldays I'd always read a tremendous amount, poetry, literature, I had a tremendous hunger to know about things. But at that moment I couldn't read any more, I couldn't look at a newspaper. Or if I did, I saw through things straight away: absolute madness, what we're all doing. And more than a little, absolutely everything! Honestly, you become so sharp, you take a scalpel to everything and laugh your head off. And at the same time you cry your eyes out. I remember standing on the bridge over the river Waal and seeing all those cars driving past, it was just like a film, the world was a sort of film. Nothing in it is real. You can touch it, but it isn't real. That sadness about the world is maybe more appropriate to the 1960s, when everyone was concerned about that. But because your ego dies off, you have no identification at all left with all those emotions. Pop music, for example, about love and desire and so on, you can feel it in theory, but you no longer identify with it. Or fear, you can feel that, but always as an experience; it doesn't make you afraid of anything. That's really not important any more. You can trot out a whole story about everything you experienced this morning, that you cut your-self shaving, or that you had an argument with your father; all completely unimportant. You can feel compassion for someone else, but you sit oppo-site him and look at him, and the other person falls almost silent, because he suddenly sees how it's just his own story that he's trapped in. And if you don't look out you get all kinds of shit thrown at you, because the other person doesn't know what's happening to him! I lost a great many friends as well, some of them deliberately. You're completely renewed, right down to your last cell, it's really a total metamorphosis. At the point when I went to live with Ellen I knew that I had to create some distance. It was really a rigorous break with all sorts of people, with my own past, my own life story. Some things I just didn't want any more. I realised later that it doesn't have to be so radical, but in my case it was so.

Ellen often talked about two things, the perceiver and the perceived. That came from vedanta, and at the time I didn't understand the first thing about it! I was simply one, period. Later on I understood it better, when I had come through it. The Upanishads made an immmediate impression on me; the other woman introduced me to that. She'd studied medicine first and then psychiatry, and after that she took up spirituality. When I went to stay with them I no longer read at all, but she had a very good translation and it really got through to me, that was really what I experienced. I could simply see it, the One, it was recognition, a deepen-ing at that moment, real joy. I lived a lot in the garden, I was bursting, I wept from sheer joy, from sorrow, from beauty. The recognition of beauty, pure beauty. In psychology or psychiatry there'll be a concept for it, religious mania or something. It's also strange how that experience of the truth, and that seeing through the world ... it is described in the Upanishads, but reading about it is not the same. That's the crazy aspect of this sort of thing of course, that it can't be communicated, other than in the experience. When it comes down to the essence of things, language no longer exists. You can make sentences and words, but they fade away. Everything fades away. You look at it, and it dissolves before your very eyes. It really exists beyond language. During the time that I withdrew at home, I just wanted to know where my thoughts came from. That's how I ended up with the ineffable, of course. I surrendered to something, yes, it was a sort of abyss, a great void, nothingness; I didn't know where I would come out. I only knew instinctively that I had to do it.

I could cope with quite a lot in the past, I wasn't afraid of getting a mild psychosis or whatever. Maybe because I smoked cannabis for a while, from the age of fifteen for three years, just about every day. At a certain point it made me paranoid and I stopped there and then; I didn't enjoy it any more. Some people are more receptive and in my case that might be through drugs, or through different experiences; being brought up with women, for example. That could have turned out quite differently, but in my opinion it really developed my feminine side. My intuitive side. Well, at home I always had to watch my step, because I could get a clout at any time. At any rate, I could intuitively let all of those emotions surface, and then they dissolved. It turned out later, with Avatar, that that's how it worked. But I had no idea of that then. I didn't even know what spirituality was. It seemed to me that I was still at a very existential level, I didn't even know what a guru was, I'd never heard of one. Later on we talked a lot about masters, about enlightenment, you name it. I don't know if that was such a good idea in the end, but I heard about it for the first time then. Ellen was talking about masters and I thought, what are you talking about? Masters, what do you want masters for? At all! That was the special thing about my situation, that I ended up in that state of freedom with no frame of reference whatsoever.

I don't know how else I can put it, but I fell right into that experience; that's a good description of it. I didn't talk to anyone about it because that would have meant admitting my vulnerability completely. And it's difficult anyway to talk about this kind of experience. Ellen warned me about that as well; there are very few people who understand it, and you shouldn't want to convince people that you know something that they don't. I knew that intuitively as well, and it's just very pleasant to sit next to someone who understands it all as well. Then you don't need to talk about it any more. And we used to sit for hours in silence, in the kitchen, or outside. Now and then I'd ask a question, and she would answer it. Not that she was my guru, but I could surrender to her. It was an unlikely combination; a young good-looking guy like myself, living with two older ladies.

After a while though I felt, now I should go and do something in the world again. But what? That was a whole learning process. Ellen had paintings on the walls by someone who became a good friend of mine. I started having lessons with him and I immediately felt a lot of connection to him. Then I moved to Amsterdam so I could paint in his studio; I also managed to find a room straight away. At first I just painted in a very free style for two years, and after that I went to art college. I often do things back-to-front like that, that's odd. So I did that and then I started a family; these days I'm in a LAT relationship, where we bring the children up together. I'm now back to a more ordinary mindset; I'd be the first to admit that. The things that bothered me at the time, and that I coped with by withdrawing—I couldn't even tell you now what they were. It's no longer present in my memory. That's what time does; it's simply vanished. I found that really wonderful as well, to experience that magic. That means of course taking leave of certain patterns, so the world becomes a lot more dull, so it seems. Before that you identify with all sorts of emotions and situations and complications, or you actively reject them, when you feel that sense of separateness very strongly, as I did. And then if you suddenly arrive where you really are, some things seem very dull; you can't do them any more. Why on earth should you watch television? It all becomes very subtle and fine, very fine.

Sometimes I would come across someone who'd experienced something similar. The link with being an artist is that I saw that freedom and made a choice for the usual frame of reference. It's not something beyond myself. The real freedom is nothing but love; the rest we all just do together. I come across a lot of people who have all sorts of theories, about yoga, about reincarnation, but in that freedom that doesn't exist at all. Now I have a pretty minimalist, or nihilist view of freedom. In India of course they have millions of gods, and I think that's fantastic, but they're all inventions. When you read the Upanishads, it's all about the One. That's really my thing, that's also what I experienced—without knowing those books. The fact that I knew nothing about masters was actually really crazy; I'd read Tolstoy but knew nothing about masters in India.

According to Indian philosophy you can attain freedom in three ways: bhakti yoga, karma yoga and jnani yoga—through the heart via surrender, through your contribution to the world, and through your mind, via insight. That's the intellectual way, but it's very difficult. So I've read a lot, and now I believe I'm more concerned with karma yoga, but then I was completely taken up with bhakti. That means surrrendering to something outside of yourself, to God or something. So that's also the daftest way! Of course you're really surrendering to something in yourself, but most people don't realise that. If you're attached to the Bible, or Allah, you surrender to something beyond yourself that doesn't actually exist, or is at least not physically present. So a guru is much easier, only you have to find the right one! But a book like the Koran, that's really an impossible path, it takes so long! Ellen and I could really have a good laugh about that, because if you see the whole film, you see that a book like that just can't work. Contemplation, that could work, because it excludes other things. But you could also read the telephone directory for that! So you can have a good laugh at that, but at the same time it's really sad.

The eastern approach contains so much more knowledge about this sort of thing, so much more power of discernment as well. You can follow the path to freedom but you can also lose yourself in sorcery. Our culture doesn't have that, we don't understand those things. Those Upanishads are roughly 3000 years old, I mean that's crazy, that research, that profound perception of the human spirit, so long ago! Christianity is nothing compared to that, and all psychology as well of course. From that angle we're all so excessively concerned with our self, our self is really an invention, and we think about it endlessly. It's actually a decadent idea. And the most misused concept I know.

I was allowed to experience that freedom and afterwards, sad to say, I returned to earth. I couldn't pinpoint the exact moment but the experience of freedom closed down again every time. You end up back in your conditioning, your ego gets in the way. Because you want other people to see you, to appreciate you or something. So it didn't really take root. It's actually difficult to talk about, because I'm not experiencing that freedom now; it's all memories. I do have moments when it comes back, but never for very long at a time, and also never so deeply. Who knows, maybe I'll get back to it some time; I always feel a yearning for it, it's not something that lets me go. It's perfect love, so what else could you possibly want?

Sanne (1968)

It's not very clear where it all started, so I'll just go back to the family I come from. My father was a very emotional man who couldn't really cope with life or society. He was a musician and had a job, because he had five children and the money had to come from somewhere, but my mother worked as well. She was the queen of the family. She could calm him down a bit, but my father was really a loose cannon, he couldn't cope at all with his emotions. It was always very intense, and I found that very threatening. He wouldn't actually hit you, but the threat was always there. It didn't take much to make him angry or irritated, he was really a very sensitive man, and all those children were always too much for him. Well, my sisters mostly kept out of the way, but my line of defence was attack. As a child I really entered the fray, fighting and screaming, screaming right back. The one who screams loudest, gets to be heard. I also stood up for the others, as a child I was a sort of catalyst in that respect. But I really went for it, and that meant that I trampled on all sorts of fears. And I've only noticed in recent years how anxious I am, how much fear I have. For a while now I've been having sessions with a therapist and that's one thing that came out there. By letting it come to the surface and experiencing it, I discovered that I always suppressed my fears, although they were there, at very unexpected moments.

My mother said that as a baby I did nothing but cry. She thought I wasn't getting enough nourishment, so she'd give me sugar-and-water and so on, and then I'd be quiet for a bit. Until I was thirteen I used to go around with a dummy, hidden in a handkerchief because I was deeply ashamed of it. I cried an awful lot, there was nothing really traumatic happening but the tension was always there, because of my father. My mother didn't live beyond sixty-seven, and somehow I think that she had to swallow so much, while my father always said, 'Don't harbour a grudge,' he just spat everything out. Just like that, splat. So my mother carried the whole family, with her heart problems and all. That sort of tension, I'm very sensitive to that, as a baby I was always on the alert, and later on as well: Oh lord, here comes dad, he's home, he's home, kids, turn the music off!

They said that I was an odd child. I can remember that when I was four I was constantly preoccupied with death. If we had pets or a fish that died, I'd conduct whole ceremonies. Funerals, down at the bottom of the garden. My father would play the organ, my sisters would walk behind, just like at a real funeral, and we'd go and bury the fish. That sort of thing. I also lived in a fantasy world, because every time I got hysterical and screamed a lot, as children do, I was locked in the cellar. My father and mother couldn't cope with it. Especially my father, because of course that confronted him too much with his own carry-on. And in the cellar I had my own fantasy world, which I retreated to. There would always be this man, a very old man with grey hair and a beard, and he always said things like: it's going to be all right. That sort of thing. That was my own little secret, it calmed me down. My mother said quite early on, you're deluded, you're mad, don't be so hysterical. I also vividly remember my teacher at school once asking me where I lived. And I said, 'I don't live around here.' So the teacher was concerned and asked, 'Don't you still live at home, then?' She checked that with my mother, who naturally said, of course she lives here. But I didn't live there, I just knew that one day I'd be collected, and that I would leave. That I was only there temporarily, to play. I was completely immersed in that world. So I think that's how I dealt with it as a child. Through fighting, or through my fantasy world.

We were brought up in a very religious way as well. Protestant, church every Sunday. My mother was more relaxed about it, it was only my father who used the Bible as a sort of touchstone in his life, but a completely twisted version of it. That's why he wouldn't let me dance, for example. We had a huge painting hanging in the hall: the road to heaven, that was the narrow path, and the road to hell was a very broad path, with people dancing along it. And from the age of four I wanted to learn ballet! Well, I had to do it all on the sly, because my mother had no objections. She had an excuse ready, she'd say, 'She's going to piano lessons.' So lying was the order of the day. But my mother had wanted to go dancing herself in the past, when she got to know my father. In the end she went on her own, because he was against it. He said something recently about that, actually, that my mother had been right, that it's actually allowed. Anyway, hell was full of people dancing, and my father always said, 'If you dance you'll go to hell.' And yet he was a musician himself, an organist and pianist, and earned money by it. He once played in an orchestra, but it was mainly in churches, always in a religious context. Classical music was allowed, so Bach, Mozart, the whole caboodle, and psalms and so on, that was allowed. But woe betide you if it was anything a bit different, that made him explode. That damned rubbish! That bloody music of yours! To him we were devils. Especially me, the others were more tame. My next youngest sister has a wild streak, but when I was a bit older I even entered the fray about that dancing. I said, 'If I *don't* dance, I'll go to hell.'

In my teenage years I did some crazy things, impulsive things, that were pretty scary in hindsight. For example, I was a photographic model for a while, and it's all about money and sex in that world. At one point a man invited me to come to Paris and work there. And I left the next day, just like that. And the world I ended up in, well, it was really a sort of underworld. Drugs, and having sex with men just to get on in life. One day this man brought a couple of others home for a sort of orgy, and I fled in the middle of the night and took a taxi to the Gare du Nord. Back in the Netherlands I had my name taken off all the modelling bureaus' books, at that point I knew: now it's time to quit. I was about 21 at the time. I had known already about all the drugs and stuff in that world, but the *loneliness* of it as well, the *isolation*, really *dreadful*! It's all so superficial. I think that the fear somehow creates excitement as well, and then I end up in that struggle, as if to say: no one's going to get the better of me any more, I can stand up for myself. And the other extreme is that I make a radical decision, now I'm going to pack it in. In the past I always kept on fighting, and because I do that a lot less these days, the fear comes much closer to the surface. And a lot of distrust as well. Because my father never taught me: come along darling, put your faith in life. No, everyone was a bastard. And as soon as the fear emerges, something happens like: I can't cope, I'm going over the edge, I'll end up with a psychosis. It makes me very fragile. And I wake up almost every morning to this fear. I come from miles away, from that area between sleeping and waking, and first of all there's nothing, and it's fairly quiet. Then I become more awake, and then it happens. And recently I've just lain there and let myself feel it, I go right into it, when I dare.

Moments like that, when I think I'm going mad, begin with something very physical, something happens in my solar plexus. It feels like a mouse running round inside a wheel, unable to stop. A completely physical sensation, I know it all too well. And then I become a bit, well, I call it autistic; I can't really make contact any more. I talk gibberish and I'm all over the place. I understand what I'm saying myself, and also that it's weird. Besides that, I perceive things differently, my sensitivity is heightened. And sometimes my skin becomes painful to touch. And I start compulsively ringing up friends, for example, just to make contact. I often get answering machines, or I don't feel like explaining things and then they don't understand. Some people do, because they've been there themselves, and then there's a sort of rapport for a while. But in the middle of the conversation I think: I should hang up now, because I'm all on my own with this anyway. And then I start pacing up and down. That stops after a while, sometimes after a couple of hours, sometimes after three days. A bit shorter recently, because I'm on to it more quickly. I know it so well from the past. Those were the times that I became hysterical, or started screaming really loudly. I'm still capable of that, when my boyfriend's on the phone, I might suddenly start screaming very loudly. Very dramatic. At one level it creates more space for me, and at another level quite the opposite. It often just takes me more out of myself, because I go to such extremes and really let myself go. And sometimes when he's been here and goes away again, I cycle after him. I once cycled after him to the station, and halfway there I realised: Sanne, what on earth are you doing? So I just let him go. I was dead beat afterwards, from constantly demanding recognition.

Once I really flipped, and it seemed almost as if I subconsciously wanted to. That was four years ago, I gave a party, and although I'd had a trembly sort of feeling the whole time, I'd eaten very little and felt shaky, I went and smoked a joint. And then I flipped completely. I was totally out of it, I no longer had any idea where I was. Luckily I had a friend with me, who told me where I was and what was happening. He looked awful … ! He looked as if he was dying. He had a sort of death mask on, and my own head felt as if it was completely open, as if the pores were wide open, and the sweat was really pouring out. At one point he laid me down in a tent, and I believe I made frantic love with him. Because I asked him: please, hold me tight and make love with me, because then I'll get back to my body! That did me a lot of good. But that was such an intense experience … After that I went to my doctor, I wanted to go to an anthroposophical clinic, as an out-patient. I took part in a biography group there, where you go back into your past, once a week. That gave me structure, which was a good thing, otherwise I'd be all over the place. I was working as usual then, I've had my own practice for ten years now, I give massage therapy, and I do wall-paintings for nurseries, I did all of that. And I was pre-scribed a preparation of copper, that has a protective effect. While I was in that biography group, I got cervical cancer on top of everything. They gave me a tremendous amount of support, with Iscador injections as well, I reacted well to that.[1] I had the operation and they managed to get the tumour out completely. I was glad that I was with them, because I felt their support every week. It was focused on me there, on what they call ego-strength. Left to myself, I would rather have dissolved, I really didn't want to take on any form whatsoever. My feelings about that fluctuated, I also put up some mute resistance, but the group noticed that I became increasingly present as the year went on. After that I did a course to strengthen my identity. It all starts with the senses, so, smelling, tasting, seeing, hearing—because you've missed that phase as a child. And I found that a good method, much more sensitive after all that regular psy-chiatry. But then I thought: bloody hell, what on earth am I doing? I'm also trying to let go of my identity at the same time! And it never went very deep anyway. I achieved much more in my individual sessions with that therapist. I've known her for ten years or so, and with her it was a much more subtle sort of exploration: what is it really about?

That moment when I flipped was a real turning point in the whole pro-cess. Before that I'd mainly learned to recognise my mechanisms: what do I do to suppress that fear? But after that I couldn't cope any more, I knew: now I have to do something about it. I can't go on like this, because there's a sort of terrorist inside me, who runs the whole show and sabotages everything; my relationships, my love life, my trust, everything. Then I realised: all right, I'm responsible for that fear, but if I no longer go on the offensive, what can I do instead? So I started to just be aware. I remember for example that during a session with my therapist I completely gave in to the fear and began to tremble all over, and that she reached out her hands to me and asked me to give her my hand, and that I simply didn't dare to. So it had a lot to do with trust. But it's always there. It's really always there. By experiencing it like that in those sessions, I become more familiar with it. If I don't do that, it will get the upper hand. Then I stop eating, the kilos drop off, I still get up in the morning and do things, but I start transferring the fear to my relationship. There's a sort of thirst for recognition underlying that, as if to say: are you still there? I project all of those things on to him then, I start claiming, all those sort of distortions. That fear is the main theme of my relationship. And I just find it really difficult to live with that fear, to find a sort of still point within it. I can feel the tears coming now. I'm so familiar with the distortions, and there are moments when I feel I'm going mad! Or: all right, I'll go mad then. Then I'll be done with it. I'll just get completely psychotic, and let everyone see me like that, then I won't have to hide it any more. I have the feeling somehow that I try to adjust to society, that I try to be someone, or to be an autonomous, independent woman in my relationships. Or to remain a free woman. But then I think: I'm not like that at all! Because underneath everything I'm just frightened, and anything but autonomous and independent. I know that I'm also a mad woman, the way I live. Friends of mine often call me 'the witch of the woods'. When I tell people how I live, and that I shower outside, that's crazy and different, isn't it? That doesn't bother me any more, I think it's quite funny, actually. I think that's what the tears are about, my longing to be there completely, madness and all. And that it's often impossible—or that I think it's impossible, because people regard me in a certain way. Because if I say I've had my own practice for ten years, they say, 'You? What do you do then?' In that shack of yours? As if there are two personalities, one woman who is mad and free and independent, and one who also wants to be connected to society. I've got more than that of course, but I have to draw a dividing-line there somewhere.

I still smoke the odd joint, as a sort of medicine. Sometimes I wake up about four in the morning, that's what they call 'the hour of the wolf'. Well, sometimes I'm overcome by this mortal fear, I'm all too familiar with that. Recently I've just been laying my hands on my body and feeling: okay, it's all right. And just being very kind to myself. So many ideas come to the surface and I can get so hooked by them that I sometimes feel: I'm going mad! And having a joint like that sometimes helps me to relax, the ideas vanish and it's all simply about what I feel. So in recent years I've really been feeling what it does to my system, and how it makes me lash out at other people, and become destructive. Usually I lash out viciously with words, but on one occasion I physically attacked my father, and called him a murderer and so on. And later on, in relationships with men, I sometimes began to thump them and beat them away from me, out of pure fear, or because they came too close. They didn't even need to do much to provoke me. If the other person breaks the contact that's a tremendous trigger. The main underlying reason is that I'm being abandoned, that there's no connection any more. And in my fear of course I have no connection with myself any more. Everything, my love, my trust, withdraws, and all that's left is a frightened little bird. And that has to do with life. When I get up in the morning, life is knocking at the door. And at that time of day I have all sorts of things to do. Contact people, get things done. Whereas at night I'm free. I really like the winter, it's dark by four o'clock, and then the nights ... Then I can write, paint, late into the night. Two years ago a friend of mine died, I looked after her for five days, until she died, and it was absolutely the right place for me. And out of all her friends she'd chosen me, and now I know why. Somehow I'm so used to death. I told her: I'll take you as far as the gateway, and I'll be there. We lay low for five days, well: sheer peace. No emotion at all. There was feeling, and sometimes I shed tears, because she wouldn't be there in that form any more. But I could be there for her completely. Not the slightest fear, nothing.

With my father I do in fact have a special bond, because he's also such an anxious man. So I recognised that in him as well, there is a sort of connection at a spiritual level. And he's changed a lot since the death of my mother, he talks about his fears, I find that really remarkable. As a child of four he was taken from his mother and put in the coal-shed, because his father had died. Then he and his brother were put into foster care, and he wasn't allowed to see his mother any more, because she couldn't cope with it. And every time he talks about it, he cries. And now his wife has been taken away. I do talk sometimes about my anxiety and mistrust, but I don't feel like really explaining it. My underlying feeling about that is: did I ever have any rapport? With my parents, with the whole world, I just feel cheated.

As boys my father and his brother once walked along the motorway together, because they wanted to commit suicide. They wanted to die. And the brother did go a bit mad, he joined a cult. That's how people talk about him as well: the man's mad, a cult! It probably wasn't a cult at all, my mother was very ready to label something voodoo or something like that. But my father was as mad as a hatter himself, he'd spend hours sweeping the street, for example. His mind would be so chaotic that he'd start sweeping, that would calm him down. But every leaf and blade of grass had to be in place. We had a big house at the edge of the woods, so luckily there weren't many people living nearby. But of course, there were always leaves lying around! You got used to it, you'd think: okay, there he goes again, leave him be, everyone's mad in their own way. For a long time in fact I was the only one who could see: Christ, what a sensitive man. How he's struggling. And how pathetic he is as well. He hasn't got any friends either, actually, and now he's glad that he's got five children; we look after him quite a bit now that my mother's dead. His biggest fear was always that he'd be left on his own, and that's exactly what happened. But I feel that he's coping really well. That's also my experience, as soon as you really dare to make contact with your fear, it turns out not to be too bad. If you become one with it, there is a very deep connection somehow, or it arouses love as well.

I went into therapy when I was quite young, some time after my twentieth birthday, when I put my modelling days behind me. Because I just got into a rut, with men and so on, I was always so afraid to make a commitment. And I started to explore that. I did year-long courses, emotional bodywork, and later on tantra, I've been running women's groups for years in that. So all in all that's a certain direction. In the past I used to go and see my parents, and my mother in particular used to say: what on earth has become of you? She couldn't see it as a good thing. For a while I had to detach myself from her, she found that very difficult at the time. But at one stage I was on a particular track and you can't get off! There's really no way back, and I don't want that any more. No way. Even though things haven't got easier for me since then, definitely not. I've read an awful lot of books and texts, done all sorts of workshops, been to gurus in India and what have you, but I discovered that everything I read turned out to be very short-lived. Only through experiencing everything, and just feeling hurt or suffering pain in my relationships, I realised at one point: well, I could stick with my old pattern, but I also have the possibility of doing something else, or of just being there. That's what I've gained. Experiencing it like that makes me feel that I'm richer or more mature. That I have choices. And also that I look much less for the answer in other people. That with everything that happens I don't start trying to help, save or conversely to blame the other person. Because now I'm aware of a gap, between the event and my old reaction. Like my grandma used to say, just count to ten. So then I don't automatically rush into a reaction, but I experience the gap more as: ow, this hurts, I'll just concentrate on this a minute. Instead of: you bastard! So that's what I've gained. Through this I feel much more authentic as a person in any case, so I care even less about what they all think of me.

For four years or so I've been in a woman's group, with that therapist. Four times a year we have a long weekend together, we do a few exercises, but mainly we just settle into our experience and follow it. That's such a delicate process! And we confront everything, really fantastic. And apart from that, what I like doing best is dancing. As regards work, I could probably do counselling for the terminally ill at a hospice, but I work twenty hours a week as it is with mentally handicapped people. They're mad in a nice way, and while it doesn't make me exactly happy, I like doing it. But when I dance, that's great. That's really great. I give dancing lessons on Thursday mornings, free expression dancing, and that's what I'd really like to do every day, from ten in the morning to six in the evening or something. I just began with a flyer, no pretensions. Of course I did dancing from the age of four to the age of nineteen, clasical ballet and modern ballet, that's a good basis. But I wasn't allowed to go to ballet school, so I found my own way, for two years I trained in free expression dancing. There's not much money in it, but that doesn't matter much to me, I haven't got any money anyway! And it makes me so happy! With the group of people I have, between twenty-five and sixty-three, a lot of women and only one man, and all so different. It's just continual exploration. Usually we're so taken up by a sort of rush and by our patterns, and here we discover other ways to move, and how to dance our lives.

Ronald (1973)

What I remember about my teenage years is that everyone considered themselves a certain sort of person, with a personality and a certain style. At least that's how it seemed to me. My classmates for example all had very definite pictures: he's like this and she's like that. They saw each other as pictures, in pigeonholes, clearly defined. And I experienced myself primarily as space, or as an observer, I didn't have such a clearly defined idea of who I was. That's why I think people didn't really know: who is Ronald? That became more and more of a problem for me, because the gap widened, I noticed that. As a child you live more through your perception and in space, you're much more connected to that, and you realise that about each other. That's always stayed in my memory. I had one particular friend who recognised that as well. He stayed at my house now and then, and we would lie awake at night in the dark, and have tremendous fun with certain situations we saw appearing in our mind's eye. After a while the distinction between his perception and mine would dissolve. We would see what happened at the same time, as if we were looking through one pair of eyes. And my interest lies mainly in that sort of perception. It's always been like that. But my classmates didn't understand me, and I didn't understand them either. My life went on, of course, but at a certain point it went badly wrong. My experience and how I came across no longer tallied with how others wanted me to behave, how I ought to be. So I started wondering, what's going on, what's wrong with me?

I was twenty-one when I was called up for military service, and that's where it went wrong. Because there they really put you in a straitjacket. Sergeants barking commands like that, I couldn't cope with that. I was there for two weeks, then I went home to my parents and said, I'm not going back. I was in a complete panic: I can't do anything right there, they don't even see me, what am I doing there? I don't belong there! Well, the people there could see that for themselves. All that marching and so on, I couldn't get the hang of it. To put it in *new age* terms, I couldn't *ground* myself there. And then you're just a head on legs. So I had a talk with an army medical officer, a psychologist, and it all went quite quickly, I was allowed to go home, on extended leave. But with the proviso: do something about it.

So I went to my family doctor, and that's how I got into the circuit, mainstream and alternative all mixed up together, for a number of years. For the mainstream side, I went to the RIAGG. I had talks with psychologists, did group courses, assertivity training, two social anxiety groups, and psychiatric daycare. The psychologists talked about depersonalisation, they also found me contrary, because I always pulled in the opposite direction. I also tried things in the alternative sphere, on my own initiative, because I found that the out-patient treatment wasn't helping enough. And during sessions with psychologists or one of those groups I noticed: they were missing something. I was convinced: there is a golden key. It must exist. It's somewhere. And none of you can see it. I was totally convinced of that. After that I trained as an aura healer. Then at one point I came across eastern philosophy, Krishnamurti, Nisargadatta. Another member of the group introduced me to advaita vedanta. During that period I started reading books. *Initiation* by Elisabeth Haich, that was a real eye-opener for me. I read that book and I was completely amazed. This is it! It's all in here! This is me, it makes sense. Finally, after all those years—it was February '98 when I read that—everything fell into place. I'm not mad after all! That's what I thought. I'm not mad after all!

For a long time I had thought I *was* mad. Because that therapy made me more and more anxious, that was the crazy thing. You only actually realise that years after you've stopped having it. But if you fix your attention on something, it becomes bigger. And this is how it went: in the weekly sociotherapy group discussion, you had to have a topic. And I sat there, and I didn't have a topic. So I just invented something. Ronald's turn: well, I'm frightened of going outside. Agoraphobia, say. So I invented that, and the invented fear then became real. Because that's how it works. And at one point it got so bad that I became paranoid, the energy surged upwards, I felt just as if I was about to … pfff … shoot skywards. Then I was put on medication, Orap.[1] That was under the supervision of a psychiatrist. But when I read that book, I discovered: hey, I'm not mad after all. Then I got my self-confidence back and I said, I'm going to stop taking the medication. That inner knowledge was finally validated, that feeling really came from within. And I also knew, you are all concerned with the exterior, with the personality. But seeing, perceiving, which was very pronounced in me even as a child, that eludes you. I don't hear anyone talk about that. That's never validated. Not by your parents and not by your teachers, you have to find it out for yourself. And I found all of that in advaita. Later on I wrote a letter about it to the psychologist who treated me, but of course he brushed it aside. It was complete abracadabra to him. It didn't fit into his scheme of things, at any rate.

I did that group for two years, ending in '98. Then I finished with mainstream altogether. Now and then you find people like Jan Foudraine, who want to do something about it, but then that's like social work in the trenches.[2] I see the mental health services as medieval. So much ignorance and self-interest. Then I continued with the alternative circuit. First I trained as an aura healer. I didn't finish that, incidentally, I quit in the last year. Partly because my experience didn't tally with their approach. It didn't feel right. I said to the teacher, you're concerned with images, with visualisations, but you pay no attention to perception, to what is always present, stillness, space. And that is the basis; the rest springs from that. He said at one point, 'Yes, all right, you don't actually need this training.' Ah well, it's the established order, that's their bread-and-butter, they can't just scrap it. But in fact they're having people on. It was never really clear to me whether they knew what I was talking about. I did get that validation in advaita circles, at *satsangs* and so on, with Jan Koehoorn for example.[3] I once did an advaita week led by someone else on the island of Schiermonnikoog, but halfway through the week I'd had enough of it. There was a group of people around him who'd apparently been going around with him for years, as a sort of hangers-on, disciples. People from all over the Netherlands who came running to see him wherever he was, but had no idea what it was all about. The last straw for me was that you had to go to this little chapel in the evening, he would be presiding at the altar and you had to go and sit in front of him, one by one, and then there was a sort of ritual. That really wasn't my kind of thing. I'd had enough by then so I left.

Anyway, I read *Initiation*, that was spot on. You can read the book in different ways, it has many layers. That whole Egyptian business, that doesn't really interest me. But 'you yourself are God, you are everything', that does, and especially her interpretation of that observation. Elizabeth Haich describes brilliantly from her own perspective not only how she experiences things, but also how she observes other people's reactions to her. I'd never read anything like that, and I recognised myself in it. That perception *is me*, and people only react to the form, to what I also see. I see my hand just as another person would see it. And yet another person refers to my hand as: that's you. After *Initiation* I was reading Krishnamurti and someone from my course mentioned books by Shri Nisargadatta Maharaj. They pare things down to the bone, he said — or even to the marrow! Well, I thought it was terrific. At first I thought, oh, Nisargadatta Maharaj, that'll be another one of these fake gurus, these hocus-pocus gurus. So off I went to the library for one of his books, and well … I thought it was fantastic! Direct, from A to B, no messing around and really sharp, terrific! I've also got a couple of video tapes of him. Yes, I found it really fantastic. And it's not a religion either, you see, not something that's been thought up. That's the great thing about it. It's just a validation: this is how things are. I have shelves full of books by Nisargadatta, and whatever you read, that's how it is. It validates my own experience. In a certain sense that knowledge made my life easier, because the panic of 'I have to be someone' faded away. That fear hasn't completely left me yet, but now I understand the underlying mechanism. It still bothers me that I'm coming from such a different perception, from that silence, and other people are not. They often find me vague, but I find *them* vague, because being an observer, that's not something they recognise. They don't realise that this all happens spontaneously, the body and talking, it's automatic. The conscious element, that's only the silent observer, that presence. What I suspected, and what was later validated, that's where I find peace. That never leaves me, it's my most profound self. Whatever anyone says, that observation is stable, and always present.

I've met a number of people who give *satsang*, but at a certain stage I stopped going to them. All right, if someone comes to the area I might go. But at a certain point it's all clear, and you've just got to get on with your life, you've got to earn your living. In 2001 I did a professional training course in desktop publishing. That was all the rage here in the north of Holland, with the result that there's masses of unemployed DTP-ers these days! I had a couple of jobs in that field, short-term, the longest was for eighteen months. And last year it fell to my lot to set up a mobile computer service, as a freelance.

I still read a bit about advaita vedanta sometimes, for validation. Spirituality, for me that's my own experience. My girlfriend calls them 'free-range chickens', all those people who go searching everywhere. I went through that period as well, all that alternative stuff, Touch for Health, haptonomy, reiki, singing bowls, the child in yourself, you name it. I've tried all those things but now, I don't need that any more. That was before advaita. I always had the feeling, you're all missing the point. Advaita vedanta is very simple. There is the side that is known, and the side that knows. And a lot of things can be classed as the side that is known. Ideas—someone comes up with this argument or with that opinion, those are all thoughts, so that is all on the known side. And it's difficult to make that clear on the internet forum or with friends, because they can't distinguish within themselves between that which perceives and that which is perceived. Ideas and lines of thinking, they can never be that which knows. My girlfriend understands this, luckily; otherwise I'd find it hard to have a relationship with her. It's important to me that she acknowledges this, otherwise it would be nothing more than an exchange of images. In my opinion that explains why a lot of people split up; after thirty years they find out that they've had nothing but an image of each other. They've never had any essential contact.

Last year I discovered another aspect of spirituality. Namely, that I'm an HSP; a highly sensitive person. That's also a bit of a trend, but I found it very helpful to read about it and make contacts in that field. It also confirmed my feeling that I'm not mad: I'm sensitive. It's all connected. The theory is that HSPers are born with a more extensive or more sensitive nervous system, so it's something physical. I can't remember how I got on to it, but I started reading about it and there is a website about HSP with a forum, it's got a few thousand members. So you can write to that, and you see people face-to-face at meetings. That's where I met my girlfriend. I have a LAT relationship with her, she lives in the south. In her case, other people's thoughts get through to her as well, that's quite a problem for her. She's trying to find her way through it. You're more aware of what's going on around you. Sounds, or things you see, I notice that so often. In social situations, if I mention something I've noticed, other people say, 'Oh, I didn't hear that at all.' It's as if things are much more muted with other people, so they don't get through. My girlfriend and I notice that there are a lot of *over-sensitive* people among them. We make a distinction between highly sensitive and over-sensitive. A trauma can make you sensitive to certain things, so that you're easily triggered. A friend of mine is an example of that, in my view. He was very traumatised in the past, bullied a lot and so on, and that made him over-sensitive, but you couldn't really call him an HSP. He also has social anxiety. The difference is slight, but a highly conscious person sees and hears a lot, they get a lot of impressions, they have to process a lot. You're not quick to judge, or you see things from various points of view. So in HSP circles you see people who are really highly conscious, who see all sorts of things, while a non-HSP doesn't observe the half of it.

In my social life I generally don't talk about this sort of thing. My acquaintances see me as 'Ronald', they've got a certain image of me, and that's what I am for them. And you've just got to take part in all that role-playing, otherwise you'll end up very lonely. At first I was very excited at discovering all of this, and I told everyone about it. You want other people to see it as well, of course, you want the validation. And I thought, honestly, this is so huge, this is so fantastic, you've got no idea what you're missing! But at a certain point people get fed up with it, and then I have less and less urge to talk about it. But sometimes people get interested in it all the same, that's really great. Recently for example I saw a book lying around at a friend's house, *Thinking and Consciousness* or something like that. I leafed through it a bit and what do you think, it was all advaita!

You're alone at several levels; your personality, your body and even your perception is only one 'thing'. Put it this way, it would be nice if you came across more people in life who also recognised that. On the subject of mystical experiences, I've also had the experience of feeling a mass of energy within my chest, vroom! That has happened once or twice, a very intense experience, to see and feel what it is like very directly. The first time was in Assen in '96, when I was standing talking to one of the male nurses. I'd been reading *The Celestine Prophecy* in the bus, that was all the rage at the time and I was completely immersed in the atmosphere of that book.[4] I was having a conversation with him and suddenly it came over me, that feeling of oneness, of love. A strong flowing sensation here round my heart, the heart chakra was wide open or something like that, a tremendous amount of love, a completely physical feeling, vroom! And a sense of spaciousness in this area, and also a tremendous degree of clarity. I could see with total clarity the other person's perception — or *the* perception, it's not your perception or mine, it's universal. And I saw that the man was completely unaware of it, that perception didn't show in his eyes. It was just something automatic; a body that can talk. It's one of those moments, you simply Know without a shadow of doubt: that's how it is. Not like going to church and the preacher saying something and you think, oh, how interesting, that sounds quite plausible. Through an experience like that you Know. That's it. In the literature they call it the suchness of things. Being. Suchness, I find that a lovely word. There's not really a good word for it in Dutch.

I've also had some experience of drugs, but that's artificial, of course. Cannabis doesn't appeal to me, I've smoked a joint three or four times, but I could take it or leave it. But those magic mushrooms, they were something else. That was when I was reading *Initiation*. I made a pint of tea with the mushrooms, but I didn't know how many to use, so I put the whole packet in. You can make tea from it and then throw the mushrooms away, but you can also eat the things. So I drank the tea and the first few minutes I felt nothing, so I thought, oh well, I'll eat the things as well. So I sat down and after twenty minutes or so I thought, I'll go and do something else, nothing's happening. Suddenly the girl next door left her flat, slamming her front door shut, and that cut through me like a sword—BAM! I thought wow! What is this? I'd got some vitamin C and orange juice ready, in case it went wrong, because that lessens the effect. But what happened next I'll never forget, then you end up in the suchness. Not in thinking this or that any more, no, it is as it is. The most important thing that sticks with me is that you are everything. There's only one ... everything is one ... All separateness, that's all illusion. And if you're not under the influence of drugs, now in my normal waking state, then there's also that difference from other people, who do not come from this perception. But it's not as strong as in that heightened state of consciousness, that's really extreme. In fact it frightened me. In my mind's eye I could see the image of my body, as if that was the One. The ego was tremendously inflated. My self-image, Ronald, this head, this face, I saw it all before me: that is the One and all. Well of course that's rubbish. At least I hope so! You never know, of course ... yeah, watch out ...! What stuck in my mind is that I made all of that, I Myself am the cause of all things, that is all I. A very big I. And an aloneness, a loneliness. A devastating one-ness, that there is only one; really awesome. And I saw designs, geometric patterns. There came a point where I thought, okay, that's enough, because in a way you stay in control. So I drank the orange juice and lay down on my bed. I slept for a couple of hours and when I woke up I was all right again. Back to my cramped everyday waking consciousness.

A couple of years ago I set up a website, in order to clarify things a bit for myself. You get so little validation. So you could argue: if you're so sure about it, why do you need so much validation? But that would be nice, wouldn't it, simply because it's so seldom validated, only in books. Sometimes I get good reactions on the website. There are also articles by a psychologist in Brabant, it seems that we think the same way about this sort of thing, and about mainstream therapies and psychology. The site isn't finished yet by a long chalk, but never mind, I'm in no hurry. The paradoxical thing about advaita is that it can only be seen or recognised immediately. People have to be ready to see it, you can't force it. If something is on the known side, such as language or mathematics or a theory, you can explain it and support it with arguments. But this is something in people themselves, you can't ... Like swimming, you can stand on the side, but you only know what it is when you jump in the water. And even that you can do to someone else, you can push them in. But with perception and being a witness ... the interest has to come from someone themselves. While someone who's never been pointed in that direction, or come into contact with it, won't even know that it exists. That's always a bit paradoxical. And that's why there are people who bring it into the open and give *satsang*, but there are also people who choose to remain silent. I don't intend to do anything with it either ... because then you get into the whole discussion of 'are you enlightened? Are you self-realised?' That sort of thing. Well, I never have an answer to that.

In recent years a group of people has been working on establishing a link between science and spirituality. Last week I read in a book on Internet, *Ontwakende zielen* (Awaking Souls) by Robert Yo, something that mystics also say: silence, it is silent and at the same time it's fizzing with activity. You're in the world as a human being and you experience separateness, because 'over here' doesn't experience what is 'over there'. And yet there is something that experiences both. Or if you put one glass of water here and another glass of water there, they're both water, and yet they're two separate things. I find that tremendously fascinating. And it also gives me answers to questions that bother me. Lynn McTaggart wrote a book, *The Field*, and there's Fritjof Capra. You pick things up everywhere. For myself I always find: the more I read, the more ballast I can jettison. A question of not developing, but de-enveloping. The further you get, the more you realise that it's all theory, all on the known side, and that only one fact remains standing, and that is Being itself. Suchness. And that goes on continually. Of course I'm also enormously conditioned. That's also a paradox, I always experience both. When someone talks to me, I experience 'talking' and 'listening', and yet you're also dealing with separateness. That's always a bit difficult.

Life just flows on and takes no notice of what we think as humans, whether we call what's standing there a beech or a birch or an oak. They're all assumptions, concepts, words. You become more and more conscious how many assumptions there are, you see that every day, in the paper, on television. That makes things difficult. When you see the oblivious way people do things, it creates irritation. I think that's why I sometimes come across as a bit odd, why I react in unexpected ways. And then you can't explain it, that's the frustrating thing. So for me it's a question of adapting in order to deal with people who confine themselves to thinking. It's easier with people who perceive more. But you can't start explaining to everyone you meet: 'do you realise that you are perception?' They'd see you coming!

As a little boy I was quite often feverish, poorly. My earliest memory is of becoming conscious of a dimensionless dot. Very small, but also very large. An absolutely immeasurable, dimensionless something. At such times I was in a completely different place, and my body and my parents, they were somewhere else. Miles away, but also very close, very strange. At the same time I realised that my parents didn't know. They talked to that body they called Ronald, that was lying there being ill on that bed; all they could see was a sick little boy. I've mentioned it since, but my mother was much less aware of things then, of course. I've seen it described in the literature, I couldn't tell you where, but I realised that I recognised that. That's my earliest memory, but it was fading then. Very occasionally it happens spontaneously, but now I can evoke it in meditation. In bed at night when I'm completely relaxed it sometimes comes back. You can lie down and allow your body to rest so much that at a certain stage you no longer have any sense perceptions. You think things like, oh yes, there's an arm lying around here somewhere, but you can't feel it. I can sometimes get into that state then, that dimensionlessness. And if I just sit down and close my eyes, I can evoke it sometimes. But there's also some fear attached. Like, what weird sort of thing is this? Your thought processes have nothing to hold onto. Now the earth is always there, gravity, and in that place there is nothing, no gravity, there's only big-small, there's no other way I can describe it. Words fall short. But it crops up in the literature. In the past I used to try and explain these things to the people around me, but it was very difficult, you can't explain it. Recently I was talking to friends about it, but they couldn't make head or tail of it. They weren't even interested in it, because they don't recognise it.

Dee (1938)

I was born in Indonesia, where my father was a missionary. I was a wanted child, I really was a wanted child. But that came with an awful lot of anxiety and tension on the part of my parents. In my early years I had a very strong bond with my father, because my mother had to look after my oldest brother. He had diptheria, and before the war that meant that she had to go into isolation with the child, while she was pregnant with my sister. My father had to work, of course, so I was put in the care of an *babu* (nurse). And for me the *babu* was my mother. I was still very young, my mother had weaned me, more or less, because she was expecting my sister. But I wasn't really ready to be weaned, and the *babu* breastfed me herself, against my mother's orders. And she gave me my first experience of real love.

Apart from this my parents had little chance to bring me up. The Japs ruled the roost. When I was four, we went to the camp. My father was already in the men's camp, we'd been there once, and he'd ordered me to take care of the other two. I had an older brother, after him came the twins, they died at birth, then there was me, and then my little sister. After that there were a couple of stillbirths, owing to the war; that wasn't talked about, but as a child I understood that. Mother was never around in the camp, as she worked as a nurse with the infectious disease cases. I had to look after the others, there was someone who kept a bit of an eye on us, and mother looked in now and then. But I did the washing, I got the food, I was indestructible and they were always ill. Well, were they always ill, or was it just an easy way out? You start wondering about that afterwards.

All of us survived. I was almost eight then, and I weighed less that ten kilos. But I was the strongest of the lot. I didn't recognise my father, I didn't believe for a minute that he was my father. Then came the insurgency and the colonial police violence that followed, so we were being shot at and we had no idea that we were free. And then we arrived in the Netherlands. I remember going to church for the first time. The minister got up in the pulpit, there were hymns and prayers, and then he started his sermon with: hurray, we're still alive! Ah yes, but how? From that time onwards my father was always depressed, my mother must have been rather less depressive, so to us she seemed normal. But when I look back … it went like this: my father got up at six o'clock, lit the stove, and when we children came down, he went back upstairs. We still ate together, but that always ended in an argument, with my father stamping away upstairs. In a family like that, no other sort of contact is possible.

My mother came from a family with a lot of children, eight of them survived but I think there had been twice as many. Every time a baby was born, she had to rock the cradle, and every time something happened. Once she couldn't get a baby to keep quiet, and she rocked it so hard that it flew out of the cradle. She put it back in, and the next day it was dead. Never talked about, of course. She couldn't get attached to children, that became clear to me when I came back from Africa. I suddenly saw that she hated little children, and I began to understand why we were all so damaged. There was no love. But I also realised, oh, but I have known love. When my youngest brother was born, nine years after me, my mother didn't care for him properly. We had a one-roomed basement flat, one big bed, a stove, a table, and nowhere else to put a cradle. But when she had fed the baby, she would put him in the cradle and start doing something else. Then the little chap would lie there crying, his face all red from the stove, and I'd say, 'Mam, Jantje's too hot! Shall I move him?' No, that's his place and he'll just have to put up with it. Well, can I put him on the big bed, then? And I'll sit beside him so he can't fall off. And can he have some water? So then I got spoons and boiled water and so on, and I began to take him over more and more, and he really became my child.

When we came home from school we would have a cup of tea together, and then Father would go back upstairs. 'Mina, I'm going to have a lie-down'. Then Mother made the dinner and I looked after the little ones, I darned the socks, everything was still rationed so I unpicked clothes and knitted new ones, and I was constantly doing things around the house. And on Sundays I cleaned up and when they went to church I changed all the beds, vacuumed the place and dusted, then they came home to a clean house. And my youngest brother was always under my feet. On Mondays I didn't go to school, because that was washing-day. So I went on Tuesday. They never said anything about it, because well, it was necessary.

When we came to the Netherlands I was put in the second class. What's 1 plus 1? Well, how should I know? A cousin of mine went to the same school and she taught me to write and do sums after school. I learned to read meanwhile, because in the second class there were masses of children who were still learning their letters. I wasn't stupid, but my Dutch was poor, because before the war I'd been with the *babu*, and the Japs forbade us to talk Dutch. My mother refused to speak the *babu*'s language, but because she was away so much I learned very little Dutch. So they must have thought I was a bit backward or something. I was already the odd one out, there was only one other child from Indonesia at school, but she used to faint at the drop of a hat, she had fits and god knows what, so she was even weirder. We were weird as well, because at school they called us: pauper's brats, nit-heads, that sort of thing. Anyway, my parents were strict Calvinists, church twice a day on Sundays, prayers and Bible reading three times a day, and once more before you went to bed. And this was a sin, that was a sin; mentally saying to your sister, 'Drop dead' — that was a sin. My parents also believed in accepting no help from the state. But there was no food! I was only fifteen when I came home one day and found that they'd plundered my post office savings account. And then something happened inside me. I'd experienced love with the *babu*, and through that I realised at that moment: God exists. Everything rests on your shoulders at the moment, you have to be strong, you must show love. So I started working, as a nurse. And I was confirmed the same year, because I simply knew that someone existed. It was all very childlike, very naïve.

In fact, there was never a time when things could have been put right, all I knew was chaos. Anyway, when I left home I started work, caring for the mentally handicapped. Well, the matron had cancer and everyone else had to look after her, so there I was, a fifteen-year-old caring for thirty-five mentally defective children, some of whom were mothers themselves. Unbelievable! That went on for a year, and somehow or other I ran things. There were also some very crazy situations, where one of them got into a state—well, that's what we called it, one of them would start a fight, and then it was every man for himself. I'd shove her into the laundry chute, close it and report it. Then the director would come along, get her out of the laundry chute and say, 'It's up to you, either you take a dose of BCL or it's back to the laundry room.'[1] And that child—they'd call her that child—would get bromide or luminal, and go out like a light.[2, 3] Well, at times like that you just wanted to be a cog in the wheel. I'm talking about 1955, what did they know in those days?

After that I went into ordinary nursing. I'd had no secondary education of course, but they saw that I wasn't backward, that I passed my exams. I was a bit of an odd one out, because I was confused and with my background I couldn't make friends easily. I did have one friend, though, she lived in the same town, and I was just like one of the family. I was regarded as one of the little kids, I was fed just as they were, and they looked after me. So I had a sort of family life there and that was pleasant. After that I did my midwife's training, and it was there, with the couples who came to have their babies, that I saw what love is. My soul began to yearn for that. Because I'd never had anything like that. It was confusing as well of course: why isn't it like that with us? I couldn't understand, even at the age of twenty-one, why there was no love between my parents. After training I worked in the deaconesses' nursing home in Hilversum for a while. The gynaecologists treated me as a midwife, but the deaconess on the maternity ward didn't like that, so she had me scrubbing out the cupboards. There was a fuss about that and I left after a couple of months, and started working as substitute midwife, here there and everywhere. That went well, but I also felt a bit confused. I saw of course how some children came into the world deformed, and couldn't understand how that was possible if there was a God. Then someone from the church rang and asked if I wanted to go to Ruanda. And I did, I'd always wanted to do mission work. As a child I'd always wanted to go back home, and Indonesia was home but I couldn't go back there, so I might as well go somewhere else in the tropics. But there too I felt confusion on all fronts. Ruanda is largely a Christian country, only nothing made sense, they were always at war with each other. I was still naïve enough to think I could change that.

I lived there in a little house in the country, in the back of beyond. A wood stove to cook on, no fridge. I taught and looked after the sick, so I had a girl who cooked and made bread. People arrived at seven thirty, first you had prayers with them, and then you did your rounds to see who was in a bad way. Everyone else had to take their turn. At a certain stage I really felt like a puppet. You weren't allowed to teach birth control, while children were dying because they were born too close together. And the tribal wars disrupted the agricultural rhythm. Before I spoke the language well enough to find that out, and to teach with those flaps of flannel: at the new moon in January you have to sow sorghum in that old bean field … well, it soon makes you think: what am I doing here? We'll grow the carrots here and have them carry water from the river up the hill, but we should be doing something else altogether! I did birth control and a lot of other things all the same, and it became more and more clear to me: I don't believe like they do. I couldn't pray any more like the others did, and I couldn't believe in sin any longer. Then I started suffering from culture shock and I became more and more confused, and then the war really started to play up. It had been dormant all this time, then years later you get an eruption like that. So I applied for extended leave, and I came back to the Netherlands in 1971, after seven years. In the meantime Women's Lib had made its mark, and society was totally transformed. What used to be strictly forbidden was now the order of the day! And during that leave, I fell in love with Karel.

Well, that did nothing to lessen the confusion. I became more and more averse to the Church, because the Church wasn't love at all, the Church was a puppet show! For that reason I didn't want to go back to Ruanda. So I married Karel, and became his children's stepmother. But then came the confusion: love is sex. Somewhere deep inside I knew perfectly well that I was falling back into a familiar position. I sometimes say, my software was programmed wrong, all that knowledge made no sense in the world outside. Because I knew that the Japs were no good, but if I wanted to do something to the Japs, my mother would be punished. That kept surfacing in all sorts of ways. And yet I thought that's how life has to be, I adapted to Karel in thousands of ways, and didn't realise I was just letting myself be used. Men had the right to go to bed with their wives. You're not allowed to say: I don't want to. I also had no concept of where my body ended and someone else's began. It was like that in the camp as well, of course. Well, of course I wanted love, and to Karel love was sex plus a tiny amount of comradeship, but that was it. No being soulmates and that sort of thing … I could get through to him less and less. And I felt more and more: I don't just want to do the housekeeping, only to be told that you don't find the toilet clean enough, and that I haven't cooked enough food for the guests. It became clearer and clearer to me on all fronts: you've got to get out. But I didn't dare to, I was far too frightened.

That went on for years, and then in '87 everything was turned on its head. It started with the death of my mother, through a medical error. And because I'm in the medical world myself, I could no longer say, 'Don't worry, just go to hospital.' The ground under my feet had vanished. It ended in discharge on medical grounds, and in one of my talks with the medical examiner the war was mentioned. He suggested that I'd only heard about it from hearsay ... But I said, 'Hearsay? If you're put in a camp at the age of four you can remember that!' Then I went to a psychiatrist and he told me: Karel is okay and you're confused. But things were already going wrong: Karel wasn't okay. And I couldn't sweep things under the carpet any more. The whole war, that medical error, everything I thought I'd done wrong, etcetera, I couldn't place it any more. And I walked around in a fury all the time. Other people had already told me, you're so aggressive, you provoke aggression. And I always met with aggression, but I had no idea that it came from me.

Anyway, after I'd got over it a bit, my husband had a nervous breakdown. When you try to change, those around you have to work with you, whether they want to or not. And so we moved to France. He wanted to live abroad at some stage, we found a lovely place with a view of the Cévennes, and that's where we went to live. That's where my mind began to clear at last. I read a book by Coëlho, *The Pilgrimage to Santiago*, it was actually a short novel with all sorts of exercises, and I started doing them. In the first exercise he says, 'If you do this exercise, you are bound to grow.' And I did the exercise, and sure enough, I started growing. For example, in one of these exercises you lie on the ground, completely folded up, and you imagine that you're a seed, and you start to drink water. You start to swell and you have to force your way through the hard earth, with a green tip pointing upwards. Imagine the tremendous power in that little seed! And then you stand up, and you become a tree trunk, you feel the wind and so on. I did that several times, and every time I felt awed by the fact that such a little seed can come up out of the ground, and there were all sorts of things that played a part. I'd developed a stoop, went to see a doctor, he worked on my bones and set me upright again, and then I went to a physiotherapist and he said, 'When you change your physical attitude, you have to change your mental attitude as well, that goes hand in hand.' That exercise brought me back to my roots, and so I started defying Karel, things like: look, mate, I'm not your servant! So I started arguing with him, about what was going on inside of me, but then you get all of those stupid things, it's only about power. He started really bossing me about, of course everybody noticed that, but I just let it all happen. And you'd never get a compliment out of him. One day I let a pan of rice burn. He was furious, he stayed furious for three days, he wouldn't speak to me. And I, like a fool, didn't say to him after one day: listen Karel, if you can't get over that pan of rice, I'm going to a hotel! No, I tried everything to win him round. I even humiliated myself at one stage! Time and again. And yet somewhere I knew that I had to go through something to become more clear. And then, very gradually, I found help, from very unexpected sources.

One night in '95 I had a dream. It was an apparition, in fact, of three men. To me it was very real, I was awake, and I could see the men actually standing there in the room. And they said, 'You went to sleep with the thought, "I want to die". We've come for you. Unless you're not ready.' I said, 'Yes,' but I added, 'If there's no other way out.' Then they said, 'You need to start thinking clearly. We can give you answers, but your questions must be clearer.' And then they vanished.

Some religions talk about angels, others about patriarchs, and Buddhism talks about enlightenment, but it's all the same thing. In this life we no longer know which way to turn, because no one accepts any more that there is a higher power, and that it can intervene. And that it doesn't do away with your responsibility, but it can draw your attention to it. The message: you need to think more clearly, that obviously came from outside. I couldn't give myself a shake and say, 'You mustn't die. And if you can't go any further, we'll take you with us, because you've had enough.' Very short, very to-the-point, but also very clear. You need a lot more words to explain it than were actually spoken at the moment. I would have died at that moment, I know that for sure. I would have had a cardiac arrest or something, if I'd said yes. There was also the shock of feeling, yes, but I haven't yet done what I should have! It's not finished. I've still got heaps of things to do, it's not yet clear to me.

I didn't have anyone to talk to about it, of course. My sister was always going on about her past lives: I stood at the foot of the cross, I was once a hermitess, walled-up in a church, and people responded by saying: you're mad. When this happened I knew I wasn't mad, and yet the thought occurred to me: I'm going mad. Because it was beyond ordinary experience. After that I had other times when something became clear to me, without apparitions, and I just said, 'That is true.' For me it had to do with the place. There was a very beautiful wide view over the Cévennes and the Ardèche, it was a few hundred metres above the Rhône, and sometimes you saw those snow-covered peaks. Absolutely gorgeous. If some places are a gateway to heaven, that's definitely one place where Jacob's ladder might have stood. Sometimes when I sat there, often at moments when I was just sort of meditating, or ... I don't know, I just

started thinking about something and then something became clear to me.
Or I'd be doing something and suddenly have to sit down and listen. And
then something became clear to me that I just couldn't get around. Something that I'd always denied suddenly became as clear as day. So that I
said, I don't know how, but that's how it is. I experienced that something
existed, a higher power — and whether you want to call that God or Allah
or Buddha, that doesn't matter. Then I experienced a tremendous love,
that I absolutely couldn't place. So I just called it 'the Pot of Love'.

Around that time I had another woman's child in the house for nearly a
year, she was having problems and I looked after her child. I could invest
all my love in that child, and he really started to blossom. Meanwhile of
course I was tugging away even harder at Karel, and in September '98 I
said to him, 'Now we really have to talk, and something in our relationship has to change, otherwise I'll have to leave.' Not long afterwards a
woman knocked on our door, and said, 'I can't go home or I'll be murdered.' So of course you say,'Sleep here then, we'll talk about it tomorrow.' And she stayed. And Karel fell in love with her. And I said to him,
'Karel, she's got to get out of this house. I can see that you love her, but
she's dependent on you now, so the two of you can't take it any further.'
But no, he fell for it like a lovesick mooncalf, and pretty soon I moved into
the spare room. Then her ex began to utter threats and there turned out to
be all sorts of suspicious things about it all, so then I decided: get the hell
out of it. Sit up and finally take notice for a change! Finally do what those
men said, work it out for yourself! So I packed my suitcase and headed for
Holland.

Well, there I was, I had nowhere to live, I had nothing, and I really
didn't know where I was any more. Luckily I soon got a place in a sort of
service flat. Meanwhile Karel told everyone in the village that I'd gone
mad. I was rung up by an acquaintance who thought it was a bit odd, I
told her I wasn't mad, just very confused. A couple of weeks later the
woman left Karel, he wouldn't give her any money. So then we were left
to sort out the mess. He was still in France. And then came the whole
struggle, with everything that had been wrongly programmed in my
head, through the war, through my way of coping with it, things I didn't
understand. A whole process started up that I really didn't know how to
deal with. So in '99 I went into therapy in Oegstgeest, at Centrum '45.[4]
Well, they asked all sorts of questions, but I couldn't bring up this story. I
didn't try, I knew already. It wasn't possible. That was because of the
other people in the group, the directors, the therapists. I would have been
labelled psychotic, in need of medication, and I didn't want that. I wasn't
psychotic, I was confused. Sometimes I wondered: am I manic-depressive
after all? Because my moods could change just like that. But I got over it

without medication, apart from taking sleeping pills now and then, because I got extremely exhausted. And very gradually I became more and more clear in my mind. My God, the time it takes before it finally dawns on you! And you're thinking all the time: I'm mad. I'm mad. But I began to see, for example, that I had behaved towards Karel as a house-keeper, so why shouldn't he treat me as one? And I thought myself that what I did wasn't good enough, and my way of loving wasn't good enough, and that I was stupid. Well, he'd been to grammar school and university, and I'd only been to elementary school. But how can someone respect you if you don't respect yourself? So it got through to me that Karel had humiliated me tremendously, and now one of the people in the group was also doing that all the time. She used to say things like, well, dear, you don't understand anything – and she did spiteful things behind my back. Then one day I had a nasty dose of flu, but I went to the centre anyway, I was so worked up! And that morning I said, 'Listen, I'm not going to be insulted by anyone any more, and that means you too!' I didn't get through the camp for nothing, I didn't get away from Karel for noth-ing, and now it's over! I won't let anyone humiliate me any more!

That evening at home I developed a really high temperature, and sometime in the middle of the night I got up and started making a pot of tea. I took it back to bed with me, and then I burnt myself. Because I lost consciousness through the fever, and spilled the whole pot of tea over myself. My temperature was already low when I woke up, but I managed to ring the doctor before I lost consciousness again, and then the ambu-lance came. And in that ambulance, I'll never forget that, the 'Pot of Love' began to overflow. I had second- and third-degree burns on my chest and my belly and I began to feel intense pain. They put me on a drip and gave me painkillers, and it took them half an hour to find me a place in a burns unit. And there it became clear to me: whatever happens, it doesn't really matter if you die, because now you're much more clear in your mind. You know that there are other things, but you don't have to die. You can if you like, but you don't have to. You can get over it. So then I decided: we'll keep going. This is just a hitch.

Well, it was some hitch, but still, they were incredibly caring towards me. People who choose to work in a burns unit – it stinks, it's nasty, people are seriously ill – you can only do that if you have a big dose of love to back you up. And compassion. Because in nursing they always have to hurt peo-ple, however hard they try not to, and then the swearing that goes on! But all the same, I felt that love through the closeness, I never felt alone for a moment. It also became clear to me that I still loved Karel, but that Karel didn't love me any more. Because at one point he rang up: I'm coming to see you. I said, 'No, come in two or three hours' time, because I've just have morphine, while they take off the old dressings, then they put me in a sort of water solution and then put the new dressings on. Come a bit later.' No, then I won't have time for you. Well, then I realised, all sorts of people have come to see me, from my therapy group, vague acquaintances, but Karel can't be bothered to come? And you still think he loves you? You just fell in love with that good part of him, that everybody has. But he's not the sort of person you can live with. Later on we got a divorce, of course, and I really got a life of my own. He comes here occasionally and then I see, my God, man, what a mess you're in. And how I'd like to straighten you out! But I've waited long enough, I can't do any more for you. What I really regret though is that I can't go to that gateway place any more.

I went on reading that sort of book. Drawing on my Christian background I said, 'If there's a God, He'll make that clear to me.' And that's just what He did! So I read all sorts of things. The Tibetan Book of the Dead next to the Bible, and I take from it whatever makes things clearer to me. I also read a lot of psychological books. One book that really clarified things for me is by Riekje van Boswijk-Hummel, about how you suppress your emotions and how they then re-emerge stronger than ever. That really applied to me, of course, with my fury at being humiliated. But nowadays I rarely have aggression directed against me. And the clarity has made love much more free. Not love in the sense of sex, but of compassion, loving. That selflessness of Christ, that disinterestedness. In my case I experienced that with the *babu*, and later with the apparition, pure agapè.[5] For me, parts of the Bible now say quite different things from what they used to. One very striking example is: love thy neighbour as thyself. The Church always interpreted that as: more than yourself. I didn't know any better. But no, what it says is: as yourself. It doesn't say: other people more. Every person is a being, and every being has a part of that love, however hidden it may be. And whatever name you give it. And that part is worth it in a person. And there's also that bit of love in Karel, only he can't reach it by any manner of means.

So I've often thought during my life: I'm going mad, I am mad, everyone says I'm mad—and at the same time I knew, I'm not. But then, they didn't know the background. And then I say, well, I'm only flesh and blood, to what extent is every sort of madness really confusion? Some confusion has a chemical cause, but this was really a question of not understanding. That isn't to say that I wasn't suffering from mental distress, or that I didn't have moments when I thought: let's put an end to it, an end to this life because I don't understand the first thing about it, it's driving me completely mad! The difference between what I knew and what happened outside, it just didn't tally, it didn't make sense!

For me it's been a long quest. And when I stop and think about it, about that wretched little creature that struggled its way through, well, it brings tears to my eyes. I think damn it, when I see one of those children whose parents really understand it ... When you see a child like that, surrounded by love, you think well, I didn't have anything like that, or very little. That's not jealousy, it's an observation. But it includes a deep understanding of myself, for example: is it surprising that you've had such a hard time? That because of that, others have found you a difficult person to deal with? You can't expect others to think from within your frame of reference.

My younger brother had a very bad start of course, my mother only weighed forty-five kilos when she was carrying him. He can scarcely cope with life physically. He's very glad when I go and see him, but it's actually all a bit too much for him. But he has really developed that bit of love, he also has a really nice wife. I would like to see his pain within the framework of the broken family we grew up in. His hatred of God, his cutting himself off from anything at all. For him, reincarnation would be the dirtiest trick that life could play on him. But I can't do much about that.

There are very few people who know about that experience of mine. My daughter-in-law knows, she's a very open person. She knows a lot as well, and she brings the children up in a very loving way. Those children are also just as open, after those burns one of her little boys, he was three at the time, said, 'Mammy, Dee's got a pain.' So I said, 'Yes, Dee's got a pain, but your mammy can't do anything about it at the moment.' And mammy stroked his head and said, 'Apart from just being here. And knowing about it.' So those children are getting a fantastic upbringing, and to some extent I'm getting mine. One I never had. Learning really silly things, like: how do you say hello? What do you say when someone gives you something? No one ever gave me anything! How to say 'thank you', I didn't know the first thing about it. And if that's your attitude to life, you'll be an odd-one-out. So the fact that people often thought, what a weird type, well, I can quite understand that now.

In 2001 I finished going to the therapy group. I'm not always equally cheerful, that's hardly possible. And I also have moments when I long for someone of my own age. But there you are, that's not easy, people of my age are often so set in their ways. But I see a lot of the grandchildren, so it would have to be a LAT relationship. Now I've got all the time in the world for the spiritual development I need to undergo, and to go on exploring that bit of knowledge or bit of God or the Buddha or the 'Pot of Love'. And of course, those who ask shall receive. And that's very simple, if a child speaks to you, to respond with love. But also to think ahead, like: of course you can come and see me, but you must tell mammy where you're going. My biggest hope lies in my relationship with children. But it can also be like what happened recently, in the woods, with a woman who was in some sort of trouble. I said hello to her and I felt something welling up, as it were, and I only said a few words and she began to pour it all out. So then I said: shall we sit down for a minute? And then just get it off your chest. People have also been there for me at times like that.

Ferri (1949)

I was in IT for twenty-eight years totally wrapped-up in my job, day and night. I'd been working as director of an IT company for the last twelve years, when I suddenly started suffering from burn-out. That was really intense, I had a complete breakdown and from that moment on I couldn't do a thing. I couldn't read a book, couldn't pick up the phone, I didn't dare have people round or speak to them, I couldn't do a thing. The result of all this was that I found myself in a tremendous depression, and had to seek help. That's how I ended up going to a psychologist. And sure enough, he told me that it wasn't just to do with my job, but also my childhood, my personality, but I shrugged it off. I also went to a psychiatrist for quite a while, and he put me on Seroxat for just under a year. I didn't work during that time, I just went to work on a therapeutic basis at one point. But as head of a company, doing three days a week just doesn't work. Everyone still drops in on you, and you have no authority anyway, because your colleague is standing in for you. So that didn't work, and I realised that I simply wasn't ready to go back. One day I saw an article in a magazine, *Management Team*, about Pieter ter Haar and his centre, the Ark. That appealed to me. So I went to the Veluwe district for three days, and was confronted for the first time with a whole new way of looking at myself, and how I tick. Because at a certain stage that was my biggest question. Who am I really? I no longer knew. What I really wanted to know was: on a scale of 100, is 80% of me a depressive, negative, irritating prick, to coin a phrase, and 20% a nice friendly guy, or is it the other way round? Because I no longer had the faintest idea. Pieter and his work began to play a very important role in my life. I arrived there with two other people, and on the first day he started saying things to me like, 'You're completely focused on yourself, you only think of yourself.' I thought: how dare you say things like that to me! That's an outright insult! I got so angry that I rang my wife that night and said, 'Look, I'm not standing for any insults! I'm coming home tonight. This is a load of rubbish!' But my wife said, 'No, wait a bit and see how it goes tomorrow.' So I went to bed and in the middle of the night I woke up and the film unrolled before my eyes again. So I said to myself, 'Maybe he's right, maybe it's true. I'll just go on with it.'

Well, something had happened on that very first evening. One of the others was talking about his family at one stage, and he began to cry his eyes out. As for me, I hadn't cried for years, couldn't remember the last time. So this man was sitting there crying and when he finally stopped, I said, 'I envy you, I wish I could cry as well. That would be wonderful.' The next day I was down for energetic therapy, physical therapy. It was based on love, don't ask, that's what they said. Went to the woman's room, she started tugging at my body and digging her elbows in my back, talking to me all the time, about the past, about my childhood, about everything I'd experienced. I said to her, 'I think I have no feelings.' That's what I thought, I have no feelings. I couldn't reach them, anyway. Then she said, 'On the contrary, you're very sensitive, only you don't realise that yet.' I didn't believe a word of it, but at one point I burst into tears, I really loosened up. I can't remember ever crying like I did then. Unbelievable … and I came out of it like a new man. I thought: what on earth's going on? I still get gooseflesh when I talk about it. It gave me such a liberated feeling! I immediately felt one hundred per cent better. I told the other two men about it, because they were next in line. And they had the same experience, fantastic!

So I was there for those three days and they also gave me a lot of tools: look, you must read these books, and try doing that. For me it was a totally new world that I'd never heard of, that I'd never believed in — never. I was brought up as a complete atheist. Church — nobody was interested in that in our house. It was bad news because it only led to wars, and all sorts of clichés like that. So I didn't get anything in the way of spirituality. Plenty of negativity, I was brought up on that, because my father had a pretty negative character. My mother didn't, luckily, but my father was cynical about the world. People were bad by definition, everything was bad. That naturally had an impact on me. I was always really cynical as well. On the outside I was usually really nice and fun and friendly, but I didn't feel like that inside. When I came home after that weekend I felt a bit better, but I didn't understand anything that had been said. So I started reading books. *Love Without Conditions*, I really ploughed through that book.[1]

I also went back to my psychologist and my psychiatrist, who continued seeing me, and I had to deal with all sorts of awful things at work. It came down to the fact that people wouldn't co-operate with my re-integration process, so I took them to court about it. I didn't win or lose, but in the courtroom I was made out to be the biggest loser to work there in twenty-five years. That really hurt me, I felt really damaged. So I went back to Pieter, who said, 'Come for a six-day retreat to my house in France. With five others, all people like you, with good jobs and a certain sort of problem that they can't solve. You're spiritually inclined, but you don't realise that yet.' I was pretty sceptical about it, but I went anyway. In October '99 I went to France and that turned out to be a real revelation. Pieter has a background in Pathwork, and his method involves talking, physical therapy and yoga, which they use during that week to peel off all your layers like onion skins.[2] I didn't know what was happening to me. The main theme was the Transformation Game; his wife supervised that.[3] And every day you played that with the five of you. Fantastic! You peel yourself completely, skin after skin. Now I know how that works, but of course I didn't know that then. One after another, all high-fliers in the business world, you saw them completely ... phew ... day after day. Crying and laughing. And that happened to me too, of course. Through the heights and the depths. After the game you just carried on together, eating together, Pieter would read something aloud and there was a fantastic atmosphere, really great! Because of course I'd been really depressive during that period, and this had a huge effect on me. I gained a lot of insight about myself ... About negative inclinations, for example, something like that came up there again. Two of the men couldn't get along at all, and one afternoon I discussed one of them with the other. During the night I realised that that theory didn't hold water at all, because I'd also seen a totally different side to this guy. The following day I said so, and the next thing we knew, those two were behaving like the best friends in the world during yoga. For a joke we asked if they were going to amalgamate! I thought that was really wonderful, and I realised: I had a part in that. But it also made me realise that at first I'd just gone around gossiping about it, in order to get the upper hand somehow — and yet it had just made me feel bad inside.

So that sort of insight made me feel good for a while. But I'm a perfectionist, I had very high standards and if I didn't live up to them, I felt worthless. That's how it was then. So I fell into a slough of despond again. During our meal on the last night we all told how we saw each other. In my case everything apparently seemed fine, but that's not how I saw it myself. Next we were told to write down a couple of things: what insights did you acquire this week? What are you going to do with them? And: do you have any more questions? So I went to bed and dreamt that I was in a sailing boat and fell overboard. I felt absolutely dreadful. I was really low. They tried to steer the boat in my direction but I said: don't bother, I'm at my wits' end. I remember that clearly. I thought: I'm at my wits' end. I've been to psychologists, to psychiatrists, I've taken medication, I've read books, I've been to Pieter ter Haar in the Veluwe and now I've come here to France, I really don't know what else I can do. I'm at my wits' end. Literally. It dawned on me what that means. And then I thought: I'm going to end it all, I don't want to go on like this. That's still engraved on my memory: I don't want to go on living like this. In the past, during one of these depressive periods, I had once actually felt the urge to drive my car into a tree. Then I woke up, and my pen hovered above my notebook, intending to record the insight: I'm at my wits' end, there's no solution for me, I'm going to pack it in. But I couldn't write it down. For one reason or another I couldn't do it. Then I lay down again and a tremendous peace came over me. Really weird. A tremendous peace. That conclusion: I'm at my wits' end, that gave me a tremendous insight into myself. Finished, I've finished. Somehow that made me feel good. I let go. And then it happened. I'd reached rock bottom, and from one moment to the next it suddenly swung, from nothing, completely in the opposite direction. I had *no idea* what was happening. Zoom, zoom, zoom! I lay there sweating, trembling, from head to foot. I thought: what's going on here? Zoom, zoom, zoom! And a voice that kept saying to me: 'I have the power to bring people together.' In connection with what happened the day before, probably. 'I have the power to bring people together'. That experience kept going through me. I was confused. And I found it terrific, unbelievable! Never experienced anything like it! It was—honestly—an unlikely experience.

So, I just lay there and after a while it ebbed away. Then I got my notebook and wrote down the insight: I have the power to bring people together. And the question: what's going on here? I fell asleep again, woke up at about five or six, and then realised what had happened. I thought, that was just a dream. But I also remembered: I wrote something down. So I got my notebook and read what I'd written: what's going on here? So it wasn't a dream, it had really happened! And I realised, this isn't normal. Even though it was lovely, it was so uncontrollable, I found it frightening! So I got into a complete panic. I got dressed, ran downstairs and said, Pieter, I've gone mad. I've gone stark staring mad, I should be put in a madhouse, because weird things are happening to me. I don't dare to drive home, I just can't do it, because I'm completely cracking up! Pieter said, 'Why, what's happened?' So I told him the whole story and then he began to laugh! He said, that's fantastic, mate! Congratulations! There's no need to be afraid, this is very important for you. You've started on the whole process, that's terrific, you need to cherish it! At first I didn't know what he was talking about. I also went to his wife, who said the same thing, that my feelings were getting a chance at last and that I'd managed to get through to my core, as you might say. And that touched me tremendously; still does, every time. I realised then: so it does exist! All that nonsense you've heard about, or that people make such a fuss about, it really exists! That's how I summarised it.

We were going home that day and I had agreed to go and play golf with Pieter that morning in Montélimar. I still felt completely upset, said I couldn't do it, and on the golf course I didn't hit a single ball at the first five holes. I stood there shaking all over. But suddenly it started to get better, I could let go. Then I got completely into the flow, and I can't remember ever hitting better shots in my life. I hit one good shot after the other, each was better than the last. And so did Pieter. But at one point his knee gave way, he couldn't turn any more, he couldn't do anything any more. I said, look, let's call it a day, because it won't work with you in that state. But he kept going. And he kept making better shots, better and better. And every time he said: if I'd stopped, I'd never have known I could hit such good shots. Well, after that we said goodbye and the way I felt then ... I loved everyone and everything, I saw things around me I'd never seen before! It looked completely different! I just felt completely ... absolutely everything! And I loved him as well, I kissed him when I left, all that sort of thing that I'd never felt before. I drove home on cloud nine, absolutely unimaginable. On the way home I stayed in a hotel overnight, I sat there on my own at the dinner table, looking at a photo of Pieter's place. The six of us had made a painting of it and given it to Pieter and his wife on the last evening. Everyone had cried their eyes out. I sat there looking at the photo, with great pleaure. The waiter saw the photo and said, 'What a great photo, did you take that yourself?' 'Yes,' I said, 'isn't it terrific?' I had that photo enlarged and it's been hanging on my wall for years now, it's very precious to me.

When I lay in bed in that hotel I kept waking up with the urge to write and write and write. I wrote down things that made me think later: where on earth do you get all this wisdom from? Wonderful. The next day I drove home and strange things happened then as well ... at one point I suddenly turned off the motorway at a different point from what I had intended. A bit further along on the left-hand side of that road there'd been an accident, and mad though it may sound, I knew somehow that the accident would happen there. I was meant to see that, that's what I think. So crazy. But it didn't surprise me any more. When I got home I felt completely transformed. I'd lost all my negativity in one go. I'd never had the experience of being completely positive, about myself, about everything. The next day we had a tournament at the local golf club and everyone said, 'Hey, you look radiant!' So I said, 'Yes, that's how I feel as well.' My wife and I were playing against another couple in this competition. The woman had a very negative attitude. Before she hit the ball she'd say,

'This one's bound to go in the water.' So I said, 'No, you're going to hit it over the water,' and she did hit it over the water. And then she said, 'Gosh, you're right.' Or: 'You're going to hit this one over the bunker,' and then it did go over the bunker. She said, 'It's such a pleasure to play with you!' I felt that too. And it went so far that those two made it to second place. I found that so fantastic! I wasn't remotely interested in my own game, yet in the past that was the only thing I cared about.

That euphoria lasted for a week. I had been warned by Pieter: you can't hang onto it, but now you know that it exists. And he was right about that, because it faded after a week and I ended up in the same old misery. So I became depressed again, but I started working on it! I started immersing myself in the subject like mad, I started reading books, Deepak Chopra for example, I've seen every television documentary about it, Tibetans, everything under the sun.[4] I wanted to know *more* about it. And that succeeded in laying a foundation, because I no longer automatically rejected belief. I didn't believe in the traditional religious way, I believed in that power from within, in that universal energy. That really exists, I've experienced it myself. And that means that I'll never go beyond my critical point again. And I didn't, either, not even in my relationship. In the past I really laid the blame on other people. I've caused people a lot of pain through that. And it was always the other person's fault in my relationships. That doesn't happen any more, and it's wonderful. Not that I'm never irritated or negative, but it no longer gets the upper hand.

Last year I was faced with a tumor and I thought: this is my ultimate test. Now I really have to show that I have made spiritual progress. And that paid such huge dividends! My father was 88 and had trouble with his bowels, it turned out to be a rectal tumor. He had an operation and that went well, but he died suddenly a week later of complications: pulmonary embolism. Dreadful! At one point he mentioned certain symptoms and I thought, oh, I've got that as well. And it turned out to be true! So I had the same operation, completely the same. I was afraid of complications, of course, and I was given injections until the last minute to prevent blood clotting. I lay there in hospital and two days later I had tremendous pain, I could only lie on my back, had bedsores, and of course I felt terrifically ill. Then I started having those experiences again. I was lying there in bed and I felt those waves of energy flowing through me once again. Waves and crying. In the meantime I'd been working as a volunteer at the hospital, that was one of the things I'd started doing. So I lay there like a king, everyone knew me of course. Then this little woman came in and saw me lying there in tears. So she said, 'Does it hurt that much, do you feel so bad, son?' And I said, 'No, I feel like the happiest man in the world, but I can't explain!' I felt so on top of the world! How is it possible? Every time I talk about it I feel cold shivers. It kept coming back, and each time I drew such strength from it that ten days later I was back at home.

Six months later I had to go back for a second operation. That turned out more drastic than I had expected, I was confined to hospital for twenty-eight days, with complications, intestinal obstruction, all very problematic. The nursing staff left much to be desired, and I got irritated with the specialists, until I thought: all right, mates, sort it out, I'm just going to lie here. And as soon as I let go, it began again, that's roughly how it works. That power started welling up inside me, whoosh whoosh! It lifted me up completely. Every time that I talk about it I get gooseflesh again. A friend of mine came to see me, someone from the group in France who I still have contact with. He'd had a similar experience. We sat there by my bed, hand in hand, and we just kissed each other; we didn't give a damn what other people thought. And then it started again. He understood and we both sat there crying with joy. Fantastic!

At first I was always searching for it, I wanted that feeling again. Only it's not on tap, it's not mine to command. But when I need it most, it's there. For example, my wife has a niece, she's a doctor these days, and she's very much involved in this as well. On the evening that I heard that I had bowel cancer, she was supposed to come and stay for the weekend, to talk about a book. At first we wanted to cancel it but we let her come after all, and she became one of the few people I told about my experience. Wow, what a weekend that was! And yet I'd just heard that I had cancer! It was simply fantastic! We sat there and cried together, but also from sheer joy and power! Later, when I was in hospital for the second time, she'd gone to do work experience in Australia, and she rang up at the very moment that I was having a hard time. In the middle of that conversation it came over me again. I lay there for fifteen minutes without being able to utter a word. Then one of the nurses came in and saw me in tears and trembling on the phone, and she asked, 'Can I help you?' And I said, 'No, I feel fantastic, go away.' So she must have thought I'd gone round the bend. But my niece understood and said, 'Oh, I'm delighted for you.' Really special. It still affects me when I talk about it. And whether I'm mad or not, that doesn't bother me at all.

I was never afraid of it again, I just enjoyed it and was only too grateful for it. Since then incidentally I've had it regularly. An emotional film ... bull's-eye! A fine piece of music ... bull's-eye! If I'm listening to Mahler's Third, say, the last part, with Edo de Waart, it happens again, my heart's fit to burst. That never used to happen to me, I always said, 'Oh, rubbish.' So it's terrific of course to have that now. If you could never talk about your feelings or yourself, and then suddenly you can. And that inner knowledge, that power within, every one has it in them, they must have.

Only problem is, can you reach it? That's how it goes. I'd like to enable everyone to feel it, because I think, if everyone had that feeling, the world would be a different place. I've experienced that for myself, I realise the value of it. Something in my consciousness has apparently shifted, maybe just a tiny bit, but still enough to give me a completely different attitude to life. I see things quite differently now, I behave quite differently with people, have a lot more friends now. I had friends in the past, but deep inside I didn't feel anything for them. I didn't realise that then; now I do. It gives me quite a different feeling and of course that works both ways. I notice that people confide in me much more these days. I work as a volunteer for a foundation. The guy who runs it has become a sort of friend. When he has a problem he always says to me, 'You're one of the few people I'm telling about this.' And I think to myself, well, you wouldn't have done that four or five years ago.

As for going back to work, after a while I didn't want to any more. The work I used to do no longer appeals to me. At first of course I felt: back to work, must must must get back to work, status, ego—I mean, it really was a good job. But once I was out of circulation I enrolled at the hospital as a volunteer. I really wanted to work with the patients' radio, as radio was one of my old hobbies, but it had just closed down. So I started collecting and bringing back patients, from the ward to the examination room. And besides that I started working for an institution, tremendous fun, that place. We act as mediators between sporting organisations and charities, with a group of volunteers and a lot of famous sportsmen and—women who work with us. What my family thinks of this U-turn I don't know, but of course they saw what was happening to me. From that time onwards I started watching the Reverend Schuller, that's another thing. Well, once I wouldn't have touched it with a barge-pole! Couldn't stand it! My in-laws used to watch it and I would think, Christ, what a load of rubbish! The crazy thing is, from that moment on I didn't believe in a God as he presents it, but the way in which he presents it, based on the love inside people, that really appeals to me. He studied psychology as well, by the way. I still watch him. I'm very lucky that my wife is on the same wavelength. After my breakdown, she explored all sorts of things herself, and when I came back from France I offered her a trip like that as well. So she's been there as well, six days, with five other women. She had a terrific time as well. Not with the same experience as I had, but at least she totally understands what it's all about.

During my depression I went to see that psychologist. He referred me to a group called 'Vermoeide Helden' (Weary Heroes), at the RIAGG in Rotterdam. Eight men, all people of a certain standing who had lost their work through a burn-out. I'm still a member, quite frankly not so much because I need it for myself, but more because I find it interesting to see how those two psychologists tackle everything. And also because I feel that I'm making a very valuable contribution. Just by saying things that those psychologists don't say. I told my story there once, I went completely over the top. Crying, trembling, everything, going through the whole experience again. At one point the man next to me fell into my arms and burst into tears, he thought it was such a terrific story. He said, 'I envy you because you've experienced this.' And odd to relate, the psychologists said nothing at all. They couldn't make head or tail of it! And they didn't come back to the subject with me. But they do see me as a very valuable member of the group, I know that. It doesn't really bother me, but I sometimes say to them, 'A bit more confrontation on your part wouldn't be out of place.' I really confront people now and then. And the funny thing is, they never call me to order, yet they can't make head or tail of it! I find that so odd! Because the way I see it, people come to that group because they've got problems. I recognise that of course, because I've had them myself. But you never get any further than a bit more insight into the problems, how they stem from your childhood. Because they don't focus on solving problems! It stops there! Just sitting there listening, and accepting that you are what you are, that doesn't get you anywhere! And that whole transformation business, that's just a phase further, to put it simply. Just a bit above that. But you have to put some effort into it!

Joyce (1948)

I went through an inner crisis which had been threatening for some time. The most difficult thing about it was that it was all purely atmospheric. Really unpleasant. Like sensing that it's going to rain, while looking at a blue sky. Animals notice that sort of thing, before a thunderstorm, for example. That's what it felt like. Gradually I dared to face that feeling. I went on living, I got on with things, and all the time that was going on. Even before it really started, I felt that I didn't know if I would get through it. As I sank further in, that gradually lessened. And I grew within it. I merged with it. I had this saying that I often used, which was: I am ready to die. That gave me strength. But I think that my boyfriend at the time was scared to death. In '99 I was very ill, I had pulmonary embolisms, it was really touch-and-go. My boyfriend had already told my eldest children: bear in mind that she might die. I was furious about that. Because that was all his projection. I knew I wasn't going to die, not physically. And I wanted to leave hospital, because something happened that made me think: now I have to get out of here. I felt that I had arrived in another world, one that had more to do with physical death. So I left, and when I got home I collapsed, right in front of him. He went into a total panic! Because he'd told my children that I might die, and mentally he was already clearing out my house—we don't live together. Then I got really angry. I slept downstairs, I couldn't manage the stairs. I felt as if my body was divided in two, I had no feeling below the waist. When I came out of hospital, there was an owl roosting near the house. Every evening. I wrote about it, and when I was better and started teaching again soon afterwards, the owl vanished, gone without a trace.

Some time later I read a book by Pema Chödrön: *Doen waar je bang voor bent* (Doing what you're afraid of). That's what I was doing, that kept coming back. Because I was ready to die, I started living with more awareness. It had nothing to do with exciting things beyond myself. It was just looking myself in the eyes. So I made a picture-book, I got all the newspapers and cut out the film adverts for an Italian film, 'Io non ho paura'—I'm not afraid. Until I had a hundred of them. So these strips of paper were all over the place, and I used them as chapter headings. Dreadful and beautiful, both sides of the coin. I am adventurous, so that played a part, although I felt this made it a bit gruesome. But unconsciously I was ready for it.

I also suffered a tremendous amount of pain, physical pain, and that surprised me. I thought, I'm in so much pain … I was doing a short Buddhist course and the monk who was leading it asked: is it pain or is it suffering? And I realised: it's pain, it's not suffering. It felt as though everything in my body had moved to another place. As if my whole skeletal system had been reorganised. As if it all had to be put together all over again. That pain lasted two years. It was continuous. And it was everywhere. I had everything checked out at the time. I'd overstrained something, at work and so on, but that's a different matter altogether from that pain. It was also really weird how it was there one minute and gone the next. Once, when I was having a conversation with a monk, I felt no pain at all. He found that quite logical, because I was talking to him at the time, so I was doing something. And that made sense, because I was detaching myself more and more from doing things, I wasn't numbing myself any more. I entered completely into the pain. Sometimes it felt as though I was being skinned alive, stripped, as if the flesh was being ripped from my bones. Then I really learned how to relax, and I could start using that.

For quite a while I would only sleep outside, in the garden, I had to be outside, I couldn't stay in the house. There's a connection, because I did go roaming once, through Sardinia, and I thought it had to do with the sort of countryside. Then I came back and people asked me whether I was home-sick, but I said: no, because I've discovered something in myself. I could see myself in that island, I didn't leave it behind. During that period there was a lot of death around me. My boyfriend and I were going away with my caravan, which I kept on a farm in the province of Drenthe, with a young farmer. I had a really intense conversation with the farmer while I was there, about life. And shortly after the summer he died in an accident. That's really weird. Because while I was having that conversation with him, I knew. Because I was operating at such a different level. And there was a dog run over on the motorway nearby as well. In fact I was sur-rounded by crosses. A week later someone asked me if I would do some graphics with a group as part of an engagement party. Weird, I seemed to be able to keep on working and existing at that level. I was hiring a Baptist church for the occasion, and on the way there with my grandson we saw a woman who'd been run over, she was just lying there under a blanket. It just went on and on like that! And then I thought: I must be careful, I must be very, very careful! And yet I knew it would be all right. But I had to keep very much on the alert, and that's what I did. It didn't take over. I was right in the middle of it, and at the same time I was an observer. After a while I had more time on hand, and I withdrew to my shed. That was in 2004.

The previous year my brother, who I hardly knew, had dropped in one day. He'd built a threshold for the shed, to keep the water out. Because when you have one of those cloudbursts here in the summer, the front street is completely flooded and it gets completely waterlogged here at the back. I can still see him doing it, down on his knees. I stood there watching and I thought, God, it's not just a shed any more. It's something else. So I called it my temple. We insulated it, I wrote a poem on the bare wood, and then we put the floor in. So that's where I went and lived. And I cried like mad, for no reason. I don't know if it was my own sadness, I don't think so. It was more like something that lived in my body, just like the tsunami, I kept thinking about that. That's what I felt like, period. So desperate, and then that breaking out, a sort of bursting open, it's sheer violence. And really physical. Sometimes when I was with someone else, that water would suddenly gush out of me, through what was happening. I didn't feel that it had anything to do with me. It wasn't really suffering, either, not really, that would be putting a name to it, and that wasn't it, it was indefinite. It was an event, an exorcism. That sounds odd to other people, of course. At one stage I did actually think: should I start taking medication? I didn't want any help because that would prevent me from experiencing what I could experience, in perfect solitude. I slept well and I wasn't depressive, but I didn't know where it would end. So I'd just sit there and I had two tiny little windows, so I could see outside; that was good. A lot of people came to the front door as well, but I can't hear anything back there, I can't hear the telephone either. I didn't realise that at the time. But if the car and the bike were there, people used to wonder where I was. Afterwards I did have contact now and then, there were also people who said, 'Come and stay here.' They found it scary. A friend from Switzerland came to my door, but I didn't hear her. When she got back home she rang up and said, 'This won't do, you must come here.' I thought it very kind of her, but I knew I shouldn't do it. And afterwards she said that she'd hoped I wouldn't do it! That she'd never have been able to cope with it! We really laughed about that. It was good to know that people were there, as long as they left me alone. I knew that I mustn't abandon 'It'. And I didn't, either, I just stayed put, for three whole months.

I was very fragile during that time. And I found contact with other people difficult, it was as if I had only a thin membrane around me. I remember occasionally saying to my boyfriend, 'I don't know whether I'll make it.' That's what I felt, you see: I don't know whether I'll make it. I didn't understand it completely myself, and yet somewhere deep inside I did. And I wanted it as well; it was an opportunity. In a certain way I was completely ready for it, and underlying everything there was still a tremendous trustfulness. But it was certainly difficult, and it was intense. That's why I stayed on the alert every day, I was really shadowing, witnessing myself. I did sleep in the house, but I'd go back to the shed in the morning, I had a sort of rhythm. And I did nothing at all, really. While as an artist, I feel: you have to produce something. All I did was to write and draw something in a little book of children's songs, dating from the 1800s. On some pages there are chairs flying through the air. I drew with juice, from elderberries or gorse, anything as long as it was fluid. I still paint with that. Strange things were happening around me as well, and I think they were all connected. During that time I was looking after my grandson nonetheless, one day a week, I get on really well with him. Tacit understanding. He was two years old at the time. And I built a huge fire here on the hearth. Really huge! And for days I wandered around the house naked. Wonderful! Oh, that was really wonderful! Yet I never thought, I hope no one sees me.

After a while I felt that it was calming down a bit. It just flowed away, I can't even recapture it any more. Then I thought, oh, in September I have to start work again. I was supposed to start teaching again. And that made me think: what on earth can I do, I can't do anything. But I have to earn my living. Another factor was: will they still want me? Who I am, who I'm becoming, I've got nothing to give, I really have no idea! Who's going to pay for that? That sort of thing. But it just fell into place, I was very open about it all. It's a strange fear. Because you lose, and you have nothing. But I had no trouble in accepting that about myself. Losing is an art. But it was difficult making contact with the world again afterwards. It's very intimate, you're really a child again, it's almost impossible to approach you as an adult woman. So of course I had all sorts of associations with incest, it was all so sensitive. Just sitting it out alone, that was all right, but with other people, that made me really awkward, that didn't work very well. And I think that phase isn't over yet. Since then I dare more to show who I really am, though. Especially the not-knowing and the vulnerability. I'm self-employed, I have to support myself through teaching and selling my art. But later on I bought a Buddha statue, for example, I never do that sort of thing! I walked past a shop window in Amsterdam and I saw that statue standing there, and I started crying. I went inside and asked about the statue, it was a female Buddha, from Burma. I can hear myself asking how much it cost. Well, a tremendous amount! And I cried my eyes out. And the owner said, 'Oh, she really speaks to you!' And, 'Even if you only pay five euros a month, she's yours.' And she cost 4000 euros! She's still there, I've only got a photo of her. And up to now I've paid about 300 euros of it. And after that I bought a ruin in Picardy, in France, just as expensive. And I don't even speak French. All because of my shed experience. I just let it all happen.

That's the wealth I've gained from that shed. I've become freer, I've broken down walls. And that's really good. I'm not trying to interpret it, or put in in some frame of reference. I enjoy it now, though I didn't at the time. Because I didn't know whether I would come through it whole. No, not *whole*. Come through it *healed*, that's it. Crying is not sadness, it's letting rivers rush through my body and really rinse it out. Sort of like sitting it out, until the sea, or a volcano, has calmed down again. After that someone gave me a book, *Autobiography of Red*, by Anne Carson, about the fire within us, that burning, that smouldering, that can devour you if you don't know how to deal with it. It's not visible through the garment of flesh, but we are neighbours of fire. A marvellous book, and it has to do with this sort of thing. The liberation of the spirit. I've achieved a sort of inner peace, even when it's hectic all around me, there is something in me that stays constant. And I didn't have that before. Not even long ago; that was sleeping, that wasn't being awake. Now I can surrender more to the motion which doesn't come from me—something like that. I notice that when I … What it is, is what is flowing through me right now. That.

In that shed I passed right through matter, I experienced: there is no matter. There was all sorts of stuff in the way, and I was just dissolving it! How on earth can you describe that? It's within me, there's nothing beyond me. And there I was, just doing that. Alchemising … those substances! Fermenting! Fermenting, and bubbles, and then it would go quiet again, and then it would start again. All very physical. When people feel pain, they think that there's something wrong, but it's just that something is going to happen! Something is breaking loose. Or you're becoming aware that something is too firmly fixed. Later on I really had to laugh about it. Afterwards, when I suddenly came into contact with advaita, I thought: yes, that's true. Recognition. Now it mainly gives me pleasure. In other people, and in myself. And there's no longer any distinction, between pain and pleasure. You make your home together, you live together, work intensively and lots of pleasure. When I started doing visual work, I needed visual images to exist in the world. Or to broaden myself, or to find myself again, or to have something in my hands. And that's all passé. What I experience with people now, in teaching as well, is a lot of fun. Because we dare to dig so deeply, and then back to normal, right as rain! You can do that in two and a half hours, that's incredible. But that comes through being open to it. That's a really large part of it, in that shed; wow, that was quite something. It was really a sort of 'holy madness'. And I also felt a yearning. I read Meister Eckhart. I come from a Catholic family — a Catholic upbringing would be putting it too strongly. I went to a Catholic primary school, run by nuns, and that's when it started falling apart. Those are the images that come back; I saw the people, and I saw what was inside of them. Those were two separate worlds. I never saw any truth there, what I saw was deception, people hiding behind a mask. In a way I had to be healed of that. I once taught in the Tiltenberg Centre, where you have to sleep in those little cells, that brought it all back to me, that atmosphere.[1] At primary school they used to tie me to my chair with a rope, because I was high-spirited and used to sing.

I remember that there were times in the past that I wasn't complete, that I dissociated, I wasn't there. As a child, and even later. After my time in the shed a memory resurfaced of when I took my eldest child to nursery, and my feet didn't touch the ground. I was walking on air. And everything was pink. First of all it was a shock, then it became quite pleasant. Floating, the colours, everything! And you go on cooking, and you go on living. It was all very agreeable, and I think it lasted about four months. Until one day I suddenly fell out of it, and found myself on the ground again. I couldn't understand it. And I thought it was horrible! I found it absolutely *horrible*! Everything was drab again. Everything was grey, hard, at that moment. I also often thought that I was mad, I wrote that everything was fine, and I could manage everything well, but I didn't fit in, in the world or in the family. I found it difficult to live ... oh, how can I put it ... I just couldn't be there completely.

I was always doing visual things, I taught, with a slight difference. Until I experienced things with people that I didn't understand, things of this sort. Then I realised: making an image is not making an image. An image comes into being. In society you have many layers of making images, making pictures of what you see. Where an inner process and the outside world meet. At a certain stage I didn't want to go on making images. I put it into words as well: I want to get away from matter. I can still hear myself saying that. Then the building where I have my studio was sold. Something that I couldn't stop myself came to an end. It happened. So I started a course at the centre of creative and expressive therapy in Amsterdam, and they gave me a teaching job straight away. I did that for a long time, in Finland as well, and other places abroad. I also worked for a long time as a creative therapist in the psychiatric sector. I could always understand the people I worked with really well. I could always put myself in their shoes very easily, I could work with schizophrenics and with people who'd just come out of a psychosis. And there were women who'd had a baby and gone into a depression and couldn't look after the baby. It was about a sort of transformation process, I was given enough scope to work it out. You had to keep up a sort of production line, so many places a day, but working one-to-one I was still able to achieve what I wanted. It was based on art, a sort of performance, or singing, or materials, and using the body. If people were falling apart, for example, you just had to let that happen, and at some point it would come all right by itself. Sometimes people were under medication that was supposed to keep them going, but not always. You can't work with people who are being kept numb. An approach like that didn't always meet with official approval, but if it worked in practice, it was allowed. After anti-psychiatry there was a period where the prevailing idea was 'just push people through it'. I've never believed in that. That is so arrogant. It also depends tremendously on which therapist or psychiatrist you have. I've also had therapists in my groups who'd been doing it for forty years, and were completely unreachable themselves; my god! But in everything I did, I found images less and less important. They do come about, but for me it was increasingly about the landscape, being outside somewhere with people.

And now I'm working on that hovel in the Ardennes. That has something to do with that, and with the shed as well. I only realised that afterwards. There's not much to it, otherwise I'd never have been able to buy it. A cottage that used to house two families, because there's two chimneys. And a bread oven. A basket-maker used to live there. The ceilings are low, you have to duck your head when you go in the door. And the loft is really lovely, you can see the trees from there, that's gorgeous. When I bought it

I got a sort of bill through the post, the electricity had been used. I thought, oh God, asylum seekers have moved in! Maybe a whole family of them! Well, we'll just have to make friends ... fantastic things like that! I talked to my brother, he's ten years older, I'm just getting to know him. He said, we must go there! Then it turned out that it was just some sort of initial payment, a connection charge. My brother asked: are we not going, then? I said, 'We're going all right!' With that caravan attached to his car, in February: ice, snow, icicles. We roughed it there for a week, on camp-beds, in a right clutter! But he made one room windproof and watertight. So we slept in one room, and in the middle of the night I heard him say, 'If your mother could see you now.' And we got down to work, and then he said, 'I'm happy. It's marvellous. It's travelling through time.' The whole family turned topsy-turvy, because he was always the odd one out at home. And I have no idea what he's really like! One morning I woke up, I opened the door, and there were a whole lot of cows. And they'd just been at the hay, so one of them had what looked like an enormous hat on! It looked just like a bridal couple—I was very taken up with bridal couples at the time. A bridal cattle-couple; they were so lovely standing there, and so matter-of-fact. And I thought: I've never had such nice neighbours.

Like my time in the shed, I can't really say much about this, except that it was good. We're going to go back, he's the only man who wants to, he feels something as well, something happens, we heal each other. We liberate each other from old times, the clots dissolve. It gives us space, and the old pleasure. There's also a bit of land behind it, with trees, and someone has offered to build me a tree-hut there, complete with doors and windows. Recently I said to some of my pupils: I've noticed that I'm happiest on the margin between humans and animals. And I've lived half out-of-doors here of course, but the contact there, with the earth and nature, there's no comparison. I used to miss that here as well, though I can stand it better now. But I need it, otherwise I can't cope. In the natural world things crystallise in me. During the night too, and in the twilight.

This year I dreamt of a bride and a white puma. In the last three years I didn't dream at all, but now it's starting again. So that's what I called the book I was working on then: *the bride and the white puma*. I woke up, it was a Sunday, very early in the morning, it was snowing, really heavily, and I love snow. And I was perfectly happy. I woke up because in the dream I saw my mother just before she died, and just like watching a film being wound backwards, I saw her as mother, as the wife of my father, as a girl, until she got back to the age of about five. I saw her standing by her father's knee, at the age of my oldest grand-daughter. That whole thing with animals, like the owl and the puma, I've never really gone into that, because it's all so normal to me, but it seems a bit shamanistic. Not long ago I read a book by Castaneda again, *The Art of Dreaming*. I got the book six years ago, but now I'm reading it in one go, after my own trip.

As an adolescent I was already living away from home, in the Hague. But I was too young and at one stage I had Interpol searching for me. The same brother found out where I was and I can still hear him say, 'What she needs is a good hiding.' So I'm a jailbreaker. My own way, often at risk of life and limb. That was more in the material world then. And now I see that it all happens at a completely different level. And I'm very happy about that. The other things were all an overture, just practising! This way after a certain point I could experience and exist at many more levels in my life. And it goes on and on, it's being continually refined. My sister, for example, has to keep to a safe distance, otherwise she finds it all too much. But I notice that something within me seems to have broken through, which makes it possible to get through all those compartments after all. I find meditation very soothing when times are hard, in order to find a sort of resting point. So that I can rediscover what is obstructing me, what drives me mad. Someone round here has had an old chapel for nineteen years now, and you can do a sitting and walking meditation there a couple of days a week, that's really good.

In the past I used to feel isolated, because other people didn't understand or sympathise with these things. That's all over now. Completely disappeared. In the long term, what I experience in that little house, that could also be open to other people, but not more than one or two at a time. And at what point ...? And there's going to be a hut in the air, and if I live to see the day, another one under the ground. I live my art, and I want to share it. There is a past, that blows like a warm breeze through the present. That makes me move more freely. This morning I based my work on: let's lend our ears, in order to hear! Because I notice, if you really dare to share, to lend your ears or your eyes, you're no longer imprisoned in your own judgement. Making an image in order to see it and let it go. Judging things cuts you off. And then there's no room for anyone else. And I really finished with that way of judging, during that last period.

Afterword

In this book, my aim above all has been a head-on approach to a subject that is generally confined to the margin, be it to the left or the right. At close range the matter appeared as a collection of loose ends. From even closer, dots came into view; the challenge then became to try to connect these, and I hope the reader would find that this has worked out, here and there. But the observations and overtures in this book are far from the last word on the subject. In fact, I hope that this introduction will lead to reflection, to discussion, and to further exploration, in both theory and practice. And may there be no holds barred for the time being, as we are unlikely to find real answers if we stick to the existing frames of reference, and we may need to turn ourselves inside out to really assimilate the implications of the facts, ideas and intuitions surrounding spiritual crises.

In order to open the door to further exploration, we must have something to sample to begin with. Do such things as spiritual crises exist in the first place? And if so, do they have a particular flavour? In my opinion, the eighteen episodes published here carry enough weight to answer the first question with a 'yes'. These first-hand accounts form part of a larger collection, which was comparatively easy to assemble. Though these episodes differ considerably as regards content, 'colour' and 'flavour', they share a number of themes and related patterns. Other than in the earlier, strictly academic phase of this whole project, however, I have omitted a qualitative analysis at this subsequent stage. Whereas the subject matter of spiritual crises is already familiar to the transpersonally trained readers of my academic study, for a broader reading public it seemed more appropriate to introduce the phenomenon as such.

Although conceptually speaking this territory is still largely uncultivated, it is anything but untrodden. Many have entered it at various points, have wandered around in it for shorter or longer periods, and departed at completely different points; many have left memoirs and directions about it. Others have inspected the territory from outside, at long or short range, and expressed their speculations about it. In the process the traditional frameworks of science and religion have taken up opposing positions, as thesis and antithesis. Where classical science has tried to vindicate itself by throwing out the soul and all its extraordinary phenomena, theistic religion has attempted to entrench itself by locking up these phenomena, and appropriating their prospective morality. If each side would only open its doors, we would at least have a fresh breeze. Now within psychology there have been earlier speculations that mental crises also have a creative component, which is not so much about coping or functioning more successfully, as about human potential itself. Images of such a profoundly transformative process also emerge from the eighteen episodes described in this book; images of a flowering, an unfolding, rather than the recovery or repair of a crippled state of affairs.

Transpersonal psychology is based on a possible, ontological, dynamic *raison d'être*, which is reflected in individual human lives—and in everything else, as it happens. In this respect the professional field is akin to certain philosophical movements, and in the light of new developments in the neuro-sciences and interdisciplinary consciousness research, the theme of such a *raison d'être* is becoming increasingly relevant. The levels at which reality appears to us, at which we perceive and construe it, continually present themselves in a new light. The relationship between consciousness, mind and body is a crucial issue in this respect, and at the present stage of this ancient quest the perspective on who we are appears to be shifting once more. Just as it does in spiritual crises. Now the doors that have been set ajar in this book do not give us access to answers alone. If we recognise spiritual crises as a phenomenon, for example, is the concept of divine madness that Plato named 'mania' at all useful to us? And what is the 'madness' that is not a disease, as posited by Michel Foucault? Can quantum physics and the neuro-sciences really explain deviations from the prevailing paradigm of the psyche? What self-healing powers do body and mind possess, and how can we best gain access to them? What are the facts and fictions behind the modest hype of high sensitivity? Which forms of spirituality entail risk, for whom, when and why? How can a human being remain sane when the world is going mad?

Spiritual crises seem to demand the utmost of us. Clear judgement and a good rapport between all our cognitive powers are a *conditio sine qua non* if we are to better understand and help those who end up in such crises, and to learn something about the human riddle in the process. For you cannot expect the taste of an apple in a pear. And you can eat all kinds of things with a knife and fork, but with a bowl of soup in front of you, you're really better off with a spoon.

Notes

Introduction

1 American Psychiatric Association (2001), p. 379.
2 Freud (1930).
3 GAP (1976).
4 Mandel (1980).
5 Quotation from interview with Dr Mrytle Heery, in http://www.psychotherapy.net/interview/Albert_Ellis (retrieved September 2009).
6 Lukoff, Lu & Turner (1992).
7 Decuypere (1986).
8 Schreurs (2001).
9 GAP (1976).
10 Blok (2004).
11 Blok (2004).
12 Schreurs (2001).
13 Blom (2003).
14 Kuhn (1962).

1 Emanuel Swedenborg and the Question of Diagnostics

1 Translated from Van Calcar (1882), p. 40.
2 Translated from Van Calcar (1882), p. 41.
3 Swedenborg (1988), *Arcana Cœlestia/ Heavenly Secrets*, 4528, §2
4 Swedenborg (1988), *Arcana Cœlestia/ Heavenly Secrets*, 4628, §2
5 Clemm (1767).
6 Ernesti, vol. 8, p. 874.
7 From correspondence with Cuno, see http://www.swedenborgdigitallibrary.org/ES/epic42.htm
8 Kant (1766).
9 Maudsley (1869).
10 Howden (1873).
11 Hitschmann (1949).
12 Jaspers (1922).
13 Dewhurst & Beard (1970).
14 Leonhard (1992).
15 Johnson (1994).

16 Foote-Smith & Smith (1996).
17 Bradford (1979), p. 379.
18 Rosenhan (1973).
19 *Drömboken*, published in Stockholm (1859); most recent English edition *Swedenborgs Dream Diary*, by Swedenborg Foundation Publishers (2001).
20 Translated from Van Calcar (1882), p. 48.
21 Translated from Van Calcar (1882), p. 55.

Diana

1 Wicca, natural religion, partly based on tradition from 'pagan' traditions such as witchcraft, partly designed by the British author and esoteric Gerald Gardner (1884–1964). Wiccan motto: perfect love, perfect trust.
2 This must be the book published by Gopi Krishna in 1970, *Kundalini: The Evolutionary Energy in Man*. See bibliography.
3 See particularly *The Seth Material* by Jane Roberts, in bibliography.
4 Atlantic, as the language of the mythical lost island of Atlantis.
5 *shakti*, another term for kundalini energy, which is identified with the goddess Shakti, the consort of Shiva, see also Chapter 4, 'The self in creative chaos'.
6 Deepak Chopra, Indian doctor and author, lives in the USA.
7 Stichting Correlatie. An appeal within the framework of research into 'voice-hearers', carried out from 1987 under direction of Prof. Romme. It is not known why the contact in this case was not taken further; the personal information was probably not recorded properly (Romme, verbal communication).

Hans

1 *satsang*, spiritual meeting led by a teacher.
2 Cisordinol, brand name of classic anti-psychotic drug with zuclopenthixol as active ingredient.
3 *saddhu*, Hindu ascetic.
4 Hans Laurentius, Dutch advaita teacher.
5 Shantimayi (1950), American by birth, teacher of eclectic school for self-realisation.

Josine

1 Rosicrucians, The Rosicrucian Order A.M.O.R.C, esoteric society.
2 Sri Aurobindo (1872–1950), Indian philosopher, poet, writer and teacher.
3 *I Am That, Talks with Sri Nisargadatta*, transcribed and edited by Maurice Frydman, originally published by Chetana Publishing, Bombay, 1973.
4 Adi Da (1939–2008), writer and teacher of self realisation, also known as Bubba Free John, Da Free John, and Da Love-Ananda; born as Franklin Albert Jones in the USA.

2 The Scientific View: Ego as the Measure of all Things

1 Ockham's Razor, logical principle, called after the English Franciscan friar William of Ockham (*c*. 1285–1349), who held: *entia non sunt multiplicanda praeter necessitatem*, roughly translated as: the simplest explanation is the best. In the development of scientific theory this principle has always been respected, namely as an invocation to cut off any factor that does not play an obvious, quantifiable part. Because it is connected to the opportunity to use

measurements as the basis for empirical statements, there is also by definition a relationship to the technological state of affairs.

2 van der Molen et al. (1997), p. 255 (translation JN).

3 van der Molen et al (1997), p. 169 (translation JN).

4 Apart from serving as textbook material, the controversial 'Little Albert experiment' has also taken on a life of its own as an urban myth. For a critical review of the whole affair, see Harris (1979), or http://htpprints.yorku.ca/archive/00000198/01/BHARRIS.HTM (retrieved September 2009)

5 Chadwick et al. (1996).

6 Likert (1932). Likert Scale: psychometric instrument introduced by the American organisational psychologist Rensis Likert (1903–1981) for the measurement of attitudes. The most used version comprises five possible responses to a proposition, ranging from 'agree completely' to 'disagree completely'. Research data which has been collected in this way, is then subjected to statistical processing by other, quantitative methods.

7 Freud (1913).

8 Lamothe (2004).

9 James (2003).

10 van der Molen et al. (1997), pp. 254–5.

11 Winnicott (1955-6).

12 Sofair (1972).

13 Dabrowski (1972).

14 Romme & Escher (1999).

15 Wallin (2007).

16 Clay (1996), pp. 170–1.

17 Bock (2000).

18 Bock (2000), p. 18.

19 Redfield Jamison (1994).

20 Duke (1992).

21 Kaplan (1964).

22 Hay (1990).

23 McCready & Greeley (1976).

24 Fiselier, Van der Waal & Spijker (2006).

25 Kurtz, Karry & Sandhu (2003).

26 Flew (2003), p. 240.

27 van Lommel (2001).

28 Flew (2003), p. 241.

29 Account found at http://www.issc-taste.org/arc/dbo.cgi?set=expom&id=00075&ss=1 (retrieved September 2009), in TASTE, The Archive of Scientists' Transcendent Experiences.

30 Flew (2003), p. 241.

31 Bleuler, E. (1894), p. 166.

32 Csikszentmihalyi (2003), p. 43.

33 Csikszentmihalyi (2003), p. 45.

34 Chalmers (1995).

35 Quoted in van Belzen (1989), pp. 47–8.
36 Quoted in van Belzen (1989), p. 48.
37 Quoted in van Belzen (1989), p. 50.
38 Bentall (2003).
39 Hurlburt (1990).
40 Hurlburt & Heavey (2006).

Frans

1 Wolter Keers (1923–1985) introduced the nondualistic teaching of advaita vedanta to the Netherlands. Among others, Keers translated the classic *I Am That, Talks with Sri Nisargadatta*, see Josine, note 3.
2 Ma Anand Sheela was for many years the right-hand aide of Bhagwan Sri Ragneesh. She ran the commune in Oregan (USA), giving rise to various scandals in the process. The commune fell apart, Bhagwan fled and was deported. Sheela served a twenty-nine-month prison sentence.
3 Avatar, particular form of personal and spiritual training.
4 Alexander Smit (1948–1998), teacher of advaita vedanta.
5 Jan van Delden (b. 1950), teacher of advaita vedanta, former student of Wolter Keers.

Sandra

1 Haldol, brand name of classic antipsychotic drug with haloperidol as active ingredient.
2 MPD, multiple personality disorder.
3 Akineton, brand name of biperiden hydrochloride, inhibits nervous system, thus controlling motory disorders caused by other medication.
4 SPV (Sociaal psychiatrisch verpleegkundige): social psychiatric nurse.
5 Hashimoto's thyroiditis: chronic auto-immune thyroid inflammation, partly genetically determined.
6 Hypo state: hypomanic episode of bipolar-II disorder (see 10).
7 Neurofeedback: training method to influence the operation of the central nervous system via operant conditioning of the electroencephalogram.
8 Delta waves, slowest brainwaves, frequency between 0.5 and 4 Hz, associated with the deep, recuperative stage of sleep.
9 HSP, Highly Sensitive Person.
10 Bipolar-II, type of manic depressive disorder with alternating depressive and hypomanic episodes.

Karin

1 ITIP, Instituut voor Integrale Toegepaste Psychologie (Institute for Integral Applied Psychology).
2 Susan Frank, teacher of advaita vedanta.
3 Bioresonance, alternative healing method, focuses via electro-acupuncture on disturbances in organ-specific resonance patterns.
4 Jalal ad-Din Rumi, Persian mystic, theologist and poet (1207–1273), whose followers founded the Mevlevi order of 'Whirling Dervishes'.

3 Window on the God-experience: Beyond the Precincts of the Church
1 Platvoet en Molendijk (1999).

2 Rocquet (2000).

3 Blok (1956), pp. 48-9.

4 James (2003) pp. 303-4, excerpt from *The Dark Night of the Soul*, book 11, Saint John of the Cross.

5 van der Leeuw (1933).

6 van der Leeuw (1924).

7 Faesen (1998), p. 223

8 Noll (1985).

9 Schilling (1998), Scivias III, 1.

10 Hadewych (2003).

11 Harris (1995).

12 American Heritage Dictionary (2000).

13 Desiderius Erasmus, *In Praise of Folly*, originally *Stultitiae laus*, first published in 1511.

14 Porter (1991).

15 Feuerstein (1990), p. 6.

16 From: *Hymns for the Drowning* by A. K. Ramanujan, quoted in McDaniel (1989), p. 31.

17 Nigg (1956).

18 Freeman (1998).

19 *mullah*, Islamic spiritual leader.

20 Shah (1969).

21 Al-Hamadhani (1982).

22 Jalaludin Rumi, quoted by Helminski (1998). Rumi was a Persian mystic, theologian and poet (1207-1273), whose disciples founded the Mevlevi order of 'Whirling Dervishes'.

23 Leeming (1979).

24 Feuerstein (1990).

25 Caplan (1999), p. 146.

26 See http://www.leelozowick.com/

27 Hijweege (2004).

28 Ganzevoort (1994), p. 217.

29 Teresa of Avila, quoted in James (2003), p. 305.

30 Degenhardt (1967), p. 116.

31 Casey (1934).

32 Translation by Stephen Patterson and Marvin Meyer, from *The Gospel of Thomas Collection*, Gnostic Society Library.

33 idem.

34 Anabaptists, persecuted movement from the reformation period which advocated adult baptism among other things, and thus can be regarded as the forerunners of the Baptist, evangelical and Pentecostal churches.

35 Ganzevoort (1994), p. 229.

36 Boisen (1959).

37 Schreurs (2001).

38 According to data from the Leiden faculty office. From: *Godsdienstig gedrag, Een onderzoek naar de mogelijkheden voor de bestudering van godsdienstig gedrag in de Nederlandse godsdienstwetenschap, voornamelijk aan de hand van het werk van*

Th.P.van Baaren. J. P.Janssen, published on:
http://home.planet.nl/~janss281/godsdienstwetenschap_en_gedrag.html
(retrieved September 2009).

39   Otto (2002), p. 70.

40   Hafiz, translated by Daniel Ladinsky (1996), p. 5.

41   Underhill (1911).

42   Chirban (2001).

43   Jean de Labadie ((1620–1674), of French birth, Catholic monk who became a Protestant preacher, dismissed because of his excessive zeal, founded the Labadist sect in Amsterdam, which was driven from Holland and ended up in Germany.

44   van der Leeuw (1924), p. 18.

45   James (2003), p. 30.

46   idem, p. 13.

47   Wundt (1874).

48   James (1890).

49   See Kim, A. (2006), http://plato.stanford.edu/entries/wilhelm-wundt/ (retrieved September 2009).

50   James (1926), pp. 393–4.

51   James (1902).

52   Bucke (1901).

53   James (2003), p. 122.

54   idem, p. 122.

55   James (1890), p. 185.

56   Zuylen, B. J. van der (1976), p. 410.

57   McCready, W. C. and Greeley, A. M. (1976).

58   Hay, D., (1990).

59   Greeley, A. & McCready, W. (1975).

60   Thomas, L. E., and Cooper, R. E. (1978).

61   van Belzen (2004).

62   Raymond F. Paloutzian, Craig W. Ellison, *Spiritual Well-Being Scale*, 1982.

63   Mommaers & van Bragt (1995), p. 109.

64   idem, p. 110.

65   *samsara*, the eternal cycle of rebirth on earth, in the reality of the multiplicity of manifestations.

66   Victoria (1997).

Theo

1   Willem Frederik Hermans: influential, controversial and award-winning Dutch author, translator of *Tractatus Logico Philosophicus* by Ludwig Wittgenstein

2   *Tao te Ching*, classical Chinese Taoist text from the 6th century BC.

3   *chakra*, Sanskrit for 'wheel', each of the seven centres between the base of the spine and crown of the head, which are a major part of the body's energy system.

4   *I Ching, Book of Changes*, oldest classical Chinese text, handbook for the use of sixty-four hexagrams as oracle.

5 *A Course in Miracles*, recorded in writing between 1965 and 1972 on the basis of an inner voice, ascribed to Jesus Christ, which was experienced by the American psychologist Helen Schucman (1909–1981).

6 *dojo*, (Japanese), training school.

7 CAD (consultatiebureau alcohol en drugs): advice bureau for alcohol and drug addiction.

Leonor

1 King Solomon, see Old Testament, 1 Kings 3: 4–15.

2 Kuan Yin, Chinese form of the buddha of compassion (Avalokiteshvara), portrayed as a woman and worshipped as a goddess.

3 *bodhisattva*, someone who follows the path of enlightenment in order to lead all other living creatures to nirvana; particularly prevalent in Mahayana Buddhism.

4 *sesshin*, period of intense meditation, Zen retreat (Japanese).

5 Chi Kung, or Qigong, aspect of traditional Chinese hygienics, via co-ordination of breathing, physical posture and exercise.

6 Vocation Sunday, Catholic day of prayer on the fourth Sunday after Easter, introduced in 1964 by Pope Paul VI, for vocations to ecclesiastical functions and the religious life.

Jeroen

1 Goes, historic town in the province of Zeeland.

2 Thomas à Kempis, *The Imitation of Christ*.

3 Mgr. Louis de Raeymaeker (1895–1970), author of *Inleiding tot de wijsbegeerte en tot het thomisme* (introduction to the philosophy and to Thomism).

4 Karlfried von Durckheim (1896–1988), German diplomat who expressed his inspiration by both Meister Eckhart and Zen in forms of therapy.

5 Hugo LaSalle (1898–1988), German Jesuit who discovered Zen while a missionary in Japan, became a Zen master and in 1968 began to propagate in in western Europe.

6 Gerta Ital, German writer on Zen meditation.

4 The Transpersonal Perspective: The Psychology of Being

1 Bucky (1992).

2 Steuchius (1540).

3 Huxley (1945).

4 Coxhead (1985), pp. 7–8.

5 Bucke (1901).

6 From: 27th edition of Bucke's *Cosmic Consciousness* (1973), introduction by George Moreby Acklom: *The Man and his Book*.

7 Laski (1961).

8 Maslow (1964).

9 Stace (1960).

10 Staal (1975).

11 Grof (1980).

12 C. G. Jung , *The Structure of the Unconscious*, quoted in Rowan (2005).

13 Assagioli (1977).

14 Almaas (1995).

15 Proprioception: subjective physical perception.
16 Visser (2001).
17 Grof & Grof (1989).
18 Grof & Grof (1990).
19 David Lukoff, see http://www.spiritualcompetency.com
    For the online course *DSM-IV Religious & Spiritual Problems*, see
    http://www.spiritualcompetency.com/dsm4/dsmrsproblem.pdf (retrieved
    September 2009).
20 Silverman (1970).
21 Dabrowski (1964).
22 Grof & Grof (eds.) (1989).
23 Boisen (1962).
24 Ellenberger (1970).
25 Laing (1972).
26 Perry (1974).
27 Hutton (1994).
28 Boorstein (1996).
29 Rowan (2005).
30 Gardner (2002)
31 James (2003), p. 282.
32 Katz (1978), pp. 26–7, author's italics.
33 Woods (1980), p. 5.
34 von Eckartsberg & Valle (1980), p. 101.
35 Waldron (1998), p. 104.
36 idem, p. 106.
37 Laski (1961), pp. 91–2.
38 Puhakka (2000), p. 13.
39 Ferrer (2000), pp. 223–4.
40 idem, p. 227.
41 *atman*, the true self, individual potential of Brahman, cf. soul.
42 *jiva*, the embodied, manifest self, cf. ego.
43 Castillo (1998), p. 226.
44 idem, p. 227.
45 idem, p. 228
46 Thapa & Murthy (1985), p. 84.
47 Jansen & Van Vugt (eds.), (2006).
48 'Cognitie en Gedrag (Cognition and Behaviour)', NWO (Dutch Organisation
    for Scientific Research) theme till end of 2008. Next theme, 'Hersenen en
    Cognitie (Brain and Cognition)', 2007–2013.
49 Paraphrase of quotation from Indian doctor and writer Deepak Chopra, see
    for example:
    http://www.skeptic.com/reading_room/debates/afterlife.html (retrieved
    September 2009).
50 Steven (2000), p. 109.
51 Moustakas (1994).
52 Stevens (2000).
53 Valle (1998).

54   Mindfulness meditation, form of meditation in which attention is not concentrated anywhere in particular, but all physical, emotional and mental activity is observed without judgement or evaluation.

55   Davidson et al. (2004).

56   Murphy & White (1995).

57   Wade (2004).

58   Demares & Krycka (1998).

59   van Lommel et al. (2001), p. 2041.

60   Ring & Cooper (1999).

61   van Lommel et al. (2001).

62   Campbell (1974), p. 306.

63   Avalon (1953).

64   Sannella (1976).

65   Bergin (1991), p. 401.

66   Vanderkooi (1997).

67   Greyson (1993).

68   Ossoff (1993).

69   *ayurveda*, traditional Indian teaching on health.

70   Hansen (1995).

71   Bentov (1977).

72   *siddhi*, extrasensory power.

73   Brett (2002).

74   Chadwick (2001).

75   'Positive' and 'negative' are used here as qualification of an affect, not as differention of pathological symptoms.

76   Kusters (2004), p. 52.

77   Kusters (2004), p. 119.

78   Kusters (2004) p. 128.

79   Chadwick, Birchwood & Trower (1996).

80   Claridge (1997).

81   Andrew et al. (2008).

82   Romme et al. (2009).

83   Woodruff (2004).

84   De Bruijn, in Romme & Escher (1999), pp. 31–40.

85   Siddle et al. (2002).

86   Kusters (2004), pp. 113–14.

87   Ram Dass, Second Conference on Buddhism and Psychotherapy, New York, 13 October 1988. Quoted in Agosin (1992).

88   *maya*—derived from Sanskrit 'ma' ('not') and 'ya' ('that'), referring to our mistaken tendency to take physical reality at face value.

89   Wapnick (1969), p. 64.

90   VanderKooi (1997), p. 34.

91   Kalweit (1992), p. 214.

92   Podvoll (1992).

93   Lukoff (1985).

94   Bragdon (1990).

95   Lukoff (2001).

96 Baars (1993).
97 Quoted in Heisenberg (1971), p. 206.
98 Janssen & Van Vugt (2006), p. 15.
99 Pribram (1971).
100 Velmans (2000).
101 Metzinger (2003).

Egmont

1 Sri Chinmoy (b. 1931), Indian philosopher and teacher of the Sri Aurobindo tradition, based in New York since 1964.
2 Michael Maier (1566–1622), German doctor and alchemist.
3 ITIP, Instituut voor Integrale Toegepaste Psychologie (Institute for Integral Applied Psychology), see Karin, note 1.
4 Vogelenzang psychiatric hospital in Bennebroek, now part of the GGZ inGeest mental health institution.
5 Haldol, brand name of classic antipsychotic drug with haloperidol as active ingredient.
6 Ink blot test: projective personality test devised by the Swiss psychiatrist Hermann Rorschach (1884–1922).
7 Semap, brand name of classic antipsychotic drug, whose active ingredient is penfluridol.
8 Orap, brand name of classic antipsychotic drug, whose active ingredient is pimozide.
9 *The Great Chicago Fire*, 8–10 October 1871. The story of the cow is probably no more than an urban legend; speculations based on extensive research suggest a key role was played by opposite neighbour Daniel Sullivan, nicknamed 'Peg Leg' because of his wooden leg. See http://www.thechicagofire.com/

Mariet

1 Parlementaire Onderzoekscommissie Sekten (The Parliamentary Research Commission into Cults). The survey led to controversies and court cases, and subsequently to legislation to combat harmful sectarian organisations.

Tanja

1 Alexander Smit (1948–1998), teacher of advaita vedanta.
2 Nisargadatta Maharaj (1897–1981), Indian teacher of advaita vedanta.
3 Uppaluri Gopala Krishnamurti (1918–2007), aka 'U.G.', enigmatic Indian mystic – not to be confused with Jiddu Krishnamurti (1895–1986), for many years the predestined world teacher of the Theosophical Society.
4 *satsang*, spiritual meeting led by a teacher.
5 Gangaji (b. 1942), woman teacher of advaita vedanta, born as Toni Roberson in the USA.
6 Tony Parsons (b. 1933), British speaker on non-duality.
7 Hans Laurentius (b. 1964), teacher of advaita vedanta.

Peter

1 Avatar, particular form of personal and spiritual training.

Sanne

1 Iscador, anthroposophical remedy based on mistletoe.

Ronald

1 Orap, brand name of classic antipsychotic medicine with pimozide as active ingredient.
2 Jan Foudraine, psychiatrist and writer, main voice for the Dutch antipsychiatry movement, see Introduction.
3 Jan Koehoorn, teacher of advaita vedanta.
4 James Redfield, *The Celestine Prophecy*, best-stelling New Age novel from 1993.

Dee

1 BCL: mixture of bromium, potassium and luminal, that puts people to sleep for twelve hours or more.
2 Bromide or potassium bromide, 'tranquillizer'.
3 Luminal: brand name for phenobarbitone, barbiturate used as tranquillizer.
4 Centrum '45: national treatment and expertise centre for victims of persecution, war and violence.
5 Agapè: the unconditional love described in the Old Testament, propagated by Christ as the love of God.

Ferri

1 *Love Without Conditions: Reflections of the Christ Mind*, Paul Ferrini.
2 Pathwork, particular form of personal and spiritual training.
3 Transformation Game, board game that serves as metaphor and structure for profound reflection. Developed by the spiritual community in Findhorn, Scotland: there is also a version for (business) organisations.
4 Deepak Chopra (b. 1948), Indian doctor based in the USA, mainly famous as writer on subjects including spirituality, quantum physics, much read in the business world.

Joyce

1 Tiltenberg, major seminary and training centre for religious education in the diocese of Haarlem.

Bibliography

Agosin, T. (1992). 'Psychosis, Dreams and Mysticism in the Clinical Domain' in F. Halligan & J. Shea (eds), *The Fires of Desire* (New York: Crossroad).

Al-Hamadhani (1982). *Vernunft is nichts als Narretei* (Tübingen: Erdmann).

Almaas, A. H. (1995). *Essence with the Elixir of Enlightenment: The Diamond Approach to Inner Realization* (Newburyport, MA: Weiser Books).

American Heritage Dictionary (4th ed.) (2000). (Boston: Houghton Mifflin Company).

American Psychiatric Association (1994). *Diagnostic and Statistical Manual of Mental Disorders* (4th ed.) (Washington, D.C.: Author).

Andrew, E. M., Gray, N. S. & Snowden, R. J. S. (2008). 'The Relationship Between Trauma and Beliefs About Hearing Voices: A Study of Psychiatric and Non-psychiatric Voice Hearers', *Psychological Medicine* 38, 1409–17.

Assagioli, R. (1977). *Psychosynthesis, A Manual of Principles and Techniques* (New York: Penguin Books).

Avalon, A. (1953). *The Serpent Power: Being the Shat-chakra-nirûpana and Pâdukâ-panchakâ: Two works on Laya Yoga*, Trans from the Sanskrit by Arthur Avalon (John Woodroffe) (Madras: Ganesh).

Baars, B. J. (1993). 'How does a stream of consciousness that is relatively simple, serial, and limited in capacity emerge from a brain that is largely unconscious, complex, and massively parallel?' in E. Marsh (ed.), *Ciba Symposium on Experimental and Theoretical Foundations of Consciousness*, 174 (London: Wiley Interscience).

van Belzen, J. A. (1989). 'Psychiater tussen praktijk en wetenschap. De fenomenologische psychologie in de psychiatrie volgens H. C. Rümke', *Psychiatrie en maatschappij* 13, 45–59.

van Belzen, J. A. (2004). 'Spirituality, Culture and Mental Health: Prospects and Risks for Contemporary Psychology of Religion', *Journal of Religion and Health* 43: 4, 291–316.

Bentall, R. (2003). *Madness Explained: Psychosis and Human Nature* (London: Allen Lane).

Bentov, I. (1977). *Stalking the Wild Pendulum: On the Mechanics of Consciousness* (New York: E. P. Dutton).

Bleuler, E. (1894). 'Versuch einer naturwissenschaftlichen Betrachtung der psychologischen Grundbegriff', *Allgemeine Zeitschrif für Psychiatrie und Psychisch-gerichtliche Medicin* 50, 166

Blok, G. (2004). *Baas in eigen brein: 'antipsychiatrie' in Nederland, 1965–1985.* (Amsterdam: Nieuwezijds).

Blok, J. A. (trans..) (1956). *Oepanisjads* (Deventer: Kluwer).

Blom, J. D. (2004). *Deconstructing Schizophrenia: An Analysis of the Epistemic and Nonepistemic Values that Govern the Biomedical Schizophrenia Concept* (Amsterdam: Boom)

Bock, Th. (2000). *Psychosen zonder psychiatrie: inzichten en levensperspectieven van mensen met een gedeeltel?k of geheel onbehandelde psychose* (Amsterdam: Candide).

Boisen, A.T. (1959). 'Religious Experience and Psychological Conflict', *Journal of Pastoral Care* 13, 160–3.

Boorstein, S. (2000). 'Transpersonal Psychotherapy', *American Journal of Psychotherapy* 54: 3, 408–23.

Bradford, D. T. (1999). 'Neuropsychology of Swedenborg's Visions', *Perceptual and Motor Skills* 88, 377–83.

Bragdon, E. (1990). *The Call of Spiritual Emergency: From Personal Crisis to Personal Transformation* (San Francisco: Harper & Row).

Bucke, R. M. (1901). *Cosmic Consciousness* (Philadelphia, Innes & Sons).

Bucky, P. A. & Weakland, A. G. (1992). *The P Albert Einstein* (Kansas City: Andrews & McMeel).

van Calcar, E. (1882). *Emanuel Swedenborg, de ziener* (Den Haag: H. C. Van Calcar).

Campbell, J. (1974). *The Mythic Image* (Princeton, NJ: Princeton University Press).

Caplan, M. (1999). *Halfway up the Mountain: The Error of Premature Claims to Enlightenment* (Prescott, Arizona: Hohm Press).

Casey, R. P. (1934). *The Excerpta ex Theodoto of Clement of Alexandria. Studies and Documents 1*, pp. 40–91 (London: Christophers).

Castillo, R. J. (1998). 'Culture and Dissociation' in R. J. Castillo (ed.), *Meanings of Madness* (Pacific Grove, CA: Brooks/Cole Publishing Company), pp. 226–33.

Chirban, J. T. (2001). *Sickness or Sin? Spiritual Discernment and Differential Diagnosis* (Brookline, MA: Holy Cross Orthodox Press).

Clay, J. (1996). *R. D. Laing: A Divided Self. A Biography* (London: Hodder & Stoughton).

Clemm, H. W. (1767). *Vollständige Einleitung in die Religion und gesammte Theologie* (Tübingen: Johann Georg Cotta).

Chadwick, P., Birchwood, M. & Trower, P. (1996). *Cognitive Therapy for Delusions, Voices and Paranoia* (Chichester, UK: John Wiley & Sons).

Chalmers, D.J. (1995). 'The Puzzle of Conscious Experience', *Scientific American* 273: 6, 80–7.

Committee on Psychiatry and Religion (1976). *Mysticism: Spiritual Quest or Psychic Disorder* (New York: Group for the Advancement of Psychiatry).

Coxhead, N. (1985). *The Relevance of Bliss. A Contemporary Exploration of Mysticism* (London: Wildwood House).

Csikszentmihalyi, M. (2003). *Flow: de psychologie van de optimale ervarin* (Amsterdam: Boom).

Dabrowski, K. (1972). *Psychoneurosis is not an Illness* (London: Gryf Publications).

Davidson, R. J., Lutz, A., Greischar, L. L., Rawlings, N. B. & Ricard, M. (2004). 'Long-term Meditators Self-induce High-amplitude Gamma Synchrony during Mental Practice' in *Proceedings of the National Academy of Sciences of the United States of America* 46, 16369–73.

Decuypere, J. (1986). 'Ziek of Mystiek?', *Tijdschrift voor psychiatrie* 28: 10, 719. (Meppel: Boom).

Degenhardt, I. (1967). 'Studien zum Wandel des Eckhartbildes', *Studien zur Problemgeschichte der antiken und mittelalterlichen Philosophie* III (Leiden: Brill).

Demares, R. & Krycka, K. (1998). 'Wild-animal-triggered Peak Experiences: Transpersonal Aspects', *Journal of Transpersonal Psychology* 30: 2, 161–77.

Dewhurst, K. & Beard, A. W., (1970). 'Sudden Religious Conversion in Temporal Lobe Epilepsy', *British Journal of Psychiatry* 117, 497–507.

Dodds, E. R. (1951). *The Greeks and the Irrational* (Berkeley: University of California Press).

Duke, P. (1992). *A Brilliant Madness: Living with Manic-depressive Illness* (New York: Bantam).

von Eckartsberg, R., & Valle, R. S. (1980). 'Heideggerian Thinking and the Eastern Mind', *Re-Vision* 3, 100–10.

von Eckartsberg, R. (1998). 'Existential-phenomenological Research' in R. Valle (ed.), *Phenomenological Inquiry in Psychology: Existential and Transpersonal Dimensions* (New York: Plenum Press), pp. 21–61.

Ernesti, J. (ed.) (1767). *Neue Theologische Bibliothek*, Band 8, p. 874. Leipzig Zie http://www.wlb-stuttgart.de/referate/theologie/swpm2899.html.

Faesen, R. (1998). 'What is a Mystical Experience? History and Interpretation', *Louvain studies* 23: 3, 221–45.

Ferrer, J. N. (2000). 'Transpersonal Knowledge: A Participatory Approach to Transpersonal Phenomena' in Puhakka (ed.), *Transpersonal Knowing* (New York: State University of New York Press), pp. 213–52.

Feuerstein, G. (1990). *Holy Madness: The Shock Tactics and Radical Teachings of Crazywise Adepts, Holy Fools, and Rascal Gurus* (New York: Paragon House).

Fiselier, J. A., van der Waal, A. E. & Spiker, J. (2006). 'Psychiatrist, Patient and Religion: More than Simply Coping', *Tijdschrift voor Psychiatrie* 48: 5, 383–6

Flew, A. (2003). 'Near-death Experiences' in Kurtz, P., Karry, B. & Sandhu, R. (ed.), *Science and Religion: Are they Compatible?* (Amherst, NY: Prometheus Books).

Foote-Smith, E. & Smith, T. (1996). 'Emanuel Swedenborg', *Epilepsia* 37: 2, 211–18.

Freeman, M. (1998). 'The Wide-spun Moment', *Parabola* 23, 9–35.

Freud, S. (1913). *Totem und Tabu: einige Übereinstimmungen im Seelenleben der Wilden und der Neurotiker* (Leipzig: Heller).

Freud, S. (1930). *Civilization and its Discontents* (London: Hogarth Press and the Institute of Psycho-Analysis).

Ganzevoort, R. R. (1994). *Een cruciaal moment; Functie en verandering van geloof in een crisis* (Zoetermeer: Boekencentrum).

Gardner, H. (2002). *Soorten intelligentie, Meervoudige intelligenties voor de 21ste eeuw* (Amsterdam: Nieuwezijds).

Greyson, B. (1993). 'The Physio-kundalini Syndrome and Mental Illness', *Journal of Transpersonal Psychology* 25: 1, 43–58.

Grof, S. (1980). *LSD Psychotherapy* (Pomona, CA: Hunter House).

Grof, S., & Grof, C. (ed.) (1989). *Spiritual Emergency – When Personal Transformation becomes a Crisis* (New York: Jeremy Tarcher/Putnam).

Grof, S., & Grof, C. (1990). *The Stormy Search For The Self: A Guide To Personal Growth Through Transformative Crisis* (New York: Jeremy Tarcher/Putnam).

Hadewijch, (2003). *Visioenen* (red. J. van Mierlo) (Antwerpen: De Vlaamsche Boekenhalle).

Hafiz (1996). *The Subject Tonight Is Love: Sixty Wild & Sweet Poems of Hafiz* (trans. Daniel Ladinsky) (New York: Pumpkin House).

Hansen, G. (1995). 'Schizophrenia or Spiritual Crisis? On "raising the kundalini" and its Diagnostic Classification', *Ugeskrift for laeger* 31:157, 4360-2 (Kopenhagen: Den Almindelige Danske Laegerforening).

Harris, N. (1979). 'Whatever Happened to Little Albert?', *American Psychologist* 34: 2, 151-60.

Harris, P (ed.) (1995). *Fire of Silence and Stillness: Anthology of Quotations for the Spiritual Journey* (Londen: Darton, Longman & Todd).

Hay, D. (1990). *Religious Experience Today: Studying the Facts* (London: Mowbray).

Heisenberg, W. (1971). *Physics and Beyond* (New York: Harper and Row).

Helminski, K. (1998). 'I Will Make Myself Mad', *Parabola* 23, 9-14.

Hitschmann, E. (1949). 'Swedenborg's Paranoia', *The American Imago: A Psychoanalytic Journal for Culture Science*, 45.

Hijweege, N. M. (2004). *Bekering in bevindelijk gereformeerde kring: een psychologische studie* (Kampen: Kok).

Howden, J. C. (1873). 'The Religious Sentiment in Epileptics', *Journal of Mental Science* 18, 482-97.

Hurlburt, R. (1990). *Sampling Normal and Schizophrenic Inner Experience* (New York: Plenum Press).

Hurlburt, R. T. & Heavey, C. L. (2006). *Exploring Inner Experience* (Amsterdam: John Benjamins).

Hutton, M. S. (1994). 'How Transpersonal Psychotherapists Differ From Other Practitioners: An Empirical Study', *Journal of Transpersonal Psychology* 26: 2, 139-74.

Huxley, A. (1945). *Perennial Philosophy* (New York: Harper & Brothers).

Jackson, M. & Fulford, K. W. M. (1997). 'Spiritual Experience and Psychopathology', *Philosophy, Psychiatry and Psychology* 4: 1, 41-65.

James, W. (1890). *The Principles of Psychology* (New York: Holt).

James, W. & James, H (ed.) (1926). *The Letters of William James* (Boston: Little & Brown).

James, W. (1902). *Varieties of Religious Experience, a study in human nature: being the Gifford lectures on natural religion delivered at Edinburgh in 1901-1902* (London: Longmans, Green & Co).

James, W. (2003) *Vormen van de religieuze ervaring: een onderzoek naar het wezen van de mens* (Amsterdam: Abraxas).

Janssen, J. & van Vugt, J. (ed.) (2006). *Brein en bewustzijn: Gedachtensprongen tussen hersenen en mensbeeld* (Budel: Damon).

Jaspers, K. (1922). *Strindberg und Van Gogh: Versuch einer pathographischen Analyse unter vergleichender Heranziehung von Swedenborg und Hölderlin* (Leipzig: Ernst Bircher).

Jibu, M. & Yasue K. (1995). *Quantum Brain Dynamics and Consciousness: An Introduction. Advances in Consciousness Research* (Amsterdam: Benjamins).

Johnson, J. (1994). 'Henry Maudsley on Swedenborg's Messianic Psychosis', *British Journal of Psychiatry* 165: 11, 690-1.

Kalweit, H. (1992). *Shamans, Healers and Medicine Men* (Boston: Shambhala).

Kant, I. (1766). *Träume eines Geistersehers, erläutert durch Träume der Metaphysik* (Königsberg: Johann Jacob Kanter).

Kaplan, B. (1964). *The Inner World of Mental Illness* (New York, Harper & Row).

Katz, S. T. (1978). *Mysticism and Philosophical Analysis* (London: Sheldon Press).

Kuhn, T. S. (1962). *The Structure of Scientific Revolution* (Chicago: Chicago University Press).

Kurtz, P., Karry, B. & Sandhu, R. (2003). *Science and Religion: Are they Compatible?* (Amherst, NY: Prometheus Books).

Lamothe, R. (2004). 'Freud's Envy of Religious Experience', *The International Journal for the Psychology of Religion* 14: 3, 161–76.

Laski, M. (1961). *Ecstasy: A Study of Some Secular and Religious Experiences* (London: The Cresset Press).

Leeming, D. (1979). 'The Hodja', *Parabola* 4: 1, 84–9.

van der Leeuw, G. (1924). *Mystiek* (Baarn: Hollandia-Drukkerij).

van der Leeuw, G. (1933). *Phänomenologie der Religion* (Tübingen: Mohr).

Leonhard, K. (1992). 'Swedenborg in seiner konfabulatorisch-phonemischen Paraphrenie' in *Bedeutende Persönlichkeiten in ihren psychischen Krankheiten: Beurteilung nach ihren eigenen Schriften und Briefen* VIII, 235–75 (Berlin: Ullstein Mosby).

Likert, R. (1932). 'A Technique for the Measurement of Attitudes', *Archives of Psychology* 140, 55.

van Lommel, P, van Wees, R, Meyers, V. & Elfferich, I. (2001). 'Near-death Experience in Survivors of Cardiac Arrest: A Prospective Study in the Netherlands', *The Lancet* 358, 2039–45.

Lukoff, D. (1985). 'The Diagnosis of Mystical Experiences with Psychotic Features', *The Journal of Transpersonal Psychology* 17: 2, 155–81.

Lukoff, D., Lu, F., & Turner, R. (1992). 'Toward a More Culturally Sensitive DSM-IV: Psychoreligious and Psychospiritual Problems', *Journal of Nervous and Mental Disease* 180: 11, 673–82.

Lukoff, D. (2001). 'Typology of Spiritual Problems, DSM-IV Religious and Spiritual Problem', *Internet Guided Learning course*, 3.2. http://www.spiritualcompetency.com/dsm4/lesson3_2.html (dd. februari 2007).

Mandel, A. J. (1980). 'Toward a Psychobiology of Transcendence' in Davidson & Davidson (eds), *The Psychobiology of Consciousness* (New York: Plenum).

Maudsley, H. (1869). 'Emanuel Swedenborg', *Journal of Mental Science* 15, 169–98.

Maslow, A. (1964). *Religions, Values and Peak Experiences* (New York: Kappa Delta Pi).

McCready, W. C. & Greeley, A. M. (1976). *The Ultimate Values of the American Population* (Beverly Hills, CA: Sage).

Metzinger, Th. (2003). *Being No One, The Self-Model Theory of Subjectivity* (Cambridge, MA: MIT Press).

van der Molen, H. T., Perreijn, S. & Van den Hout, M. A. (1997). *Klinische psychologie: theorieën en psychopathologie* (Groningen: Wolters-Noordhoff).

Mommaers, P., van Bragt, J. & De Smalen, W. (1995). *Ruusbroec in gesprek met het Oosten; mystiek in boeddhisme en christendom* (Kampen: Kok).

Moustakas, C. E. (1994). *Phenomenological Research Methods* (Thousand Oaks, CA: Sage Publications).

Murphy, M. & White, R. A. (1995). *In the Zone: Transcendent Experience in Sports* (New York: Penguin/Arkana).

Nigg, W. (1956). *Der christliche Narr* (Zürich: Artemis).

Noll, R. (1985). 'Mental Imagery Cultivation as a Cultural Phenomenon: The Role of Visions in Shamanism', *Current Anthropology* 26: 4, 443–61.

Ossoff, J. (1993). 'Reflections of Shaktipat: Psychosis or the Rise of Kundalini? A Case Study', *Journal of Transpersonal Psychology* 25: 1, 29–42.

Otto, R. (2002). *Het heilige* (Amsterdam: Appelbloesem Pers-Abraxas).

Platvoet, J. G. & Molendijk, A. L. (ed.) (1999). *The Pragmatics of Defining Religion: Contexts, Concepts and Contests* (Leiden: Brill).

Podvoll, E. M. (1992). *De verlokkingen van de waanzin: nieuwe inzichten over psychose* (Cothen: Servire).

Porter, R. (1991). *De zin van de waanzin, een sociale geschiedenis* (Amsterdam: Veen).

Pribram, K. H. (1971). *Languages of the Brain: Experimental Paradoxes and Principles in Neuropsychology*, Series in Experimental Psychology (Englewood Cliffs: Prentice-Hall).

Pribram, K. H., Yasue, K. & Jibu, M. (1991). *Brain and Perception: Holonomy and Structure in Figural Processing* (Hillsdale, NJ: Erlbaum).

Puhakka, K. (2003). 'An Invitation to Authentic Knowing' in Puhakka, K. (ed.), *Transpersonal Knowing* (New York: State University of New York Press), pp. 11–30.

Redfield Jamison, K. (1994). *Touched with Fire: Manic-depressive Illness and the Artistic Temperament* (New York: The Free Press).

Ring, K., & Cooper, S. (1999). *Mindsight: Near-death and Out-of-body Experiences Blind* (Palo Alto: William James Center for Consciousness Studies).

Rocquet, C. H. (2000). *Ruusbroec: een inleiding tot zijn persoon en tijd* (Zoetermeer: Meinema).

Romme, M. A. J. & Escher, A. D. M. A. C. (1999). *Stemmen horen accepteren: verschillende manieren van omgaan met stemmen in je hoofd* (Baarn: Tirion).

Romme, M. A. J., Escher, A. D. M. A. C., Dillon, J., Corstens, D. & Morris, M. (2009). *Living with Voices: Fifty Stories of Recovery* (Ross-on-Wye, UK: PCCS Books).

Rosenhan, D. L. (1973). 'On Being Sane in Insane Places', *Science* 179, 250–8.

Rowan, J. (2005). *The Transpersonal – Spirituality in Psychotherapy and Counselling* (London: Routledge).

Sannella, L. (1976). *Kundalini: Psychosis or Transcendence?* (San Francisco: Sannella).

Schilling, R. (1998). *Hildegard van Bingen, Bazuin van het levende Licht, 1098–1179*, (Baarn: ten Have).

Schreurs, A. (2001). *Psychotherapie en spiritualiteit, integratie van de spirituele dimensie in de therapeutische praktijk* (Assen: Van Gorcum).

Shah, I. (1969). *Wisdom of the Idiots* (London: Octagon Press).

Sofair, T. (1972). 'Positive Disintegration and Constructive Change in Schizophrenia', *The American Journal of Psychoanalysis* 32: 2, 170–6.

Staal, F. (1975). *Exploring Mysticism: A Methodological Essay* (Berkeley: University of California Press).

Stace, W. T. (1960). *Mysticism and Philosophy* (Philadelphia: J. B. Lippincott).

Steuchius, A. (1540). *De philosophia perenni sive veterum philosophorum cum theologia christiana consensu libri X.*

Stevens, R. (2000). 'Phenomenological Approaches to the Study of Conscious Awareness' in Velmans, *Investigating Phenomenal Consciousness: New Methodologies and Maps* (Amsterdam: John Benjamins), pp. 99–120.

Swedenborg, E. (1988). *Arcana Caelestia, Principally a Revelation of the Inner or Spiritual Meaning of Genesis and Exodus* (trans. from Latin by John Elliott). (London: Swedenborg Society).

Thapa, K., & Murthy, V. (1985). 'Experiential Characteristics of Certain Altered States of Consciousness, *The Journal of Transpersonal Psychology* 17: 1, 77–86.

Underhill, E. (1911). *Mysticism: A Study in Nature and Development of Spiritual Consciousness* (London: Methuen).

Valle, R. (ed.) (1998). *Phenomenological Inquiry in Psychology: Existential and Transpersonal Dimensions* (New York: Plenum Press).

Vanderkooi, L. (1997). 'Buddhist Teachers' Experience with Extreme Mental States in Western Meditators', *Journal of Transpersonal Psychology* 29: 1, 31–46.

Velmans, M. (ed.) (2000). 'Investigating Phenomenal Consciousness: New Methodologies and Maps', *Advances in Consciousness Research* (Amsterdam: John Benjamins).

Victoria, B. A. (1997). *Zen at War* (New York & Tokyo: Weatherhill).

Visser. F (2001). *Ken Wilber, denken als passie* (Rotterdam: Lemniscaat).

Wade, J. (2004). *Transcendent Sex: When Lovemaking Opens the Veil* (New York: Paraview).

Waldron, J. L. (1998). 'The Life Impact of Transcendent Experiences with a Pronounced Quality of Noesis', *The Journal of Transpersonal Psychology* 30: 2, 103–26.

Wallin, D. J. (2007). *Attachment in Psychotherapy* (New York: Guilford Press).

Winnicott, D. W. (1955-6). 'Clinical Varieties of Transference', *International Journal of Psycho-Analysis* 37, 386.

Woodruff, P. W. (2004). 'Auditory Hallucinations: Insights and Questions from Neuroimaging', *Cognitive Neuropsychiatry* 9, 73–91.

Woods, R. (ed.) (1980). *Understanding Mysticism* (New York: Image Books).

Wundt, W. (1874). *Grundzüge der physiologischen Psychologie* (Leipzig: Wilhelm Engelmann).

Reduchowski
for treatment
symptom treatment
√ ... industrial